The Economics of the Global Response to HIV/AIDS

Markus Haacker

Durban,
July 2016

To Robert,

at IAEN 2016.

OXFORD
UNIVERSITY PRESS

OXFORD

UNIVERSITY PRESS

Great Clarendon Street, Oxford, OX2 6DP,
United Kingdom

Oxford University Press is a department of the University of Oxford.
It furthers the University's objective of excellence in research, scholarship,
and education by publishing worldwide. Oxford is a registered trade mark of
Oxford University Press in the UK and in certain other countries

First Edition published in 2016
Impression: 1

Published in the United States of America by Oxford University Press
198 Madison Avenue, New York, NY 10016, United States of America

British Library Cataloguing in Publication Data
Data available

Library of Congress Control Number: 2015956476

ISBN 978-0-19-871804-8

Printed in Great Britain by
Clays Ltd, St Ives Plc

Acknowledgements

This book builds on work conducted from 2000, when the author was employed at the International Monetary Fund (through 2008), and since then includes consultancies with the World Bank and intermittently with UNAIDS from 2008, and stints visiting the London School of Hygiene and Tropical Medicine, the University of Oxford, and the Harvard T.H. Chan School of Public Health. Over the years, many individuals have contributed to the work this book builds on, by collaborating or providing their support, including (in alphabetical order) Arnab Acharya, George Alleyne, Abdoulaye Bio Tchané, Charles Birungi, Mark Blecher, Mariam Claeson, Paul Collier, Francis Cox, Stefan Dercon, Shantayanan Devarajan, Steven Forsythe, Nicole Fraser, Thembi Gama, Marelize Gorgens, Brigitte Granville, Robert Greener, Teresa Guthrie, Keith Hansen, Malayah Harper, Peter S. Heller, Keith Jefferis, Erik Lamontagne, Elizabeth Lule, Khanya Mabuza, Faith Mamba, Ernest Massiah, Nokwazi Mathabela, Bill McGreevey, Gesine Meyer-Rath, Anne J. Mills, the late Philip Musgrove, Regina Ombam, Mead Over, David E. Sahn, Iris Semini, Pierre Somse, John Stover, Nertila Tavanxhi, Jacques van der Gaag, Alan Whiteside, David Wilson, Derek von Wissell, and Jonathan Wolff.

During the writing of the book, the work has greatly benefitted from the hospitality and academic resources of the Harvard T.H. Chan School of Public Health and the support from Rifat Atun. Michael Obst provided excellent research support through all stages of the work. The work on the book did not receive any financial support. Aspects of the book build on work under-taken under contract to the World Bank (especially the interpretation of policy commitments under the HIV/AIDS response as fiscal liabilities and the work on the cost-effectiveness of medical male circumcision) and UNAIDS (examples drawing on the analysis for the Kenya HIV/AIDS investment case, some of the content on domestic financing of HIV/AIDS responses). Sarah-Jane Anderson, Geoffrey Barrow, Sergio Bautista, Íde Cremin, Katharine Kripke, Gesine Meyer-Rath, and Stephen Resch provided access to some of their data and ongoing work. Yogan Pillay gave permission to utilize data from South Africa used in the discussion of HIV/AIDS policy design in Chapter 10. Nelson Musoba granted permission to reprint material from the Uganda HIV investment case. Theo Vos advised on the availability of Global Burden of Disease data.

I would like to thank my wife Veronika, who took much of the strain from writing this book, for her patience and support. I regret that I could not spend more time with my two young sons, Otto and Ivan, over the year the book was written, and hope that one day you will take pride in this book.

Contents

Contents

List of Figures

List of Figures

List of Tables

1

Introduction

HIV/AIDS has been the largest adverse health shock in recent history. The only health shocks it is sometimes compared with, in terms of the magnitude of the impact, are the European Plague of the fourteenth century or the 1918 influenza. In some countries, life expectancy declined by up to two decades owing to HIV/AIDS, reversing all the health gains achieved since the 1950s.

HIV/AIDS has also been unique in terms of the international response it has elicited. Reflecting concerns not only about the health impacts, but also about the economic and social consequences, political stability, and security, HIV/AIDS at times became a dominant issue in global health and development policy—resulting in the establishment of several major international organizations (most notably UNAIDS and the Global Fund), and very significant financial commitments to the global HIV/AIDS response, rising from US$300 million in 1998 to US$8 billion by 2011, when it accounted for 40 per cent of health-related aid and 5 per cent of total aid.

The global HIV/AIDS response has transformed the consequences of HIV across developing countries. As of the mid-2015, 15.8 million people were receiving treatment in low- and middle-income countries, including many countries where treatment would arguably be inaccessible to all but a small minority to this day. As a consequence, mortality among people living with HIV now stands at about 4.5 per cent across developing countries (a decline of about one-half), and below 2 per cent in some of these countries. As the quality of treatment has also improved, people living with HIV in developing countries can hope to reach old age and have a near-normal life expectancy (including several decades of living with HIV), provided they initiate treatment relatively early during the progression of the disease.[1] HIV/AIDS is thus transitioning into a chronic disease across the developing world.

Over the last years, the policy discourse on the global HIV/AIDS response has shifted in two ways. The first shift is exemplified by the UNAIDS investment framework, signalling a shift from a 'commodity approach' focusing on expanding access to HIV/AIDS services significantly and quickly and the challenges of doing so in countries with weak health systems, to an emphasis on effectively utilizing the evidence gained on what works best in terms of reducing HIV incidence in the design of HIV/AIDS programmes and aligning the HIV/AIDS response with the national (or sub-national) drivers of HIV transmission (Schwartländer et al., 2011). In part, this shift reflects demands from donors for increased accountability and efficiency. While the shift has broadly coincided with the global financial crisis, and tighter budgets in donor countries have contributed, it also builds on the evidence base accumulated during the first stage of the scaling-up of the global HIV/AIDS response.

Second, the emphasis of the global response to HIV/AIDS has shifted from an objective of providing 'universal access' to treatment and other HIV/AIDS-related services to 'ending AIDS',[2] motivated by the evidence on and potential for reducing HIV incidence through 'treatment as prevention' and medical male circumcision. Even more than in the 'investment framework', the perspective is forward-looking. HIV policies and interventions are motivated and assessed not only in terms of the best ways to achieve their immediate objectives, but also in terms of the implications for the trajectory of HIV/AIDS in the long term.

Defining Economic Focus

This book applies an economic perspective to the global response to HIV/AIDS by analysing the economic and development implications of HIV/AIDS and the HIV/AIDS response, and applying economic analysis to the assessment and design of HIV/AIDS interventions and programmes. The approach reflects a number of purposes and considerations:

- The global HIV/AIDS response was in part motivated by concerns about the epidemic's social, economic, and development impacts—based on general notions of the impacts of health shocks and early evidence on the impacts of HIV/AIDS. To what extent have these concerns borne out?

- HIV/AIDS—an extremely large health shock—offers an opportunity to review and refine general hypotheses on the economic consequences of health shocks, especially as reverse causality is less of an issue for HIV/AIDS, compared with endemic tropical diseases like malaria.

- To what extent has the impact of HIV/AIDS intersected with economic inequalities and barriers to economic development? What was the impact of the global HIV/AIDS response in mitigating the adverse health consequences across countries?

- How did the financing of the global HIV/AIDS response evolve, and what is the outlook on its financial sustainability?

- What are the consequences of a shortfall in global HIV/AIDS funding for aid-recipient countries, and how can these be mitigated in this context?
- Considering the impacts of the global HIV/AIDS response and its costs, has HIV/AIDS received too much money? (And what priors does this question imply?)
- HIV/AIDS and the response to it are characterized by extremely long time frames, owing to long survival and HIV transmission dynamics, and HIV infections cause spending commitments which extend over decades. Under these circumstances, what is the best way of assessing the effectiveness and cost-effectiveness of alternative HIV/AIDS strategies?
- How can the cost-effectiveness of specific HIV prevention interventions best be evaluated, taking into account dynamic effects ('downstream' infections averted among sexual partners, but also the risk that a beneficiary of an HIV prevention intervention becomes infected later)?
- Assessing the cost-effectiveness of male circumcision and treatment as prevention is particularly challenging, as the HIV prevention benefits are spread over the life of a recipient.
- What are the consequences of the scaling-up of treatment for assessing the cost-effectiveness across HIV prevention interventions?
- What is the best practice to assess the efficiency of specific HIV/AIDS programme spending allocations, and using results on the cost-effectiveness of specific interventions to inform optimal programme design?
- What are the lessons from public finance on domestic financing and the sustainability of a national HIV/AIDS response?

Structure of the Book

The book is divided into three parts. Part I addresses the global impact of HIV/AIDS; Part II discusses the course, impact, and financing of the global response to HIV/AIDS; and Part III deals with questions regarding the design and financing of national HIV/AIDS programmes.

Part I starts out with a discussion of the health impact of HIV/AIDS (Chapter 2), including a review of the state of the global epidemic, its contribution to the burden of disease, and its distribution across countries. While HIV/AIDS is less correlated with barriers to economic development than TB or malaria globally, it stands out as the impact is extremely severe in specific countries. The chapter also discusses recent trends such as the partial recovery in life expectancy owing to increasing access to treatment and the 'graying'

3

of AIDS. Chapter 3 addresses the impacts of HIV/AIDS on households and individuals. It reviews the social determinants of HIV/AIDS and the impacts on affected individuals and households (including orphans), and closes with a discussion of the impacts of HIV/AIDS on poverty and mortality. Chapter 4 starts with an overview of the macroeconomic consequences of HIV/AIDS, covers the modelling of and the empirical evidence on the impacts of HIV/AIDS on GDP per capita and economic growth, and discusses the economic evaluation of health shocks like HIV/AIDS.

Part II provides a bird's eye perspective on the global response to HIV/AIDS. Chapter 5 begins with a review of the course and state of the global response to HIV/AIDS and of its financing. This is followed by an analysis of the costs of the HIV/AIDS response across countries and the role of external financing in containing the domestic financing burden associated with the HIV/AIDS response. Finally, the chapter discusses the sustainability of the HIV/AIDS response, focusing on economic aspects, but also covering the epidemiological and political dimensions of sustainability. Chapter 6 focuses on the impact of the global HIV/AIDS response, beginning with a discussion on approaches to measuring this impact and challenges of attribution. This is followed by a discussion on achievements, focusing on HIV prevalence among young people (as a measure of changes in HIV incidence) and the consequences of the scaling-up of treatment. The final section relates the outcomes and costs of the global response and addresses whether 'the HIV/AIDS response has received too much money'.

Part III is intended as a toolbox for applying economic analysis in the design of HIV/AIDS programmes. In particular, the objective is to refine the analysis of the cost-effectiveness of HIV/AIDS programmes and HIV prevention interventions to take into account the transition of HIV/AIDS into a chronic disease. Because the coverage of antiretroviral therapy (ART) (at least as far as the most pressing medical needs are concerned) is fairly high in many countries, the returns to investment in HIV prevention in terms of health outcomes like deaths averted or life years gained have diminished. At the same time, investments in HIV prevention carry *financial* returns—savings in terms of the averted costs of treatment and other HIV/AIDS-related services caused by an HIV infection, and therefore contributions to the financial sustainability of the HIV/AIDS response. Part III, among other points, addresses how to capture these savings in the evaluation of HIV/AIDS programmes and interventions, and takes into account that they are spread over long periods, even decades.

Chapter 7 places cost-effectiveness in the context of the global HIV/AIDS policy discourse, broadly starting with the UNAIDS 'investment framework', and distinguishes various objectives of HIV/AIDS interventions and dimensions of cost-effectiveness. It then shows how the health consequences of HIV infections diminish, and the financial consequences increase, as treatment coverage and eligibility expand, and illustrates the consequences for the cost-effectiveness of HIV prevention interventions.

Chapter 8 develops a forward-looking analysis of the costs of HIV programmes, interpreting the policy objectives of the HIV/AIDS programme as spending commitments towards people living with HIV. New HIV infections add to these spending commitments. The chapter provides an example for integrating *spending commitments* in the analysis of the *costs* of alternative HIV/AIDS policies, and interprets the outcomes of HIV/AIDS policies against national development objectives (including a discussion of 'economic returns' to HIV/AIDS programmes).

Chapter 9 is by far the longest chapter of the book, and discusses the cost-effectiveness of specific HIV prevention interventions. It sets out with an illustration of transmission dynamics and the dynamic effects of averting an HIV infection, and discusses the cost-effectiveness of various (types of) HIV prevention interventions:

- Condoms, as an example of an HIV prevention measure which has a one-off effect, and used to illustrate differences in the effectiveness of HIV prevention measures across age groups.

- Measures targeting key populations, building on a 'modes of transmission' framework. The intention is to illustrate how the effects of investments in HIV prevention depend on sexual risk behaviour, taking into account dynamic effects which may augment or diminish the effect of an HIV prevention intervention over time.

- The cost-effectiveness of medical male circumcision is difficult to assess because it reduces the risk of contracting HIV over the remaining lifetime of a person undergoing male circumcision. The effects of medical male circumcision on HIV incidence therefore depend strongly on the age at circumcision, and they are spread over decades.

- Treatment, in addition to its health and survival effects, affects the risk of passing on HIV for the remaining lifetime of a person receiving it. It is thus characterized by similarly long time horizons as medical male circumcision, but an assessment of the cost-effectiveness has to take into account the direct health benefits and the impact on HIV transmission simultaneously.

Chapter 10 brings together the programme-level discussion in Chapter 8 and the analysis of specific interventions in Chapter 9, addressing how to interpret estimates of the cost-effectiveness of specific interventions, and their health and financial returns, in order to determine optimal HIV/AIDS programme spending allocations through iterative procedures or more formal optimization approaches.

Chapter 11 returns to the issue of financing the HIV/AIDS response, discussing the financing needs and the sustainability of the national HIV/AIDS response applying a domestic fiscal perspective. This is complemented by discussion of current efforts to improve the financial sustainability of HIV/AIDS responses by improving their efficiency, and a review of various sources of domestic funding of the HIV/AIDS response.

Chapter 12 summarizes some of the lessons from the economic analysis of HIV/AIDS and the HIV/AIDS response developed in this book.

Supplementary material on the book, including pointers to commentary and related work, some underlying material, updates, and corrections, will be available on a dedicated website: www.hiveconbook.com.

Part I
The Global Impact of HIV/AIDS

Part I addresses the global impacts of HIV/AIDS from three angles. The most immediate impacts of HIV/AIDS are the health impacts (Chapter 2), such as increased mortality of people living with HIV, and the consequences for health indicators for the population overall, such as life expectancy. However, the global response to HIV/AIDS has also been motivated by the projected social and economic consequences of the epidemic. Chapter 3 discusses the consequences of HIV/AIDS for affected households; and Chapter 4 reviews the macroeconomic impacts (e.g. on economic growth and GDP per capita).

2

Health Impacts of HIV/AIDS

The most direct consequences of HIV/AIDS are the increased mortality and morbidity caused by the epidemic. For many purposes, the buck may stop here—it is a no-brainer that a drop in life expectancy exceeding 10 years, or a prospect of one-in-three for a young adult of contracting HIV at some stage in life and suffering premature death, represent a devastating decline in living standards.[1]

Nevertheless, the economic repercussions of these health consequences exacerbate the impacts of HIV/AIDS, and may pose economic and development challenges in their own right. For example, health shocks are a principal cause of descents into poverty, and much of the concerns regarding macroeconomic consequences rest on the fact that the disease has a disproportionate effect among young adults.

Barriers to economic development, in turn, have shaped the health consequences of the epidemic, and the global response to HIV/AIDS was partly driven by concerns about the social and economic consequences of the epidemic in less-developed economies, as well as indignation about the absence of treatment in these countries while it was already prolonging the lives of people living with HIV (PLWH) in advanced economies.[2]

As an entry point to the economic analysis offered in this book, the chapter provides an overview of the state of the epidemic and the health impacts of HIV/AIDS, and places the impact of HIV/AIDS in context, for example compared to other significant health shocks or to other diseases.

The State of the Epidemic

HIV/AIDS is a relatively new disease. The first cases of what is now called the acquired human immunodeficiency syndrome (AIDS) were documented in 1981 among gay men in the United States, and the human immunodeficiency virus (HIV) was established as the cause of AIDS by 1984. The epidemic soon

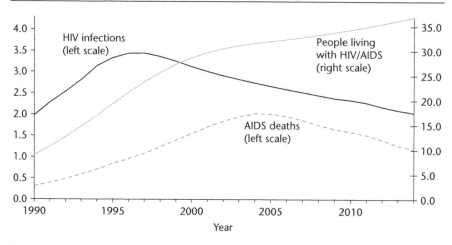

Figure 2.1. The global course of HIV/AIDS (millions)
Source: UNAIDS, 2015c.

became recognized as a global phenomenon, and the scale of the epidemic became apparent, notably in sub-Saharan Africa where earlier disease outbreaks in the 1970s and 1980s were attributed to HIV/AIDS in retrospect.[3]

By the late 1980s, the epidemic had spread globally, and it is estimated that about 9 million people were living with HIV/AIDS in 1990 (Figure 2.1). The epidemic continued to escalate, and the number of people living with HIV/AIDS reached 20 million by 1996 and 30 million by 2002. Subsequently, the number of people living with HIV increased steadily, but more slowly, reaching 36.9 million by 2014. Because of growing population, though, HIV *prevalence* (the share of people living with HIV in the population) has remained broadly constant, globally, over the last decade.

These trends reflect a number of developments both in HIV incidence (the annual rate at which people become newly infected) and AIDS-related mortality. The explosive growth in HIV incidence until the early 1990s is characteristic of a new epidemic that hits a population. The subsequent slowdown and decline in HIV incidence from the mid-1990s can be attributed to several factors. First, an increasing number of people, especially those adopting high-risk sexual behaviour (e.g. men who have sex with men, sex workers), become infected.[4] Therefore, the susceptible population (those who could still become infected) shrinks overall, and the share engaging in high-risk behaviour in the susceptible population declines. Apart from these composition effects, it is plausible that behaviour change (e.g. increased condom use, or reducing the number of casual sex partners) has played a role in the decline in HIV incidence since the mid-1990s, brought about by a combination of experience (witnessing the impacts of HIV/AIDS) and policy (information about HIV transmission risks, promoting HIV prevention). Available studies suggest a divergent picture on the extent to which these different factors have contributed to the decline in HIV incidence across countries.[5] It is worth noting that immunity after surviving an initial infection, which plays an important role in the course of epidemics like influenza, plays no role with regard to HIV/AIDS, as HIV/AIDS so far is not curable.

More recently, medical interventions aiming to reduce the risk of HIV transmission have become more important. These interventions include prevention of mother-to-child transmission of HIV (by providing treatment to pregnant women and mothers, to reduce the risk of HIV infection for the baby in utero, during birth, and by breastfeeding), male circumcision (which reduces the risk of acquisition of HIV by circumcised males), and antiretroviral treatment (which, by suppressing the virus, reduces the probability of passing on HIV, in addition to the health benefits for the person receiving it). These interventions are among the cornerstones of current HIV/AIDS policies (Schwartländer et al., 2011; UNAIDS, 2014c), and are discussed thoroughly in Part III of this book.

The second factor underlying trends in the number of people living with HIV is AIDS-related mortality. HIV/AIDS is a non-curable disease, which—in the absence of treatment—results in death, although with an unusually long lag averaging about 8 years from the time of infection, with high variability. For this reason, the number of AIDS-related deaths continued to rise long after the number of HIV infections started to decline, and AIDS-related mortality among people living with HIV rose from 3.5 per cent in 1990 to 6.4 per cent in 2004 (Figure 2.2). At about this time, the international effort to extend access

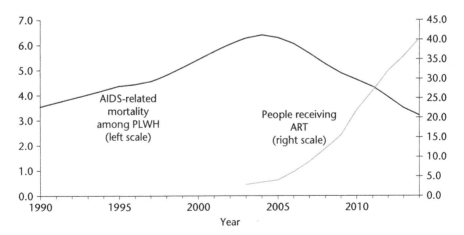

Figure 2.2. Treatment access and AIDS-related mortality (per cent of people living with HIV)

Source: Author's calculations, based on UNAIDS (2015c) and WHO/UNAIDS/UNICEF (2013).

Table 2.1. The global distribution of HIV/AIDS, 2014

	People living with HIV	People receiving treatment	HIV prevalence[a]	New HIV infections	AIDS-Related deaths	AIDS-related mortality
	(Units)	(Units)	(Per cent, ages 15–49)	(Units)	(Units)	(Per cent of PLWH)
Global	36,900,000	14,900,000	0.8	2,000,000	1,200,000	3.3
Asia and the Pacific	5,000,000	1,800,000	0.2 (<0.1–1.1)	340,000	240,000	4.8
Caribbean	280,000	120,000	1.1 (0.3–1.9)	13,000	8,800	3.1
Jamaica	29,000	9,100	1.6	1,500	1,300	4.5
Eastern Europe and Central Asia	1,500,000	280,000	0.9 (0.1–0.6)	135,000	62,000	4.1
Latin America	1,700,000	790,000	0.4 (0.2–1.8)	87,000	41,000	2.4
Middle East and North Africa	240,000	32,000	0.1 (<0.1–1.6)	22,000	12,000	5.0
Sub-Saharan Africa	25,800,000	10,700,000	4.8 (0.3–27.7)	1,350,000	790,000	3.1
Botswana	390,000	240,000	25.2	13,600	5,100	1.3
Kenya	1,370,000	760,000	5.3	56,000	33,000	2.4
Homa Bay (ages 15+)			25.7			
Wajir (ages 15+)			0.2			
Mozambique	1,540,000	650,000	10.6	88,000	45,000	2.9
Niger	52,000	11,000	0.5	1,300	3,400	6.5
Nigeria	3,390,000	750,000	3.2	228,000	174,000	5.1
South Africa	6,840,000	3,080,000	18.9	338,000	138,000	2.0
KwaZulu-Natal (2012)			27.9			
Western Cape (2012)			7.8			
Swaziland	214,000	110,000	27.7	9,600	3,500	1.6
Western and Central Europe and North America	2,400,000		0.3 (<0.1–0.3)	85,000	26,000	1.1

Source: UNAIDS (2015a) for country-level and global regional data, Shisana et al. (2014) for sub-national data from South Africa, and National AIDS Control Council of Kenya (2014) for sub-national data from Kenya.

[a] Numbers in brackets show point estimates for countries with the lowest and highest HIV prevalence within region. For some countries, no national data are publicly available, regional averages may therefore lie outside the range of reported country-level data.

to treatment across less-developed countries took off with the WHO's '3 by 5' initiative (to extend access to treatment to 3 million people across low- and middle-income countries by 2005). From a very low base, treatment access expanded to about 15.0 million (40 per cent of people living with HIV) by the end of 2014. As a consequence, AIDS-related mortality among people living with HIV globally has declined to 3.2 per cent in 2014.[6]

The global figures, however, mask the fact that HIV/AIDS is distributed highly unequally across regions, countries, and even within countries (Table 2.1). Almost 70 per cent of people living with HIV/AIDS reside in sub-Saharan Africa, where average HIV prevalence is 4.8 per cent as of 2014. The other global regions with elevated HIV prevalence are the Caribbean (1.1 per cent) and

Eastern Europe and Central Asia (0.9 per cent); in all other global regions HIV prevalence averages less than 0.5 per cent.

The regional averages in turn mask a wide dispersion across countries, notably in sub-Saharan Africa where HIV prevalence ranges from 0.3 per cent (Madagascar) to 27.7 per cent of the population of ages 15–49 (Swaziland). National estimates, too, can be very misleading indicators of the state of the epidemic. In Kenya, provincial HIV prevalence rates differ by a factor of 100. In South Africa, provincial HIV prevalence rates range from 7.8 per cent in Western Cape to 27.6 per cent in KwaZulu-Natal, and, on the sub-provincial level, HIV prevalence in the East of South Africa is almost 10 times higher than in the West (Shisana and others, 2014).

One important lesson from the data presented in Table 2.1 regards mortality. Location matters for survival prospects among people living with HIV. Globally, AIDS-related mortality was 3.3 per cent among people living with HIV in 2014. In Europe and North America, it was only 1.1 per cent in 2014, suggesting that people living with HIV have a fairly good chance of reaching old age. In contrast, AIDS-related mortality among people living with HIV is between 5 and 6.5 per cent in the Middle East and North Africa, and in selected countries in sub-Saharan Africa. As for other aspects of HIV/AIDS, the experience in sub-Saharan Africa is not uniform, as evident from the mortality rates for Botswana (1.3 per cent), Swaziland (1.6 per cent), and South Africa (2.0 per cent) which are far below the regional average (and lower than average AIDS-related mortality among PLWH across Latin America).

Placing the Impact of HIV/AIDS in Context

The global response to HIV/AIDS has been motivated in part by the perception or recognition of HIV/AIDS as a disaster, and the discussion of the health impacts of HIV/AIDS provides some pointers as to why this is the case. The 2001 'Declaration of Commitment' by the United Nations General Assembly Special Session on HIV/AIDS was motivated by concerns 'that the global HIV/AIDS epidemic, through its devastating scale and impact, constitutes a global emergency and one of the most formidable challenges to human life and dignity'. Piot (2005), then Executive Director of UNAIDS, framed HIV/AIDS as 'one of the most serious threats to our prospects for progress and stability—on a par with such extraordinary threats as nuclear weaponry or global climate change'. The 2008 *World Disasters Report*, published by the International Federation of Red Cross and Red Crescent Societies, focused on HIV/AIDS and took a more nuanced view, proposing that 'for a number of countries (all at present in sub-Saharan Africa) and for a significant number of groups of people where the epidemic is concentrated, the HIV epidemic is undoubtedly a disaster'.

While these assessments are not only based on the direct health consequences of HIV/AIDS, but also on its economic and social consequences, most of the latter can be attributed to the health impacts. As a first step to validating statements regarding the extraordinary development challenges posed by HIV/AIDS, it is useful to place the health impact of HIV/AIDS in context. This is done here in two directions—(1) reviewing the most significant adverse health shocks recorded globally since 1950, and establishing the role of HIV/AIDS or other factors to such shocks, and (2) comparing the contribution of HIV/AIDS and of other diseases commonly associated with low levels of development to the global burden of disease.

Table 2.2 summarizes the most significant health shocks (measured by a decline in life expectancy from a previous peak) recorded globally since 1950, based on estimates by the United Nations Population Division. These data are available in 5-year averages only,[7] the period estimates may therefore distort the impacts of shocks of short duration. The two most significant shocks (Cambodia in the 1970s and Rwanda in the early 1990s) are episodes of extreme violence (with a partial contribution of HIV/AIDS in Rwanda). Overall, however, the list is dominated by countries suffering the impacts of HIV/AIDS, in addition to further episodes of violence, famine, and economic crises.

Moreover, the health shocks associated with HIV/AIDS are among the most persistent shocks. Of fourteen shocks extending over at least four 5-year periods, eleven are associated with HIV/AIDS. The remaining three are of a much smaller magnitude and were caused by economic disruptions (Kazakhstan, North Korea, Russia). If the cumulative impact is applied, the four worst episodes, and eight of the worst ten, are caused by HIV/AIDS.

These comparisons suffer from one important shortcoming—they do not capture factors which have a persistent impact on health outcomes, such as economic underdevelopment and endemic diseases such as malaria. From a broad public health or development perspective, the analysis based on *reversals* in life expectancy therefore falls short.

Nevertheless, HIV/AIDS stands up there with (and mostly ahead of) some of the most notorious catastrophic shocks to health outcomes and living standards recorded since 1950. What distinguishes HIV/AIDS additionally is the fact that the shock is persistent. This is a significant aspect of the epidemic from a policy perspective. As Whiteside and Whalley (2007) observe, HIV/AIDS in many countries exceeds thresholds defining disasters applied by various organizations, and does so year after year.[8] Emergency assistance, however, tends to focus on mitigating and reversing the consequences of specific shocks, for example in the aftermath of natural disasters or of armed conflict. The current policy discourse on HIV financing, and its transition to a sustainable funding model, can therefore be interpreted as a transition from an *emergency* response—with relatively generous availability of funding—to a

Table 2.2. Large adverse health shocks, measured by drop in life expectancy

Country	Principal cause(s)	Period	Duration (5-year periods)	Drop in life expectancy[a]		
				Peak	Average	Cumulative
Cambodia	Violence	1970–80	2	−27.5	−15.8	−31.6
Rwanda	Violence, HIV/AIDS	1985–2000	3	−26.6	−11.3	−34.0
Zimbabwe	HIV/AIDS, economic crisis	1990–	5(+)	−20.9	−13.4	−66.9
Lesotho	HIV/AIDS	1995–	4(+)	−16.3	−12.3	−49.1
Botswana	HIV/AIDS	1990–2010	4	−13.8	−7.2	−28.7
Swaziland	HIV/AIDS	1995–	4(+)	−13.3	−10.3	−41.1
South Africa	HIV/AIDS	1995–	4(+)	−10.1	−6.9	−27.7
Zambia	HIV/AIDS	1980–2005	5	−9.1	−6.0	−29.8
Timor-Leste	Famine, violence	1975–1985	2	−8.8	−4.4	−8.8
Kenya	HIV/AIDS	1990–2010	4	−8.1	−5.2	−20.7
Namibia	HIV/AIDS	1995–2010	3	−7.8	−3.9	−11.8
Dem. People's Republic of Korea	Famine, economic crisis	1995–	4(+)	−6.5	−2.6	−10.2
Côte d'Ivoire	HIV/AIDS	1990–	5(+)	−6.1	−3.6	−17.9
Congo, Rep. of	HIV/AIDS	1985–2005	4	−5.4	−3.4	−13.8
Central African Republic	HIV/AIDS	1990–	5(+)	−5.4	−2.9	−14.5
Uganda	HIV/AIDS	1980–2005	5	−5.1	−2.7	−13.4
Syrian Arab Republic	Violence	2010–	1(+)	−4.9	−4.9	−4.9
Sierra Leone	HIV/AIDS, violence	1985–2000	3	−4.9	−3.6	−10.8
Iran (Islamic Republic of)	Violence	1980–85	1	−4.6	−4.6	−4.6
Vietnam	Violence	1970–75	1	−4.6	−4.6	−4.6
Kazakhstan	Economic disruptions	1990–2010	4	−4.5	−2.8	−11.3
Russian Federation	Economic disruptions	1990–2010	4	−4.2	−3.0	−12.2

Source: Author's calculations, based on UNPD (2015). Attribution of causes are the author's.

[a] Drop in life expectancy is measured by decline in life expectancy from previous peak. The average drop is the average difference to the previous peak, the cumulative impact the sum of the differences from the previous peak. Especially for health shocks of a longer duration, the drop in life expectancy understates the impact, because life expectancy would have *grown* from the previous peak otherwise.

situation in which HIV/AIDS policies are competing for funding with other *endemic* health and development challenges.

Apart from concerns about the *scale* of the impact of HIV/AIDS in some countries, the global response to HIV/AIDS has in part been driven by concerns that the health consequences of HIV/AIDS would undermine state capacities and economic development gains in some of the *poorest* countries. This perception was fuelled by the fact that the epidemic is concentrated in sub-Saharan Africa. This link has always been a gross over-simplification—national HIV prevalence rates in sub-Saharan Africa range from about 0.5 per cent to 28 per cent as of 2014 (UNAIDS, 2015c), and the countries facing the highest HIV prevalence rates overall contain some of the most advanced economies on the continent.

Moreover, there are other diseases which are also associated with low levels of development (notably malaria)—even if HIV/AIDS is associated with low levels of economic development, this may not be a distinguishing feature of the epidemic. Indeed, among communicable diseases HIV/AIDS is not a disease particularly associated with a low level of development (Table 2.3). More than one-third (38 per cent) of AIDS-related deaths occur in low-income countries, a higher rate than for communicable disease overall. On this count, however, malaria is more strongly associated with barriers to development, with 41 per cent of the disease burden occurring in low-income countries. At the other end of the income distribution, 23 per cent of HIV/AIDS-related deaths occurred in high- and upper-middle-income countries in 2010 (compared to 12 per cent for TB (tuberculosis) and only 1 per cent for malaria).[9] A similar picture emerges with regard to sub-Saharan Africa. About 80 per cent of deaths from HIV/AIDS occur in low-income countries. However, this is lower than the burden of disease overall or from communicable diseases occurring in low-income countries in sub-Saharan Africa (about 90 per cent), and much lower than the respective share of low-income countries in deaths from malaria and neglected tropical diseases (98 per cent).[10]

Irrespective of whether HIV/AIDS is associated with low levels of economic development, the mortality data summarized in Table 2.3 reflect the substantial addition to the global burden of disease caused by HIV/AIDS. Globally, one in forty-one deaths could be attributed to HIV/AIDS in 2013. In low-income countries, one in eleven deaths was caused by HIV/AIDS. The magnitude of the impact of HIV/AIDS was much more pronounced in sub-Saharan Africa, where one in nine deaths was AIDS-related in low-income countries, and one in four in high- and middle-income countries.

Averages of disease burden across countries could mask extreme outcomes in specific countries. To gain a better understanding of how the burden of HIV/AIDS and other infectious diseases is correlated with the level of economic development, Figure 2.3 plots mortality attributed to tuberculosis, malaria, and HIV/AIDS across the global population, ordered by country-level GDP per capita. In addition to the severity of the impact of these diseases in the respective countries (the height of the respective bars), the figure also shows the distribution of the global burden from these three diseases (represented by the areas enclosed by the bars).

From this perspective, the disease associated most strongly with a low level of economic development is TB. For low- and lower-middle-income countries, TB contributes about 0.03 to 0.05 percentage points to mortality (for comparison—total mortality is typically around 1 percentage point), for upper-middle- and high-income countries this drops to zero.[11] There are a

Table 2.3. Burden of disease, by cause, across countries (2013)

Income Group/Region/ Country	Cause of death					
	Total	Communicable	HIV/AIDS	TB	Malaria	NTDs
			Total deaths			
All countries	54,753,000	8,797,000	1,345,000	1,305,000	854,000	142,000
High-income countries	12,639,000	677,000	38,000	36,000	700	4,000
Upper-middle-income countries	15,368,000	1,109,000	269,000	117,000	13,000	18,000
Lower-middle-income countries	21,343,000	4,580,000	530,000	900,000	490,000	83,000
Low-income countries	5,404,000	2,432,000	508,000	252,000	351,000	38,000
Sub-Saharan Africa	8,552,000	4,089,000	1,108,000	354,000	712,000	47,000
High- and middle-income countries	825,000	380,000	222,000	34,000	13,000	1,000
Low-income countries	7,727,000	3,709,000	886,000	320,000	699,000	46,000
	Distribution of disease burden across countries (per cent of total deaths by region)					
All countries	100.0	100.0	100.0	100.0	100.0	100.0
High-income countries	23.1	7.7	2.8	2.8	0.1	2.8
Upper-middle-income countries	28.1	12.6	20.0	9.0	1.5	12.7
Lower-middle-income countries	39.0	52.1	39.4	69.0	57.4	58.5
Low-income countries	9.9	27.6	37.8	19.3	41.1	26.8
Sub-Saharan Africa	15.6	46.5	82.4	27.1	83.4	33.1
High- and middle-income countries	1.5	4.3	16.5	2.6	1.5	0.7
Low-income countries	14.1	42.2	65.9	24.5	81.9	32.4
	Distribution of disease burden across countries (per cent of total deaths by cause)					
All countries	100.0	16.1	2.5	2.4	1.6	0.3
High-income countries	100.0	5.4	0.3	0.3	0.0	0.0
Upper-middle-income countries	100.0	7.2	1.8	0.8	0.1	0.1
Lower-middle-income countries	100.0	21.5	2.5	4.2	2.3	0.4
Low-income countries	100.0	45.0	9.4	4.7	6.5	0.7
Sub-Saharan Africa	100.0	47.8	13.0	4.1	8.3	0.5
High- and middle-income countries	100.0	46.1	26.9	4.1	1.6	0.1
Low-income countries	100.0	48.0	11.5	4.1	9.0	0.6

Source: Author's calculations, based on Institute for Health Metrics and Evaluation (2014). Income groups are based on the World Bank's classification contained in World Bank (2015). NTDs = Neglected tropical diseases.

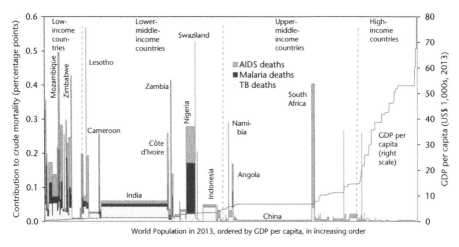

Figure 2.3. AIDS, malaria, and TB deaths, and economic development (contribution to crude mortality, percentage points)

Note: Dividing lines between income categories (broken lines) approximate World Bank classifications.

Source: IHME (2014) for mortality and population data, World Bank (2015) augmented from IMF (2015) for GDP data.

few outliers at higher levels of GDP per capita, but these can be attributed to high HIV prevalence in the respective countries. (TB is not only a prime killer of people living with HIV, in which case it would be counted as an AIDS-related death in Figure 2.3; because of high vulnerability to TB of people living with HIV, and the infectious nature of the disease, high HIV prevalence is associated with an increase in the number of active TB cases across the population, including people *not* living with HIV.)

Malaria is also predominantly associated with very low levels of economic development, with the exception of a few outliers, where GDP is inflated by high oil revenues (Nigeria, and—to the right of the 'South Africa' bar—Gabon and Equatorial Guinea). With these exceptions, virtually all countries where mortality attributed to malaria exceeds 0.1 percentage points have a GDP per capita of less than US$1,400 as of 2010. However, among countries with such a low income, the impact of malaria is heterogeneous, ranging from negligible levels to mortality rates exceeding 0.2 percentage points (Burkina Faso, Guinea-Bissau, Mali, and Mozambique).

One thing that the burden of HIV/AIDS has in common with those of malaria and tuberculosis is its absence (as a significant contributor to mortality) in high-income countries (with the exception of Trinidad and Tobago, the Bahamas, and newly-rich Equatorial-Guinea, with a combined population of 2.4 million), a result not only of relatively low HIV prevalence, but also of superior access to treatment. Apart from this, the most distinguishing features of HIV/AIDS are the highly uneven distribution across countries (slightly tilted towards low-income countries) and the very severe impacts of the disease in a limited number of countries (in line with the previous observations on the causes of large health reversals overall).

Overall, the findings from this review of the magnitude of the health shock caused by the HIV/AIDS epidemic is consistent with the nuanced approach of the 2008 *World Disasters Report*, whereby 'for a number of countries...the epidemic is undoubtedly a disaster'.[12] Specifically, it is the cause of many of the most severe reversals in life expectancy recorded globally since 1950. However, in comparison with diseases like tuberculosis or malaria, the adverse impact of HIV/AIDS is not particularly associated with low levels of economic development.

Health and Demographic Consequences

The summary data on the state of the epidemic per se do not carry much information on the social and economic consequences of HIV/AIDS. The previous section took the discussion forward by placing the impact of HIV/AIDS in context, exploring causes of large reversals in life expectancy or comparing the burden of disease from HIV/AIDS with that from other diseases. The present section analyses some of the health and demographic consequences of HIV/AIDS in more detail, with an emphasis on consequences of HIV/AIDS relevant from an economic perspective.

To this end, it is necessary to explore specific country data and estimates in more detail. Three countries were selected for this review—Botswana, Kenya, and Jamaica, differing considerably in terms of the state and scale of the epidemic (as summarized in Figure 2.4), but also representing different economic settings.[13]

- *Botswana*, with an estimated HIV prevalence (ages 15–49) of 25.2 per cent as of 2014, is among the countries with the highest HIV prevalence globally, even though HIV prevalence has declined considerably from its peak of 29.1 per cent in 2001. As of 2014, an estimated 392,000 people were living with HIV, out of a total population of 2.2 million. Annual adult HIV incidence is estimated to have peaked at 5.4 per cent in the mid-1990s, but has fallen to 1.4 per cent as of 2014. AIDS has been and continues to be a principal cause of death in Botswana. Annual AIDS-related deaths peaked at 18,800 (out of a total population of 1.8 million) in 2002, in which year it accounted for about two-thirds of all deaths. Botswana is one of the wealthiest countries in sub-Saharan Africa, with a GDP per capita of US$7,500 in 2014. It has been a leader in extending

19

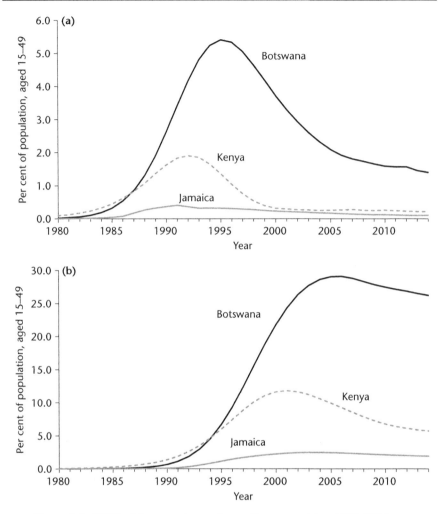

Figure 2.4. HIV incidence and prevalence, three countries, 1980–2014

Source: UNAIDS (2015a) and, for Jamaica, UNAIDS (2014d).
(a). HIV incidence
(b). HIV prevalence

access to treatment across the population (with considerable external support), and 244,000 people (62 per cent of people living with HIV, and 11 per cent of the total population) were receiving treatment at the end of 2014. Owing to declining HIV incidence in previous years, and the steep increase in treatment, the number of AIDS-related deaths has declined to 5,100 as of 2014 (a decline of almost three-quarters from a peak of 18,800 in 2002).

- In *Kenya*, HIV prevalence (ages 15–49) stood at 5.3 per cent as of 2014, not very far from the regional average for sub-Saharan Africa (4.8 per cent), and down from a peak of 9.8 per cent attained in 1997. Within Kenya, however, HIV/AIDS is distributed very unevenly, with HIV prevalence close to 1 per cent in some districts in the north east (bordering Somalia and Ethiopia) to over 20 per cent in some districts in the south west, by Lake Victoria. Approximately 1.4 million people, out of a total population of about 45 million, were living with HIV in 2014. Adult HIV incidence peaked in 1993 at 1.8 per cent, and has since declined to 0.25 per cent. AIDS-related mortality peaked at 125,000 deaths, or 0.4 per cent, in 2003, when it accounted for almost one-third of all deaths, but has since declined to around 33,000 in 2014, with one in eight deaths attributed to HIV/AIDS, partly reflecting the step increase in access to treatment in recent years—as of the end of 2014, 755,000 Kenyans living with HIV were receiving treatment.

- *Jamaica* has much lower HIV prevalence than the other two countries chosen as examples, estimated at 1.6 per cent of the population (ages 15–49) in 2014. HIV transmission is mainly heterosexual, but the country is also experiencing a serious HIV epidemic among men who have sex with men, who account for 4 per cent of the male population but close to one-third of all HIV infections (JNHP, 2012). In 2014, 29,400 people were living with HIV/AIDS (down from 34,400 in 2001), and 1,500 new HIV infections occurred (down from 4,400 in 1991). The number of Jamaicans receiving treatment has increased to 9,100 in 2014. AIDS-related deaths (1,300 in 2014), accounted for 6 per cent of total deaths, but AIDS is an important cause of premature mortality among adults, accounting for about one-quarter of deaths in the 15–49 age group.

The most common indicator of the magnitude of an HIV epidemic is HIV prevalence, the share of people living with HIV in a population—typically the population aged 15–49, because the impact of HIV/AIDS is concentrated in this population. HIV prevalence, however, is a misleading indicator of the scale of the epidemic, because it is an average across the population, which masks the fact that HIV prevalence is still very low among young people, and that it may have declined because of HIV/AIDS-related mortality in older cohorts. Measuring the scale of the epidemic by HIV prevalence is therefore similar to measuring the magnitude of a wave by its *average* height, whereas one would also want to know its *peak* height—that is, in the present context, the share of a cohort expected to contract HIV or die from AIDS-related causes.

The *prospect* for members of an age *cohort* of contracting HIV/AIDS at some stage during their life may therefore provide a better measure of the severity of the epidemic, and helps to interpret the data on average HIV prevalence across the population. This measure is also important from an economic perspective—some of the economic analyses of the impact of HIV/AIDS emphasize the link between health risks and incentives to invest in education, and this issue plays a role in the literature on the effects of HIV/AIDS on economic growth.

The risk of contracting HIV at some stage in life in the three study countries is illustrated in Figure 2.5 for individuals born in 1980.[14] The figure starts in 1995 (when these individuals are assumed to commence sexual activity at age 15 in the Spectrum software underlying the estimates). These estimates thus do not include prevention of mother-to-child transmission. However, the advantage of focusing on sexual transmission from age 15 is that the comparisons across countries or over time are not affected by large differences in infant and child mortality for reasons other than HIV/AIDS.

In Botswana, the share of the cohort born in 1980 who contracted HIV by 2014 is estimated at 40 per cent for men and 46 per cent for women. While most HIV infections in this cohort have already happened, the share of this cohort to eventually contract HIV is estimated to rise to about 45 per cent for men and 55 per cent for women, roughly twice the level of HIV prevalence in this period.[15] A similar picture emerges for Kenya and Jamaica. In Kenya (HIV prevalence up to 10 per cent in this period), 6.1 per cent of men born in 1980, and 7.2 per cent of women, are estimated to have contracted HIV since entering adulthood, and this rate is expected to grow over the coming years to 7.2 per cent (men) and 9.5 per cent (women) of this cohort. In Jamaica, a national HIV prevalence of 1.6 per cent translates into a lifetime risk of contracting HIV of 2.1 per cent for women, and close to 3.4 per cent for men born in 1980.[16]

In line with declining national HIV incidence over the last two decades, the lifetime risk of contracting HIV has also declined steeply. For the cohort born in 1970 and entering adulthood (age 15) in Botswana in 1985, the lifetime risk of contracting HIV was about two-thirds for men and three-quarters for women. (Members of this cohort were in their mid-20s when national HIV incidence peaked at over 5 per cent.) For young adults who are in their early 20s in Botswana now (cohort entering adulthood in 2005, born in 1990), the lifetime risk of contracting HIV has declined steeply, to 33 per cent for men and 39 per cent for women. In the other two countries, the projected lifetime risk of contracting HIV has declined as well—to 4.8 per cent (men) and 5.7 per cent (women) in Kenya, and 2.5 per cent (men) and 1.2 per cent (women) in Jamaica for the cohort born in 1990.

One of the distinguishing features of HIV/AIDS—similar to other sexually transmitted diseases, but unique among major causes of mortality—is the fact that the impact is concentrated among *young* adults. Indeed, in many countries, the age profile of mortality changed from a U-shape (with high mortality

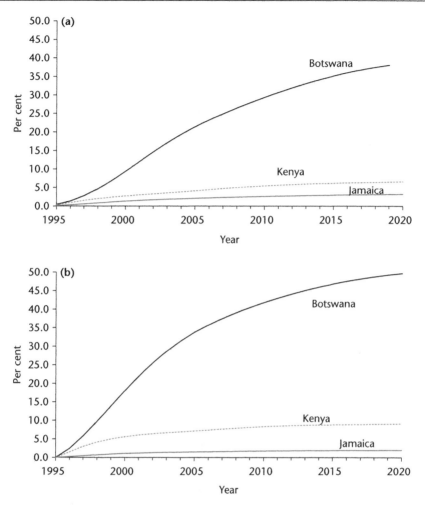

Figure 2.5. Accumulated HIV infection risk, three countries, 1995–2020

Source: Author's calculations, based on UNAIDS (2015a) and, for Jamaica, UNAIDS (2014d).

(a). Accumulated projected HIV infection risk for male individual at age 15 in 1995

(b). Accumulated projected HIV infection risk for female individual at age 15 in 1995

in infancy and old age, but low mortality in between), to a W-shape, with mortality around ages 30–40 among the highest. This aspect of HIV/AIDS has also driven concerns about the economic and social consequences of HIV/ AIDS, as young adults are among the economically most productive members of society and frequently leave behind orphans.

The extremely severe impact of HIV/AIDS on young adults in countries with high HIV prevalence is apparent from the data on mortality by age for

Botswana (Figure 2.6). As of 2000, mortality increased steeply from about age 20, and exceeded 2 per cent for the 30–39 age group, which—in the absence of HIV/AIDS—would have faced an annual mortality of about 0.3 per cent. In this year, HIV/AIDS was also a dominant contributor to child mortality. By 2014, the impact of HIV/AIDS on mortality at ages 30–39 had dropped by three-quarters (to about 0.5 per cent). While HIV prevalence in this age group has declined (from 48 per cent to 36 per cent), most of the drop in overall mortality reflects the expansion of treatment, cutting AIDS-related mortality among people living with HIV in this age group from 5.2 per cent to 1.4 per cent. Nevertheless, HIV/AIDS remains a dominant source of premature deaths among adults. Also noteworthy is the near-disappearance of HIV/AIDS as a cause of child mortality.

In Kenya—with a much lower HIV prevalence—the 'AIDS bump' in the age profile of mortality has largely disappeared. The principal cause, as in Botswana, is the steep decline in mortality among people living with HIV (dropping from 10 per cent annually to 2 per cent of the population at ages 30–39). However, HIV/AIDS still accounts for one-third of all deaths at ages 30–39. Even in Jamaica, with a much lower HIV prevalence than in the other two countries, there is a pronounced impact of HIV/AIDS on mortality among young adults, accounting for the majority of all adult deaths for those aged 25–44 in 2000, and about one-third in 2014.

One of the consequences of the improved survival of people living with HIV/AIDS, and of declining HIV incidence, is the fact that people living with HIV are—on average—getting older. This 'graying of AIDS' was first recognized in countries like the United States, but—owing to the steep declines in AIDS-related mortality experienced over the last decade—is becoming a global phenomenon.[17] This development has policy consequences on at least two dimensions. First, while international institutions like UNAIDS are now seeing the 'beginning of the end of the AIDS epidemic' (UNAIDS, 2014c), this does not apply to the number of people living with HIV/AIDS, and managing the needs of people living with HIV/AIDS will remain a public health challenge in many countries for decades. Second, HIV/AIDS may complicate the management of diseases associated with old age, and vice versa, resulting in new types of HIV/AIDS-related health challenges.

As an example for this 'AIDS transition', that is, a kind of demographic transition among people living with HIV/AIDS,[18] consider the evolving age structure of people living with HIV in Botswana, chosen here because it started extending access to treatment across the population early, and is therefore more advanced in this age transition than other countries (Figure 2.7).

Regarding the processes underlying the 'AIDS transition', it is useful to distinguish mother-to-child transmission and HIV infections among adults.

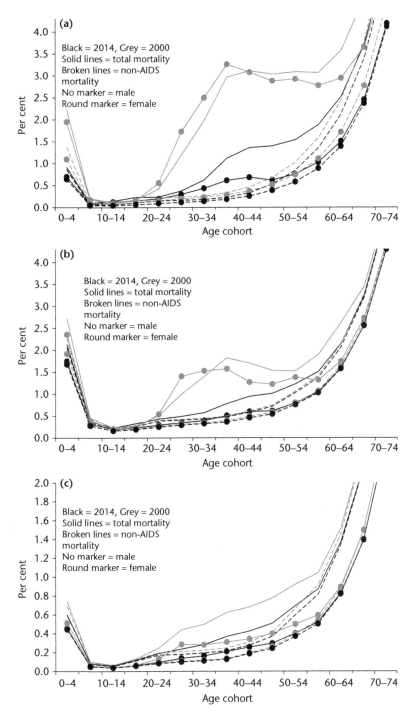

Figure 2.6. Age profile of mortality, three countries, 2000 and 2014

(a). Botswana: Mortality by age, 2000 and 2014
Source: UNAIDS (2015a).

(b). Kenya: Mortality by age, 2000 and 2014
Source: UNAIDS (2015a).

(c). Jamaica: Mortality by age, 2000 and 2014
Source: UNAIDS (2014d).

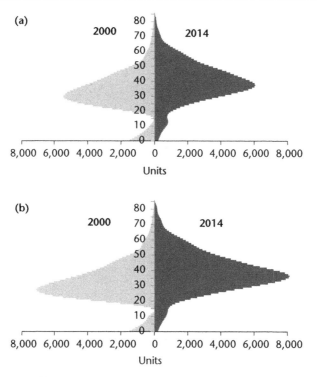

Figure 2.7. Age profile of people living with HIV, Botswana, 2000 and 2014
Source: Author's calculations (intrapolation), based on UNAIDS (2015a).
(a). Men
(b). Women

For infants and adolescents, the 'end of AIDS' in Botswana is indeed near. The number of new HIV infections through mother-to-child transmission has declined to a very low level, and children who have become infected in recent years have a good chance of surviving for many years. Among adults, HIV infections among the youngest cohorts have declined, and survival has improved. These two factors have resulted in a considerable shift in the age distribution of people living with HIV. Between 2000 and 2014, the average age of a person living with HIV in Botswana increased by about six years, from 33 years to 39 years for men, and from 32 years to 39 years for women. This means that people living with HIV now are much older on average than the adult population (aged 15+) overall—HIV/AIDS in Botswana has turned into an epidemic primarily affecting older adults. As the two factors underlying this trend (declining HIV incidence, and substantial progress in extending access to treatment) can be observed in many other countries, this case study illustrates a trend that can be observed globally.

The bulk of the discussion of the impact of HIV/AIDS in the three countries considered here was geared towards looking behind some of the aggregate indicators of the impact of HIV/AIDS. The remainder of the chapter reconnects to the earlier discussion of the impact of HIV/AIDS on life expectancy across countries. The analysis will (1) assess more precisely the impact on life expectancy of HIV/AIDS (i.e. the change against a counterfactual without AIDS) for the three countries and (2) address the role that the expanding access to treatment has played.

'Life expectancy at birth' is used as an indicator of the state of health, for two reasons. First, it plays an important role among development objectives in many countries. Second, unlike average mortality rates, it does not depend on the age structure of the population.[19] 'Life expectancy at birth' is commonly defined as the expected duration of an individual's life, projected from birth, assuming that current age-specific mortality rates would remain the same forever. It is thus a summary indicator of the current mortality profile across the population, but not a forward-looking life expectancy of a concrete cohort.

The estimates for the three countries covered show a large impact of HIV/AIDS on life expectancy, and a partial recovery in recent years. The losses in life expectancy peaked around the year 2002, at 20 years for Botswana, 8 years in Kenya, and 3 years in Jamaica. At the high end, these findings illustrate the catastrophic shocks to life expectancy in some countries discussed earlier. At the low end, the estimates illustrate that even in countries where HIV prevalence is only at 1 or 2 per cent, the impact of HIV/AIDS on health outcomes is by no means negligible.

Regarding the rebound in life expectancy observed in all three countries in Figure 2.8, it is possible to distinguish three factors.[20] First, even without the scaling-up of treatment, the gap would have narrowed somewhat, owing to declining HIV prevalence. Second, the most important factor is without doubt the increased access to treatment, which goes a long way towards reversing the losses in life expectancy. However, even in countries with near-universal treatment access, a considerable loss of life expectancy remains, and further substantial progress in reversing the health impact of HIV/AIDS would need to come from bringing down HIV incidence. Third, mortality among people receiving antiretroviral treatment remains much higher than for the general (non HIV-positive) population. While the scaling-up immediately reduces mortality among people living with HIV/AIDS, a rebound in mortality overall (and thus life expectancy) can occur as an increasing share of the population receives ART, and this factor appears to be the cause of the rebound shown in Botswana.

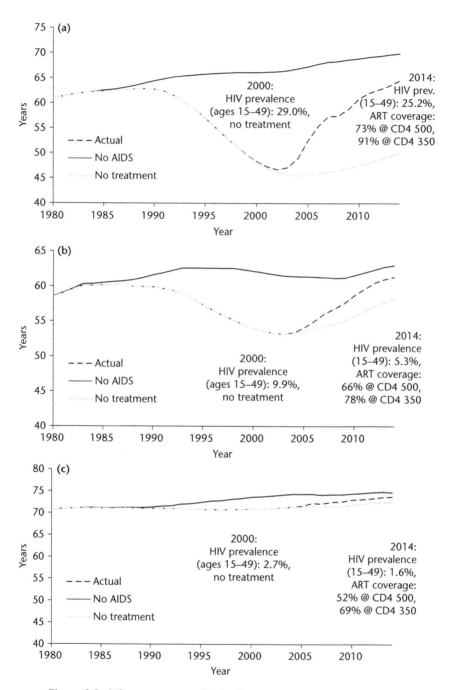

Figure 2.8. Life expectancy at birth, three countries, 1980–2014

Source: Author's calculations, based on UNAIDS (2015a) for Botswana and Kenya, and UNAIDS (2014d) for Jamaica.
(a). Botswana
(b). Kenya
(c). Jamaica

Some Notes on the Impact of the Global Response

The impact of HIV/AIDS is mediated through the policy response to the epidemic, which may contribute to changes in HIV incidence (through interventions affecting risk behaviour or reducing HIV transmission) and survival of people living with HIV (most obviously through improved access to treatment). Examples for the role of policy in shaping the impact of the epidemic discussed in this chapter include the declines in HIV incidence experienced globally and in most countries; the steep reversals in life expectancy, followed by a partial recovery, experienced in many countries; the reduction in mortality among people living with HIV; and the improved availability of treatment in low- and middle-income countries.

These changes lead to important new questions, and are relevant for the economic analysis offered elsewhere in this book. The first question regards attribution—how much of the observed changes in the state of the epidemic and in health outcomes can be attributed to the policy response? Second, how successful has the global response been in combatting the epidemic and mitigating its consequences, especially across less developed countries? These questions are addressed in more detail in Chapter 6 on the 'Impact of the Global Response to HIV/AIDS'. Third, reduced mortality and morbidity among people living with HIV/AIDS modify and generally reduce the social and economic impacts of HIV/AIDS, and it will be important to keep this in mind in the discussion of the social and economic consequences (Chapters 3 and 4). Finally, the changing health impacts of HIV/AIDS, owing to the global response, also have implications for the outcomes of HIV policies—most importantly, the health outcomes (e.g. life years saved, or deaths averted over some policy period) of HIV prevention interventions are diminished. These questions are addressed in Part III of the book, especially in Chapters 8 and 9 dealing with aspects of cost-effectiveness.

3

Impact on Individuals and Households

The impact of HIV/AIDS on the livelihoods of affected households and individuals,[1] and the interactions between HIV/AIDS and poverty, have played an important role in the global policy discourse, in terms of building global support, and in shaping HIV/AIDS policies. For example, the 2006 UN 'Political Declaration' states that 'in many parts of the world, the spread of HIV/AIDS is a cause and consequence of poverty, and that effectively combating HIV/AIDS is essential to the achievement of internationally agreed development goals'. Beegle and de Walque (2009) point out that 'understanding the demographic and socioeconomic patterns of prevalence and incidence of HIV/AIDS in Sub-Saharan Africa is crucial for developing programs and policies to combat HIV/AIDS'.

This chapter discusses the impacts of HIV/AIDS on households and individuals, and the links between HIV/AIDS and socioeconomic factors like poverty and inequality, from several angles.

The first section, 'The socio-economic gradient of HIV/AIDS', addresses the *social determinants of HIV/AIDS*, that is, the extent to which the impact of HIV/AIDS is correlated with social and economic factors. This point is relevant for the repercussions of HIV/AIDS from an economic development perspective, the health policy challenges posed by HIV/AIDS, and the design of HIV prevention policies.

The second section, 'The economic consequences of HIV/AIDS for households and individuals', reviews the evidence on the *impacts of HIV/AIDS on affected individuals and households*, discussing the impacts on households of people *living* with HIV, the consequences of deaths (HIV/AIDS-specific, but also drawing on literature on the consequences of deaths more generally), and the effectiveness of ART in reversing the adverse economic outcomes.[2]

The *impact on orphans* is treated separately in the third section of the chapter, because the impact of HIV/AIDS on this group is not well captured by studies focusing on households affected by HIV/AIDS (as many of them are reared in other households), and because there is a large body of literature dealing with the consequences of orphanhood in general.

The last section addresses the *impacts of HIV/AIDS on poverty and inequality*. These are potentially different from the impacts of HIV/AIDS on households and individuals because of changes in the composition of households over time and especially following a death, interactions between households, and the consequences of increased mortality for poverty headcounts and possibly poverty rates.

The Socioeconomic Gradient of HIV/AIDS

Much of the early concerns regarding the potential adverse development impacts of HIV/AIDS were motivated by the fact that the epidemic primarily affects young adults, especially women, and its apparent concentration in developing countries and in sub-Saharan Africa. UNAIDS (1998) observed that '89 per cent of people with HIV live in sub-Saharan Africa and the developing countries of Asia, which between them account for less than 10% of global gross national product', and a report commissioned by the World Bank and the European Commission (Ainsworth and Over, 1998) observed that 'nine out of 10 people infected lived in developing countries, and two-thirds of those infected lived in the poorest countries of sub-Saharan Africa'.

The academic literature of the day provided a less clear-cut picture. Whiteside (2002) describes a vicious cycle whereby 'poverty increases the spread of HIV and AIDS increases poverty', and concludes that 'directly tackling poverty remains the primary goal'—'poverty alleviation will address the impact of AIDS', and 'will feed into prevention of further infections'. In contrast, Halperin (2001) pointed out that 'many of the African countries most affected by HIV were and are among the most economically developed', and that 'studies from several developing countries have found that HIV rates tend to be higher among people with greater income and education levels'.

Over the following years, gross statements on the association between poverty and HIV/AIDS were superseded by a more nuanced understanding of the global distribution of HIV/AIDS (and of the economies of Africa). For example, UNAIDS (2006) observed that 'the worst-hit countries today are not necessarily the poorest. Southern Africa, with the world's highest HIV prevalence, includes the most economically developed countries in sub-Saharan Africa. Generally, these countries have higher levels of education, gross domestic product and access to water and sanitation than other parts of the continent. However, they also tend to have greater economic inequality and large numbers of people living in poverty, both of which have been clearly associated with HIV transmission.'

Such statements are based on the observed correlations between HIV prevalence and economic indicators like GDP per capita, poverty rates, or summary

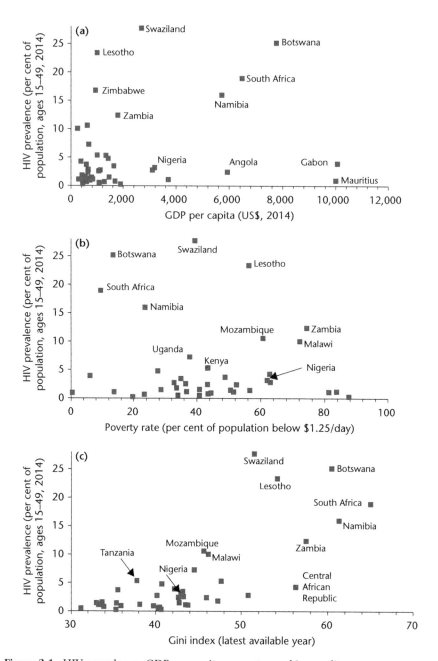

Figure 3.1. HIV prevalence, GDP per capita, poverty, and inequality

Source: UNAIDS (2015a) for HIV prevalence, and World Bank (2015) for GDP per capita, poverty rates (latest available year), and Gini index.

(a). HIV prevalence and GDP per capita across sub-Saharan Africa

(b). HIV prevalence and poverty across sub-Saharan Africa

(c). HIV Prevalence and inequality across sub-Saharan Africa

indices describing the extent of economic inequality, which are illustrated in Figure 3.1 for sub-Saharan Africa in 2014.[3] For the correlation between HIV prevalence and GDP per capita, a mixed picture emerges. Most countries are clustered at fairly low GDP per capita and HIV prevalence. The main exceptions are South Africa and countries adjacent to or surrounded by it, and a number of countries with relatively high income but very low HIV prevalence—either oil-rich countries or small island countries.[4] Regarding poverty, the five countries with the highest HIV prevalence (Botswana, Lesotho, Namibia, South Africa, and Swaziland) have at most average poverty rates.[5] Perhaps the clearest picture emerges for inequality—the highest HIV prevalence for countries with a Gini index below 43 (the regional median) is 5 per cent, and for countries facing extremely high HIV prevalence (about 14 per cent or higher) the Gini index is also very high in a regional or global context.

Statistically, there is a weak positive correlation between HIV prevalence and GDP per capita, a negative correlation between HIV prevalence and poverty rates, and a positive correlation between HIV prevalence and the Gini index. If all three economic variables are included in a regression, only the Gini index comes out positive, while GDP per capita and poverty have statistically and economically insignificant coefficients.[6]

In summary, there is no obvious link between macroeconomic indicators of poverty (poverty rates, or low GDP per capita) and HIV prevalence. Indeed HIV prevalence appears highest in countries with low poverty rates. However, the analysis suggests a robust correlation between HIV prevalence and inequality, as measured by the Gini index. The critical question is whether this correlation can be interpreted as a causal link, and there are some reasons for caution in this regard.[7]

- While there are some theoretical or empirical underpinnings of a link between susceptibility to HIV and inequality, most of this literature regards *gender* inequality or 'groups that have been marginalized socially, culturally, and often economically, such as injection drug users, sex workers, migrants, and men who have sex with men'. The national distribution of income is not a good proxy for such inequalities.[8]

- A link between HIV and economic inequality is more plausible regarding the role of transactional and age-disparate sex (the 'sugar daddy' phenomenon), which are frequently quoted as contributors to the risk of acquiring HIV especially for young women. The empirical relevance of this factor, though, is unclear.[9]

- The results are highly dependent on the experience of Southern Africa, notably the closely integrated countries South Africa, Botswana, Lesotho, Namibia, and Swaziland. Both inequality and high HIV prevalence could reflect specific other factors at work across this region.

The early presumptions about the link between HIV/AIDS and poverty were tested when the results from the first Demographic and Health Surveys (DHSs) including data on HIV status became available around 2005. Shelton et al. (2005) observed that HIV prevalence was higher in the wealthier segments of the population in Tanzania and Kenya.[10] Mishra et al. (2007), based on DHSs from eight countries, also concluded that 'adults in the wealthiest quintiles have a higher prevalence of HIV than those in the poorer quintiles', and that this positive correlation could not be explained by some other factors like place of residence or education.

These findings were corroborated by later studies, based on a larger set of DHS data. Parkhurst (2010) does not find a clear correlation between HIV prevalence and wealth quintile—HIV prevalence tended to increase with wealth in low-income countries, but not in countries with higher GDP per capita. The latest such review (Hajizadeh et al., 2014, based on twenty-four DHS data sets) finds that HIV/AIDS was concentrated among people with higher socioeconomic status in the majority of countries for both men and women; only in Senegal and Swaziland was HIV prevalence higher among individuals in poorer households.

The focus on wealth and income in the literature on the socioeconomic gradient of HIV/AIDS masks several aspects of the socioeconomic profile of the epidemic which are relevant both from an economic development and a policy perspective. The ones consistently appearing in the literature are the impacts of HIV/AIDS on women, the role of education, and differences in the impact of HIV/AIDS by location.[11]

Where heterosexual transmission of HIV dominates, the majority of people living with HIV are women, and women tend to become infected earlier than men—a point illustrated in the discussion of the evolving age profile of HIV/AIDS in Botswana and of HIV/AIDS-related mortality in Botswana and Kenya (Chapter 2). In sub-Saharan Africa, it is estimated that 59 per cent of adults living with HIV are women as of 2014 (UNAIDS, 2015c), and Harris et al. (2014) note that the median female-to-male ratio in adult HIV prevalence from DHSs across twenty-five African countries is 1.64. For young women (ages 15–24), estimated HIV prevalence across sub-Saharan Africa (2.5 per cent) is almost twice as high as for men (1.4 per cent; UNAIDS, 2015c). Some of these differences are commonly attributed to there being a higher risk for women than for men of contracting HIV through vaginal intercourse.[12] Biological factors alone, however, cannot explain the large difference in HIV prevalence between men and women—country-level female-to-male ratios in adult HIV prevalence in DHS data from sub-Saharan Africa range from 1.3 to 2.2 (Harris et al., 2014) or 0.9 to 2.3 (Magadi, 2011).

Magadi (2011) provides a thorough empirical analysis based on DHS data from twenty countries focusing specifically on gender disparities. Among the factors she identifies are age at first sex—for women, especially an age of first sex of 15 or less was associated with higher HIV prevalence. HIV prevalence among women who had never married was higher (but lower among men). Completing primary education was positively associated with HIV prevalence for women, but not for men. Male circumcision—a factor that reduces the risk of contracting HIV for men—also explains some of the variation. Even after controlling for these and other factors, HIV prevalence comes out much higher for women than men, especially at young ages.

Among the factors that have been credited for relatively high HIV prevalence rates among young women are age-discordant matching (women entering sexual relationships with older men, including the 'sugar daddy' phenomenon), and the need to engage in transactional sex for material or survival reasons. A correlation between HIV *prevalence* among women and partners' age has been established in a number of studies. However, Harling et al. (2014) show that larger age differences between partners are not associated with a larger risk of *acquiring* HIV in KwaZulu-Natal, suggesting that the correlation between HIV prevalence and partners' age observed elsewhere does not reflect a causal link.

Access to education features prominently in the HIV/AIDS policy discourse. According to UNAIDS (2014c), lack of education is among the 'obstacles that block adolescent girls and young women from being able to protect themselves against HIV', and the World Bank has observed that 'a good basic education itself ranks among the most effective—and cost-effective—means of HIV/AIDS prevention', and described education as 'an effective "Social Vaccine" against HIV/AIDS'.[13] Thus, lack of education appears as one of the obstacles to HIV prevention and a contributor to vulnerabilities to HIV, and improved access to education is seen as a contributor to effective HIV prevention strategies.

The evidence regarding the association of HIV prevalence and education, however, is not consistent with this view. Fortson (2008) concludes that 'better-educated respondents are more likely to be HIV-positive' according to DHS data from Cameroon, Kenya, and Tanzania (but obtains small and insignificant coefficients for Burkina Faso and Ghana). Magadi (2011), and Magadi and Desta (2011), find a positive link between access to education and HIV prevalence, especially for women, based on pooled DHS data from twenty countries. Asiedu et al. (2012) suggest that the association between education and HIV prevalence is positive in Malawi, but negative in Lesotho, Swaziland, and Zimbabwe.

Overall, the picture from these cross-sectional data is more consistent with a view of basic education as a contributor to social (and sexual) opportunity, rather than a contributor to HIV prevention in its own right. In contrast, some experimental or quasi-experimental studies suggest that cash transfers to keep girls in school could be effective in preventing HIV infections among these girls (e.g. Baird et al., 2012; Behrman, 2015).[14] To reconcile these different bodies of evidence, it will be necessary to gain a better understanding of the dynamic effects of interventions to keep young people in school on HIV acquisition—to what extent do the direct and behavioural effects persist into adulthood?[15]

Household data including data on HIV prevalence have also advanced the understanding of differences in HIV prevalence across locations (which in turn have motivated more targeted approached to HIV prevention, as documented by the emphasis placed on the role of location by UNAIDS (2014c)),[16] and of their social and economic correlates.

Magadi (2013), using data from twenty DHS studies, addresses the association of HIV/AIDS and poverty, differentiating between urban and rural areas. While other authors have not found a clear association between HIV prevalence and wealth on the national level, Magadi finds that this masks 'that the urban poor in sub-Saharan Africa have significantly *higher* odds of HIV infection than their urban non-poor counterparts, despite poverty being associated with a significantly *lower* risk among rural residents' (her emphasis). Large differences in HIV prevalence may also occur *within* urban areas. Madise et al. (2012) estimated that HIV prevalence in two Nairobi slums was at 11.8 per cent, about twice the rate as estimated for the (non-slum) urban population in the DHS.

An interesting variation of the work on location and HIV prevalence is a paper by Feldacker et al. (2010), combining DHS data for Malawi (which include precise spatial information) and area-level socioeconomic data, who find that HIV prevalence for women is negatively correlated with distance to a major road or to a major city. High spatial disparities were also observed by Tanser et al. (2009) in KwaZulu-Natal, with HIV prevalence ranging from 6 per cent to 36 per cent across locations and the highest rates observed close to a major road, while 'more inaccessible rural areas' had the lowest HIV prevalence rates.

A shortcoming of the empirical literature on the association between HIV/AIDS and income based on DHS data is a lack of evidence on the link between HIV/AIDS and inequality, which plays a large role in the policy discourse and studies using cross-country data. This reflects the difficulties in constructing sub-national indices of inequality, especially as the wealth indices reported in DHS studies cannot be interpreted easily in terms of inequality. Durevall and Lindskog (2012), focusing on HIV prevalence among a sample of women in Malawi, get around this problem by combining DHS data with data from a household income and expenditure survey to obtain regional inequality indices for consumption. They report a positive association between the risk of HIV infection and inequality. While HIV prevalence for wealthier individuals was higher, the respective coefficients tended to be statistically insignificant.

While most of the evidence on socioeconomic aspects of HIV/AIDS is from cross-sectional studies, the dynamics of the epidemic have changed very considerably over the last two decades, and a number of studies suggest that the burden of HIV/AIDS has been shifting to households with lower wealth or education. Lopman et al. (2007), for example, observe that HIV prevalence declined most, and HIV incidence was lowest, for the wealthiest individuals in Manicaland (Zimbabwe) in 2001–03. A review of published studies by Hargreaves et al. (2008) finds that 'HIV prevalence fell more consistently among highly educated groups than among less educated groups'. Based on data from countries where more than one DHS data set was available, Hargreaves et al. (2013) conclude that the burden of HIV/AIDS is shifting towards people with lower educational attainment.

One challenge that is common to almost all of the studies of socioeconomic correlates of HIV/AIDS arises from the fact that they draw on data of HIV prevalence.[17] If mortality among people living with HIV is correlated with socioeconomic status, then HIV prevalence could give a misleading picture of differences in the impact of HIV/AIDS depending on certain socioeconomic indicators. Specifically, it is conceivable that HIV prevalence understates the impact of HIV among the poor, because the poor die because of AIDS more quickly.[18] However, mortality among poor people is also higher across the board, so this argument could cut both ways.[19]

This shortcoming reflects that most of the evidence on the socioeconomic gradient of HIV comes from cross-sectional studies, whereas inference on trends in HIV incidence requires longitudinal studies, identifying individuals who *become* HIV-positive. While some such studies are available, most do not provide an analysis of economic correlates of HIV incidence.[20]

Looking ahead, the most important challenge to understanding the socioeconomic correlates of HIV/AIDS is that HIV prevalence increasingly becomes a policy-determined variable, reflecting access to treatment. To the extent that access to treatment is correlated with socioeconomic indicators, HIV prevalence can be a misleading indicator for the impact of HIV/AIDS per se—higher treatment access and thus lower mortality among some socioeconomic group would result in higher HIV prevalence in this group, while the impact of HIV/AIDS in that group is actually reduced as those contracting HIV survive for longer.

The Economic Consequences of HIV/AIDS for Households and Individuals

The analysis of the economic consequences of HIV/AIDS for affected households and individuals (i.e. people living with HIV and their households) poses a number of challenges. The relevant time frames are very long, and the consequences of HIV differ very considerably according to the stage of disease—especially since HIV/AIDS, owing to widespread access to antiretroviral treatment, has evolved into a chronic disease. Moreover, the composition of households changes, obviously following a death, but also for demographic and economic reasons. The discussion approaches the economic consequences of HIV/AIDS from three angles. It covers the impacts of HIV/AIDS on individuals living with HIV and their households, and addresses how these impacts have changed over the last years; reviews the literature on the consequences of deaths (HIV/AIDS-specific and in general), and discusses the impact of orphanhood.

Most of the evidence on the *impacts of HIV/AIDS on affected individuals and households* comes from cross-sectional studies, comparing the situation of affected households with that of reference cases, and looking at aspects like household incomes, the level and composition of expenditures, and the situation of household members.[21]

With regard to income and economic status, the literature on the socioeconomic gradient of HIV/AIDS (reviewed in the previous section) shows that households affected by HIV/AIDS are not systematically worse off across countries. Because this correlation reflects both socioeconomic differences in HIV *incidence* and the economic *consequences* of HIV/AIDS, it is not a clean indicator of either factor. However, in the absence of a clear negative correlation between HIV status and economic status, it is hard to argue that HIV/AIDS has a strong negative impact on household incomes. To clearly separate the two factors, a longitudinal dataset—tracking households affected by HIV/AIDS over time, ideally from the time of infection, and also containing households not affected by HIV as reference cases—would be required. Owing to the nature of the epidemic, such data are very rare.

The (statistically) weak impacts of HIV/AIDS on the incomes of affected households may reflect that HIV status is not a good marker of losses in capabilities, as the latter are concentrated over a fairly short period preceding the death of a person living with HIV. Fox et al. (2004) document this point analysing the productivity of tea pluckers in Kenya in the months and years preceding death or retirement for medical reasons (i.e. individuals were too sick to work at all). A statistically significant impact of HIV/AIDS became apparent only 1½ years before termination, and tea pluckers earned about one-sixth less in the two years preceding termination. This means that most people living with HIV—2 years or more away from death—would not show any productivity decline.

This study preceded the availability of treatment (other than for AIDS-related opportunistic infections). As treatment mitigates and reverses the health consequences of HIV/AIDS, productivity losses and the associated income losses are also reduced, as documented in several studies.[22] Bor et al.

(2012) observe that employment for a group of Batswana patients had fallen by 38 per cent in the 2 years preceding initiation of treatment. Four years after initiation of treatment, 85 per cent of patients were still alive, and employment had returned to 90 per cent of its baseline level. Based on data from Kenya, Goldstein et al. (2010) report similar findings, and point to improved nutritional status and school attendance among children in patients' households.[23]

Larson et al. (2013) follow up on the earlier study from Kenya (Fox et al., 2004), focusing on the impacts of treatment (Figure 3.2). The impacts of HIV/AIDS—in terms of attendance and especially of the quantity of tea plucked—become visible about one year before workers initiate treatment, and there is a speedy (but only partial) recovery once individuals are on

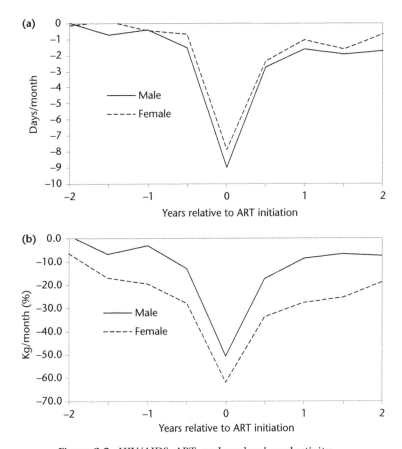

Figure 3.2. HIV/AIDS, ART, and workers' productivity

Note: Losses are shown relative to outcomes in a reference group.

Source: Larson et al., 2013.

(a). Loss in days working per month (days)

(b). Loss in kilograms harvested per month (per cent)

treatment. In addition to reduced attendance and productivity on the job, the changes also reflect that some sick individuals (especially women) are shifted to physically less demanding tasks.[24]

The findings by Larson et al. (2013), Bor et al. (2012), and Goldstein et al. (2012) also have implications for the impacts of HIV/AIDS as treatment coverage and eligibility improves. In the study by Larson and others, it appears that people living with HIV initiate treatment very late during the disease, close to the point at which they would die or no longer be able to work.[25] If more effective HIV surveillance, or changed health-seeking behaviour, results in earlier initiation of treatment, the adverse impacts of HIV/AIDS—and the rebound following initiation of treatment—shown in Figure 3.2 would be reduced very considerably.

The impacts of HIV/AIDS on the expenditures of affected households are better documented. Some expenditure items can be directly attributed to HIV/ AIDS treatment and care. Meaningful analysis can therefore be conducted by assessing the expenditure patterns of households affected by HIV/AIDS, without necessarily requiring data on reference cases (otherwise similar households *not* affected by HIV/AIDS) or pre-HIV expenditure patterns for affected households.

The most important cost of HIV/AIDS to households affected by HIV/AIDS is the cost of accessing and obtaining care and treatment. These costs can absorb a substantial share of household resources, even where antiretroviral therapy is available free of charge. Beaulière et al. (2010), based on data from Côte d'Ivoire collected in 2007, estimate that health expenditures for the HIV-infected individual averaged US$14 per month (about 4 per cent of average household income of US$314). About one quarter of the costs went towards antiretroviral therapy, one-quarter to travel expenses, and one-half to other medical expenses (which increased steeply at lower CD4 counts). Mahal et al. (2008) apply propensity score matching to compare health spending in households affected by HIV/AIDS in Nigeria in 2004 to a sample of otherwise similar households not affected, finding that out-of-pocket expenses for HIV/AIDS-related healthcare accounted for about 30 per cent of household income.[26]

As the costs of care and treatment account for the bulk of HIV/AIDS-related expenditures to households, an alternative way of obtaining estimates of the costs of HIV/AIDS to households is through data on patients accessing care (bearing in mind that these are a subset of people living with HIV). Pinto et al. (2013) estimate that the costs of accessing care amounted to US$2.55 at a 'centralized care' site in Malawi (where average monthly personal income was US$58), of which travel expenses accounted for US$1.33. At a 'decentralized care' site, costs of accessing care were lower (US$1.48), mostly because of lower travel expenses (US$0.37), but patient incomes were also much lower (US$28 per month). Each visit to the clinic cost about 7 hours (at either site), of which one half was spent at the clinic, and the rest on travel. Cleary et al. (2013) estimate the monthly costs to ART patients in South Africa at ZAR 81 (9.4 per cent of average household income). In this study, the burden to households is more severe in rural areas, where spending on self-care (non-prescription and traditional medicines) and transportation is much higher.

Insurance plays a small role in the literature on the impact of HIV/AIDS on households, because in countries with high HIV prevalence treatment is generally provided free of charge, and because the coverage of insurance has been low in most of these countries, and access limited to the wealthiest households and the formal sector. (E.g. in South Africa, access to insurance is very low outside the top three deciles of the income distribution.)

More difficult to measure are non-financial impacts of HIV on the welfare of household members, as financial resources are allocated to care and treatment and household members devote time to care. Alkenbrack Batteh et al. (2008) show that children had fewer meals and had to take on more responsibilities in households affected by HIV/AIDS in Cambodia. Similarly, Heymann and Kidman (2009) report that parents with HIV/AIDS care-giving responsibilities spent less time on their children, and older children had to take on additional responsibilities in the household. The literature on the impacts of antiretroviral therapy also provides insights on the impacts of HIV/AIDS on household members. Goldstein et al. (2010) find that treatment initiation in Kenya has been associated with 'substantial improvements... in the nutritional status and school attendance of children in patients' households'. This latter finding on the effectiveness of ART can also be read as a statement about the consequences of HIV/AIDS—because treatment tends to be initiated when the patient is already severely ill, the estimates in reversals of outcomes owing to treatment provide snapshots of the impacts on households of caring for a severely ill member.

The *death of a household member* is a traumatic experience, and a watershed in terms of the socioeconomic consequences of HIV/AIDS for the household. It often occurs when household resources have already been stretched by care for a terminally ill person, and results in substantial additional expenses. Following the death, the consequences are less clear—children may lose a parent (discussed in the section on orphans, later in this chapter), the household loses a source of income, but the deceased also no longer absorbs household resources on care or normal living expenses. Looking further ahead, the household composition may change, for demographic or economic reasons.

Methodologically, the death of a person living with HIV divides two bodies of literature—studies focusing on people living with HIV or households containing such a person, and studies of the consequences of mortality. Most of the latter do not distinguish between HIV/AIDS and other causes of death explicitly, but frequently cover countries or areas in which HIV/AIDS is a dominant cause of premature mortality among adults.[27]

The study by Ardington et al. (2014) is unique as it looks at households before and after a death, distinguishing AIDS-related deaths from those due to other causes, based on a large longitudinal dataset from KwaZulu-Natal. They find that 'households in which members die of AIDS are systematically poorer than other households', but that 'these households were poorer long before members fell ill with AIDS'. AIDS-related deaths had an impoverishing effect on households, which was very similar to the effect of a sudden death—that is, absorption of household resources by care and treatment preceding a death did not play a large role in this sample. Funeral expenses can explain some of this impoverishing effect, while the loss of an employed member did not significantly contribute to it.[28]

Among the most immediate consequences of a death are the costs of funerals. For KwaZulu-Natal, Case et al. (2013) observe that households on average spend the equivalent of an annual income on funerals, but that these costs differ according to the status of the deceased—funeral expenses for women and distant relatives are lower. The bulk of funeral expenditures (about 90 per cent) were financed by household members, although one-quarter of households needed to borrow, and about one quarter of the deceased (typically elderly) had a funeral policy.

It is plausible that the consequences of a death for the household depend on the identity of the deceased, for example, his or her role in the family and the contribution to family income. However, even if a main breadwinner dies, the income loss does not need to be permanent, as other family members may take on new responsibilities or as new members join the household. The most substantial study addressing these points is a paper by Mather et al. (2004), which summarizes the findings of five related studies focusing on rural households in Kenya, Malawi, Mozambique, Rwanda, and Zambia, respectively, usually with a time horizon of around 5 years.[29]

Mather and others point out that the majority of deceased prime-age adults are not household heads or spouses, and that a disproportionate number of casualties are among younger female dependents. Some households appear to be able to attract new members to replace deceased prime-age adults, but this ability appears diminished for poor households or households suffering the death of a household head or spouse. The identity of the deceased also affects the economic consequences of a death. In Kenya, for example, 'the death of a male household head is associated with larger negative impacts on household crop production, non-farm income, and asset levels'. These larger effects may reflect the missing contributions of the deceased household head, but they could also be the consequence of a limited ability of widows to control household assets.[30]

Beegle et al. (2008) span an even wider time horizon, utilizing a large survey tracking individuals from about 2,000 households over 13 years (1991–2004) in Kagera (Tanzania). As deaths occurred throughout this period, it is possible to draw inference on how the impact of adult deaths evolves over time. They find that the death of a prime-age adult results in a drop in consumption of 7 per cent in the first five years following a death, but that this drop becomes smaller and statistically insignificant later on.[31] Seeley et al. (2008) complement the quantitative studies discussed earlier with an in-depth ethnological study of 26 households from Uganda, designed to throw some light on the role of interactions between households—factors that cannot be captured by an empirical analysis taking the household as a unit of account. They find that households affected by HIV/AIDS in general have been able to get by, partly owing to changes in household composition and support received from communities.[32] At the same time, the focus on 'households affected by HIV/AIDS' (i.e. containing a person living with HIV/AIDS, or having experienced an AIDS-related death) falls short in terms of capturing the impacts of HIV/AIDS on households overall, as support to related households has been a drag on the resources of other households as well.

Overall, the evidence reviewed here is consistent with the conclusions drawn by Seeley et al. (2010) from about 20 years of empirical work on the effects of HIV/AIDS on rural communities in East Africa: 'People have undoubtedly suffered terrible personal loss and distress, but those who have survived have got by, they have drawn on support from family, friends and from local organisations to rebuild livelihoods.... From today's perspective, the AIDS epidemic seems not to have had the profound long-term impact in this part of East Africa that was predicted 20 years ago.'

Orphans

One of the distinguishing features of HIV/AIDS is that it affects primarily young adults. High AIDS-related mortality therefore results in a steep increase in the number of orphans. Apart from the direct consequences for the children affected, concerns about the repercussions of an increasing number of orphans (such as economic collapse or a potential 'crime time bomb') have played a role in the HIV/AIDS policy discourse.[33]

UNICEF (2014) estimates that globally 150 million children, or 7 per cent of the young population of ages 0–17, were orphans (defined as children who have lost at least one parent) as of 2012, and that 18 million were orphaned as a consequence of HIV/AIDS. In line with the burden of disease, most children orphaned by HIV/AIDS are located in sub-Saharan Africa (about 15 million), where they account for one-quarter of all orphans. The impact of HIV/AIDS on

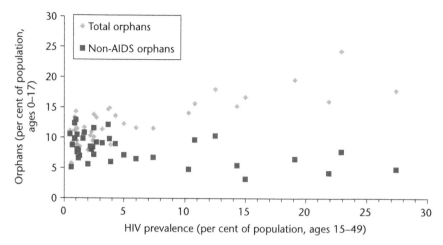

Figure 3.3. Orphan rates and HIV prevalence, 2013

Source: Author's calculations, based on UNICEF (2015). Data cover most countries in sub-Saharan Africa, Haiti, and Papua New Guinea.

orphans, however, is distributed very unevenly across countries (as is the case for the impact of HIV/AIDS more generally). While orphans may account for over 10 per cent of the young population in some least developed countries even without the contribution of HIV/AIDS,[34] orphans account for at least 13 per cent and up to 24 per cent of the young population in countries with an HIV prevalence exceeding 10 per cent (Figure 3.3).

The aggregate figures, however, mask several aspects of the impact of HIV/AIDS on young people. First, orphan rates are low at birth, and rise with age. The number of children experiencing orphanhood at a very young age is thus lower than the average, while it is much higher for older children. For example, in Zimbabwe, an orphan rate of 24 per cent in 2004/05 reflected a rate of 8 per cent for ages 0–4, 28 per cent for ages 0–14, and 36 per cent at ages 15–17.[35] Second, a disproportionate number of children orphaned by HIV/AIDS are 'double' orphans (having lost both parents). This is rare for children orphaned for other causes (9 per cent of those orphans), but common for children orphaned by HIV/AIDS of whom 31 per cent where double orphans in 2012 (UNICEF, 2013). Third, in cases of HIV/AIDS, parental death typically follows some period of illness, so that adverse impacts on children precede orphanhood (one reason for the focus on OVCs—orphans *and vulnerable children*—in HIV/AIDS policies).

Similar to the literature on the household impacts of HIV/AIDS, there are two types of studies addressing the consequences of orphanhood—cross-sectional studies, frequently drawing on DHS data, and longitudinal studies following a cohort into and through orphanhood.

Bicego et al. (2003), the first study using DHS data to address the emerging impact of HIV/AIDS on orphans, observe that orphans have a lower probability of being at the appropriate grade level in school, but are not obviously disadvantaged in terms of household wealth. Case et al. (2004) add several insights to these findings—they find that *paternal* orphans tend to live in poorer households than non-orphans (or maternal orphans), and link the disadvantage in access to education to orphans' living arrangements—'the degree of relatedness between orphans and their adult caregivers is highly predictive of children's outcomes'. Ainsworth and Filmer (2006) build on a dataset compiled from 102 surveys including data on orphans (about two-thirds are DHS data), including data from many countries outside sub-Saharan Africa. They show that enrolment rates for orphans are lower, but that the difference is small and insignificant in many countries, and that it is much smaller than differences in access to education associated with differences in wealth. Mishra and Bignami-Van Assche (2008) consider a richer set of outcomes from DHS studies—while confirming earlier findings regarding access to education, they find 'little evidence that OVC are disadvantaged in health, nutritional status, and health care'.

Among papers following orphans and the consequences of orphanhood over time, Ainsworth et al. (2005) focus on the time around an adult death, showing that an adult death may delay school attendance for maternal orphans and children in poor households, and result in lower attendance for children already in school. In contrast, Beegle et al. (2010) address the long-term consequences of orphanhood, using a sample of non-orphaned children surveyed in 1991–1994, and then again in 2004 by which time about one in five had experienced orphanhood before age 15.[36] Maternal orphanhood was associated with a loss of 2 centimetres in final height attainment and of one year of educational attainment. For paternal orphans the effects were generally similar but of lower magnitude and statistically insignificant.

One aspect that occasionally plays a role in the policy discourse on HIV/AIDS is the phenomenon of 'child-headed households'. However, the few empirical studies addressing this point do not find that it plays a large role. Hosegood et al. (2007), in a study covering Malawi, South Africa, and Tanzania, 'find no evidence that the prevalence of child-headed households is significant or has increased in the three study areas'. According to Meintjes et al. (2010), 0.7 per cent of children in South Africa were living in child-headed households (based on data collected between 2000 and 2007). Moreover, it is not plausible that HIV/AIDS had a large impact on this rate, as it has remained stable in 2000–2007 (while the estimated number of AIDS orphans has increased steeply), and as over 90 per cent of children in such households had at least one living parent.

HIV/AIDS, Poverty, and Inequality

The available evidence on the impact of HIV/AIDS on affected households does not directly translate into evidence on the impact of HIV/AIDS on poverty and inequality, for three reasons. First, studies focusing on households affected by HIV/AIDS do not capture interactions between households. For example, to the extent that households affected by HIV/AIDS receive support from other households, a study on the impact of HIV/AIDS on affected households understates the impacts on the community. On the other hand, other households may benefit, for example, if someone else takes up employment vacated by a person too sick to work or who has died. Second, HIV/AIDS—through reduced investment or access to education—could have longer-term consequences not captured by household studies. Third, poverty rates and indicators for inequality are ambiguous measures for the impact of a mortality shock, because the composition of the population changes.

For these reasons, the study of the impacts of HIV/AIDS on poverty and inequality is distinct from the study of household-level effects of HIV/AIDS, and additionally requires some economy-wide data, or a modelling suitable to assess the economy-wide implications of the evidence on the household-level effects of HIV/AIDS.

As a starting point, a look at the association between HIV/AIDS and changes in poverty or inequality is useful—if HIV/AIDS has a significant impact on poverty or inequality, it should be possible to detect it in the data. Figure 3.4 summarizes the available data, plotting estimates of annual changes in poverty rates (at the \$1.25/day poverty line used by the World Bank) and in the Gini index of inequality over some period against HIV prevalence at the beginning of the period.[37]

On this high level of aggregation, there is no clear link between HIV prevalence and changes in poverty and inequality across countries. HIV prevalence is basically uncorrelated with changes in poverty, and there is a weak positive correlation between HIV prevalence and subsequent changes in inequality. These results are robust to including some other variables (e.g. GDP per capita) in the analysis and to replacing the absolute changes of the variables of interest with percentage changes.[38] The cross-country data thus do not suggest a significant impact of HIV/AIDS on poverty, and on inequality.[39]

To reconcile the household-level evidence and the macroeconomic perspective, various studies combine estimates of the impact of HIV/AIDS across a distribution of households (drawing from a national household income and expenditure survey) with some macroeconomic model. Greener et al. (2000), in an analysis of the macroeconomic effects of HIV/AIDS in Botswana, distinguish three factors: The loss in income of households affected by HIV/AIDS

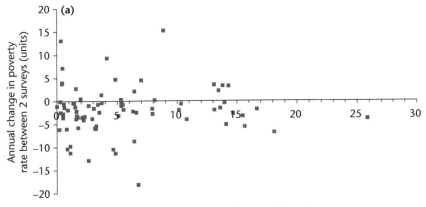

HIV prevalence (ages 15–49), year of first of two surveys

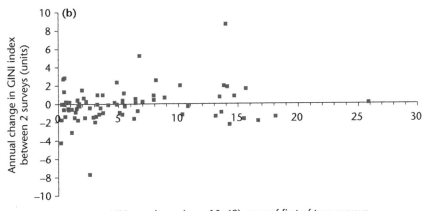

HIV prevalence (ages 15–49), year of first of two surveys

Figure 3.4. HIV prevalence and changes in poverty and inequality

Source: Author's calculations, based on World Bank (2015) and UNAIDS (2015c).
(a). Changes in poverty and HIV prevalence
  Note: Poverty rate estimated at $1.25/day.
(b). Changes in inequality and HIV prevalence

alone would increase the poverty rate by 4.0 percentage points. As some households benefit from filling jobs vacated by people who have died because of AIDS, the impact on poverty is reduced to 3.1 percentage points. However, if allowance is made for increased needs of households affected by HIV/AIDS, the impact of HIV/AIDS on poverty increases to 4.9 percentage points. This analysis—preceding the scaling-up of treatment—was updated by Jefferis et al. (2008), who estimate a much reduced impact of HIV/AIDS on poverty (1.5 percentage points), and find that antiretroviral therapy reduces the impact of HIV/AIDS on poverty by one-third to one-half.

Salinas and Haacker (2006) provide a similar analysis for Ghana, Kenya, Swaziland, and Zambia, finding that the impacts of HIV/AIDS on poverty are disproportionately large in Ghana and Kenya because of high HIV prevalence among population groups just above the poverty line. Financial support between households tends to reduce the impacts on poverty—while some households are pulled into poverty by providing financial support, the support reduces *steep* declines in household income assumed for households affected by HIV/AIDS which is the larger effect with regard to poverty. Cogneau and Grimm (2008), with a fuller macroeconomic analysis on Côte d'Ivoire, find that HIV/AIDS reduces economic growth, but it results in a very small change in GDP per capita, poverty, and inequality.

Poverty rates, though, can be a very misleading indicator for the impacts of HIV/AIDS on poverty—possibly, the most direct impact of HIV/AIDS on poverty rates is by killing people rather than through its financial costs to households, or other consequences for household members. For example, HIV/AIDS could exacerbate poverty among poor households, but if it also kills poor people more quickly than others, poverty rates and GDP per capita might improve, even though the economic and life prospects of poor people deteriorate steeply. To avoid such a 'repugnant conclusion', analyses of economic welfare in situations where changes in mortality or life expectancy play an important role frequently use some indicators describing an individual's expected living standards over his or her life, which are reduced by an increased risk of mortality (as well as income losses).[40] These issues will be discussed further in Chapter 4 in the evaluation of the macroeconomic consequences of HIV/AIDS.

4

Macroeconomic Consequences of HIV/AIDS

The global response to HIV/AIDS has been motivated partly by concerns about the potential *economic* consequences of HIV/AIDS—especially considering that many countries facing high HIV prevalence were also characterized by a low level of economic development even before the consequences of HIV/AIDS started to be felt. These concerns mirror a strand of thinking in economic development that attributes a central role to health not only in its own right, but also as a 'critical input into poverty reduction, economic growth, and long-term economic development' (Commission on Macroeconomics and Health, 2001).

Correspondingly, the *economic* returns to investments in HIV/AIDS play a role in assessing the outcomes of HIV/AIDS interventions. Do HIV/AIDS interventions, in addition to their health impacts, also contribute to attaining economic development objectives? What implications do such economic returns have for the understanding of the effectiveness of HIV/AIDS interventions? If HIV/AIDS interventions result in higher GDP and higher government revenues, do these higher revenues refinance at least some of the costs of the HIV/AIDS response? The perspective of HIV/AIDS interventions as an instrument for human and economic development also adds a tool for persuading finance ministers to spend money, providing hard-nosed economic arguments to effectively compete for funds with economic sectors like agriculture or transport (Alleyne, 2009).

At the same time, the evidence on the economic impacts of HIV/AIDS provides an opportunity for testing and refining perceived wisdom on the links between health and economic development, especially considering the large magnitude of the health shock caused by HIV/AIDS. For example, the evidence on the link between HIV/AIDS and economic growth contributes to validating or refining general conceptions about the link between health and growth.

Overview of Macroeconomic Consequences

The macroeconomic consequences of HIV/AIDS are multi-faceted. While much of the literature on the economic impacts of HIV/AIDS and this chapter's discussion focus on GDP and GDP per capita, it is useful to take a step back and consider the various dimensions of the macroeconomic implications of HIV/AIDS.

- HIV/AIDS affects material living standards, as measured by GDP and GDP per capita, most directly as a consequence of increased mortality (causing economic disruptions and resulting in a diminished population size), and as private and public HIV/AIDS spending results in diminished investment. Looking further ahead, HIV/AIDS may also affect education (and eventually labour productivity), as children in households affected by HIV/AIDS may be disadvantaged in terms of access to schooling, and as reduced life expectancy diminishes incentives to invest in education.

- A focus on GDP and GDP per capita misses out on the changing *composition* of spending. Private and public spending on the response to HIV/AIDS absorbs resources which could otherwise be used for additional investment or consumption. GDP or GDP per capita net of HIV/AIDS-related spending is thus a more accurate measure of the impact of HIV/AIDS on material living standards than GDP and GDP per capita alone.[1] This logic is sometimes applied in studies of the household-level effects of HIV/AIDS, when poverty lines are adjusted to take into account the spending needs of people living with HIV, but rarely in studies of the macroeconomic consequences of HIV/AIDS.[2]

- The impact of and the response to HIV/AIDS affect government finance. If the economy grows more slowly as a consequence of HIV/AIDS, government revenues (but also certain expenses linked to the population size) also increase more slowly. The more direct implications of HIV/AIDS, though, are for government expenditures, as the response to HIV/AIDS absorbs fiscal resources. This is the focus of Part III of this book, which discusses the available data on the financial costs of HIV/AIDS, and the financial consequences and cost-effectiveness of alternative HIV/AIDS policies and interventions. Additionally, HIV/AIDS affects government spending beyond HIV/AIDS line items, through conditions like disability or orphanhood addressed by non-HIV/AIDS-specific spending, and through the costs of the impact of HIV/AIDS on government employees.

- If the impacts of HIV/AIDS are distributed unevenly across households, poverty may increase even if GDP per capita remains unchanged or even increases.

- Some households and individuals gain as a consequence of HIV/AIDS-related mortality, e.g. benefiting from employment opportunities opened up by a death—a factor captured by macroeconomic indicators like GDP per capita, but not by studies focusing on the consequences of HIV/AIDS for affected households.

- HIV/AIDS affects the production costs of private enterprises, to the extent that increased morbidity affects the productivity of employees, or because of mortality-related disruptions. Early studies suggest that HIV/AIDS increases personnel costs by several percentage points in countries with high HIV prevalence.[3] However, in a large survey of South African enterprises, most companies perceived at most a small impact (up to 2.5 per cent) of HIV/AIDS on profits, and few considered HIV/AIDS in investment decisions (Ellis, 2006; Ellis and Terwin, 2005). The scaling-up of treatment has reduced the impacts of HIV/AIDS on production costs; and treatment has become much cheaper for companies providing it to employees.

- From a macroeconomic perspective, productivity losses caused by HIV/AIDS do not necessarily reduce the profitability and competitiveness of companies if the costs are passed on to employees through lower salaries. Chicoine (2012) provides evidence in this direction, suggesting that wages in areas which have experienced high AIDS-related mortality have declined relative to other areas in South Africa.

- The reliance of many HIV programmes on external funding raises the possibility of some 'Dutch disease' effects—i.e., the inflows of aid resulting in an appreciation of the currency and undermining competitiveness. HIV/AIDS-related aid flows, however, rarely exceed 2 per cent of GDP of the recipient country, and a large chunk of it typically finances imports of drugs and therefore does not cause external imbalances. As HIV/AIDS-related aid flows are thus small compared to overall aid flows to highly aid-dependent countries (which may exceed 20 per cent of GDP), and the empirical evidence on aid, competitiveness, and growth is ambiguous, this issue is not explored in more detail.[4]

Modelling the Impact of HIV/AIDS on Economic Growth

The first studies on the macroeconomic impact of HIV/AIDS were conducted at the World Bank in the early 1990s, after the scale of HIV/AIDS in some countries in sub-Saharan Africa had become apparent, and in response to concerns about the adverse economic development impacts of the epidemic. These studies were conducted in the tradition of the neoclassical growth accounting framework, focusing on the impacts of HIV/AIDS on productivity, savings, and population growth. While many policy-oriented studies continued to follow this mould, more recent academic studies have tended to focus on the implication of HIV/AIDS on productivity and its determinants. This shift followed the emergence of 'new growth theory', which attributes a central role to human capital (education, etc.) and individuals' incentives and decisions to invest in human capital.[5]

Many of the issues in analysing the impacts of HIV/AIDS on economic growth can be summarized using a simple macroeconomic growth accounting model.[6] In this model, the level of GDP (Y) in some year (t) depends on the economy's capital stock (K), the supply of labour (L), and labour productivity or human capital (H, which is a measure of the productivity of labour reflecting factors like education), that is,

$$Y_t = F(K_t, H_t L_t). \tag{1}$$

The level of GDP per capita,

$$\frac{Y_t}{L_t} = F\left(\frac{K_t}{L_t}, H_t\right), \tag{2}$$

depends on the capital–labour ratio and labour productivity.[7] The capital stock changes as a share (s) of GDP is invested, while some portion of the capital stock depreciates at rate δ, i.e.,

$$K_{t+1} - K_t = s_t Y_t - \delta K_t. \tag{3}$$

In this model, there are three types of effects of a health shock like HIV/AIDS on economic growth:

- The labour supply L grows more slowly, mainly as a consequence of increased mortality.[8] Consequently, GDP grows more slowly. Because a smaller labour supply means a higher capital–labour ratio, GDP per capita grows faster.

- The investment rate (s) declines, as private and public resources are devoted to coping with the impact of HIV/AIDS and the HIV/AIDS response (provided that at least a portion of this spending is financed from reduced investment rather than lower consumption). As a consequence, the capital stock K is depleted.

- The average productivity of labour (H) deteriorates because of increased morbidity, and also because human capital in the form of experience is destroyed. However, average productivity also depends on the composition of the working-age population. If HIV/AIDS primarily depleted the most educated, H would decline (setting aside other factors). In contrast, if the impact of HIV/AIDS is concentrated among unskilled workers, this factor would raise H.

- HIV/AIDS may affect households' decisions to invest in education, owing to the burden on households affected by HIV/AIDS (see Chapter 3), or because of the shortened expected life span (which reduces the period over which investments in education yield benefits). In models inspired by 'new growth theory', these effects would reduce the accumulation of human capital.

There are two summary points which can be taken from this stylized analysis. First, HIV/AIDS has a negative effect on each of the production factors K, L, and H (unless H increases, e.g. because HIV is concentrated among populations with low skills, and this effect dominates other factors) contributing to GDP, that is, there is a strong presumption that HIV/AIDS reduces GDP. Second, the impact of HIV/AIDS on GDP per capita is ambiguous—if the labour supply L declines more than the capital stock, then the capital–labour ratio $\frac{K}{L}$ may increase and result in an increase in GDP per capita.

Among the earliest studies of the macroeconomic effects of HIV/AIDS is a series of papers by or involving Cuddington,[9] addressing many of the questions appearing throughout this literature—what are the magnitude of the medical and private costs, how much of the costs are financed through savings, how and by how much does HIV/AIDS affect productivity? These studies explore a range of assumptions on the magnitude of the impact of HIV/AIDS on productivity and investment, which translate into a wide range of estimates of the impact of HIV/AIDS on growth—for example Cuddington (1993a) projected a negative impact of HIV/AIDS on GDP per capita of between 0.5 per cent and 11 per cent by 2010 (implying a decline in the growth of GDP per capita of between 0 and 0.5 per cent), but suggests that the smaller impacts within this range were more plausible. Over (1992), among other points, addresses the macroeconomic consequences of the social gradient of HIV/AIDS—if HIV/AIDS is concentrated among highly skilled individuals, the impact on GDP per capita will be exacerbated.

Some of the early studies also address the fact that many developing economies are characterized by a large informal sector, with low output per head, and a formal economy which is the main contributor to GDP.[10] However, the results on the impact of HIV/AIDS on growth from 'dual-economy models' taking account of this uneven economic structure are very similar to the more aggregated growth models described earlier.

One common finding of this class of models is that HIV/AIDS slows down economic growth, largely in line with population growth. However, with regard to GDP per capita, the impacts of HIV/AIDS largely cancel out—investment and labour productivity go down (reducing GDP per capita), but the population increases more slowly (increasing GDP per capita). For example, Roe and Smith

(2008) predict that South Africa's GDP will be 60 per cent lower than otherwise by 2053, but that GDP per capita will be reduced by only about 3 per cent.

CGE (computable general equilibrium) models are designed to provide a more differentiated picture of the impact of HIV/AIDS across sectors of the economy.[11] Across such models, the impact of HIV/AIDS on sectoral outputs is particularly severe in labour-intensive sectors or for economic activities associated with a higher risk of HIV infection (e.g. transport, mining). Where HIV prevalence differs across skill categories, the composition of labour across sectors also plays a role. Sectors primarily servicing the domestic market are also affected by a slowdown in domestic demand owing to the impact of HIV/AIDS (except for the health sector, which is facing increased demand). However, as long as the fundamental assumptions regarding the consequences of HIV/AIDS (productivity, costs, investment, population) are the same, the outcomes are very similar to the more aggregated models described before.[12]

The modelling undertaken by the South African Bureau of Economic Research (2001, also see Smit, Ellis, and Laubscher, 2006), is a special case because the analysis of the impact of HIV/AIDS is embedded in a large macroeconomic model more commonly used for analysing economic policy decisions and forecasting. The production side (distinguishing three types of labour) and the long-run dynamics of the impact of HIV/AIDS in this model are fairly simple and similar to aggregated models discussed earlier. Additionally, the model yields estimates of the impact of HIV/AIDS on key macroeconomic indicators in the short-run, including variables like inflation or the balance of payments not normally captured by HIV/AIDS impact studies.

Most recent efforts to model the growth impacts of HIV/AIDS—inspired by modern theory of economic growth—focus on behavioural responses to HIV/AIDS and the link between HIV/AIDS and the accumulation of human capital, incorporating the impacts of HIV/AIDS on fertility, the consequences of the impact of HIV/AIDS on households (especially for children), and the implications of increased mortality risks for the returns to education.

Young (2005) argues that the most important impact of HIV/AIDS with regard to growth is a decline in fertility, 'both directly, through a reduction in the willingness to engage in unprotected sexual activity, and indirectly, by increasing the scarcity of labor and the value of a woman's time.' While HIV/AIDS also affects the acquisition of human capital by orphans, the former effect dominates, and GDP per capita consequently increases.

Most studies focus on the impacts of HIV/AIDS on education, motivated by empirical work linking HIV prevalence or life expectancy to educational outcomes. For example, Fortson (2011) finds that children in areas with high HIV prevalence have completed 0.5 years less schooling, and Akbulut-Yuksel and Turan (2012) suggest that HIV/AIDS weakens the links between maternal education and children's years of schooling.

In this spirit, Corrigan et al. (2005) develop an 'overlapping-generations' model (calibrated with parameters 'typical in sub-Saharan nations') in which the impact of HIV/AIDS on parents, and the anticipated risk of contracting HIV/AIDS, affect children's education, and—on the macroeconomic level—the accumulation of human capital and of physical capital (the latter because lower human capital also reduces the returns to physical capital). In this analysis, a probability to die prematurely because of AIDS of 20 per cent results in a decline in the rate of growth of GDP per capita of 0.5 per cent. In a similar model, Ferreira et al. (2011) find that output per capita decreases by 42 per cent in Swaziland, and 18 per cent in South Africa, in the absence of treatment. If every individual living with HIV receives treatment, this loss is reduced to 24 per cent and 6 per cent, respectively.

Some studies propose that HIV/AIDS could have more negative impacts, invoking some kind of poverty traps. Couderc and Ventelou (2005) link human capital accumulation to health spending and the state of HIV/AIDS—in poor countries (where health spending is low), the impact of HIV/AIDS can then shift human capital accumulation on a downward trajectory. In the study by Bell et al. (2006), the poverty trap operates on the household level—the impacts of HIV/AIDS on affected households, and the implications for the accumulation of human capital of their children, would push families towards an equilibrium characterized by low human capital and income. Without upward mobility, HIV/AIDS then places an increasing share of the population on this negative trajectory.

Empirical Evidence on the Impact on Economic Growth

Measures of health, most commonly life expectancy, play an important role in the empirical literature on determinants of economic growth, suggesting that HIV/AIDS could have a considerable negative impact on economic growth, GDP, and GDP per capita. HIV/AIDS, however, is a disease with unusual characteristics (compared to other prime causes of mortality). The impact of HIV/AIDS on growth could therefore be different from the link between health and growth in general. Indeed, many observers have argued that HIV/AIDS—hitting primarily the most productive adults—does have a disproportionately severe economic impact. It thus makes sense to evaluate the impacts of HIV/AIDS on economic growth directly, by including in growth regressions variables specifically capturing the impact of HIV/AIDS.

In the empirical literature on the determinants of economic growth, life expectancy is often used as a proxy for human capital (the factor H in the illustrative model, above). In fact, its role has been such that Sala-i-Martin (1997), testing the robustness of the impact of some sixty-two variables proposed in the literature as determinants of growth, considered life expectancy as one of three sacrosanct variables which a priori would have to appear in any sensible growth regression.[13]

Bloom et al. (2004b), in a widely quoted paper focusing on the role of health (i.e. life expectancy) in an otherwise standard growth regression, conclude that an additional year of life expectancy is associated with an output gain of 4 per cent. To illustrate the implications this would have for a country severely affected by HIV/AIDS, consider the example of Kenya (Chapter 2), with a decline in life expectancy of about 7 years between 1990 and 2002. This loss in life expectancy would result in an output loss of 37 per cent, and a decline in annual growth of 3.8 percentage points over this 15-year period. Life expectancy subsequently rebounded strongly, largely because of improved access to treatment, and this would have added 5 percentage points to annual growth during the recovery period, a 9-percentage point swing from the period in which the impact of HIV/AIDS escalated. However, GDP growth in Kenya—and in other countries facing large HIV epidemics—did not exhibit such large swings correlated with the impact of HIV. The experience of the growth impact of HIV/AIDS is thus more consistent with health as a contributor to capabilities in the long term (e.g. as described by Case and Paxson, 2009, or Weil, 2007), rather than the interpretation of indicators like life expecctancy as proxy for productivity permeating the macroeconomic growth literature.[14]

Some empirical studies follow a 'two-step' approach, (1) linking economic growth and some health indicator, and (2) the health indicator to the impact of HIV/AIDS. McDonald and Roberts (2006) link GDP per capita to variables like investment, secondary school enrolment and—as a measure of health—'predicted infant mortality'.[15] The latter was estimated in a second equation, with HIV prevalence as one of the explanatory variables. Combining the impact of HIV prevalence on infant mortality, and of infant mortality on growth, they estimate that a 1 per cent increase in HIV prevalence reduces the level of GDP per capita by 0.6 per cent in sub-Saharan Africa through 1998. If HIV prevalence escalates from zero to 10 per cent in about 15 years, this would mean that the rate of growth declines by about 0.4 per cent over this period. Outside Africa (with much lower levels of and less variation in HIV prevalence), the impact of HIV/AIDS on growth is unclear.

Two other studies also follow such an 'indirect' approach. Dixon et al. (2001) include 'predicted life expectancy' in the growth regression, and link it to HIV prevalence in a separate regression. Their findings are inconclusive—showing a negative impact of HIV on life expectancy, but no clear link between life expectancy and growth. According to Bonnel (2000), HIV/AIDS affects the quality of macroeconomic policies (according to the World Bank's policy ratings), which in turn affect economic growth,[16] resulting in an impact of HIV/AIDS on economic growth as high as 0.7 percentage points (for an HIV prevalence of 8 per cent) and 2.6 percentage points (for an HIV prevalence of 20 per cent).

Other empirical studies follow a 'direct approach', that is, directly inserting HIV/AIDS-related variables among determinants of economic growth. An early study by Bloom and Mahal (1997), based on very preliminary estimates on the state of HIV/AIDS in 1994, did not find a significant effect of HIV/AIDS on growth.[17] Papageorgiou and Stoytcheva (2008) link the level of GDP per capita in 1986–2000 to the number of reported AIDS cases.[18] They find a statistically significant but economically miniscule effect of HIV/AIDS—for example for Botswana, the level of GDP per capita is reduced by 0.2 per cent—a blip considering that GDP per capita has increased by 170 per cent, or 5 per cent annually, between 1980 and 2000.

Werker et al. (2009) do not find 'any measurable impact' of HIV/AIDS on the growth of GDP per capita (1992–2002), obtaining very small and statistically insignificant coefficients. To address the possible endogeneity of HIV prevalence in a growth regression, they use male circumcision to identify exogenous variations in HIV prevalence across countries.[19] This approach, however, comes at a cost, as they cannot exploit the variation of HIV prevalence over time. Lovász and Schipp (2009) find a strong negative effect of HIV prevalence on the rate of growth of GDP per capita, but their findings are implausibly large at low levels of HIV prevalence (e.g. a reduction in growth of GDP per capita of 2 percentage points at an HIV prevalence of 3 per cent), pointing to misspecification, and the results are not robust.[20]

In summary, the empirical evidence on the impacts of HIV/AIDS on economic growth presents an incoherent picture. While studies following an indirect approach (postulating that HIV/AIDS affects growth through some other variable like life expectancy) frequently find a significant and large effect of HIV/AIDS on growth, most studies directly inserting the impact of HIV/AIDS into growth regressions do not find a significant impact.

The latter suggests that the impact of HIV/AIDS on economic growth has been limited. The discrepancies between studies following an 'indirect' approach (through variables like life expectancy) and those analysing the impacts of HIV/AIDS directly suggest that the impacts of HIV/AIDS on economic growth have been different from links between summary health indicators and economic growth suggested in the broader literature on health and growth.[21] This could reflect that HIV/AIDS-related mortality has a disproportionately low economic impact, compared to other diseases, but this reading is implausible because the impacts of HIV/AIDS are concentrated among the economically most active population. It is more plausible that the discrepancies reflect (1) that the correlation between life expectancy and economic growth reflects third factors (as argued by Deaton, 2006), or (2) that the correlation between life expectancy and growth reflect longer-term processes operating with long lags, for example a link from child health to adult capabilities.

Economic Evaluation of the Health Consequences of HIV/AIDS

One robust lesson coming out of the evidence on the impacts of HIV/AIDS on households and on the macroeconomic repercussions regards the scale of economic consequences—the economic repercussions of HIV/AIDS may exacerbate the consequences of HIV/AIDS for some households and communities, but they are not a cause for concern in addition to and on a similar scale as the direct health consequences of HIV/AIDS. Indeed, one economist (Young, 2005) concluded that 'the AIDS epidemic is a humanitarian disaster of millennial proportions, one that cries for assistance. It is not, however, an economic disaster.'

This view, however, is in contrast to a perspective that sees good health as an 'integral part of good development', and 'freedom from avoidable ill-health and from escapable mortality' as one of the most important development aspects, in its own right and as it enables the enjoyment of other freedoms (Sen, 1999). A focus on economic growth and income per capita as principal development indicators may nevertheless be justified when rising incomes and progress on other dimensions of well-being are closely correlated. Obviously, this is not the case with HIV/AIDS, which has had a catastrophic health impact in a number of countries, including otherwise very successful developing economies.[22] Relatedly, a narrow focus on incomes can result in a 'repugnant' interpretation (Grimm and Harttgen, 2008) of increased mortality and risks to life as a welfare improvement (because poverty headcounts or GDP per capita may improve as a consequence).

For these reasons, a number of authors use lifetime income (approximated as GDP per capita times life expectancy) as a measure of living standards. This is usefully applied by Bourguignon and Morrison (2002) to the evolving 'distribution of well-being among world citizens' from 1820 to 1992—finding that improving life expectancies across developing countries have resulted in an overall decline in inequality in lifetime incomes. The period covered, however, largely precedes the escalation of HIV/AIDS.[23] Anderson (2005) applies a similar analysis to the experience of sub-Saharan Africa in the 1990s (when mortality rates increased steeply in many African countries). GDP per capita stagnated in the region over this period, and there was 'little apparent change in inequality indices' across countries. However, on the basis of lifetime income, living standards deteriorated substantially, while inequality across countries declined (because many countries with high HIV prevalence are relatively wealthy).

The most common approach to assessing the impact of changes in life expectancy or mortality on living standards, though, is the 'value of statistical life'.[24] This estimate of an economic valuation of a life would be based on the compensation individuals would demand for taking on dangerous assignments,[25] or the additional costs individuals would accept for improved safety (e.g. installing airbags). Social valuations, for example in government guidelines on assessing investments in road safety or health regulations, are a secondary source of information.

One feature that is common to essentially all estimates of the value of statistical life is the fact that the value of a statistical life is considerably higher than the expected remaining lifetime income, typically by a factor of around 3–4—individuals would want to be compensated for taking on additional mortality risks by much more than the expected loss in lifetime earnings because of the higher risk of death.[26] This is an important lesson from the empirical literature on the value of statistical life, because it suggests that welfare assessments of the consequences of HIV/AIDS based on the reduced lifetime income underestimate the adverse consequences of a mortality shock.

The 'value of statistical life' has been used to assess the welfare gains from medical research (Murphy and Topel, 2006), the evolution of global inequality in living standards (Becker et al., 2005), and the contribution of rising life expectancy to living standards through long periods of development (Crafts, 2007; Jamison and others, 2013).[27] These studies typically find that the contributions of increasing life expectancy to living standards were of a similar magnitude as the contributions of economic growth, and offer an attractive framework to study the consequences of *adverse* health shocks as well.

Before discussing the costs of HIV/AIDS using the value of statistical life, it is useful to take a step back and consider some of the shortcomings of the approach:

- The value of statistical life is attractive because it attaches an economic cost to health risks. More generally, it is a *specific social valuation* of health gains (or losses) directly comparable to GDP per capita and economic growth. Potential recipients of policy advice, however, are likely equipped with social preferences that include both economic growth and health gains anyway. The value added of attaching a specific 'economic' cost to mortality may be lost to this audience.[28]

- The step from individual valuations of income and life expectancy to social valuations of GDP per capita and average life expectancy across the population is not trivial. The empirical literature suggests that the valuation of health gains differ across individuals, and that a health gain to a richer person is more valuable than a gain to a poor person. In contrast, social valuations based on the value of statistical life normally apply the same value of life to each person, irrespective of individual income.

- Most of the empirical literature on the value of statistical life is based on wage differences associated with miniscule differences in mortality risks. The increased mortality risks associated with HIV/AIDS are of a much higher magnitude, applying the empirical estimate here is akin to a problem of 'out-of-sample' projection.

- Possibly the more serious problem of out-of-sample projection regards calibrating estimates of the value of statistical life across developing countries. Most empirical estimates of the value of statistical life are from advanced economies, with a level of GDP per capita well over US$20,000, and especially from the United States. Applying these estimates to developing and especially low-income countries with a GDP per capita of less than US$1,000 involves a large leap of faith.

The latter point—that is, the assumptions different studies make regarding the value of statistical life in developing countries—plays a large role in estimates of the costs of increased mortality because of HIV/AIDS. One such study (Philipson and Soares (2005), applying the same model as Becker et al. (2005)), calibrates a model to data from the United States. In this model, the value of statistical life declines more than proportionally with income, and turns negative at a level close to the poverty line of US$1 per day—individuals below this level would be better off dead, and their estimates indeed show that HIV/AIDS—because it kills people—is improving welfare in the Democratic Republic of Congo, the only country where average GDP per capita was below this level during the period they are studying. Apart from these stark 'Swiftian' results,[29] their approach also returns comparatively low estimates of the welfare costs of HIV across low-income countries.

Most studies, however, assume that the value of statistical life is proportional to GDP per capita, in line with empirical studies by Miller (2000) or Bellavance et al. (2009),[30] and this assumption is also commonly used in non-HIV/AIDS-specific studies by authors like Becker and Elias (2007), Murphy and Topel (2006), or Jamison et al. (2013).[31] Under this assumption, Figure 4.1 illustrates how the value of a decline in life expectancy, in terms of an equivalent drop in income, is calculated, and provides examples of the impact of HIV/AIDS for selected countries. For this illustration, it is assumed that a drop in life expectancy by 1 per cent is valued like a drop in income of 3.5 per cent, broadly consistent with empirical estimates of the value of statistical life.

Under these circumstances, even a loss in life expectancy of 'only' one year (1.3 per cent), as in Jamaica, results in a decline in living standards equivalent to a drop of 5 per cent of GDP per capita. In Kenya, a loss of 1.7 years is equivalent to a loss of 9 per cent of GDP per capita, while in Botswana life

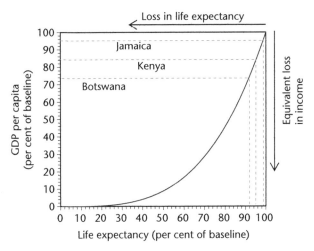

Figure 4.1. Drop in life expectancy and equivalent income loss, applying 'value of statistical life', 2014

Source: Author's calculations, using UNAIDS (2015a, 2014d).

expectancy declines by 5.4 years, equivalent to a loss in living standards of 25 per cent of GDP per capita.[32] These numbers (estimated for 2014), though, represent a large rebound from the peak impact of HIV/AIDS on mortality. For 2002, the estimated loss in life expectancy for Botswana, Jamaica, and Kenya is 20 years, 3 years, and 8 years, respectively (Figure 2.8), equivalent to a loss in GDP per capita of 71 per cent, 13 per cent, and 40 per cent.

Using similar techniques, Bloom et al. (2004a) estimate that the health impact of HIV/AIDS in Africa was equivalent to an income drop of 15 per cent as of 2000. Crafts and Haacker (2004) arrive at estimates of the welfare costs of HIV/AIDS of up to 80 per cent of GDP (for Botswana, near the peak of mortality experienced there), and also point out that changes in life expectancy at birth could understate the welfare effects of HIV/AIDS—age-weighted analysis based on *remaining* life expectancy for each age returns higher estimates.

Part II
The Global Response to HIV/AIDS

The global response to HIV/AIDS has been motivated by perceptions not only about the health impacts of HIV/AIDS, but also by concerns about its economic and social consequences. In turn, the response to HIV/AIDS has shaped the consequences of the epidemic, and many of the economic issues addressed in this book are in part a consequence of policies pursued over the last decades. The global response to HIV/AIDS also poses a number of economic questions in its own right. It has evolved into a major aspect of global development assistance. Looking back, and looking ahead in terms of the sustained funding of the HIV/AIDS response, it is important to assess the 'returns to investment' and the rationality of observed global spending patterns. Do the outcomes of the global HIV/AIDS response justify its costs? And is the observed global pattern of HIV/AIDS funding rational, taking into consideration the burden of disease and the capability of countries to fund an effective HIV/AIDS response?

These issues are addressed in two chapters. Chapter 5 provides an overview of the global HIV/AIDS response—focusing on the evolving policy discourse, the emerging institutions, and the funding of the global HIV/AIDS response. Chapter 6 assesses the impact of the global response towards 'ending AIDS' and mitigating its consequences, and in terms of overall health outcomes, and discusses whether the global HIV/AIDS response has received too much money.

5

History and State of the Global Response to HIV/AIDS

This chapter provides a narrative of the global HIV/AIDS response and its financing, and a discussion of the current policy discourse on the financing and sustainability of the HIV/AIDS response. The first section provides a brief review of the global response to HIV/AIDS, intended to provide background for the economic analysis offered across this book. The second section takes stock of the financing of the global HIV/AIDS response. The chapter closes with a discussion of the outlook and current policy discourse on the financing and sustainability of the HIV/AIDS response.

The Course of the Global Response

It is useful to divide the course of the global response to HIV/AIDS in three phases. The first phase began in the mid-1980s with the emergence of HIV/AIDS, includes the establishment of UNAIDS, and extends to the 'tipping point' in about 2001, when HIV/AIDS became recognized as a global health and development challenge of the highest order (Piot, 2012). The defining theme of the second phase is the drive to provide universal access to treatment and other HIV/AIDS-related services, and was characterized by rapid expansion in the coverage of treatment, and a steep increase in global funding for HIV/AIDS (including the emergence of the Global Fund and PEPFAR, now the two dominant players in global HIV/AIDS funding). The transition to the third and current phase was more gradual, and involved several elements—a changed perception about the future availability of funding; a steep decline in HIV/AIDS-related mortality across countries owing to improved access to treatment; a re-orientation of HIV/AIDS programme design around the UNAIDS 'investment framework', and the establishment of a forward-looking narrative towards the 'end of AIDS'. At the same time, the exceptional role of HIV/AIDS in the global development policy discourse has been transformed, as documented in the 2015 Sustainable Development Goals.

Following the first reports on the medical condition that was to become known as HIV/AIDS, the epidemic was primarily considered a health problem of rich countries. At the time of the first International AIDS Conference in 1985, only 17,000 cases had been reported, mainly in the United States, and HIV/AIDS was considered predominantly a disease affecting male homosexuals and injecting drug users. However, evidence soon emerged of the presence of HIV/AIDS in a number of African countries and of the role of heterosexual transmission of HIV, although the scale (and especially potential) of the epidemic across Africa continued to be under-appreciated.[1]

Once the global dimension of HIV/AIDS began to be understood, a Global Programme on AIDS (GPA) was established at the WHO, and the WHO became the lead agency on the response to HIV/AIDS in the UN system.[2] The epidemic, however, transcended the traditional area of expertise of the WHO in several ways. First, as HIV/AIDS is primarily a sexually transmitted disease, HIV transmission and prevention were tied to numerous social, cultural, and economic factors, including evolving attitudes towards sex, urbanization, or the role of prostitution.[3] Second, as effective treatment was unavailable even in the most advanced countries, the early HIV/AIDS response strongly focused on effective HIV prevention and its social aspects rather than on medical aspects.

For these reasons, and because of the concerns about the potential of HIV/AIDS in reversing development gains in some least developed countries, the economic and social consequences of HIV/AIDS—much more so than for other health conditions—played an important role in the global HIV/AIDS policy discourse, and as early as 1988 a major conference on the 'Global Impact of AIDS' addressed the numerous facets of its social and economic consequences.[4] In addition to the relevance for HIV/AIDS programme design, the potential role of the evidence on economic and social consequence was recognized, for example Over and Piot (1993) pointed out that 'information on the magnitude of the economic effects of STDs on households would move the allocation of resources away from other sectors and toward the health sector'.

Economic aspects also played quite a different role in the emerging HIV/AIDS response, which met concerns about diverting resources away from other pressing health challenges in the developing world. Piot (2012) recalls that in about 1994, 'I was urging [the World Bank] to invest massively in AIDS control, but the audience was mostly economists and they blew me out of the water with arguments about cost-effectiveness and returns to investment.'[5]

One defining aspect of the global HIV/AIDS response has been the prominent role of civil society, and the involvement of people living with HIV in shaping it—creating awareness of the epidemic, building recognition of HIV/AIDS as a global health challenge, contributing to establishing treatment access as a human rights issue and pressurizing governments to extend or improve access to prevention, care, and treatment.[6]

By the mid-1990s, it had been recognized that 'the magnitude and impact [of HIV/AIDS were] greatest in developing countries' (United Nations Economic and Social Council, 1994). In light of the scale of the epidemic, and the unique challenges posed by it, the Joint United Nations Programme on HIV/AIDS (UNAIDS) was launched in 1995, to provide global leadership on HIV/AIDS, effectively coordinate the HIV/AIDS-related activities of its 'co-sponsoring' UN agencies, strengthen the capacities of national governments to develop and implement effective national strategies, and advocate greater political commitment on HIV/AIDS.[7] In addition to and in support of these tasks UNAIDS has also focused on building an extensive global data and surveillance system on the state of HIV/AIDS and the HIV/AIDS response.[8]

In terms of access to treatment (and the consequences for the health and lives of people living with HIV), the 1990s were a period of divergence between rich and poor countries. The first treatment slowing the progress of AIDS had become available in 1987, but patients tended to develop resistance fairly quickly. This situation changed around 1996, when combination therapies—combinations of different types of antiretroviral therapies—were shown to be more effective than single drugs, and also more promising in preventing the development of drug resistance.

The introduction of combination antiretroviral therapies had a dramatic effect in countries like the United States, where AIDS-related mortality dropped by more than one-half between 1995 and 1997 (from 21 per cent to 9 per cent of people who had ever been diagnosed with AIDS, Figure 5.1). At an annual cost of about US$20,000, though, combination therapy was essentially unavailable across developing countries. Piot (2012) observed that 'in 1994 nearly every AIDS patient died. This was true all over the world, but in the worst affected populations in Africa, the suffering of patients was inhuman and people died much faster.' By 2000, this was still true for Africa, whereas life prospects of people living with HIV in rich countries had improved dramatically.

Meanwhile, the situation was characterized by a dramatic escalation of HIV/AIDS, especially in sub-Saharan Africa where the number of people living with HIV had risen from an estimated 6 million in 1990 to 21 million by 2000 (about three-quarters of the global total), with dramatic inequities between rich and poor countries in terms of the consequences of HIV.[9]

These inequities, though, triggered three developments which by 2001 resulted in a 'tipping point' in the global HIV response. First, pilot projects providing antiretroviral therapy in low-income countries, under conditions

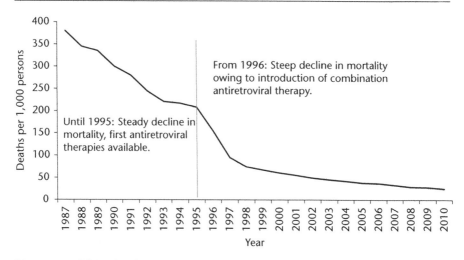

Figure 5.1. AIDS-related mortality among people living with HIV ever classified as Stage 3 (AIDS), United States, 1987–2010

Note: Mortality rates are normalized based on the age distribution of the US population in 2000.
Source: National Center for HIV/AIDS, Viral Hepatitis, STD, and TB Prevention, undated.

which could conceivably be reproduced across the health system, demonstrated the feasibility of providing antiretroviral therapy in such countries (e.g. Farmer et al., 2001), and in 2002 the WHO issued its first guidelines for the use of antiretroviral drugs in low-income settings. Second, the costs of antiretroviral drugs for use in developing countries declined steeply, owing to negotiated agreements with pharmaceutical companies (e.g. through the UNAIDS 'Drug Access Initiative'), increasing availability of generic antiretroviral drugs, and a shift in international patent law, allowing poor countries to obtain generic versions of patent-protected drugs in public health emergencies. As a consequence of these developments, the influential Harvard Consensus Statement concluded in 2001 'that on moral, health, social and economic grounds the international community should provide the scientific and financial leadership for a rapid scaling-up of AIDS treatment in the poorest and hardest-hit countries'.

The third element was a break-through in the recognition of the global impact of and the challenges posed by HIV/AIDS. Reflecting concerns about the threats to peace, security, and political stability, the UN Security Council held a session on HIV/AIDS in 2000. The United Nations General Assembly (2001) described HIV/AIDS as 'a global emergency and one of the most formidable challenges to human life and dignity, as well as to the effective enjoyment of human rights, which undermines social and economic development throughout the world and affects all levels of society'. And HIV/AIDS became a cornerstone of the international development agenda embodied in the Millennium Development Goals (MDGs), appearing in one MDG (MDG 6: 'Combat HIV/AIDS, malaria, and other diseases') and directly affecting others (notably MDG 4 ('Reduce child mortality') and MDG 5 ('Improve maternal health')).[10]

Together, these developments prepared the ground for the large expansion of antiretroviral treatment which took place from about 2004 and still continues. The 2001 UN General Assembly resolution called for the establishment of a 'global HIV/AIDS and health fund to finance an urgent and expanded response to the epidemic', which was established (as the 'Global Fund to Fight HIV/AIDS, Tuberculosis, and Malaria') soon after in 2002. In December 2003, the WHO and UNAIDS launched the '3 by 5' initiative, aiming to get 3 million people living with HIV in low- and middle-income countries on antiretroviral therapy by 2005, and setting a pattern of ambitious quantitative targets driving the global HIV/AIDS policy agenda. In January 2003, US President Bush announced a commitment to provide US$15 billion over 5 years to the global HIV/AIDS response through the President's Emergency Plan for AIDS Relief (PEPFAR).[11] The following years were characterized by a steep expansion in access to anti-retroviral treatment across low- and middle income countries (from about 400,000 in 2003 to 9 million in 2010, and 14.9 million by the end of 2014). Meanwhile, global HIV/AIDS spending increased from US$ 5.1 billion in 2002 to US$ 15.6 billion in 2008, driven by a steep expansion in external assistance from US$ 1.4 billion in 2002 to US$ 8.5 billion in 2008 (UNAIDS, 2015b).

While access to treatment expanded dramatically, success in HIV prevention was disappointing. Globally, the number of HIV infections declined from a peak of 3.7 million in 1997 to 2.6 million by 2008. However, some of this decline reflected the natural dynamics of the epidemic rather than behaviour change and the consequences of HIV prevention interventions (this issue is discussed further in Chapter 6). Moreover, in this period, there were about two new HIV infections for each person put on treatment—the efforts on scaling up treatment were not keeping up with the increasing demand, and the ongoing high numbers of HIV infections (and resulting treatment needs) prompted concerns about ballooning costs (or an 'entitlement burden', Over (2008)).

Against this backdrop, there was an urgent need and demand for more effective approaches to HIV prevention. Two approaches have since emerged as the centrepieces of effective HIV prevention strategies—*male circumcision* and *treatment as prevention*. Both approaches are not new—a link between male circumcision and HIV prevention was already hypothesized in the 1980s, evidence on the link between viral suppression (one of the conse-quences of antiretroviral treatment) and HIV transmission had been available since about 2000, and antiretroviral therapy was already being used in the prevention of mother-to-child transmission.[12]

The situation changed for male circumcision after the results of several trials became available around 2007, showing that male circumcision reduced female-to-male HIV transmission by about 60 per cent. Male circumcision subsequently and quickly became a cornerstone of HIV prevention in high-prevalence countries and especially in PEPFAR's HIV prevention strategy.

For treatment as prevention, the critical development was the release of results of a trial suggesting that treatment was reducing HIV transmission by over 90 per cent (Cohen et al., 2011). This result was politically highly significant not only because it confirmed the plausible link between treatment and HIV transmission, but because of the large magnitude of the measured effect, opening the door for systematically utilizing *treatment for HIV prevention*—providing treatment irrespective of an individual's disease progression to prevent HIV transmission. Additionally, the findings provided a powerful advocacy tool with regard to concerns about the financial sustainability of an ambitious scaling-up of treatment—at least some of the costs of treatment would be offset by later financial savings (and other gains) as a consequence of reduced HIV incidence.[13]

The period from about 2008 brought a major shift in the global HIV/AIDS response, reflecting three factors. First, the status of HIV/AIDS as one of the major health and development threats was eroding. Second, the global financial crisis introduced considerable uncertainty to the outlook on the financing of the HIV/AIDS response. Third, global HIV/AIDS policy was getting normalized, shifting from an emergency mode—aiming to expand needed HIV/AIDS services quickly, without much regard for the cost-effectiveness of alternative interventions (the 'commodity approach' described by Schwartländer et al., 2011)—into a mode characterized by increased accountability for results and emphasis on cost-effectiveness.

Although global HIV deaths remained high (declining from a peak of 2.36 million in 2004 to 1.96 million in 2009), they were seen to be on a trajectory towards much lower level (as the expansion of treatment continued). Even in countries with very high HIV prevalence, fears regarding social and economic disintegration as a consequence of HIV/AIDS had not played out.[14] Whiteside and Smith (2009) developed a nuanced view, pointing to the exceptional challenges posed by HIV/AIDS (only) in mid-prevalence countries with insufficient resources to address the epidemic and in high prevalence countries, but argued that it should be treated as a normal public health issue elsewhere. The panel convened by the 'Copenhagen Consensus' ranked HIV/AIDS as the No. 1 priority among global challenges in 2004. In a second round in 2008, HIV/AIDS no longer made the list of the top fifteen global priorities. While this outcome in part reflects the success of the global response to HIV/AIDS in mitigating the impacts and improving the outlook on the epidemic,[15] it also illustrates the changed policy environment.

The global crisis changed the HIV/AIDS policy discourse by introducing considerable uncertainty to the funding outlook. It also resulted in a more constrained fiscal environment in major donor countries—for example, in the United States and the United Kingdom the level of public debt shot up by about 40 per cent of GDP between 2007 and 2012. The global financial crisis also coincided with the beginning of a 'flat-lining' of external funding for HIV/AIDS programmes. The extent to which this can be attributed to the financial crisis is unclear. For example, the reauthorization of PEPFAR in 2008, including the funding envelope through 2013 and an increased emphasis on 'country ownership' and sustainability of programmes was already under way before the financial crisis hit (Goosby et al., 2012).

The changing political and financial environment triggered a shift in emphasis towards greater cost-effectiveness and financial sustainability of HIV/AIDS programmes. Perhaps not coincidentally, an economist (Michel Sidibé) succeeded a medical doctor (Peter Piot) as the head of UNAIDS in January 2009. The uncertain financial environment directly motivated efforts by national HIV/AIDS programmes to increase efficiency and achieve more cost-effective allocation of resources (Avila-Figueroa and DeLay, 2009).

The redirection in global HIV/AIDS policy resulted in the launch of the UNAIDS investment approach (Schwartländer et al., 2011), built around 'basic program activities' shown to be effective in reducing 'HIV transmission, morbidity, and mortality from AIDS'. The 'investment approach' frames HIV/AIDS programmes as investments, generating returns both in terms of health outcomes and in terms of treatment costs avoided as a result of reduced HIV incidence,[16] and covers a longer time frame (typically 10–15 years) than national HIV/AIDS strategy documents (up to 5 years), so that the consequences of current investments in the HIV/AIDS response in terms of changing the trajectory of the epidemic become more visible. This shift was endorsed by the Global Fund (2011a), which later required that new funding proposals should be supported by an 'investment case' (Global Fund, 2014a). Similarly, the PEPFAR (2012) 'blueprint' emphasizes 'strategic, scientifically sound investments' as one of its four pillars.

The other theme which has re-shaped global HIV/AIDS politics in recent years is the drive towards 'ending AIDS' (i.e. bringing 'the HIV epidemic under control so that it is not a public health threat' (Sidibé, 2014)), reflecting increased optimism about controlling new HIV infections. At the same time, it is part of a political strategy of leading the HIV/AIDS response through ambitious targets and emphasizing that the fight against HIV/AIDS is winnable (UNAIDS, 2014c). This strategy also flanks the 'investment approach' by defining some ultimate objectives and framing current HIV/AIDS spending as temporary investments to this end rather than open-ended spending commitments.

These policy changes occurred against the backdrop of a re-valuation of the role of HIV/AIDS in the global development policy discourse, as the response to HIV/AIDS—together with a long list of other priorities in addressing contributors to the global burden of disease—was subsumed under a Sustainable Development Goal to 'ensure healthy lives and promote well-being for all at all ages' (United Nations General Assembly, 2015).

The Financing of the Global Response to HIV/AIDS

HIV/AIDS-related external financing amounted to about US$0.5 billion in the mid-1990s, and exceeded US$1 billion for the first time in 2000 (UNAIDS, 2004). From there, it has increased steeply, to US$8.5 billion by 2008, contributing to an increase in total HIV/AIDS spending to US$ 15.6 billion (Figure 5.2). The most significant developments in external funding have been the establishment of the Global Fund (disbursing since 2003, accounting for about 20 per cent of HIV/AIDS-related disbursements in 2004–13) and of PEPFAR (since 2004), which became the dominant source of external HIV/AIDS financing (about 60 per cent of all HIV/AIDS-related disbursements in 2004–13), according to OECD (2015). From 2008, global HIV/AIDS spending has grown more slowly, as external funding has fluctuated around US$9 billion annually, and the increase to US$20 billion has been driven by domestic funding. The share of

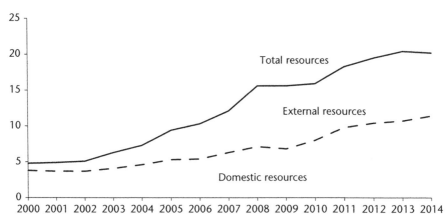

Figure 5.2. Resources available for HIV in low- and middle-income countries, 2000–2014 (US$ billions)
Source: UNAIDS (2015b).

external funding in global HIV/AIDS spending has declined to 43 per cent by 2014, from 60 per cent in 2008.

The aggregate figures, though, mask very large differences in the role of external financing across countries. Across low-income countries, external funding accounted for 90 per cent of the costs of the HIV/AIDS response as of 2014 (UNAIDS, 2015b), and among these are some of the countries facing the steepest financing challenges (relative to GDP or government revenues). In contrast, the increase in domestic resources predominantly reflects growing government commitment in middle-income countries, where HIV/AIDS generally is much less of a fiscal challenge.

National data on the costs and the funding of the HIV/AIDS response are available from most countries, and published by UNAIDS.[17] Data on *actual spending* and its financing, however, could give a misleading picture of *financing challenges*, if the extent to which financing challenges for a comprehensive HIV/AIDS response are met differ systematically across countries.[18] For example, if a country—because of lack of financial resources, capacity constraints, or the scale of the epidemic—is unable to mount an effective HIV/AIDS response, actual spending underplays the financing challenge.[19]

The available data on total HIV/AIDS spending are summarized in Figure 5.3, plotting total spending (in per cent of GDP) against HIV prevalence and GDP per capita, respectively. Neither sub-figure yields a clear picture. Spending on the HIV/AIDS response exceeds 1 per cent of GDP in all eight countries with an HIV prevalence above 5 per cent, but the highest levels of spending, relative to GDP, are recorded from two countries (Rwanda and Haiti) with much lower prevalence. At the same time, most countries where HIV/AIDS spending exceeds 1 per cent are low-income countries; the notable exceptions are Swaziland, Botswana, and Namibia—middle-income countries where HIV prevalence is extremely high.

Thus, the financing challenges associated with the national HIV/AIDS response are as much a reflection of economic factors as of the scale of the epidemic. Indeed, 80 per cent of the variation in the financial burden can be explained just by the ratio of HIV prevalence and GDP per capita,[20] with

$$HIV\ Spending\ (\%\ of\ GDP) = 37.5 * \left(\frac{HIV\ Prevalence}{GDP\ per\ capita}\right)^{0.72}$$

In this specification, a doubling in HIV prevalence is associated with an increase in HIV/AIDS spending by 65 per cent. A doubling in GDP per capita is associated with a decline in HIV/AIDS by 39 per cent relative to GDP, and an increase by 21 per cent in absolute terms. The financing challenge may increase less than proportionally with HIV prevalence because some costs (running a basic national response, certain HIV prevention measures) are incurred at low HIV prevalence rates and do not increase systematically as HIV prevalence

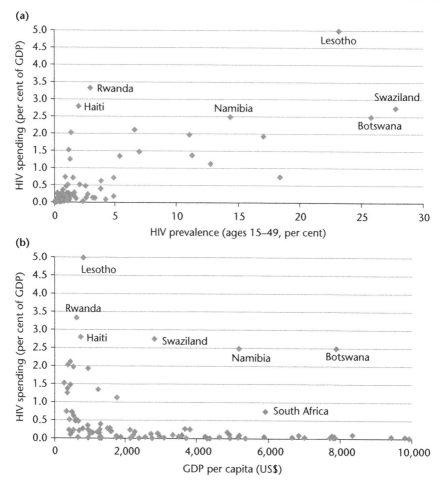

Figure 5.3. HIV/AIDS spending, HIV prevalence, and GDP per capita
Source: UNAIDS (2015c, 2015d) and World Bank (2015).
(a). HIV spending and HIV prevalence, latest available year
(b). HIV spending and GDP per capita, latest available year

increases, and because higher HIV prevalence drives down unit costs.[21] The costs of the HIV/AIDS response increase with GDP per capita (but less than proportionally so that the costs in per cent of GDP decline) because salaries account for a substantial proportion of the cost.

In this way, the patterns shown in Figure 5.3 can largely be explained in terms of the variation of HIV prevalence and GDP per capita across countries. In comparison with the middle-income countries (with GDP per capita around US$6,000 to US$8,000) facing extremely high HIV prevalence (between 15 per cent and 27 per cent), a number of low-income countries face much lower HIV prevalence (between 1 and 15 per cent), but their level of GDP per capita is much lower (at between US$270 up to about US $1,000). Because the unit costs of HIV/AIDS services *relative to economic capacities* are so high in these countries, the financing burden (relative to GDP) comes out as high as or even higher than in the high-prevalence countries.

The high costs of the HIV/AIDS response in numerous countries under-score the role external financing has played and is playing in enabling the global HIV/AIDS response. This applies especially to low-income countries, where the impact of HIV/AIDS tends to compound other pressing health challenges, and where domestic government revenues (not only in abso-lute terms but also in relation to GDP) tend to be lower. The role of external assistance, and its consequences in terms of containing the domestic financing burden of the HIV/AIDS response, is illustrated in Figure 5.4.

The rate of external support differs widely across countries, from 0 to 100 per cent. There is, however, a clear pattern across countries with different income levels—in most low-income countries, the rate of external support is around 90 per cent. It then declines steeply, by about 6 percentage points for each additional US$1,000 in GDP per capita (see empirical analysis in next section). In some regards, external assistance for HIV/AIDS programmes thus resembles development assistance for health overall—the most severe finan-cing challenges (relative to economic capacities) tend to occur in low-income countries which are also receiving considerable external assistance in other areas, and where health outcomes are low—even without the impact of HIV/AIDS. However, in comparison with the role of external assistance in general, the rates of external financing for HIV/AIDS responses are higher.[22]

External financing—with few exceptions—has been effective in reducing the domestic financing burden of the HIV/AIDS response across countries (Figure 5.4.b). In almost all countries, domestic financing has been reduced to less than 0.3 per cent of GDP. The exceptions are a number of Southern African middle-income countries (Botswana, Lesotho, Namibia, and Swazi-land) characterized by very high HIV prevalence and high GDP per capita. These latter countries, though, receive very little external assistance outside the area of HIV/AIDS. While external financing of the HIV/AIDS response does not bring the domestic financing burden down to the levels observed else-where, the rate of external financing of HIV/AIDS spending in these countries (between one-third and three-quarters) is nevertheless high considering their economic circumstances.

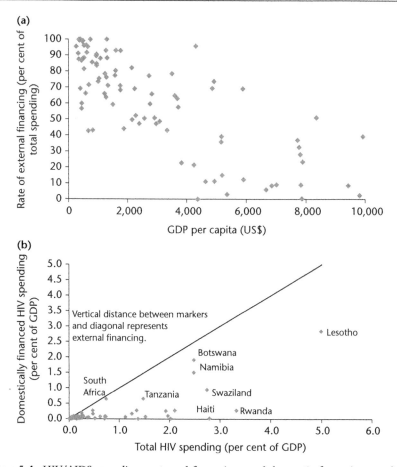

Figure 5.4. HIV/AIDS spending, external financing, and domestic financing needs
Source: UNAIDS (2015d) and World Bank (2015).
(a). Rate of external financing HIV/AIDS programmes and GDP per capita, latest available year
(b). Domestically financed and total spending on HIV/AIDS programmes, latest available year

Outlook on Financing and Sustainability

Building on a perception that the trajectory of costs of HIV programmes was not sustainable (United Nations General Assembly, 2011), the policy discourse on the HIV/AIDS response over the last years has shifted to improving the efficiency of the HIV/AIDS response (discussed at length elsewhere in this book), shifting 'from emergency to sustainability' (Global Fund, 2011c) or from reaching epidemic control to maintaining that control (PEPFAR, 2014c), and developing sustainable financing scenarios, based on principles like 'shared responsibility', 'global solidarity', and a 'fair share' in HIV/AIDS financing (African Union, 2012; Buse and Martin, 2012).

One crucial aspect of this sustainability agenda is the policy discourse on sources of funding. Where would the money come from? What domestic contributions can reasonably be expected from countries receiving external support for their HIV/AIDS responses?

To appreciate the contribution (and limitations) of the economic perspective developed in this book with regard to sustainability, it is useful to first distinguish several different aspects of 'sustainability':

- *Epidemiological sustainability:* Are the investments in the HIV/AIDS response effective in containing the epidemic and contributing to the ultimate objective of 'ending AIDS'?

- *Financial sustainability:* Do the financing numbers add up in the short-to-medium term (e.g., financial solvency of an HIV/AIDS 'strategic plan')?[23] Is there a credible financing scenario in the longer run, i.e. is the HIV/AIDS strategy financially sustainable? The latter question is particularly pertinent where donors signal that they wish to limit their future support and the national government (or other parties) would have to take on an increasing share of the costs of the HIV/AIDS response.

- *Political sustainability:* Does the HIV/AIDS programme enjoy the political support (including but not reduced to financial commitments) of the key players? Is the narrative of the global HIV/AIDS response suitable to ensure continuing support from main donors? Is the HIV/AIDS response aligned with broader health policy objectives? To what extent is 'country ownership' present, and is there a credible path to increased domestic ownership (and financing) of the HIV/AIDS response?

These different aspects are related. Epidemiological sustainability contributes to financial sustainability; epidemiological and financial sustainability underlie political sustainability, and political sustainability is a prerequisite for financial sustainability. Most of the discussion in Part III of this book deals with the interplay of epidemiological and financial sustainability (the returns, in terms of health outcomes, to investments in the HIV/AIDS response, and how these investments affect financial sustainability). Chapter 6 deals with aspects of the political sustainability of the global HIV/AIDS response. The remainder of the present chapter reviews aspects of the policy discourse on the financing of the global HIV/AIDS response.

Much of the global policy discourse on sustainable financing focused on appropriate contributions of national governments, as well as the role of donors in enabling effective HIV/AIDS responses where these would pose an unusually large and unsustainable burden to national governments. Most of the related literature on the scope for increased domestic financing of the HIV/AIDS response applies some kind of benchmarking, comparing HIV/AIDS-related spending across countries or applying some criteria on how much countries can be expected to contribute to the costs of the national HIV/AIDS response.

One such approach is the DIPI ('Domestic Investment Priority Index') developed by UNAIDS (2010a, 2010c) for the 2010 'Report on the Global AIDS Epidemic', which has been used frequently in publications by UNAIDS and others (e.g. Global Fund, 2013a). The DIPI is calculated as the ratio of (domestically financed) public expenditure on the HIV/AIDS response (in per cent of government revenues) and the number of people living with HIV (in per cent of the national population). This index is used by UNAIDS as a benchmark to identify countries that 'need to invest more in their AIDS responses'.

The DIPI (and its use as a benchmark for domestic contributions) is problematic because it is inconsistent with the empirical evidence on drivers of the costs of the HIV/AIDS response across countries.[24] As shown in the previous section, *HIV/AIDS spending increases less than proportionally with HIV prevalence*. This means that countries with low HIV prevalence are characterized by a high DIPI—the 'top performers' are Madagascar (HIV prevalence 0.5 per cent) and the Czech Republic (HIV prevalence 0.04 per cent), and the country with the highest HIV prevalence among the top twenty countries is Burundi (HIV prevalence 1.3 per cent). Using the DIPI as a benchmark for identifying countries that 'need to invest more in their AIDS responses' thus means that countries with *high* HIV prevalence should shoulder a *higher* share of the costs of the national HIV/AIDS response than low-prevalence countries, a demand running against the principle of 'global solidarity' endorsed by UNAIDS elsewhere, and contradicting policies of other institutions engaged in the HIV/AIDS response like the 'new funding model' of the Global Fund.[25]

To avoid such shortcomings, it is generally preferable to empirically control for a number of variables which plausibly affect domestic financing of the HIV/AIDS response, as in the analyses by Galárraga et al. (2013) and Haacker and Greener (2012, discussed further below).[26] Galárraga et al. (2013) combine an empirical analysis of domestic contributions to the HIV/AIDS response with an analysis of current availability of resources versus resource needs estimates provided by UNAIDS. In their preferred specification, domestic funding for HIV/AIDS per person living with HIV increases with gross national income per capita, and is also higher in countries with a high level of HIV/AIDS spending (relative to gross national income).

The analysis by Galárraga et al. (2013) thus allows a benchmarking of domestic spending on HIV/AIDS with expected spending (from their regression), and—where actual spending falls short of estimated needs—offers insights on the extent to which aligning domestic contributions with their expected levels would close the financing gap.

There are, however, two principal shortcomings to this approach (as pointed out by Galárraga et al. (2013)). First, it offers little explicit guidance on how to close funding gaps (except in situations where aligning domestic contributions to the estimated benchmark would be sufficient). Second, there are limitations to using empirical benchmarks based on a regression as normative guides to how much a country should contribute. Some variables may contribute to explaining the variation in the domestic HIV/AIDS financing across countries, but it would be inappropriate to include them in a policy rule. For example, domestic HIV/AIDS spending may be correlated with (non-HIV/AIDS) health expenditure because the government places great weight on health in general, but penalizing this government by reducing external financing for this reason would be problematic.

The alternative to benchmarking domestic HIV/AIDS spending based on observed spending patterns and plausible determinants across countries is to apply some indicators for the capability to pay. Resch et al. (2015) provide a very useful introduction to this approach, and their general approach is used here to organize the discussion (though the interpretation of the bullets is the author's, and differs substantially from theirs). Starting out from UNAIDS' estimates of resource needs for the HIV/AIDS response in twelve countries in sub-Saharan Africa until 2018, they discuss the potential contribution of domestic financing to meeting these resource needs, distinguishing three factors:

- Economic growth (assuming that government revenues and domestically financed HIV/AIDS expenditures would increase in line with GDP).
- Increasing domestic spending on health (e.g. using the Abuja target as a benchmark).
- Allocating resources to HIV/AIDS in proportion to the burden of disease.

The contribution of economic growth is critical for an analysis of the costs and financing of the HIV/AIDS response over long periods, especially as many African countries facing high HIV prevalence also experience high growth rates. For example, economic growth in Kenya is expected to grow at about 7 per cent annually, and 40 per cent overall, between 2015 and 2020. If this rate persists, GDP in 2030 will be 2.7 times as high as it is today. For given projections of the costs of the HIV/AIDS response, increasing domestic resources owing to economic growth are thus a big part of the picture. In the recent 'investment case' analysis for Kenya, for example, the absolute costs of the HIV/AIDS response are projected to increase by 40 per cent between 2020 and 2030, but because they increase slower than GDP, the costs decline from 1.8 per cent of GDP to 1.5 per cent of GDP.

The contribution of GDP growth to financing the HIV/AIDS response, however, is tempered to the extent that increasing GDP *per capita* results in higher salaries and unit costs of HIV/AIDS services. In Kenya, for example, the increase in GDP (7 per cent annually) primarily reflects growth of GDP per capita (4.2 per cent) rather than population growth (2.7 per cent), and at this rate GDP per capita increases by 86 per cent through 2030. Taking into account how increasing salaries may affect the costs of the HIV/AIDS response is thus crucial for projecting costs and assessing the financial sustainability of the HIV/AIDS response.

In this area, though, there is a disconnect between modellers with an epidemiological background (rarely including macroeconomic considerations explicitly) and those with an economic background, illustrated for example in an exchange between Over (an economist who spent decades at the World Bank) and Stover (an accomplished epidemiologist). While Over and Garnett (2012) link projected treatment costs to GDP per capita in an analysis of the cost-effectiveness of treatment, Stover (2012) considers this approach as 'unique' and 'innovative', and does not follow it. As a result, Stover finds 'benefit to cost ratios that are about three times higher' for treatment as prevention than the ones estimated by Garnett and Over. These discrepancies illustrate that accounting for macroeconomic factors like increasing salaries in cost projections plays a large role in estimating the financing burden and the cost-effectiveness of HIV/AIDS programmes and interventions.

The discussion of *increasing budget allocations to HIV/AIDS* is usually divided into increasing budget allocations for health overall (and allocations for HIV/AIDS within this envelope) and increasing HIV/AIDS-specific allocations. The prominence of the first approach reflects that HIV/AIDS and broad health advocacy intersect in it, and—at least regarding sub-Saharan Africa—that the Abuja target provides a benchmark to evaluate current budget allocations. In the Abuja Declaration (Organization of African Unity, 2001), African Heads of State pledged 'to set a target of allocating at least 15 per cent of our annual budget to the improvement of the health sector'.

This commitment, however, was made in the context of high optimism about the course of official development assistance, shortly after the MDGs were launched, and the Abuja declaration made reference to the commitments by donors to devote 0.7 per cent of national income to development assistance. Like the latter, the Abuja target had little practical relevance—public health spending has stagnated at about 11 per cent of government revenues (unweighted average) across sub-Saharan Africa since about 2006, and this stagnation likely reflects a decline of domestic resources devoted to health as the data of public expenditure include some of the increase in external assistance for health (and especially HIV/AIDS) which took place over this period.

One political challenge associated with the Abuja targets is the fact that they place much emphasis on the countries devoting a relatively high share of government expenditures to health (the seven countries meeting the Abuja target as of 2013), but not those where the share of health in government spending is *far* below the Abuja target (in 2013, nine countries in the region did not even meet half of the Abuja target, with public health spending accounting for less than 7.5 per cent of government expenditure). Perhaps for these reasons, the Abuja targets do no longer play a role in the policy discourse in the region, as illustrated by the African Union's 'Roadmap' for the HIV/AIDS, TB, and malaria response (African Union, 2012) which makes no reference to it, and Piot (2012) comments on the 2001 targets observing that 'I always pushed for ambitious goals, but I tried also to avoid totally unrealistic ones, which can in fact be demoralizing instead of inspirational.'

The third benchmark commonly used for appropriate domestic investments in the HIV/AIDS response is the *burden of disease from HIV/AIDS* in comparison to other diseases. (This will be discussed further in Chapter 6.) While it is tempting to argue that spending on HIV/AIDS should be 'in proportion' to spending on other diseases, the share of HIV/AIDS in the burden of disease is not necessarily a good benchmark, because much health spending cannot be directly attributed to specific diseases, the burden of disease is endogenous and the result of investments in public health and specific diseases, and the cost-effectiveness of available interventions in terms of achieving desired health outcomes differs. Nevertheless, different allocations to HIV/AIDS across countries with similar circumstances can be interpreted in terms of the priorities the government assigns to the HIV/AIDS response, or play a role in convincing governments of appropriate HIV/AIDS investments. Along these lines (and taking note of some of the drawbacks just described), Resch et al. (2015) apply a 'conservative' benchmark for the share of public health spending going to the HIV/AIDS response of one-half times the share of HIV/AIDS in the disease burden. Empirical analyses of determinants of domestic HIV/AIDS spending, incorporating some measure of the burden of disease, can also be interpreted as benchmarks for appropriate HIV/AIDS investments, as in the work by Galárraga et al. (2013).

Approaches benchmarking domestic HIV/AIDS spending against current measures of the burden of disease, fiscal, and economic capacities miss out on one distinguishing aspect of the HIV/AIDS response—spending needs are highly persistent, extending over decades.[27] The HIV/AIDS response, in terms of its financial consequences, is radically different from a severe but short-term shock like the Ebola outbreak of 2014/15, which resulted in a steep fiscal cost—but over only about 2 years. The government could conceivably accommodate a fiscal shock of, say, 2 per cent of GDP over such a short period, for example by running a higher fiscal deficit when the shock occurs and spreading the costs over a longer period. However, it is much harder to do so if the fiscal shock persists over several decades, as in case of the HIV/AIDS response.[28] To capture this persistence in the spending needs of the HIV/AIDS response, some studies interpret the spending commitments under the HIV/AIDS response as a financial liability which needs to be paid off over a long period.[29] This analogy—discussed further in Chapter 11—then provides an opportunity to link the analysis of the financial burden posed by the HIV/AIDS response to the literature on the sustainability of public debt.

The approaches discussed above apply some benchmarks to *domestic* financing of HIV/AIDS programmes, and derive conclusions on external funding needs to 'plug the holes'. An alternative approach focuses on the role of *external* financing across countries and estimates policies pursued by donors. For example, Haacker and Greener (2012) analyse the share of external funding in the financing of HIV/AIDS programmes across countries, depending on variables such as GDP per capita, income status (as classified by World Bank), HIV prevalence, perception of government effectiveness, and country size.[30] According to this work (updated here based on the most recent data for ninety-eight countries, with similar results), the policies pursued by donors can be summarized by a simple rule (with t-ratios in parentheses):

$$External\ Funding\ (percent) = 76.7 + 12.2 * LIC - 0.0063 * GDP\ per\ capita$$
$$(21.3)\quad (2.8)\qquad (-10.5)$$

That is, an additional US$1,000 in GDP per capita is associated with a drop in the share of external funding by 6.3 percentage points, and low-income countries (*LICs*) receive an additional 12.2 per cent (compare Figure 5.4.a). This equation explains 65 per cent of the variation in external financing. If HIV prevalence is added to this equation, the coefficient is small and insignificant. The absence of a clear link between HIV prevalence and the rate of external financing does not mean that donors disregard HIV prevalence—countries with higher HIV prevalence tend to run larger HIV/AIDS programmes, in these countries donors provide a larger *absolute* amount of funding, but do not make a *disproportionately* higher contribution to larger HIV programmes.

High rates of external support leave countries vulnerable to a decline in the availability of external funding, and this applies in particular to a number of low-income countries which are among the countries facing the steepest financing challenges (relative to their GDP) and where the HIV/AIDS response is predominantly financed by external grants (e.g. Burundi, Haiti, Liberia, Mozambique, and Rwanda). Haacker and Greener (2012) discuss how donor policies would need to be adapted in case of a shortage of external financing in order to prevent an excessive domestic financing burden, finding that donor policies would need to be adapted in two ways—reducing the rate of external funding more steeply for countries with higher GDP per capita, and funding a disproportionately higher share of the costs of the HIV/AIDS response in countries with high HIV prevalence.[31] The 'new funding model' of the Global Fund introduced in 2011 (Global Fund, 2011c, 2013b, 2014b) can be interpreted as a step in this direction, defining requirements for domestic counterpart financing between 5 per cent (for low-income countries) and 60 per cent (upper-middle-income countries), and excluding countries with relatively high income from funding unless the disease burden is sufficiently high. The stepwise approach adopted by the Global Fund, though, introduces large differences between countries under similar economic circumstances (e.g. one just below and the other just above the income threshold between low- and middle income countries), and a rule varying counterpart requirements more gradually with the level of GDP per capita would be more efficient.

6

Impact of the Global Response to HIV/AIDS

This chapter attempts an evaluation of the outcomes of the global HIV/AIDS response—direct outcomes such as coverage rates of treatment, mortality among people living with HIV, or reduced HIV incidence, and their implications for broad health outcomes such as overall mortality and life expectancy. In line with the discussion of the health impact of HIV/AIDS, which highlighted that the impact of HIV/AIDS is highly concentrated across countries, much of the emphasis will be on the impacts of the global HIV/AIDS response across countries. A concluding section discusses whether investments in the HIV/AIDS response have been effective and whether the global HIV/AIDS response has received 'too much money'.

Challenges of Attribution

To appreciate the effectiveness and cost-effectiveness of the global response to HIV/AIDS, it is first necessary to identify its outcomes—not a straightforward task, because key aspects such as HIV incidence are normally observed only indirectly, and causal attribution of changes in HIV incidence to interventions is not straightforward.[1] Assessing the impacts of an HIV/AIDS programme therefore typically involves some modelling—linking policy variables to indicators of the state of the epidemic which are the outcome of some separate modelling (such as the estimates of the state of HIV/AIDS published by UNAIDS) or complementing estimates of the direct effects of an intervention with some epidemiological modelling to obtain population-level effects of an intervention or policy.

Reflecting these challenges, numerous approaches have been utilized to evaluate aspects of the impact of the HIV/AIDS response.

- Empirical analyses, identifying the impacts of specific interventions
  - on the individuals targeted, and sometimes also
  - across their communities.

- Empirical analyses, relating outcomes to inputs of the HIV/AIDS response
  - relating health outcomes or coverage of HIV/AIDS services to spending on the HIV/AIDS response, or
  - relating health outcomes to programme indicators such as the coverage of certain HIV/AIDS services.
- Modelling to distinguish natural epidemiological dynamics from factors which could be attributed to interventions.
- Analyses using an epidemiological model to map assumptions on the effectiveness of various interventions into projections of the population-level effects of HIV/AIDS policies.
- Informal approaches, testing narratives of the course of the epidemic against available socio-economic data.

The principal examples on the impacts of specific interventions on HIV incidence are the trials on the effectiveness of specific HIV prevention interventions like treatment as prevention or male circumcision (discussed in Chapter 9).[2] Such evidence forms the basis of the modelling of the impact of HIV prevention interventions; it is also usefully complemented by non-experimental empirical studies seeking to capture the impacts of HIV prevention interventions over time or across the population. For example, Gray et al. (2012) show that effectiveness of male circumcision was maintained over five years following a trial, and Auvert et al. (2013) document a decline in HIV prevalence following an expansion of male circumcision. A number of evaluations of the Avahan initiative in India documented the impacts of interventions focusing on female sex workers and condom use (Deering et al., 2011), HIV prevalence among female sex workers (Alary and others, 2014), and HIV prevalence across the population (Arora et al., 2013).

Focusing on the link between outcomes and aggregate HIV/AIDS-related spending across countries is attractive because it yields direct estimates of 'returns to investment' of the HIV/AIDS response. Also, programme-level spending data may contain overhead expenses and reflect inefficiencies and wastage that may not appear in data on specific interventions or in facility-level data. On the other hand, aggregated programme-level data blur the effects of underlying interventions and introduce additional data noise. The power of cross-country analyses, however, is relatively low. Data on the state of HIV/AIDS are available from UNAIDS (2015c) for 120 countries, and aggregate HIV/AIDS spending data are available for most of these countries at least for some years. However, between most countries there is little variation in terms of the scale of the epidemic—HIV prevalence (ages 15–49) exceeds 1 per cent in only forty-eight countries. On the downside, while spending data are convenient measures of the intensity of the HIV/AIDS response overall or across major programme categories (e.g. prevention), such aggregation blurs the effects of underlying interventions and introduces additional data noise.

One example for an evaluation of the HIV/AIDS response on the most aggregate level is the study by Nunnenkamp and Öhler (2011), which compares trends in HIV incidence and deaths between countries which have received large amounts of aid, or otherwise. They find that large levels of aid have not been associated with a significant decline in HIV incidence. The impact of the results on the link between aid and AIDS deaths are stronger— aid from the United States especially (which has a large treatment component) has been associated with steeper declines in AIDS deaths. The weak results on the effects of aid on HIV incidence may reflect that much of the variation in aid reflects differences in treatment costs. Ng et al. (2011) use data on regional spending (largely on HIV prevention) from the Avahan initiative in India, and find that higher spending is associated with a larger decline in HIV prevalence.

However, such empirical approaches to establishing the effects of HIV prevention interventions are inefficient in accounting for the underlying dynamics of the epidemic and in utilizing the substantial information on the state of the epidemic and its drivers. To address this shortcoming, researchers frequently use epidemiological models analytically—calibrating the model to available data, utilizing it to identify the most plausible causes of changes in HIV incidence, distinguishing the natural dynamics of the epidemic from factors which could be attributed to policy. For example, Hallett et al. (2006) reviewed trends in HIV prevalence in eight countries, observing that HIV prevalence may 'decline without a deliberate adoption of safer sexual behaviours', but pointing out that the observed 'changes in prevalence in Uganda, parts of urban Kenya, Zimbabwe, and urban Haiti are unlikely to be a product of these natural dynamics' and more consistent with changes in sexual risk behaviour. Following a similar approach, Johnson et al. (2012) estimate changes in HIV incidence in South Africa, and attribute most of the decline observed between 2000 and 2008 to increased condom use.

Projections of the impacts of alternative HIV/AIDS policies, such as the ones published by UNAIDS, are most commonly based on an epidemiological model ('Goals') that includes a matrix describing the effects of a wide range of HIV prevention interventions.[3] This matrix is populated based on available empirical estimates of the direct effects of specific interventions. Projections based on the Goals model are discussed elsewhere in this book, for example in the context of the UNAIDS 'investment framework' (Chapter 7), or the discussion of the optimal design of HIV/AIDS programmes (Chapter 10).

One shortcoming of the model-based evaluations of HIV policies arises from the facts that changes in HIV incidence in these models are conditioned on factors such as condom use or sexual risk behaviour, and that the impact of the HIV/AIDS response on these factors is not straightforward. For example, a decline in sexual risk behaviour may reflect personal experiences as much as HIV awareness campaigns. This uncertainty on the causes of changes in behaviour makes it difficult to attribute changes in HIV incidence to policy interventions and raises challenges for forward-looking policy scenarios aimed at controlling the epidemic.

The quantitative modelling analyses are therefore usefully complemented by studies seeking to develop fuller narratives of drivers of risk behaviours. For example, Gregson et al. (2010) document 'reductions in numbers reporting casual partners from the late 1990s and high condom use in non-regular partnerships between 1998 and 2007' in Zimbabwe, and Halperin et al. (2011) conclude that behaviour changes 'appear to have been stimulated primarily by increased awareness of AIDS deaths and secondarily by the country's economic deterioration'.

Achievements of the Global Response to HIV/AIDS

The global response to HIV/AIDS was motivated not only by the adverse health impacts of HIV/AIDS, but also because HIV/AIDS was seen as a development challenge (Chapter 5)—the magnitude of the epidemic was greatest in developing countries (ECOSOC, 1994), though not necessarily the poorest ones, and the virtual absence of treatment across developing countries resulted in steep inequities in the consequences of contracting HIV across countries. To evaluate the achievements of the global response to HIV/AIDS, it is therefore necessary to take into account not only its success in controlling the epidemic and extending access to treatment, but also the extent to which it has mitigated inequalities in the consequences of HIV/AIDS across countries and reduced economic barriers to treatment access.[4]

As a crude indicator for progress in controlling the epidemic, Figure 6.1 summarizes trends in HIV prevalence among young people (here: aged 15–24) between 2000 and 2014. Compared to HIV prevalence overall, HIV prevalence among the young is a better indicator for underlying trends in HIV *incidence*, because it reflects HIV infections which happened fairly recently, and as it is less sensitive to changes in access to treatment.

For both young women and men, HIV prevalence has declined, sometimes substantially, in almost all countries where HIV prevalence exceeded 2 per cent for women or 1 per cent for men in 2000, with particularly steep declines in Botswana, Central African Republic, Côte d'Ivoire, Malawi, Namibia, and Zimbabwe. (Note the different scales for women and men in Figure 6.1 for better readability—HIV prevalence among young men is usually about half the level for young women.) The most notable exceptions are Equatorial Guinea, where HIV prevalence among young people more than doubled,

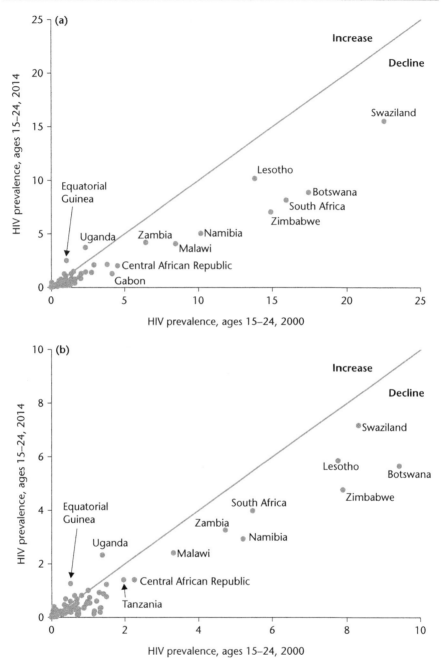

Figure 6.1. HIV prevalence among young people, 2000 and 2014
Source: UNAIDS (2015c).
(a). Females
(b). Males

and Uganda (increasing from 2.4 per cent to 3.7 per cent for women, and from 1.4 per cent to 2.3 per cent for men).

One area in which the impact of HIV prevention policies can be quantified is the scaling-up of male circumcision. The 'Joint Strategic Action Framework' of the WHO and UNAIDS (2011) envisages a steep expansion in the coverage of male circumcision in countries facing high HIV prevalence, from less than 40 per cent in 2008 to 80 per cent by 2016.[5] By the end of 2013, 5.8 million males had undergone medical male circumcision, corresponding to 38 per cent of the progress needed to reach the target of 80 per cent (WHO, 2014). Modelling suggests that this factor has reduced HIV incidence among males by more than 10 per cent in Botswana, Swaziland, Uganda, and Zambia.[6]

The most visible outcome of the global HIV response is the universal increase in access to treatment and the resulting decline in HIV/AIDS-related mortality, overcoming barriers posed by the sheer magnitude of the health shock posed by HIV/AIDS in countries with high HIV prevalence, and economic barriers in countries where scaling-up of treatment would have been beyond the means of the government and the vast majority of citizens. In fact, as of 2013, there was no obvious correlation between treatment coverage and GDP per capita across developing countries, and the principal barrier to treatment access was being located in a country with low HIV prevalence (Figure 6.2).[7] This latter result could reflect the difficulties in setting up effective HIV/AIDS services (and thus high unit costs) where there are few people living with HIV, and low political priority attributed to the HIV/AIDS response in these countries. In interpreting these coverage rates, it is important to bear in mind that treatment coverage reported by UNAIDS (2013a) is based on the WHO (2013) eligibility criteria (eligibility at a CD4 count below 500, plus some additional criteria). The most pressing medical needs, though, occur below a CD4 count of 200,[8] and treatment coverage rates at lower CD4 counts would be much higher than the ones shown in Figure 6.2.

As a consequence of increased access to treatment, AIDS-related mortality has declined steeply across developing countries. As of 2014, AIDS-related mortality across developing countries ranged from 1.8 per cent to 6.5 per cent of people living with HIV (10th and 90th percentile), and averaged 3.2 per cent (Figure 6.3). Without access to antiretroviral therapy, it would range from 5.2 per cent to 10.6 per cent, and average 7.8 per cent.[9] Thus, the drive towards universal access to treatment has so far succeeded in cutting AIDS-related mortality among people living with HIV across developing countries by well over one-half. However, it still remains higher than in the most advanced economies (e.g. United Kingdom, Switzerland), where AIDS-related mortality among people living with HIV is now lower than 1 per cent.

As the impact of HIV/AIDS is distributed unevenly across countries, and countries differ in terms of their capacities in responding to the epidemic, it is

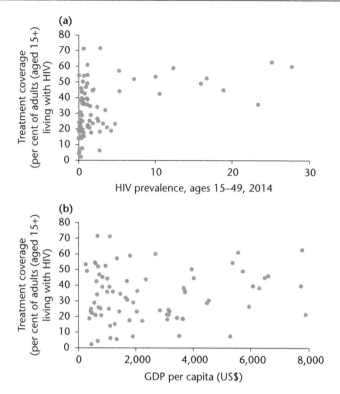

Figure 6.2. Treatment coverage, HIV prevalence, and GDP per capita, 2013
Source: UNAIDS (2015c) and World Bank (2015).
(a). Treatment coverage and HIV prevalence
(b). Treatment coverage and GDP per capita

also important to understand the impact of treatment across countries. Figure 6.3a addresses this point by lining up countries according to their GDP per capita, and weighing observations (i.e. the area of the relevant dots) by HIV prevalence and people living with HIV. Overall, AIDS-related mortality declines with GDP per capita, but this association is weak and explains little of the variation in mortality. However, there are clear differences among *countries facing high HIV prevalence*. In middle-income countries, mortality among people living with HIV ranges from 1.2 per cent (Namibia) to 2.0 per cent (South Africa). In low-income countries with HIV prevalence above 5 per cent, mortality ranges from 1.6 per cent to 3.1 per cent.[10] Overall, the principal barrier to expanding access to treatment on the country-level appears to be a lack of political priority or high unit costs of HIV/AIDS services where HIV prevalence is low (the countries with highest mortality among people living with HIV are countries facing low HIV prevalence); among high-prevalence

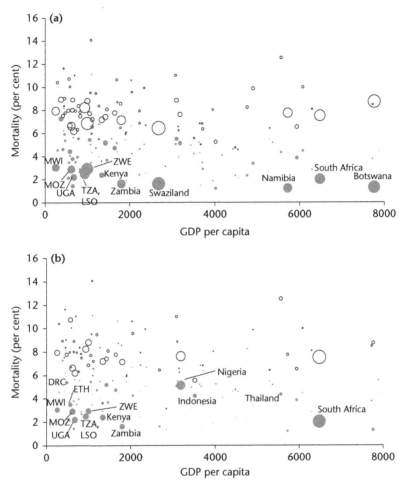

Figure 6.3. AIDS-related mortality across countries, with and without treatment, 2014

Source: UNAIDS (2015c).
(a). Weighted (bubble area) by HIV prevalence
(b). Weighted (bubble area) by number of people living with HIV
Note: Solid points represent estimates of AIDS-related mortality as of 2014, hollow points show counterfactual estimates of mortality in the absence of treatment in that year. DRC=Democratic Republic of the Congo, ETH=Ethiopia, LSO=Lesotho, MOZ=Mozambique, MWI=Malawi, TZA= Tanzania, UGA=Uganda, and ZWE=Zimbabwe.

countries, constraints associated with low economic capacities appear to be a powerful obstacle.

From a *global* policy perspective, it is also important to look at the absolute magnitude of the contribution of a country to excess mortality from HIV/AIDS (Figure 6.3.b). From this perspective, Nigeria is by far the largest contributor, accounting for almost one-quarter of excess mortality, even though HIV prevalence is only about 3 per cent—reflecting its size (3.4 million living with HIV), but also high mortality among people living with HIV in excess of 5 per cent.[11] South Africa follows with 9 per cent, owing to the magnitude of the epidemic in this country, and mortality among people living with HIV of 2.0 per cent. Other significant contributors to AIDS-related excess mortality are Mozambique (4.7 per cent of total excess mortality; 1.5 million PLWH, AIDS-related mortality of 2.9 per cent among PLWH), Cameroon (4.7 per cent; 0.7 million PLWH; AIDS-related mortality of 5.2 per cent); Tanzania (4.3 per cent; 1.4 million PLWH; AIDS-related mortality of 2.9 per cent); and Indonesia (3.7 per cent; 0.7 million PLWH; AIDS-related mortality of 4.2 per cent). (India would also belong in this group based on earlier data, but recent estimates of the state of HIV/AIDS are unavailable.)

Implications for Global Health Outcomes

The implications of the HIV/AIDS response for global health outcomes are distinct from the direct impact of HIV/AIDS discussed above for two reasons. (1) The HIV/AIDS response may affect non-HIV/AIDS health outcomes, for example positively through investments in health systems strengthening under the HIV/AIDS response, or negatively as resources are allocated from other health conditions to the HIV/AIDS response and the availability of non-HIV/AIDS health services deteriorates. (2) For an evaluation of the global health outcomes of HIV/AIDS, it is important to take into account the health context of HIV/AIDS across countries. To what extent did HIV/AIDS affect countries where health outcomes were already low before the escalation of HIV/AIDS? What are the implications of HIV/AIDS and the response to it for the occurrence of extreme negative health outcomes and for inequality in global health outcomes?

The most immediate impact of the HIV/AIDS response on health outcomes is the improved survival of people living with HIV owing to treatment, and this effect is amply documented through data on patients receiving antiretroviral therapy.[12] Beyond this evidence, estimates of the population-level effects of antiretroviral therapy are relevant for validation of the direct estimates (e.g. if the latter are compromised by loss to follow-up), assessing the significance of the HIV/AIDS response in terms of population-level health outcomes, and assessing positive or negative spillovers from the HIV/AIDS response.

Evidence on the *population-level* impact of antiretroviral therapy on mortality is limited, because it requires demographic surveillance data which can be matched to the treatment scale-up, but the available data consistently show a steep decline in mortality where treatment becomes available. In Botswana, mortality at ages 15–64 declined by almost half between 2003 and 2009. At sites in Malawi, Tanzania, South Africa, and Uganda the roll-out of antiretro-viral therapy was associated with a decline in all-cause mortality for ages 15–59 of between 21 per cent and 42 per cent (Floyd et al., 2012), owing to a decline in mortality among people living with HIV (up to 65 per cent) while there was no change in non-AIDS mortality associated with the treatment scale-up. Reniers et al. (2014), for a pooled sample (including sites from Kenya, Malawi, Tanzania, South Africa, Uganda, and Zimbabwe) with an HIV preva-lence of 18.5 per cent, document a decline in all-cause mortality from 1.9 per cent to 1.3 per cent between 2000–2003 and 2009–2011, driven by a decline in mortality among people living with HIV from 7.8 per cent to 3.2 per cent. Casting the net even wider, Bendavid et al. (2012) observe that mortality in PEPFAR focus countries has declined by 16 per cent relative to non-focus countries between 2004 and 2008.

While there is no compelling evidence that the HIV/AIDS response has been associated with changes in non-AIDS-related mortality, there is some evidence—both from health facilities and across countries, on links between the scaling-up of HIV/AIDS services and the coverage of specific health ser-vices. Brugha et al. (2010) find a positive correlation between the scaling-up of antiretroviral therapy and prevention of mother-to-child transmission of HIV, on one hand, and the delivery of reproductive health services, on the other hand, across health facilities in Zambia. Similarly, Kruk et al. (2012) observe that 'having more patients on antiretroviral treatment and HIV-related infra-structure investments, such as on-site laboratories at health clinics, were associated with more deliveries at health facilities by women not infected with HIV' across 157 health facilities supported by PEPFAR in eight African countries. Based on country-level data, Lee and Platas-Izama (2015) observe that neonatal mortality declined more slowly in fifteen countries receiving funding from PEPFAR in 2004–2009. After controlling for HIV prevalence, Grépin (2012) finds that higher levels of HIV/AIDS-related external aid are associated with lower rates of childhood immunization.

Overall, the data on broad and more specific health outcomes suggest that the HIV/AIDS response reduced overall mortality considerably in countries severely affected by HIV/AIDS. This effect in the first place reflects reduced mortality of people living with HIV, whereas positive or negative effects on health outcomes not specific to people living with HIV did not play a signifi-cant role.

The area in which the impact of the global response to HIV/AIDS across countries can be *modelled* in a straightforward manner is the decline in mortality owing to the scaling-up of treatment. Starting from a scenario describing the course of the epidemic, it is possible to ask how much increased access to treatment has improved health outcomes, and to what extent it has contributed to reversing the adverse impact of HIV/AIDS. To this end, two

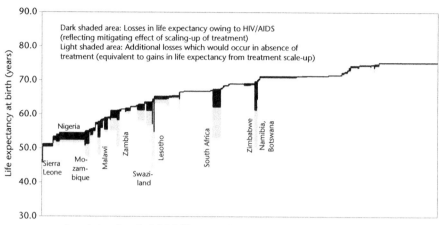

Population (total of 2.7 billion over 106 countries), sorted by life expectancy excluding impact of HIV/AIDS

Figure 6.4. Impact of HIV/AIDS and of treatment access on life expectancy at birth across countries, 2014

Source: UNAIDS (2015a) and author's calculations.

counterfactual scenarios need to be created—one excluding the impact of treatment on survival, and the other one excluding the impact of AIDS altogether.

The consequences of HIV/AIDS and the scaling-up of treatment are summarized in Figure 6.4 using life expectancy at birth as a summary indicator. The figure builds on the epidemiological work files used by UNAIDS which are available for 105 countries with a total population of 2.7 billion, accounting for 29.3 million people living with HIV in 2014 (out of a global total of 37 million).[13] While this covers only 37 per cent of the global population, the countries shown include virtually all countries globally where life expectancy is below 65 years (except Somalia and Comoros) and all countries with an HIV prevalence exceeding 1 per cent. Figure 6.4 therefore gives a complete picture of the consequences of HIV/AIDS at the lower end of the global distribution of life expectancy, and in countries where HIV/AIDS has a significant impact.

Countries are ordered by life expectancy excluding the impact of HIV/AIDS (the upper surface of the graph), and weighted by population (larger countries are represented by wider bars). The height of the dark areas represents the loss in life expectancy owing to HIV/AIDS, and the height of the light areas shows the additional loss in life expectancy which would occur without treatment (or the reversal in the adverse impacts owing to treatment).

The estimates illustrate the fact that HIV/AIDS is highly concentrated across countries, and shows the extraordinary magnitude of its impact. Without the impact of HIV/AIDS, Sierra Leone would be the only country with a life expectancy below 50 years.[14] Without the scaling-up of treatment, life expectancy would fall below 50 years in an additional four countries (Lesotho, Malawi, Mozambique, and Swaziland). The figure also illustrates the limitations of the scaling-up of treatment so far. Treatment has spectacularly reduced the impacts of HIV/AIDS by over 70 per cent in some countries (Botswana, South Africa, Zambia) and by more than half in some other countries facing very high HIV prevalence (Lesotho, Malawi, Namibia, Swaziland, and Zimbabwe). However, across all the countries shown, treatment reversed 'only' half (population-weighted average) of the impact of HIV/AIDS on life expectancy—reflecting low treatment coverage in some countries with relatively low HIV prevalence but large population (e.g. Nigeria)—so that the impact of HIV/AIDS across countries remains very significant.

Has the Global HIV/AIDS Response Received too Much Money?

Concerns on the impact of the HIV/AIDS response on health outcomes across the board can be summarized under two broad themes: (1) that the HIV/AIDS response, by absorbing scarce health sector resources, is eroding other vital health care services; and (2) that HIV/AIDS is receiving too much money relative to other pressing health challenges, and overall health outcomes could be improved by reallocating some of the funding of the HIV/AIDS response to other health services.

On the first item, it is necessary to bear in mind that even if health outcomes in other areas deteriorate as a consequence of the HIV/AIDS response, this does not necessarily reflect over-investment in the HIV/AIDS response. HIV/AIDS represented a major adverse health shock in many countries, and the fast scaling-up of the HIV/AIDS response and especially of treatment was a reaction to the often devastating consequences. Under these circumstances, reallocating some scarce health sector resources—especially those which cannot be augmented quickly like trained health personnel—to enable the scaling-up of HIV/AIDS services (and taking into account that health outcomes deteriorate in other areas) could be part of an optimal strategy from a broad public health perspective. In the longer run, though, it is less plausible that an HIV/AIDS strategy that is optimal from an overall public health perspective would have negative impacts on other health services because any *specific* resource constraints (e.g. health personnel) could be addressed by appropriate investments (e.g. training). Nevertheless, to the extent that the HIV/AIDS response absorbs public and private financial resources, it crowds out other public or private spending. However, this crowding out occurs under a *general* (and not health-specific) budget constraint, and much of the required resources would be reallocated from non-health spending, mitigating adverse consequences within the health sector by spreading the costs across policy objectives or private consumption.

Nevertheless, a deterioration in non-HIV/AIDS health services is of course problematic because of its distributional implications (the beneficiaries of the HIV/AIDS response are not necessarily the same as those losing out if other health services are eroded), many countries facing high HIV prevalence are also facing pressing health challenges across the board (see Figure 6.4, showing counterfactual life expectancies without HIV/AIDS), and because a well-defined common objective for public health policy may not exist—the objectives and incentives of major donors could be different from those of the national Ministry of Health.

By and large, major donors have taken into account health systems constraints and invested in building capacities. Health systems strengthening (with an emphasis on training and laboratory capacities, see PEPFAR (2014a)) accounted for 15 per cent (US$900 million) of PEPFAR programme expenditures in (fiscal year) 2013, and health systems strengthening is an integral component of PEPFAR's 'sustainability agenda' (PEPFAR, 2014c). At the Global Fund, the calculation of the funding envelope each country can apply for is based on the burden of HIV/AIDS, TB, and malaria (and other criteria) in that country. Within this envelope, though, most countries can allocate funding to health systems strengthening, in addition to spending specifically addressing the three diseases (Global Fund, 2014c). As a consequence, a considerable proportion of Global Fund funding can go towards health systems strengthening—Warren et al. (2013) estimate that 37 per cent of Global Fund grants were allocated to health systems strengthening—including 14 per cent of total funding going to general (i.e. not disease-specific) health systems strengthening.[15]

To what extent (and whether) the HIV/AIDS response has resulted in deteriorating health outcomes elsewhere, though, is unclear. Using data from demographic and health surveys, Case and Paxson (2011) show that access to some non-HIV/AIDS health services (antenatal care, birth deliveries, and rates of immunization for children) have deteriorated in areas where HIV *prevalence* has been high. This deterioration, however, occurred in the mid-1990s, before the HIV/AIDS *response* took off. Available studies on the impact of the HIV/AIDS response yield an unclear and heterogeneous picture. Data from health facilities suggest that reproductive health services have improved at facilities also providing antiretroviral therapy, and studies based on cross-country data find no link between increased PEPFAR funding and non-AIDS mortality, although some common health indicators (e.g. neonatal mortality, immunization rates) may have deteriorated.[16]

One channel through which the global HIV/AIDS response could erode non-HIV/AIDS health services is by absorbing funding that would otherwise support other aspects of the health system. 'Otherwise', however, implies the existence of a well-defined counterfactual. In the absence of such a counterfactual, it is only possible to assess trends in HIV/AIDS financing in relation to funding for other objectives. One such study (Shiffman et al., 2009) discusses trends in commitments of external aid on health and population policies between 1998 and 2007, pointing to the large increase in commitments on HIV/AIDS (from US$300 million to US$7.4 billion, and 5.5 per cent of the total to 47 per cent of the total). Commitments on the control of infectious diseases rose less rapidly (from US$300 million to US$2.7 billion—largely a consequence of the arrival of the Global Fund), while aid commitments on population policies and health systems strengthening stagnated in absolute terms (and their share in aid commitments dropped). Over the last years, though, this picture has changed. According to the OECD's CRS database (OECD, 2015), disbursements on HIV/AIDS have stagnated below US$8 billion between 2011 and 2013, and their share in health-related aid disbursement has declined from 40 per cent (average, 2008–2011) to 35 per cent in 2013. Instead, the weights of reproductive health care, basic nutrition, malaria, and tuberculosis have increased.

The literature addressing the impact of the HIV/AIDS response on health systems (beyond the specific health services discussed in the previous section) is exceedingly weak. Different reviews concluded that 'only seemingly anecdotal evidence or authors' perceptions/interpretations of circumstances could be extracted from the included studies'; that 'there was a paucity of robust evidence' and 'effects on health systems were rarely a focus of research protocols;' and that 'there is limited hard evidence of . . . health system impacts'.[17] Bearing in mind these shortcomings, positive impacts on health systems referred to in the literature include an increasing priority given to public health by governments, greater stakeholder participation and a strengthening of civil society, improvements in health infrastructure (e.g. laboratories) in many countries, and improvements in primary care services in some; while negative effects include distortion of national policies, onerous grant application and reporting requirements, and siphoning off of scarce personnel from other health care services.[18]

In summary, there is no clear evidence suggesting that the HIV/AIDS response had a significant positive or negative impact on non-HIV/AIDS health services—there is no obvious impact of the HIV/AIDS response on summary non-HIV/AIDS health indicators; for more specific indicators the picture is uneven. However, HIV/AIDS absorbed much of the increase in health-related aid since 2002, at least until a partial reversal most recently. While it is not clear (and doubtful, in light of the discussion of the global HIV/AIDS response in Chapter 5) whether the funds absorbed by the HIV/AIDS response would have been available for the health sector otherwise, it is nevertheless legitimate to ask whether the expansion in HIV/AIDS funding has been the best use of available funds from a global health perspective—to evaluate the success of the HIV/AIDS response so far from a broader global health perspective, and to map out its future.

There are two principal arguments suggesting that the HIV/AIDS response has received '*too much money*'. First, global funding for the HIV/AIDS response is very high in relation to its contribution to the global burden of disease (e.g. England, 2007b). For example, between 2005 and 2014, HIV/AIDS accounted for 3.7 per cent of deaths across low- and middle-income countries, and 9.8 per cent of mortality at ages 15–59 (IHME, 2014). In contrast, 38 per cent of health-related development assistance globally has been devoted to HIV/AIDS over this period. Second, the cost-effectiveness of HIV/AIDS-related interventions, and especially of antiretroviral therapy, is lower than for a number of health interventions (as documented comprehensively by Laxminarayan et al., 2006).

The amount of spending in relation to the magnitude of the disease burden offers a convenient benchmark for describing the priority attributed to different diseases. For example, the 'Domestic Investment Priority Index' used by UNAIDS to rank domestic commitments to the HIV/AIDS response is based on such a ratio (discussed in Chapter 5). There are, however, a number of problems with using the burden of disease as a benchmark. The burden of disease from different causes is endogenous and (among other factors) depends on disease-specific spending—as an intervention targeting a specific disease is scaled up, the burden of disease is diminished, and spending on that disease may appear high relative to the remaining burden of disease. Also, the costs of responding to specific diseases do not necessarily increase proportionately with the burden from that disease—for example HIV/AIDS spending appears high relative to the burden of disease in countries with low HIV prevalence (Chapter 5). For these reasons, estimates of the cost-effectiveness of the HIV/AIDS response, which focus on the *impact* on the burden of disease rather than the *remaining* burden of disease, are superior indicators for affective allocations of health funding, and are indeed used intensively in the policy discourse on the HIV/AIDS response (see Chapters 9 and 10).

One factor that has become increasingly important for the evaluation of HIV/AIDS interventions over the last 10 years is the fact that HIV/AIDS has evolved into a chronic disease in many countries. The consequences of each HIV infection in terms of life years lost have therefore declined, and the cost-effectiveness of HIV prevention interventions in terms of health outcomes has deteriorated. However, each HIV infection prevented also averts a long tail of expenditures required to meet the need for treatment and other services, which should be taken into account in the evaluation of the intervention.

For a backward looking evaluation of the effects and the cost-effectiveness of the global response to HIV/AIDS, there is surprisingly little material,[19] because of the weak evidence for the impacts of HIV prevention interventions on the population level (discussed above), and as most analytical work has been policy-oriented and forward-looking. As of 2014, the costs of the global response to HIV/AIDS had risen to US$20.1 billion, of which US$11.3 billion were funded externally (UNAIDS, 2015b). Spending on treatment amounted to US$10.0 billion in 2013, sustaining about 12 million people on treatment.[20] On average, treatment-related costs thus have fallen to well below US$1,000 annually according to these aggregate data. PEPFAR (2014b) reports similar estimates, with US$747 for adult ART patients and US$837 for paediatric treatment (both first-line), and US$1,428 for patients receiving second-line treatment. It is worth noting that these are top-down estimates which would include various indirect costs, recent estimates of facility level-costs of providing antiretroviral therapy in five African countries return annual unit costs between about US$200 and US$700 (Tagar et al., 2014).

Overall, the HIV/AIDS response has been an extraordinarily effective but also expensive global health intervention. It has resulted in a decline in AIDS-related mortality by one-half so far, and reversed catastrophic health impacts in countries with high HIV prevalence—the analysis summarized in Figure 6.4 suggests that without the scaling-up of treatment, numerous countries facing very high HIV prevalence would be among the countries with the lowest life expectancy anywhere, and the global HIV/AIDS response has already gone a long way towards mitigating and reversing these impacts.

In spite of these successes, HIV/AIDS continues to cause severe loss of life in many countries. The HIV/AIDS response also poses significant fiscal challenges, with costs well over 1 per cent of GDP, and 5 per cent of domestic government revenues in some high prevalence countries, but also a number of low-income countries with very limited domestic resources. Without external support, the gains achieved in these countries (including reversals of catastrophic losses in life expectancy in some) would be under threat. Thus, HIV/AIDS still 'is exceptional, but not everywhere' (Whiteside and Smith, 2009), and the global response to HIV/AIDS offers lessons (and a precedent) for addressing broader global health inequities (Forman, 2011).

Cost-effectiveness (while taking into account the broader objectives of health and development policy) of course remains a guiding principle in assessing the contributions of HIV/AIDS-related interventions and designing an effective response. This theme is developed in Part III of the book, taking into account the *financial* as well as health consequences of investments in the HIV/AIDS response, as well as their impacts on the course of the epidemic.

Part III
Design and Financing
of HIV/AIDS Policies

Part III discusses the role of economic analysis in the design of national HIV/AIDS programmes. Chapter 7 provides an introduction, reviewing the role of economic analysis and cost-effectiveness in HIV/AIDS programme design, and discussing the implications for cost-effectiveness analysis of the scaling up of treatment. It introduces the forward-looking analysis used throughout the book, incorporating the *spending commitments* implied by new HIV infections (and saved by HIV prevention interventions) in cost-effectiveness analysis. Chapter 8 addresses the cost-effectiveness of HIV/AIDS programmes based on overall outcomes and total spending and spending commitments. Chapter 9 discusses the cost-effectiveness of specific HIV prevention interventions, taking into account HIV transmission dynamics (beyond the immediate effect of an intervention), and the spending commitments caused by HIV infections. Chapter 10 reviews approaches to using cost-effectiveness analysis in the design of *optimal* HIV/AIDS strategies. Chapter 11 discusses the financing of national HIV/AIDS programmes, and its interactions with HIV/AIDS policy design.

7

Current Policy Challenges and Economic Perspectives

The purposes of this chapter are to position economic analysis, including analysis of cost-effectiveness, in the current HIV/AIDS policy discourse, and to provide an introduction to cost-effectiveness in the context of the evaluation of HIV/AIDS programmes and interventions. The 'investment framework' launched by UNAIDS in 2011 embeds economic concepts like 'returns to investment' and 'cost-effectiveness' in the global HIV/AIDS policy discourse, and has provided a widely applied template for strategy documents.

For cost-effectiveness analysis in support of policy design, it is important to bear in mind the objectives and preferences of the intended audience. While improving the cost-effectiveness of the HIV/AIDS response with regard to direct outcomes like HIV infections or AIDS-related deaths averted is valuable in its own right and contributes to making an 'investment case', the policy preferences of national governments are broader, and may not contain HIV/AIDS-specific outcomes directly. For effective policy design and advocacy, it is therefore necessary to connect the outcomes of the HIV/AIDS response to national health and development objectives. The next section describes the domain of cost-effectiveness analysis of HIV/AIDS programmes with regard to these wider policy objectives.

One important aspect of the cost-effectiveness of HIV/AIDS interventions is the transformation in the outcomes of such interventions associated with the scaling-up of treatment (discussed in the third section of this chapter). Consequently, the impacts on health outcomes like new HIV infections have diminished, but HIV infections result in spending needs which persist over decades. While the cost-effectiveness of some HIV prevention interventions *in terms of health outcomes* may have deteriorated, their contribution towards attaining *financial sustainability*—by containing the projected costs—of the HIV/AIDS response could be increasing.

Current Issues in HIV/AIDS Programme Design

The 'investment framework' represents a shift in the strategy for UNAIDS and other major international organizations like the Global Fund, and a departure from the policies and programmatic initiative which had dominated the global HIV/AIDS agenda roughly from 2000, characterized by the recognition of HIV/AIDS as one of the dominant global development challenges of our time,[1] unprecedented financial support,[2] and a vast increase in access to treatment[3] (see Chapters 5 and 6).

The UNAIDS investment framework in part is a response to a changed political environment. Some of the concerns regarding the potential global impact of HIV/AIDS have not borne out. Altman and Buse (2012) observe that 'in most parts of the world, AIDS is not a security or development crisis', and Whiteside and Smith (2009) observe that 'AIDS should be normalised' in most countries, that is, be 'viewed and addressed as one of many important health issues that are integrated into public health systems'. At the same time, a deteriorated fiscal outlook in the main donor countries has resulted in increased scrutiny of the results and effectiveness of global HIV/AIDS spending.

Against this context, the 'investment framework' placed greater emphasis on economic aspects of HIV/AIDS interventions and policies, such as 'returns to investment', financial and economic (in addition to health) outcomes (such as savings in treatment costs from reduced HIV incidence), improved targeting of available resources, and the financial sustainability and financing of HIV/AIDS strategies. It is *explicitly* built on an 'assessment of the existing evidence of what works in HIV/AIDS prevention, treatment, care and support', notably regarding the 'basic programme activities [which] have a direct effect on reduction of transmission, morbidity, and mortality from HIV/AIDS'—prevention of mother-to-child transmission; condom promotion and distribution; interventions targeting HIV transmission in 'key populations'; treatment, care, and support to people living with HIV/AIDS, male circumcision, and behaviour change programmes. However, the 'framework' is not cast as a prescriptive strategy, inviting adaptation as new evidence emerges.

One consequence of the increased emphasis on returns to investment, and an area in which the investment framework has been influential in shaping policy documents, is the need to adopt a fairly long time frame, for example the paper introducing the 'investment framework' adopts a time frame of about 10 years, and most strategy papers nowadays would adopt even longer time horizons. This need arises from the emphasis on the 'returns to investment'—because of the slow disease progression and transmission dynamics of HIV/AIDS, the health and economic returns to current investments in HIV prevention unfold over long periods, even decades.

Apart from offering a framework for HIV/AIDS policy design, the 'investment framework' is an advocacy tool, calling for increased investments in the HIV/AIDS response. In this regard it is not new, and resembles earlier calls by UNAIDS and other organizations for increased funding, for example the case for 'scaling up HIV/AIDS prevention programs' described by Stover et al. (2001), which also contained pointers to financial savings in treatment costs as a result of investments in HIV prevention. From an economic perspective, the advocacy role of the 'investment framework' (and country-specific 'investment cases' building on it) has two consequences. First, the relevant policy outcomes are wider than HIV/AIDS-specific or health indicators—to effectively make the case to funders for additional (or maintaining existing) resources, it is necessary to cast outcomes so that they connect to the funders' policy objectives. This is particularly relevant for interactions with national governments which have a broad policy mandate, unlike major donors like PEPFAR or the Global Fund. Second, improving the cost-effectiveness of HIV/AIDS programmes and securing funding are related. Establishing the most cost-effective spending allocations on an HIV/AIDS programme, or improving programme efficiency in other ways, is not only an exercise in making the best use of an existing budget, but feeds back into decisions on funding allocations to the HIV/AIDS response.

Operationally, one of the most significant consequences of the 'investment framework' is its absorption in the new funding model of the Global Fund,[4] which endorses and requires that applicants apply the 'HIV strategic investment approach' in funding applications (Global Fund, 2014a), 'underpinned by meticulous analysis of empirical evidence, a realistic appraisal of existing resources, and quantification of the returns of HIV investments'. It places strong emphasis on interventions addressing the needs of key populations (such as sex workers, men who have sex with men, or injecting drug users). While the largest share of funding by the Global Fund is allocated by quota, a portion of funding is allocated according to the quality of a proposal.

Substantially, the 'investment framework' has evolved in two directions since 2011. First, under the heading of 'combination prevention', the design of HIV/AIDS prevention strategies has become more differentiated. Combination prevention 'is the application of several evidence-based interventions to achieve maximum effect on population-level HIV transmission *in a specific setting*' (Jones et al., 2014, emphasis added). That is, to the principles of the 'investment approach', it adds a recognition that the drivers of HIV incidence and the intensity of the epidemic, and hence the effectiveness of alternative interventions, differ widely across population groups and across locations.[5] The second new development is the increasing role of 'treatment as prevention' in global HIV prevention strategies, including the '90-90-90' objectives[6] which forms the backbone of the UNAIDS agenda of 'ending AIDS by 2030'. This agenda introduces a new qualitative objective to HIV/AIDS strategic planning—diminishing the scale of the impact to the point that it is no longer a public health threat and the impact is minimal.[7]

Understanding Cost-effectiveness

Assessing the cost-effectiveness of HIV/AIDS programmes and interventions is challenging because of the slow disease progression and HIV transmission dynamics. HIV is a virus that affects those infected very slowly—the effects of HIV infections and HIV prevention interventions, in terms of outcomes commonly used in health economics like deaths averted or life years saved, unfold over a long period.

Moreover, the effects of one HIV infection averted could be magnified if the person under consideration could otherwise pass on HIV to his or her sexual partners or children. An empirical evaluation of the link between an intervention and an HIV infection averted may not capture such effects, because they might extend beyond the targeted population, and some of these downstream infections may occur (or be prevented) after the evaluation period.[8]

For the evaluation of the cost-effectiveness of HIV prevention interventions, these transmission dynamics have two consequences—(1) capturing the full effects of an HIV prevention intervention on HIV incidence and any resulting health outcomes requires some modelling, on top of the empirical evidence; and (2) the transmission dynamics introduce additional lags—the effects of an HIV prevention intervention, including downstream infections and the resulting health outcomes, therefore extend well beyond the typical life span of a person living with HIV.

Taking into account the transmission dynamics of the disease may also result in a lowering of the estimated effects of an HIV prevention intervention, because people *not* infected as a result of an intervention may contract HIV later on. For example, an empirical evaluation of incentives to keep girls in school may conclude that these incentives are effective in reducing HIV incidence among girls. However, in an environment where young women are at high risk of contracting HIV, these effects dissipate to the extent that the beneficiaries contract HIV later on.[9]

These challenges regarding the assessment of the cost-effectiveness of HIV prevention interventions exist irrespective of access to treatment. The scaling-up of treatment over the last decade has exacerbated the consequences of these issues for the evaluation of HIV/AIDS interventions, and also introduced new issues:

- The link between HIV prevention interventions and health outcomes (deaths, etc.) has become weaker, and is spread out over decades.

- New HIV infections carry *financial* consequences (largely, but not only, the costs of treatment) which are also spread over decades.

As of 2001, survival of a person living with HIV and receiving ART in developing countries would have been estimated at about 15 years (Stover et al., 2001), with the person receiving treatment for half of this time. In contrast, a comprehensive review of data on survival while on treatment from South Africa concludes that people living with HIV can have a near-normal life expectancy, provided that they start ART before their CD4 count drops below 200 (Johnson et al., 2013). These results are similar to results from the United States and Canada, where expected survival of a young person (age 20) living with HIV and on treatment is now estimated at an additional 55 years (that is, up to age 75) if treatment is initiated early (CD4 count above 350), about 5 years less than for the general population (Samji et al., 2013).

In summary, because of large gains in survival, measures of cost-effectiveness such as the costs per death averted over an HIV/AIDS programme period become less meaningful for assessing the cost-effectiveness of HIV/AIDS policies (because few people who become HIV infected die within periods conventionally used in policy analysis). In contrast, the financial consequences of HIV infections occurring or averted have become more pervasive.

The UNAIDS 'investment approach' takes into account these shifts by an increased emphasis on financial and economic aspects of the consequences of alternative HIV/AIDS policies. These include the financial savings from reduced HIV incidence expected as a consequence of successful HIV prevention interventions or the economic gains from the increased productive capacity of people receiving treatment.[10] These economic outcomes add an additional layer to the analysis of cost-effectiveness of HIV/AIDS interventions because they would contribute directly (financial savings) or indirectly (enhanced economic capacities) to the financing of the HIV interventions under consideration.

Figure 7.1 summarizes the different dimensions of assessing the cost-effectiveness of HIV/AIDS policies and interventions. The upper half of the figure describes the HIV/AIDS strategy and the national policy context, and the outcomes of the HIV/AIDS response, in terms of HIV/AIDS-specific indicators and also taking into account general national policy indicators. The bottom part captures the costs associated with an HIV/AIDS strategy, including HIV/AIDS-specific expenditures but also some of the wider financial consequences of HIV/AIDS-related policy choices.

	HIV/AIDS strategy	State of epidemic	Health, development, and economic repercussions
Policy formulation	HIV/AIDS policies • Treatment access (eligibility, coverage) • HIV prevention strategy • Social mitigation		National policy context • Health policy • Social policy • Economic development objectives
Outcomes		HIV incidence, prevalence, PLWH, deaths Number of people receiving treatment	National policy indicators, e.g. • Life expectancy • Child mortality • Poverty rates • Economic growth
Fiscal costs			
Current spending	Current spending on HIV/AIDS response		Implications for public spending, e.g. • Social expenditures
Future spending needs		Spending commitmentsto sustain HIV/AIDS response	• Costs of impact on public servants Implications for government revenues, e.g., from higher GDP

Figure 7.1. Framework for assessing the cost-effectiveness of HIV/AIDS policies and interventions

Within this framework, the scope of outcomes and costs included in a cost-effectiveness analysis depend on the purpose of the analysis. The most common situations are:

- Cost-effectiveness of an HIV/AIDS strategy in terms of changing the course of the epidemic or outcomes for people living with HIV. This would include reports comparing the outcomes of alternative strategies to the respective costs. Examples include a number of papers written in support of evolving global HIV/AIDS strategies (e.g. Schwartländer et al., 2011), describing or comparing the effectiveness of specific HIV/AIDS interventions (e.g. Njeuhmeli and others, 2011; or Bärnighausen et al., 2012a), or analytical papers establishing optimal strategies to attain specific objectives (e.g. Wilson et al., 2014b).[11]

- Cost-effectiveness of an HIV/AIDS strategy towards broader national health or development objectives. Some papers questioning (or defending) the scale of spending on HIV/AIDS in relation to other pressing health challenges (e.g. England, 2007; or Bongaarts and Over, 2010) fall into this category; HIV/AIDS 'investment cases' in support of national HIV/AIDS strategies typically make reference to wider policy objectives, and a number of papers attempt to quantify 'economic returns' (e.g. higher GDP) to investments in HIV/AIDS (e.g. Resch et al., 2011).[12]

- Fiscal analyses. In terms of the outcomes, these also take in the broader national policy objectives (as a Ministry of Finance would adopt). The coverage of costs, however, is wider, also taking into account public expenditures indirectly affected by HIV/AIDS (social expenditures, costs associated with the impact of HIV/AIDS on government employees), as well as the consequences of HIV/AIDS for government revenues.

- Financial analyses. Because investments in HIV prevention result in reduced treatment costs later on, they are also financial investments, which can be analysed in their own right. Depending on the financial returns to the investments in the HIV/AIDS response or specific interventions, the activity could be partially refinanced by such savings, or be cost-saving, i.e., reduce the financial burden of the HIV/AIDS response. This point is made by Stover et al. (2001) for investments in HIV prevention on the global level; examples on specific interventions include Granich et al. (2012) on 'expanding ART for treatment and prevention of HIV' and Njeuhmeli et al. (2011) for male circumcision.[13]

Treatment Access, Survival, and the Calculus of Cost-effectiveness

The expansion of treatment has transformed the consequences of new HIV infections, with implications for the assessment of the cost-effectiveness of HIV prevention interventions. As HIV/AIDS is turning into a chronic disease, the health consequences of HIV infections diminish, but each HIV infection has long-term consequences in terms of the demand for health services and the financial resources required to meet this demand.

This transition is illustrated in Figure 7.2 and Table 7.1, which show the health outcomes and financial consequences of one additional HIV infection for different treatment eligibility criteria.[14] Treatment eligibility is defined in terms of the CD4 count—the number of CD4 T lymphocytes in the blood which measure the strength of the immune system and indicate HIV disease progression. Treatment is assumed to cost US$400 annually (including drugs and all aspects of service delivery) throughout the projection period. Once an individual's CD4 count falls below the eligibility threshold, he or she is assumed to progress to treatment immediately, with a probability of 100 per cent. (For category 'Test & treat'—treatment access irrespective of CD4 count—individuals proceed to treatment right after infection.) These scenarios are analytic, more realistic ones can be derived as weighted averages of the estimates summarized in Tables 7.1 and 7.2, with more realistic assumptions on treatment coverage, and taking into account that many people living

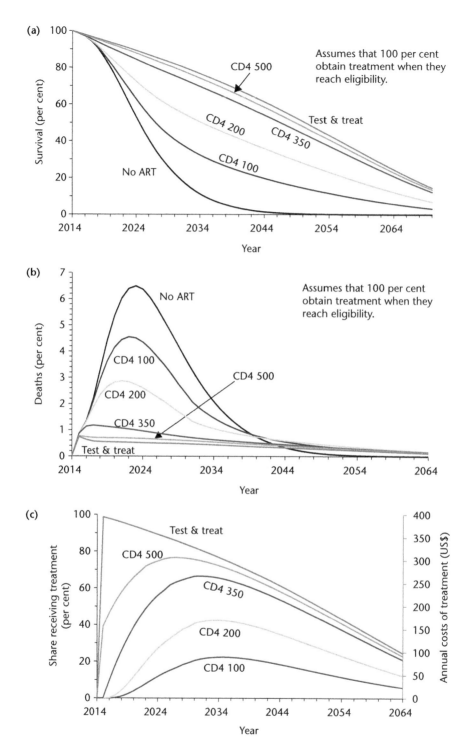

Figure 7.2. Health and financial consequences of new HIV infections with different treatment eligibility

Source: Author's calculations.
(a). Survival under different treatment eligibility criteria
(b). Projected AIDS deaths among PLWH
(c). Share of cohort on treatment, and expected treatment costs
Note: All percentages relate to cohort who contracted HIV in 2014.

Table 7.1. Health and financial consequences of one HIV infection

	Life expectancy (Years)	Projected time on treatment (Years)	Probability of dying from AIDS (Per cent)	Costs of treatment (US$)	Costs of treatment (US$), discounted at . . .		
					3%	5%	7%
No ART	12	0	93	0	0	0	0
ART from CD4 count of 100	19	7	75	2,898	1,347	874	595
ART from CD4 count of 200	25	15	56	5,818	2,734	1,796	1,241
ART from CD4 count of 350	33	25	31	9,974	4,913	3,354	2,417
ART from CD4 count of 500	35	30	25	12,108	6,389	4,588	3,481
ART at all CD4 counts	36	35	20	14,106	7,881	5,883	4,634

Source: Author's calculations. Assumes that 100 per cent of individuals progress to treatment once they reach eligibility, and that the annual costs of treatment are constant at US$400. Life expectancy is remaining life expectancy from time of infection.

Table 7.2. Treatment eligibility and cost-effectiveness of HIV prevention interventions

	Cost per HIV infection averted	Cost per AIDS death averted	Savings per HIV infection averted	Net costs per HIV infection averted	Net costs per AIDS death averted	Financial rate of return
			(Applying discount rate of 5%)			
	(US$)	(US$)	(US$)	(US$)	(US$)	(%)
No ART	3,000	3,217	0	3,000	3,217	
ART from CD4 count of 100	3,000	3,996	874	2,126	2,831	−0.5
ART from CD4 count of 200	3,000	5,348	1,796	1,204	2,146	2.1
ART from CD4 count of 350	3,000	9,690	3,354	−354	−1,144	4.8
ART from CD4 count of 500	3,000	12,229	4,588	−1,588	−6,473	6.8
ART at all CD4 counts	3,000	14,966	5,883	−2,883	−14,384	9.4

Source: Author's calculations. See Table 7.1 for underlying assumptions.

with HIV may initiate treatment later than at the point when they become eligible.

As treatment eligibility expands, survival improves—without treatment, an individual newly infected with HIV survives for about 12 years, with treatment initiation at a CD4 count of 500, survival improves to over 35 years.

Twenty years after an HIV infection, a small minority survive without treatment (11 per cent of the cohort), and mortality among the few survivors rises to about 17 per cent. With high treatment coverage and early initiation of treatment (CD4 500), 74 per cent survive for 20 years, and annual mortality at that stage is reduced to 2.0 per cent.

In fact, with comprehensive treatment coverage at a CD4 count of 350 or 500, HIV/AIDS ceases to be a predominantly deadly disease—only about one-quarter (CD4 500) to one-third (CD4 350) of individuals who become infected with HIV are projected to die for AIDS-related reasons. In contrast, 93 per cent of individuals die for AIDS-related reasons in the absence of treatment. This is the first part of the argument made earlier—as HIV/AIDS is evolving into a chronic disease, health consequences of new HIV infections diminish and are spread out over longer periods, and the cost-effectiveness of HIV prevention interventions, in terms of indicators like deaths averted over some period, deteriorates. The second part of the argument regards the consequences of new HIV infections in terms of the demand for health services and the corresponding financial costs. These commitments are drawn out over very long periods. For example, with treatment initiation at a CD4 count of 350, the individual spends an estimated 25 years on treatment, out of a remaining life expectancy of 33 years (Table 7.1).

Meeting this demand for health services comes at some cost. If the costs of providing treatment and related services amount to US$400 annually, meeting the lifetime demand for these services arising from one HIV infection results in a cost of US$10,000 if treatment is initiated at a CD4 count of 350 (Table 7.1), and the projected *annual* costs exceed US$200 for much of the projection period (Figure 7.2.b).[15] These costs are relevant not only in terms of the consequences of alternative HIV/AIDS policies, but also for the planning of HIV/AIDS policies which are cost-effective and contribute to financial sustainability. Investments in HIV prevention, at a cost, reduce HIV incidence and consequently future costs of meeting the demand for HIV/AIDS-related health services. These cost savings could refinance some of the initial investments, or more than offset them. In the latter case, the initial outlay, because of the subsequent financial returns, is cost-saving and increases the government's fiscal space.

One challenge with incorporating such cost savings in the analysis of the cost-effectiveness of HIV/AIDS interventions and policies arises from the fact that the financial savings are spread over a very long time period—several decades. A policy evaluation would therefore normally apply some discount rate, which could reflect the government's cost of borrowing, or a higher rate to account for uncertainties and the lack of liquidity of investments in HIV/AIDS.[16]

For example, for a discount rate of 5 per cent, the financial costs caused by one HIV infection come out at US$4,600 (for a CD4 criterion of 500) or US$3,350 (CD4 criterion of 350). This is just over one-third of the undiscounted costs, reflecting the long time period over which the costs are distributed. At a lower discount rate of 3 per cent, the discounted costs come out at about one-half of the undiscounted costs, and at a higher discount rate of 7 per cent they are reduced to about one-quarter of the undiscounted costs (see Table 7.1).

The two trends in the cost-effectiveness of investments in HIV prevention—the shrinking health outcomes and the more persistent financial consequences, are illustrated in Table 7.2. For an HIV prevention intervention which averts an HIV infection at a cost of US$3000, the costs per death averted increase from just over US$3000 (without treatment, as an HIV infection very likely will cause the death of the individual infected) to US$12,200 (with eligibility at a CD4 count of 500, and a low probability of just one-quarter that the individual will die of AIDS-related causes).[17] However, each HIV infection averted also saves between $0 (no treatment) and US$4,600 (CD4 criterion of 500) in treatment costs. Taking into account these savings, the *net* costs per HIV infection averted in this example *decline* steeply as eligibility increases, from US$3000 (without treatment) to minus US$1,600 (CD4 count of 500). That is, with treatment eligibility at a CD4 count of 350 or above, each infection averted at a cost of up to US$3,000 saves money.

The net costs per death saved decline even more steeply, from US$3,200 without treatment (when all HIV infections, with some lag, resulted in an AIDS-related death) and turn into a net saving of US$6,500 per death averted (with eligibility at CD4 500). The economics behind this trend, though, are somewhat counterintuitive and illustrate the declining relevance of the costs per death averted in assessing the cost-effectiveness of HIV prevention interventions—because the number of AIDS deaths averted by an HIV infection declines as treatment eligibility increases, each AIDS death is associated with the financial savings from more HIV infections—the net costs or savings per AIDS death are simply the net costs per HIV infection (increasing as eligibility improves), divided by the number of AIDS deaths per HIV infection (declining as eligibility improves).

For the analysis of the cost-effectiveness of HIV/AIDS interventions, these findings have at least two consequences. First, investments in HIV prevention—irrespective of or in addition to the health outcomes, can be sensible *financial* investments. In this concrete example, an investment that prevents one HIV infection at a cost of US$3,000 carries a financial rate of return between minus 0.5 per cent (with ART from a CD4 count of 100) and 6.8 per cent (with ART from a CD4 count of 500). Depending on the circumstances of the HIV programme and the fiscal context (including the relevant discount rate), it is thus plausible that some investments in HIV prevention enhance rather than absorb the government's fiscal space.

Second, across the scenarios illustrated in Figure 7.2, each HIV infection results in a very persistent financial cost—peaking after 13 years (with treatment initiation at CD4 500) to 21 years (with treatment initiation at CD4 100). This persistence has profound implications for the assessment of the cost-effectiveness of HIV/AIDS interventions.

For the analysis of an intervention which reduces HIV incidence at a specific point in time, a time horizon of 15 years, as is not uncommon in HIV/AIDS programme analyses, would capture much of the consequences for mortality, but only about one-half of the financial consequence. More generally, the incongruence between the time profiles of health outcomes and financial consequences means that estimates of cost-effectiveness become highly dependent on the time horizon applied.

For an intervention (e.g. male circumcision) which affects HIV incidence over a longer period (e.g. a policy period of 15 years), the analysis becomes more problematic, as many of the health consequences, and most of the financial consequences of HIV preventions averted relatively late in this period are not captured within this period.

The analysis in the following three chapters will, among other points, return to these issues, both for the analysis of specific HIV/AIDS interventions and for programme analysis. The approach utilized throughout these chapters builds on the projections of the costs caused by new HIV infections, as illustrated in Figure 7.2. Depending on the government's policy objectives (e.g. treatment coverage, eligibility) and the unit costs of providing HIV/AIDS services, these projected costs can be interpreted as a financial liability to the government, caused by a new HIV infection. Keeping this point in mind, Chapter 8 discusses the cost-effectiveness of an HIV/AIDS programme overall, Chapter 9 addresses specific HIV prevention interventions, and Chapter 10 reviews the use of cost-effectiveness analysis in determining optimal HIV/AIDS strategies.

8

Cost-effectiveness of HIV/AIDS Programmes

Analyses of the costs of proposed HIV/AIDS polices, and their cost-effectiveness in terms of attaining certain outcomes have played a central role in the development of global HIV/AIDS policy initiatives and the formulation of national HIV/AIDS programmes. Typically, these analyses would compare one or several 'scaling-up' scenarios (e.g. describing the consequences of higher coverage rates of or improved eligibility for treatment), with a 'baseline' scenario that describes a status quo. In line with the dominant role of this type of modelling in HIV/AIDS programme planning, the chapter sets out with a discussion of the approach, describing the methods and the lessons regarding the cost-effectiveness of HIV/AIDS policies.

There are several shortcomings to an analysis comparing alternative policy scenarios over some fixed time horizon. Results on the cost-effectiveness of a policy scenario are highly dependent on the time horizon, because the financial consequences of alternative HIV/AIDS policies are spread over decades. A policy analysis comparing costs and outcomes over some period (even with a 10–15 year horizon as adopted in recent UNAIDS documents) therefore misses out on much of the financial returns to investments in HIV prevention. This point is addressed in the second section of the chapter, which provides a 'fiscal space' analysis of alternative HIV/AIDS policies, fully capturing the financial consequences (including the savings that can be attributed to reduced HIV incidence) of alternative HIV/AIDS policies. (Another major shortcoming—that cost-effectiveness analyses based on programme-level costs and outcomes are a very blunt tool for identifying *optimal* HIV/AIDS strategies—is discussed in Chapter 10.)

HIV/AIDS programmes have always been motivated in part by their role in mitigating and reversing the development and economic consequences of HIV/AIDS, and the UNAIDS 'investment framework' emphasizes 'economic returns' to investments in HIV/AIDS programmes, including 'productivity gains' which would offset at least some of the costs of the HIV/AIDS response. The third section of this chapter addresses the returns to HIV/AIDS

investments against national (non HIV/AIDS-specific) development objectives, and discusses the relevance of the 'economic returns' in terms of refinancing HIV/AIDS investments.

'Returns to Investments' in the HIV/AIDS Response

Assessments of the effectiveness and cost-effectiveness of alternative HIV/
AIDS policies have long been part of global HIV/AIDS policy development
and advocacy. These assessments are typically applying the 'Goals' software, a
package designed to analyse the consequences of alternative HIV/AIDS
polices, specified in terms of coverage rates of adult and child treatment,
prevention of mother-to-child transmission, and a range of other HIV prevention interventions.[1] The 'Goals' software is part of the 'Spectrum' software and
thus tightly integrated with the 'AIDS Impact Model' used by UNAIDS and
national HIV/AIDS programmes to estimate and project the state of the
epidemic.[2]

While the examples for policy analyses discussed here address aspects of
global HIV/AIDS policies, similar analyses are regularly performed in support
of the development of national HIV/AIDS policies. Key findings of such
studies on the 'returns to investment' of alternative HIV/AIDS policies include
the following:

a) Stover et al., 2001: Assess the 'global impact of scaling up HIV/AIDS
   prevention programs.' A 'comprehensive prevention package' would
   avert 31.1 million infections at a cost of US$122 billion (US$3,900 per
   infection averted, 'which avoids an expenditure for treatment and care
   with a net present value of US$4,700 and results in savings of US$780 per
   infection averted').

b) Schwartländer et al., 2011: The 'investment framework' requires an additional investment of US$46.5 billion globally in 2011–2020, and US
   $179 billion overall, but would avert an additional 12.2 million new
   infections and 7.4 million deaths. Savings in treatment cost from HIV
   infections averted are estimated at US$40 billion, i.e., on average US
   $3,900 per HIV infection averted.[3]

c) Hecht et al., 2010: A 'rapid scale-up' scenario 'to achieve universal access
   to prevention and treatment services by 2015' would prevent 7 million
   deaths and 14.2 million infections, at a cost of US$232 billion, compared
   to current coverage trends, between 2009 and 2031. A 'hard choices'
   scenario 'concentrated on few interventions that were known to be
   cost-effective and were targeted to high-risk populations' would prevent

6 million deaths and avert 7.9 million HIV infections, and save US$93 billion compared to the 'current trends' scenario.

d) Stover et al., 2014: This article assesses the consequences of implementing the WHO 2013 guidelines for treatment eligibility,[4] compared to adhering to the WHO 2010 guidelines. Projecting forward, implementing the 2013 guidelines would require an additional investment of US $28 billion between 2013 and 2025, and avert 3.0 million deaths and 3.1 million new HIV infections in this period, compared with a policy of adhering to 2010 guidelines. The average cost per infection averted comes out at US$9,000, and the cost per death averted at US$9,600.

A number of lessons can be drawn from these comparisons. First, the costs per HIV infection averted differ very substantially across scenarios, estimated at about US$4,000 (a, b), between minus US$12,000 and plus US$16,000 (c), and US$9,000 (d). Second, the scenarios differ considerably in terms of their effectiveness in averting HIV infections vs. deaths, with a ratio of infections averted to deaths averted between 1:1 (d) and 2:1 (c, 'rapid scale-up'). Third, programme-level effectiveness masks a composite of more or less effective interventions, as illustrated by the alternative scenarios discussed by Hecht et al. (2010). Fourth, where estimates of the cost savings owing to HIV infections averted are presented, these are large relative to and may even exceed the investments in the HIV/AIDS response.

To gain better insights into the processes underlying the estimates of the 'returns to investment' discussed above, which average not only across interventions but also over time, Figure 8.1 reproduces projections of the costs of the HIV response and the number of HIV infections averted under the 'investment framework' and the 'baseline' scenario (from Schwartländer et al., 2011). There are several lessons from reviewing the projected impact of the investment framework over time.

- The impacts on AIDS deaths are not only lower than the impacts on HIV infections (as not all people living with HIV die because of AIDS), but also grow more slowly. Conclusions regarding the relative effectiveness of HIV/AIDS programmes in averting HIV infections or deaths thus depend on the time horizon.

- The cost–outcome ratios for HIV infections and deaths are declining (i.e. improving) over time. As a consequence, conclusions on the cost-effectiveness of scaling-up an HIV/AIDS programme generally depend on the time horizon applied and do not compare well across studies.[5]

- The costs of the investment framework relative to the baseline start dipping down over the last years of the projections as reduced HIV incidence starts feeding through to reduced treatment costs. This trend

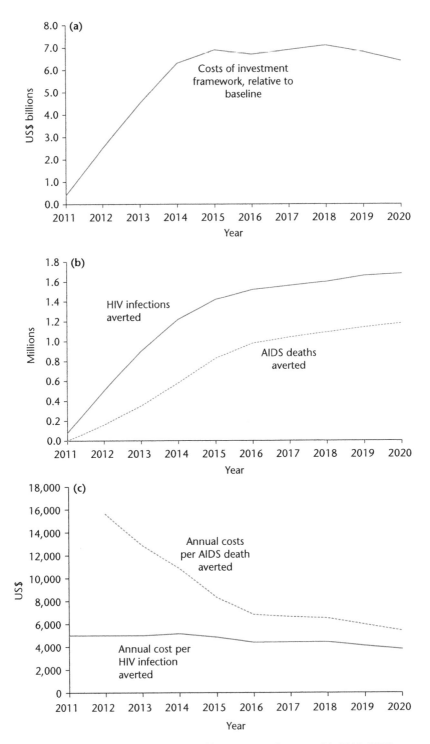

Figure 8.1. Costs and outcomes of 'investment framework', 2011–2020

Source: Author's calculations, based on Schwartländer et al. (2011).
(a). Costs of investment framework
(b). HIV infections and deaths averted
(c). Cost–outcome ratios

should become more important after 2020, as more people *not* infected with HIV in 2011–2020 do *not* seek treatment. The time horizon of the investment framework is thus too short to capture the financial savings from reduced HIV incidence.

Fiscal Space Analysis

The evaluation of the cost-effectiveness of HIV/AIDS polices and policy alternatives is not straightforward because HIV infections result in treatment needs which extend over decades, and because of the interactions between HIV incidence and treatment access. Fiscal space analysis of HIV/AIDS policies provides a tool for integrating spending *commitments* associated with changes in treatment coverage or HIV incidence in the analysis of the cost-effectiveness of HIV/AIDS policies.

Two of the papers reviewed earlier incorporated some discussion of the longer-term savings achieved by reduced HIV incidence in the analysis of the cost-effectiveness of scaling up certain HIV/AIDS policies. Stover et al. (2001) argue that the 'comprehensive prevention package' would cost US $122 billion, but return gross savings of about US$146 billion in terms of avoided treatment costs, and therefore a net saving of US$24 billion. At least at the discount rate of 3 per cent as applied in this example, the 'comprehensive prevention package' is a good (financial) investment, even before taking into account any of the health gains.

Schwartländer et al. (2011) make a similar point—the savings from HIV infections avoided under the investment framework (US$40 billion) are almost as large as the costs (US$46 billion). Compared to the 2001 analysis, with a clear division between prevention spending (not including treatment) and savings in treatment costs, the evaluation of the global scenario in the 'investment framework' is more complex. As the 2011 'investment framework' accounts for the effect of treatment on HIV infections, the line between the costs of the investment framework and cost savings from a reduced demand for treatment has become blurred. Consequently, some of the cost savings from reduced HIV incidence are already included in the projections of the costs of the 'investment framework'. Subtracting an estimate of the cost savings owing to reduced HIV incidence from the projected costs would therefore result in double-counting.[6]

Additionally, while the decline in HIV incidence under the 'investment framework' results in reduced future needs for spending on treatment, the scaling up of treatment under the investment framework results in an increase in the number of people receiving treatment, which presents a spending commitment that extends well beyond 2020 (the end of the policy period in the paper by Schwartländer et al. (2011)). Only including the projected lifetime savings from reduced HIV incidence in the analysis, but not the additional spending commitments from the increase in the number of people receiving treatment as of 2020 (resulting in a very persistent cost post-2020) is therefore lop-sided and results in an underestimate of the financial consequences of the 'investment framework'.

The concept of fiscal space is helpful in addressing these challenges in assessing the cost-effectiveness of HIV/AIDS programmes (and, similarly, specific interventions). The most common definition (Heller, 2005) describes fiscal space 'as the availability of budgetary room that allows a government to provide resources for a desired purpose without any prejudice to the sustainability of a government's financial position'. In the sphere of public health, this concept is most commonly applied to describing the availability or identifying additional resources for health, that is, the *financing* of health spending.[7] In the current context, the concept of fiscal space is applied to the *absorption* of financial resources by the policy under consideration. *Policy commitments* have spending consequences which commit future financial resources, and therefore create *spending commitments*.[8]

For the analysis of HIV/AIDS programmes and interventions this means concretely:

- Under the government's policy to extend treatment to people living with HIV meeting certain criteria, *an HIV infection causes a spending commitment* which impinges on the resource envelope available to the government to attain its policy objectives. Usually, this spending commitment can be interpreted as the present discounted value of the projected spending needs.[9]

- A policy to expand treatment eligibility implies an increased financial commitment towards people currently living with HIV/AIDS. This is a long-term financial commitment extending over decades, the government would want to know and take into consideration the magnitude of this commitment, beyond the costing of a national strategic plan (typically with a time horizon of about 4 years) or any arbitrary cut-off points.

- If an HIV/AIDS policy reduces HIV incidence compared to some other policy (for given coverage and eligibility), it creates lower new spending commitments. In a scaling-up scenario, each new HIV infection is more expensive in terms of causing new spending commitments, but overall new spending commitments would be reduced if the decline in HIV incidence is strong enough.

- The needs of people living with HIV/AIDS at the end of a policy period, whether receiving treatment or not (yet), under the government's policy commitments, give rise to a commitment of financial resources beyond the policy period. If a policy succeeds in reducing this spending commitment, this is a financial saving that can be attributed to the policies studied, and can be estimated and included in the cost-effectiveness analysis.

The principles of fiscal space analysis of HIV/AIDS programmes are illustrated in Figure 8.2, contrasting projected current costs and spending commitments following one HIV infection.[10] For example, raising treatment eligibility

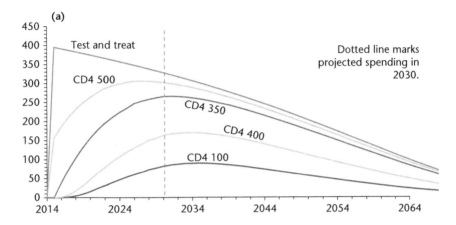

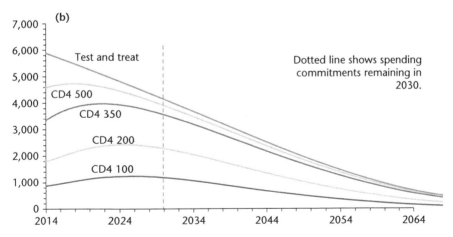

Figure 8.2. Costs and spending commitments caused by one new HIV infection

Source: Author's calculations.
(a). Projected costs of treatment caused by one HIV infection in 2014
(b). Spending commitments caused by one HIV infection in 2014
Note: Applies discount rate of 5 per cent.

from a CD4 count of 350 to a CD4 count of 500 raises the projected current costs throughout the projection horizon (Figure 8.2.a), and increases the spending commitment caused by one HIV infection from US$3,350 to US $4,600 (Figure 8.2.b). In general, the remaining spending commitment declines over time as less of the projected spending remains. However, because of the discounting, the remaining spending commitments increase initially in three scenarios—peak spending becomes more imminent and is discounted less, more than offsetting the fact that some of the projected spending has already happened.

To illustrate the relevance and implications of fiscal space analysis for the evaluation of policies over specific periods, Figure 8.2 marks projected current spending and remaining spending commitments as of 2030. Two lessons can be taken from this. First, the costs occurring before 2030, and indeed after only 5 or 10 years, are substantial. This implies that a substantial proportion of the savings from reduced HIV incidence is realized within a policy period of, say, 10–20 years. Subtracting an estimate of the cost savings from reduced HIV incidence from the projected costs over a policy period (which already contain some of the savings) therefore results in double-counting and an underestimate of the net costs of the policy change. Second, the bulk of the costs occur after 2030, and remaining spending commitments at that time are at least 85 per cent of the initial value. This means that even with a time horizon of 15 years, the financial analysis misses out on most of the consequences of any changes in HIV incidence occurring early in the policy period considered.

The evaluation of HIV/AIDS programmes, rather than the costs caused by a single HIV infection, is more complex. First, the scope of the relevant costs is wider. In addition to treatment costs, there are the costs of basic programme activities such as other measures aimed at reducing HIV incidence, medical services other than antiretroviral therapy, and mitigation of social consequences, as well as the costs of 'critical enablers' (expenditures which do not have a direct outcome, but are important for effectively delivering the basic programme activities).[11]

Second, a programme evaluation suffers from two types of cut-off problems. As noted, the financial consequences of HIV infections occurring within the programme period extend beyond it. Additionally, because the programme changes the course of the epidemic, it also has implications for the state of the epidemic and for health outcomes beyond the evaluation period. Fiscal space analysis of HIV/AIDS programmes addresses the former problem, but not the latter. While fiscal space analysis improves the analysis of the cost-effectiveness of HIV/AIDS programmes, it is not a complete solution to the problems posed by the slow dynamics and long time horizons characteristic of HIV/AIDS.

The working of fiscal space analysis of HIV/AIDS programmes is illustrated with an example from an 'HIV/AIDS investment case' for Kenya (National AIDS Control Council, 2014). The Kenyan Ministry of Health has recently endorsed the new WHO guidelines on treatment access (raising the eligibility threshold to a CD4 count of 500, with some population groups eligible irrespective of CD4 count).[12] Additionally, the Kenyan investment framework envisages an ambitious scaling-up of treatment access as well as calibrating HIV prevention efforts across risk groups and in accordance with evidence on local or regional drivers of HIV incidence.

The costs and consequences of this 'investment framework' for Kenya, compared to a baseline scenario in which HIV/AIDS service coverage remains broadly constant, are illustrated in Figure 8.3. The 'investment framework' envisages a steep increase in spending initially, with *additional* costs rising to US$570 million (0.63 per cent of GDP) by 2024 and only slowly decreasing to US$535 million (0.35 per cent of GDP) by the end of the projection period. Overall, the additional costs between 2014 and 2030 add up to US$6.5 billion (10.4 per cent of 2014 GDP, or an average 0.45 per cent of GDP annually in 2014–2030).[13]

In the HIV 'investment framework', the number of HIV infections declines steeply, by about one-half within 5 years. The number of HIV deaths declines somewhat less, by about 40 per cent. Overall, the 'investment framework' results in an increase in the number of people living with HIV by almost 150,000 by 2030 (but 570,000 less than in the baseline scenario), and a higher number (both in absolute terms and as a share of people living with HIV) receive treatment. The costs per HIV infection averted between 2014 and 2030 are estimated at US$5,800, and the costs per death averted come out at US$10,500.

From the perspective of fiscal space, the important point to note is the fact that both scenarios imply *spending commitments* which go beyond the policy period considered here. Most people who become infected in 2014–2030 will still be alive in 2030, and require treatment then or soon after. Moreover, provided they obtain treatment, many people living with HIV will survive for decades. In this specific case, both scenarios envisage fairly high treatment coverage rates, and about one-third of people living with HIV in 2030 will still be alive 30 years later (Figure 8.3.e). The policy commitment to provide treatment to people living with HIV, together with high rates of survival on treatment, thus creates a long-term spending commitment.[14]

This spending commitment is illustrated in Figure 8.3.f. For some years, spending on services to people living with HIV hovers at close to US$1.4 billion after 2030, and then slowly declines to about US$970 million by 2060.[15] (Costs decline more slowly than the number of people receiving

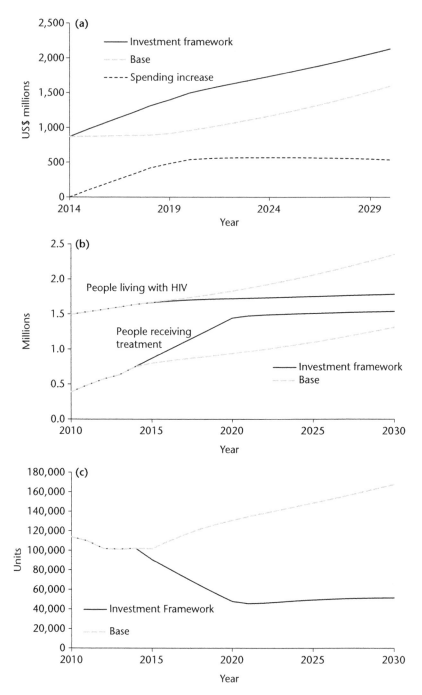

Figure 8.3. Costs and consequences of the 'investment framework' in Kenya

Source: National AIDS Control Council, 2014.

(a). Projected costs of emerging HIV/AIDS strategy, 2014–2030

(b). People living with HIV, 2010–2030

(c). HIV infections, all ages, 2010–2030

(d). AIDS deaths, all ages, 2010–2030

(e). Survival of people living with HIV as of 2030, 2030–2060

(f). Costs of services to people living with HIV in 2030, 2030–2060

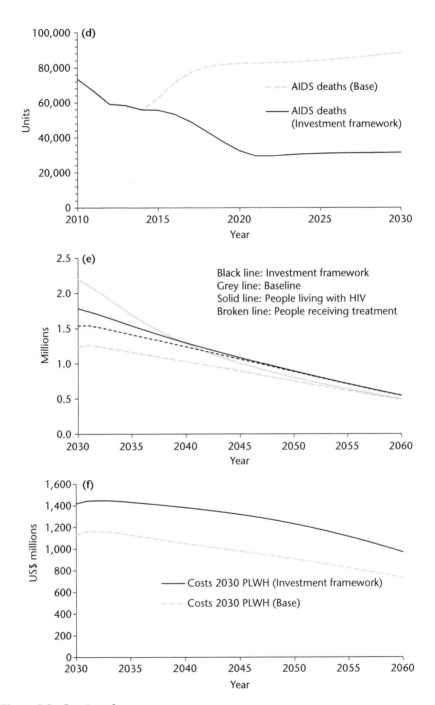

Figure 8.3. Continued

Table 8.1. Spending commitments implied by national HIV/AIDS response (US$ millions)

	Baseline	Investment framework	Difference (IF minus Base)
Total costs	29,467	40,331	10,863
Costs through 2030	14,805	21,337	6,532
Spending commitments beyond 2030	14,662	18,994	4,331
Prevention spending through 2030 (excl. treatment)	4,061	6,919	2,858
Costs of services to PLWH in 2014	12,262	20,039	7,778
Costs through 2030	7,000	10,361	3,361
Spending commitments beyond 2030	5,261	9,678	4,417
Costs caused by new HIV infections 2014–2030	13,145	13,372	227
Costs through 2030	3,744	4,057	313
Spending commitments beyond 2030	9,401	9,315	−86
		(Per cent of 2014 GDP)	
Total costs	47.0	64.3	17.3
Costs through 2030	23.6	34.0	10.4
Spending commitments beyond 2030	23.4	30.3	6.9

Note: All cost estimates as of 2014, applying a discount rate of 3 per cent.
Source: National AIDS Control Council, 2014.

treatment because unit costs are partially tied to GDP per capita and therefore increase.)

The overall spending commitments associated with the alternative HIV/AIDS policies are summarized in Table 8.1. Overall, only about half of the costs of either strategy occur before 2030, underlining the need to look at the long-term spending commitments implied by any HIV/AIDS strategy. Overall, the investment framework implies an additional spending commitment of US $6.5 billion until 2030, and an additional US$4.3 billion beyond 2030. Most of this increase is accounted for by the costs of the scaling-up of treatment—spending commitments towards people already living with HIV/AIDS increase by US$7.8 billion. The costs caused by new HIV infections in 2014 to 2030 stay largely unchanged (increasing by 2 per cent, or US$227 million). However, this masks a steep decline in HIV incidence (and resulting cost savings), while the costs caused by each new HIV infection increase steeply. In this specific case, thus, the savings from reduced HIV incidence do not go far in terms of refinancing the costs of the initial scaling-up of treatment, but at least they do offset the increased costs caused by each new HIV infection.

The cost savings from HIV infections averted are thus an important part of the financial aspects of the alternative HIV/AIDS strategies, but so are the increased spending commitments implied by higher targeted treatment coverage or expanded eligibility. Spending commitments caused by new HIV infections reflect both factors, when compared against spending commitments under a baseline scenario. Spending commitments from new HIV infections decline in a scaling-up scenario only if the decline in the number of new HIV infections dominates the increased costs arising from each new HIV infection.

Nevertheless, the cost savings from each HIV infection averted alone, and from reduced HIV incidence overall, are an important factor in the assessment and planning of an HIV/AIDS programme, because they determine the *financial* returns to investments in HIV prevention, and are therefore relevant for determining optimal investments in HIV prevention. If the costs caused by each HIV infection increase, this affects the cost-effectiveness of HIV prevention interventions, as illustrated in Chapter 7.

In the example from Kenya, the small increase in the costs caused by new HIV infections of US$227 million in 2014–2030 can be broken down in the effect of the increase in the costs caused by each new HIV infection, and the effect of HIV infections averted as a consequence of the Kenyan 'investment framework'. The former effect alone would result in an additional cost of US$10.5 billion (i.e. the costs caused by new HIV infections in 2014–2030 would rise to US$23.6 billion in Table 8.1).

However, the number of HIV infections projected in 2014–2030 declines from 2.3 million to 1.0 million, resulting in a decline in the costs caused by new HIV infections of US$10.3 billion, leading to a relatively small net increase in costs caused by new HIV infections of US$227 million. On average, one HIV infection averted results in savings of US$10,500.[16] This is a useful benchmark for assessing the cost-effectiveness of HIV prevention interventions and their potential contributions to financial sustainability of the HIV/AIDS response. Subtracting the cost savings from the costs of preventing an HIV infection yields an estimate of the net costs or savings associated with an HIV prevention intervention, and—in this example—HIV prevention interventions which avert an HIV infection at a cost of less than US$10,500 could potentially be scaled up to reduce the fiscal space absorbed by the HIV/AIDS response (while improving health outcomes).

In summary, financial savings as a consequence of reduced HIV incidence play a large role in the evaluation of HIV/AIDS policies—but so do the increased costs caused by each new HIV infection if the programme includes increasing coverage or expanded eligibility of treatment. In the particular example illustrated in Table 8.1, the latter more than offset the former, and there is a small increase in the costs caused by new HIV infections, even though the number of new HIV infections declines under the investment framework. In other cases, though, net savings could play a larger role (generally, if the decline in the number of new HIV infections is large relative to the increase in the costs per HIV infection). Irrespective of the net savings or spending commitments from new HIV infections on the programme level, the cost savings from each HIV infection averted plays as important role in programme evaluation, to guide decisions on investments in HIV prevention.

There are, however, a number of shortcomings to the approaches discussed here. Because of the long time frames required to capture the effects of HIV/AIDS-related interventions, uncertainty (in a sense more fundamental than captured by perturbations to some well-defined parameters) and the valuation of financial flows which are spread over long periods are critical issues in long-term policy analysis, but rarely addressed explicitly in the HIV/AIDS policy discourse. Another shortcoming that is shared by both approaches arises from epidemiological dynamics—the interventions during the programme period alter the state of the epidemic, and have consequences for the course of the epidemic beyond the programme period which are covered neither by conventional approaches nor the fiscal space analysis.[17]

Contribution to National Development Objectives

In some regards, quantifying the contribution of the national response to HIV/AIDS to national development objectives mirrors the analysis of the consequences of HIV/AIDS for health outcomes, the economic consequences for individuals and households and for the economy overall (Chapters 2–4). While there is a fair understanding of the consequences of HIV/AIDS on affected households, little is known about the impacts of HIV/AIDS on national poverty rates, which are a poor indicator of the impact of HIV/AIDS anyway.[18] For analysis of the effectiveness of the HIV/AIDS response, this difficulty is compounded by the fact that the benefit incidence of HIV/AIDS-related services across socioeconomic categories is not well understood. The discussion offered here on the cost-effectiveness of HIV/AIDS programmes in terms of contributing to national development objectives therefore focuses on two outcomes which can be quantified fairly well—life expectancy and GDP or GDP per capita.

Health outcomes like life expectancy or child mortality tend to feature prominently in national health and development strategies, and can serve to place the impact of HIV/AIDS in context. For example, in many countries in sub-Saharan Africa HIV/AIDS has been the dominant driver of (declines in) life expectancy (in some countries by more than 10 years), and the response to HIV/AIDS—most directly prevention of mother-to-child HIV transmission and expanded access to treatment—has gone a long way towards reversing these declines. Looking ahead, however, the scope for achieving *additional* health gains through *additional* HIV/AIDS investments has become much more limited. This point is illustrated in Figure 8.4, which contrasts the gains in life expectancy since 2000 with projected gains under a scaling-up scenario ('investment framework') and a baseline scenario. Between 2000 and

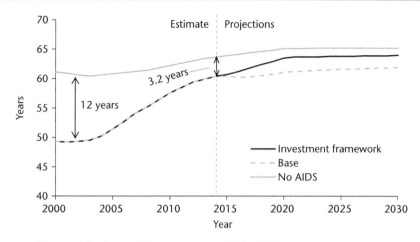

Figure 8.4. Kenya: Life expectancy, 2000–2030
Source: Author's calculations, based on National AIDS Control Council, 2014.

2014, the loss in life expectancy owing to HIV/AIDS was cut from 12 years to just over 3 years.

Looking ahead, the policies under the baseline scenario are effective in sustaining the gains in life expectancy achieved so far (the loss in life expectancy remains between 3.3 years and 4.1 years through 2030), at an average cost of 1.2 per cent of GDP. The additional 2 years (period average) gained under the investment framework would require an additional 0.45 per cent of GDP. The cost-effectiveness of the 'scaling-up' in terms of raising life expectancy is thus about two-thirds of the effectiveness of the measures included in the baseline scenario.

This example is representative of a broader trend in cost-effectiveness, when HIV/AIDS programmes have already implemented some of the most cost-effective HIV prevention interventions, and as the scaling-up of treatment shifts towards expanding eligibility to levels where treatment initiation does not have an immediate impact on mortality. However, the 'investment frame-work'—with 2 years gained at an expense of 0.45 per cent of GDP—still provides a good return in this example (while diminished from the early stages of the HIV/AIDS response), when cost-effectiveness criteria applied by the WHO or economic valuations like the ones described in Chapter 4 are applied.[19]

The most common indicators of the state of economic development, though, are GDP, GDP per capita, and economic growth, and for the assessment of the effectiveness of the national response to HIV/AIDS in contributing to national development objectives they are relevant as measures of the impact of HIV/AIDS on material living standards, and as sources of potential contributions to the financing of the national response. Regarding the impact of HIV/AIDS on these variables, it is useful to distinguish three factors:

- *Productivity gains.* If the HIV/AIDS response improves the productivity of people living with HIV/AIDS, their capability to sustain themselves and their families improves.[20] This effect raises GDP and GDP per capita by the same proportion.

- *Improved survival.* If people living with HIV/AIDS survive longer because they receive treatment, they also contribute to GDP longer. This effect raises GDP, but GDP per capita remains constant or declines (to the extent that people receiving treatment have lower productivity than healthy people). Additionally, any *death-related costs* (e.g. funeral costs) are delayed as a consequence of longer survival.

- *Broader macroeconomic gains.* These arise, for example, from cross-household dynamics or if HIV/AIDS affects access to education (and—with a considerable lag—productivity), and are discussed in Chapters 3 and 4.

For the purposes of HIV/AIDS programme evaluation, productivity gains are the most relevant gains, directly improving the material well-being of people living with HIV and their families. For the beneficiaries of treatment, the outcome resembles a social transfer, and it is legitimate to include this 'saving' as an offset in the analysis of the economic costs (i.e. the economy-wide costs irrespective of who pays) of an HIV/AIDS programme. One important aspect of productivity gains from access to treatment is the fact that their magnitude depends on treatment eligibility—as treatment eligibility expands and people living with HIV increasingly initiate treatment before they show the symptoms of AIDS, the role of productivity gains diminishes.

From a fiscal perspective (only considering the costs and gains to the public sector), the productivity gains are relevant in two ways. Some of the gains would translate into higher tax revenues (see discussion of this point under 'improved survival', in the next paragraph). The productivity gains also obviate the need for transfers like disability benefits and can therefore result in fiscal savings. However, the link between state of health, antiretroviral therapy, and eligibility introduces trade-offs for recipients of disability grants living with HIV/AIDS, which have been contentiously discussed in South Africa (see, for example, Nattrass (2006) and de Paoli et al. (2012)). As any such fiscal gains (especially regarding social grants) would be highly country-specific, productivity gains could have very small consequences for the financing of HIV/AIDS programmes and should not be included *by default* in assessments of fiscal gains arising from HIV/AIDS investments.

Economic gains from improved survival are distinct from productivity gains (where one individual and his household benefits), because the beneficiary is deceased in the counterfactual situation. Regarding the contribution to GDP, such 'economic gains' are not very interesting because a country is not richer because its population is larger, and much of the output gains from improved survival are eaten up by the surviving population's cost of living rather than providing resources which could at least theoretically serve to offset the costs of the HIV/AIDS response.

However, there are certain death-related costs, such as the costs of funerals which are delayed, possibly for decades, by treatment. The avoidance of loss of support to surviving dependents falls between the categories of gains from improved survival and death-related costs. To the extent that an individual supports dependents, his or her death is an economic loss to the surviving members of society (specifically: his or her family). Because of improved survival, such losses are not only delayed, but frequently avoided altogether—the incidence of orphanhood is reduced as AIDS-related deaths among young adults become rarer. These latter costs are more persistent than the immediate death-related costs. On the other hand, the available evidence suggests that households and individuals recover after a death, and that the loss of support to dependents is not a permanent cost.[21] In any case, the loss of support to dependents accounts for only a portion of the output losses associated with a death, because much of the deceased's income would be self-consumed if he or she were still alive.

From a fiscal perspective, output gains from increased survival result in increased tax revenues, which could be used to refinance the investments in the HIV/AIDS response. Where domestic government revenues are dominated by taxes related to the overall level of economic activity (such as income taxes, sales or value added taxes, or import tariffs), these can be approximated by the tax/GDP ratio which, for developing countries, would typically be in a range of 10–25 per cent.[22]

At the same time, increased survival also increases the demand for public services. Not all of increased government revenue owing to increased survival is therefore available to offset the costs of investments in the HIV/AIDS response. Such effects are difficult to quantify, as most of the increased demand for public services translates into spending indirectly, through political decisions and the budget process. However, it seems clear that higher tax revenues owing to increased survival are not automatically available to offset the costs of investments in the HIV/AIDS response.

The economic gains described in this section have been used by UNAIDS to advocate increased funding for HIV treatment. The most commonly quoted paper is one by Resch et al. (2011), which appears in the UNAIDS 'Investment Case Toolkit' (UNAIDS, 2013b) and other prominent UNAIDS publications, showing that 'investments in HIV treatment scale-up generate returns more than two-fold greater when averted medical costs, averted orphan care and

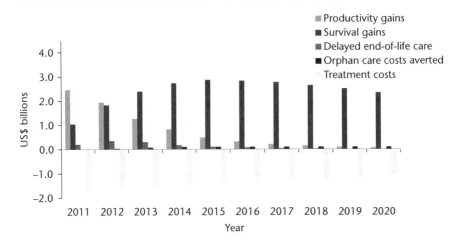

Figure 8.5. Costs of and economic returns to investment in AIDS treatment

Source: Adapted from Resch et al., 2011. Totals are based on projections for ninety-eight countries supported by the Global Fund.

labour productivity gains are taken into account' (UNAIDS, 2014a, also see UNAIDS, 2013a).

The paper by Resch et al. (2011) serves as an illustration for an analysis of economic returns to treatment, both because of its role in advocacy and because the findings can be interpreted in a straightforward fashion in terms of the general discussion in this chapter.[23] The paper produces estimates of the economic gains from keeping the cohort of individuals receiving treatment with support from the Global Fund on treatment, against a counterfactual in which treatment is terminated. Their findings are adapted here (Figure 8.5) to distinguish productivity gains (reversing productivity losses among people sick with AIDS) and gains from longer survival, which is not done in the underlying paper.[24] There are several lessons which can be drawn from their analysis:

- By far the largest 'returns to investment' are those arising from improved productivity of people living with HIV and increased survival, rather than those from deferred end-of-life care and orphan support.[25]

- Initially, the 'economic returns' are dominated by the increased *productivity* of people who would otherwise be suffering from AIDS (but still be alive without treatment). As argued above, these gains can be interpreted as 'economic gains' in a straightforward fashion. However, the magnitude of the gains, reflecting an 80 per cent productivity loss of people not receiving treatment, appears high compared to recent estimates of output losses preceding and following treatment initiation (Chapter 3), perhaps because the paper considers an atypical counterfactual scenario of treatment *termination*.

- In the longer run, the 'economic gains' are dominated by the output effects from increased *survival*, and these are larger than the treatment cost. This is plausible, given the underlying assumptions—one life year gained in this analysis increases output by about US$1,000, whereas median treatment cost are reported at US$204 (first-line) and US$1,238 (second-line).

These survival gains, however, cannot be interpreted as 'economic gains' in the sense of improved material living standards, because treatment costs (about one-half of the output gains) and the cost of living of the survivors plausibly *exceed* the output gains (especially as survivors will also bear private medical costs not included in this analysis). Thus, in the example by Resch et al. (2011), average *material* living standards, after taking into account these costs, would *decline* as a consequence of scaling up treatment. Overall, therefore, the claim by UNAIDS that *economic* gains alone more than offset the costs of treatment is implausible. (This point does not invalidate the effectiveness of HIV/AIDS investments in terms of improving *health* outcomes, and the financial returns to HIV/AIDS investments.)

Regarding the application of the findings from Resch et al. (2011) to the current policy discourse (as in UNAIDS, 2014a and UNAIDS, 2013a), it is further necessary to take into account that their paper is considering a cohort with a very poor state of health (survival without treatment of about 2.5 years, productivity diminished by 80 per cent). As treatment is increasingly extended to individuals at higher CD4 counts, many of whom may not be experiencing the symptoms of AIDS, the initial productivity gains will be smaller than in this example.

9

Cost-effectiveness of HIV/AIDS Interventions

The long time frames characterizing the HIV epidemic pose unique challenges for the analysis of the cost-effectiveness of HIV programmes and interventions. This chapter applies a forward-looking analysis to the analysis of the cost-effectiveness of *specific HIV/AIDS interventions*.

The chapter sets out with a general discussion of the effectiveness of HIV prevention interventions. On one hand, an individual who benefited from an HIV prevention intervention does not pass HIV on to others, thereby augmenting the direct effect of the intervention. On the other hand, the individual might get infected on a subsequent occasion, offsetting some of the direct effect on HIV incidence. The chapter first discusses the population-level effects of HIV infections averted at different ages, and the consequences of HIV infections averted depending on sexual risk behaviour.

The chapter then addresses the cost-effectiveness of three HIV prevention interventions—condoms, male circumcision, and treatment as prevention. These interventions have been selected not only because they are among the most important HIV prevention interventions, but also to highlight some methodological points. Condoms are an example for an HIV prevention intervention which has an impact only at a point of time. In contrast, male circumcision is a one-off intervention which provides partial protection against contracting HIV for life, the effects are thus more-drawn out than for interventions with a one-off effect. Treatment as prevention is an intervention that also has a lifetime effect. However, unlike male circumcision, it results in a recurrent cost, and increased survival—in addition to reduced HIV incidence—is immediately relevant for the assessment of the cost-effectiveness of treatment.

Population Heterogeneity and Effectiveness of HIV Prevention Interventions

HIV infections occur within a web of sexual and social relations, which is characterized by a high degree of heterogeneity across individuals and between population groups, and that also changes considerably over the course of an individual's life. The most common distinction in this regard is between different risk categories according to sexual behaviour (to be discussed in the next section). The current section addresses the role of heterogeneity within the general population, and the consequences for the effectiveness of HIV prevention interventions. At the same time, it provides an introduction to techniques that will be used later in the discussion of the effectiveness and cost-effectiveness of various HIV prevention interventions.

The model used for illustration is the ASSA2008 model of the HIV epidemic in South Africa (ASSA, 2011).[1] The purpose of the discussion is to make some general points about the effectiveness of HIV prevention interventions across the population. To this end, the ASSA2008 model is particularly useful because it can be adapted to introduce very specific changes to HIV incidence (e.g. by age, in a specific year), and track their consequences across the population and over time. The effects described here, though, are also present in other models (including the 'Spectrum' package), so the lessons are relevant more widely. It should be noted, though, that South Africa is a country facing a severe generalized HIV epidemic, and some of the findings are specific to that context.[2]

As of 2010, HIV prevalence for ages 15–49 in South Africa, according to the ASSA2008 model, was estimated at 15.9 per cent (19.3 per cent for women, 12.4 per cent for men), and HIV incidence at 1.1 per cent (women) and 0.9 per cent for men. As is well known, these aggregates mask very substantial differences in HIV incidence by age group, illustrated in Figure 9.1. For women (Figure 9.1.a), HIV incidence rises steeply from 0.3 per cent at age 14 to 3.1 per cent at age 19. Over these years, women increasingly have sexual relations with men who are already HIV-positive, explaining some of the initial increase in female HIV incidence with age. Another factor is the intensity of sexual activity, which—in this model—is assumed to peak at age 23 for women. At this age, though, HIV incidence is already declining, while partners' HIV prevalence still rises. This is explained by a third factor at work—sorting. Because women engaging in more risky behaviour are more likely to become infected early, with increasing age the composition of women not infected with HIV shifts towards those adopting less risky behaviour. Men's HIV incidence (Figure 9.1.b) peaks later, at age 25, and the distribution is shaped by the same factors—partners' HIV prevalence (although in this case sexual partners, on average, are younger), the peak in sexual activity (at age 28), and sorting.

In addition to the risk of *contracting* HIV, it is equally important for the understanding of the transmission dynamics of HIV/AIDS to understand the risk that a person living with HIV *passes it on* (Figure 9.2)—the risk of contracting HIV and the risk of passing it on are two sides of the same coin. For women living with HIV, the annual probability of passing it on is highest before

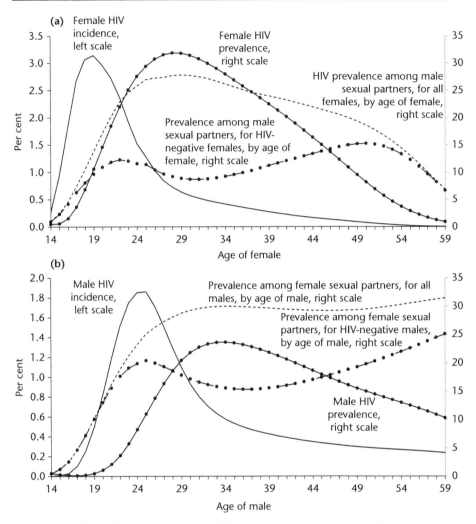

Figure 9.1. HIV incidence and partner's HIV prevalence, South Africa, 2010

Source: Author's calculations, based on ASSA (2011).
(a). Female HIV incidence and prevalence, and partners' HIV prevalence
(b). Male HIV incidence and prevalence, and partners' HIV prevalence

age 20—reflecting the fact that a person who becomes infected with HIV/AIDS early on is statistically more likely to have adopted and adopt high-risk sexual behaviour. Additionally, the shape of the curve reflects the intensity of sexual activity, which in the underlying model is assumed to increase steeply until it reaches its peak at age 23, and—to a lesser extent—HIV prevalence among male partners.

As many HIV prevention interventions do not distinguish individuals by HIV status, the unconditional probability—irrespective of HIV status—that a

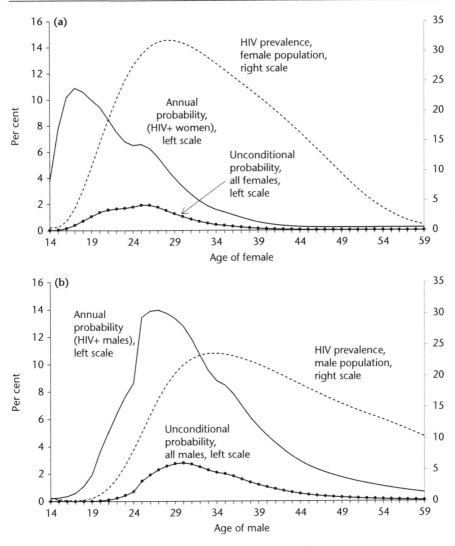

Figure 9.2. Annual probability of passing on HIV, South Africa, 2010

Source: Author's calculations, based on ASSA (2011).
(a). Annual probability of passing on HIV for females, by age
(b). Annual probability of passing on HIV for males, by age

person at a specific age passes on HIV is similarly relevant. This is calculated as the probability that a person living with HIV passes it on, times HIV prevalence in the respective age group. This probability peaks at just under 2 per cent at age 26, between the peaks of sexual activity and of female HIV prevalence, falls below 1 per cent by age 30 and quickly declines for older ages. These estimates suggest a high degree of concentration—more than one-half of female-to-male HIV infections in South Africa are estimated to involve women between the ages of 21 and 27.

For men, the situation differs in two regards. First, the probability of passing on HIV peaks at age 26 for people living with HIV, and at age 30 unconditional on HIV status, reflecting the slower initiation of and the later peak (at age 28) in sexual activity. Second, the rate at which men living with HIV pass on HIV is much higher than for women—for example, it peaks at 14 per cent rather than 11 per cent, and averages 7 per cent rather than 4 per cent, a reflection of the fact that the male-to-female transmission rate is higher than vice versa.[3] Similar to the finding for women, male-to-female HIV transmission is concentrated in a narrow age segment of the male population—more than one-half involves males between the ages of 27 and 34.

The cross-sectional analysis of the risk of contracting or passing on HIV offers very useful insights on the cost-effectiveness of HIV prevention interventions. However, the high rates of HIV transmission in some age groups imply that this analysis misses out on one important aspect of HIV prevention—the dynamic effects. These effects modify the effect of an HIV prevention intervention in two ways. First, a person who does not contract HIV/AIDS also does not pass on HIV to sexual partners and offspring—augmenting the direct impact of an HIV prevention intervention. Second, a person who does not contract HIV/AIDS because of some intervention may become infected at a later stage, reducing the impact of the intervention. As these effects work in opposite directions, it is not clear whether they augment or diminish the effects of HIV prevention interventions (and this may depend on the type of intervention).

Such dynamic effects are illustrated in Figure 9.3, showing the HIV infections averted in later years as a consequence of an HIV infection averted in 2010, for a male or female individual at age 25. As a person *not* infected with HIV also cannot pass on HIV, the effects of one HIV infection averted spread and increase over time—to sexual partners and so on, and—for women—to children. For example, one HIV infection averted for a 25-year-old woman in South Africa (Figure 9.3.a) in 2010 averts an additional 0.5 'downstream' infections. However, as or if the women may become infected subsequently, the effects of preventing an HIV infection are greatly diminished—in this example (Figure 9.3.c), there is a probability of just over one-half that the woman would become infected later on, and the 'downstream' infections averted are reduced to 0.25. In this situation, the population-level effect of averting one HIV infection, at 0.73 HIV infections averted, is therefore lower than the direct effect.

For men, the population-level effects of an HIV infection averted (excluding the risk that the direct beneficiary might contract HIV later) are higher, because of higher male-to-female transmission rates than vice versa—

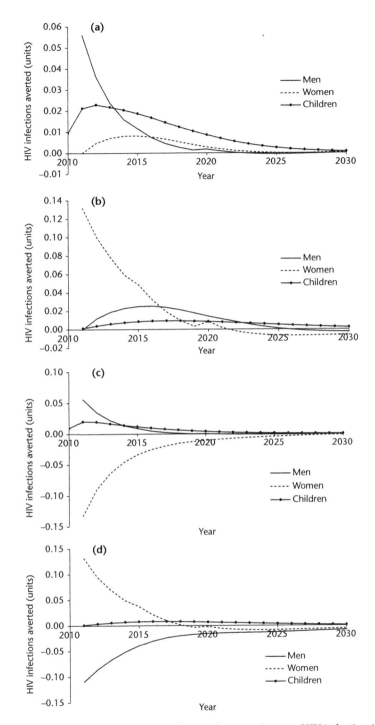

Figure 9.3. Dynamic effects on HIV incidence of preventing one HIV infection in 2010

Source: Author's calculations, based on ASSA (2011), a model of the South African HIV epidemic.
(a). Female individual, age 25, infected in 2010 (excludes risk that individual could become infected later)
(b). Male individual, age 25, infected in 2010 (excludes risk that individual could become infected later)
(c). Female individual, age 25, infected in 2010 (includes risk that individual could become infected later)
(d). Male individual, age 25, infected in 2010 (includes risk that individual could become infected later)

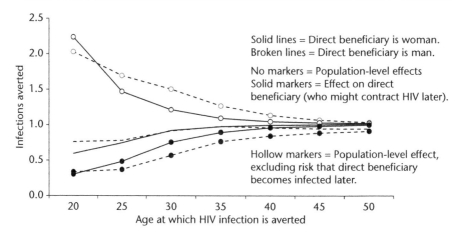

Figure 9.4. Population level effects of HIV prevention intervention that directly averts one HIV infection

Source: Author's calculations, based on ASSA (2011), tracking the consequences of one HIV infection averted in South Africa in 2010.

preventing one HIV infection averts 1.7 HIV infections overall, including an effect on women (0.4), children (0.1), and other men (0.2). Taking into account the risk of subsequent HIV infections, though, the effect is much diminished. There is a 60 per cent chance that the direct beneficiary would contract HIV later on, and the population-level effects are diminished to 0.8 HIV infections averted.

In addition to insights into the effects of HIV prevention interventions over time, the example from South Africa also contains lessons on the impacts across age groups, summarized in Figure 9.4.[4] For older adults, the total effects are similar to the direct effects—it is unlikely that a person who benefited from an HIV prevention intervention contracts HIV later on, and the likelihood that an individual in this age group infects another is also relatively small. For individuals below the age of 30, the differences between the direct effects and the overall effects are large. For the immediate beneficiaries of an HIV prevention intervention, the high risk of subsequent infections means that the effects of the intervention are reduced by up to two-thirds, and the population-level effects are lower than the direct effects. Meanwhile, the intense transmission dynamics mean that an intervention that would keep individuals from becoming infected at a later date could plausibly increase the individual and population-level effects of the intervention by a factor of 2 or 3, compared to an intervention which has a one-off effect.

South Africa, of course, is a country facing a severe generalized epidemic, and it is important to understand to what extent the findings are specific to this context. At first sight, it appears that, in a country with a low-level HIV epidemic, the risk that a beneficiary of an HIV prevention intervention becomes infected at a later time is much reduced, and that the multiplier effects (downstream effects averted) are less forceful. This intuition, however, is misleading, because of heterogeneity of transmission patterns within countries (by risk group or geographically). To the extent that there is variation in risk of HIV acquisition within a country, people contracting HIV are concentrated in populations with relatively high risk of acquiring and passing on HIV.

That this point is relevant can be seen from the national-level data on the probability of passing on HIV. For countries with an HIV prevalence of 2.5 per cent and higher, the annual probability that an adult living with HIV (ages 15+) passes it on is uncorrelated with HIV prevalence. Moreover, the average risk that an individual passes on HIV for these countries (5.4 per cent) is almost the same as for South Africa (5.5 per cent), and there is not much variation across countries.[5]

It is therefore plausible that for many countries the analysis of the population-level effects of one HIV infection averted would yield results similar to those summarized in Figures 9.3 and 9.4 for South Africa. This conclusion, however, does not carry through for countries with an HIV prevalence below 2.5 per cent—these countries are characterized by a high dispersion with regard to the probability that an adult living with HIV (ages 15+) passes it on, ranging from around 1 per cent to close to 20 per cent (Venezuela, Vietnam) with an average of 9.3 and a standard deviation of 7.7, and include countries where the epidemic is under control at low levels as well as countries where there are escalating epidemics, possibly among specific sub-populations.

Condoms

Condoms have been and remain a cornerstone of HIV prevention strategies. UNAIDS (2014b) emphasizes that 'correct and consistent use of male and female condoms remains one of the simplest and most effective ways of preventing sexual transmission of HIV', and condom use features prominently in strategies to prevent HIV infection across the population, as well as in population groups at high risk of contracting HIV, such as sex workers, gay men, or prison populations (UNAIDS, 2014c).

Condoms have conclusively been shown to reduce HIV incidence, and the correct use of a condom can vastly reduce the risk of contracting or passing on HIV. A substantial review estimates that (self-reported) consistent condom use among sero-discordant couples is associated with a reduction in HIV incidence by about 80 per cent; it is plausible, though, that this estimate is an underestimate because of misreporting or inconsistent condom use.[6] On the

population level, a number of studies of trends in HIV incidence and prevalence point to increased condom use as a major contributor to declines in HIV
incidence observed in South Africa, Zimbabwe, and India.[7]

For the analysis of HIV prevention strategies, in addition to the effectiveness
of condom use in averting HIV infection, it is equally important to understand
the effects of HIV prevention interventions on condom use. In this regard, the
evidence is mixed. With regard to female sex workers and their clients, most
studies find that interventions can achieve large increases in condom use.[8]
The evidence for the impact of interventions on condom use in casual relationships is much less conclusive, and condom use in primary partnerships
remained low unless one partner was knowingly HIV-infected or at high-risk.[9]

One aspect that is common to the studies of interventions geared towards
promoting condom use is that the understanding of the *cost*-effectiveness of
such interventions is very limited.[10] In addition to the difficulties of interpreting self-reported data on condom use, and the resulting uncertainty in the link
between measured condom use and HIV transmission, this reflects that many
HIV prevention interventions (e.g. voluntary counselling and testing) are
aimed at reducing sexual risk behaviour in general, and do not only promote
condom use.

With these shortcomings in mind (which it cannot resolve), the analysis
below illuminates three aspects of the cost-effectiveness of condoms, applying
some of the tools and considerations developed in Chapters 7 and 8, and in
the previous section.

- How do the direct effects of condom use on HIV incidence differ across
  the population? The effects, among other points, depend on the likelihood of sexual interactions between sero-discordant agents, which differs
  across age groups or according to some other individual characteristics.

- What are the population-level effects, as opposed to the direct effects? An
  individual who does not contract HIV also does not pass it on (augmenting
  the direct effects of an HIV prevention intervention), but may contract
  HIV following the intervention (partly reversing the direct effect of the
  intervention, and limiting pass-on effects). As in the above discussion of
  the consequences of HIV *infections*, it is plausible that these factors also
  play a role in the assessment of the effectiveness of HIV *prevention* interventions (i.e. the chain from prevention interventions to HIV infections
  averted directly, and then to the population-level effect on HIV incidence).

- What are the financial consequences of increasing the utilization of
  condoms? How do the costs add to the fiscal space absorbed by an HIV/
  AIDS programme, and (through the financial savings from reduced HIV
  incidence) what is the potential for containing the fiscal space absorbed
  by an HIV/AIDS programme?

Continuing the example from South Africa in the previous section, Figure 9.5 summarizes the impact of condoms on HIV incidence. For each age, the utilization of condoms is assumed to be spread across risk groups, in line with the amount of sexual activity and assumptions on condom coverage in the respective groups. To capture the effects by population age, Figure 9.5 is

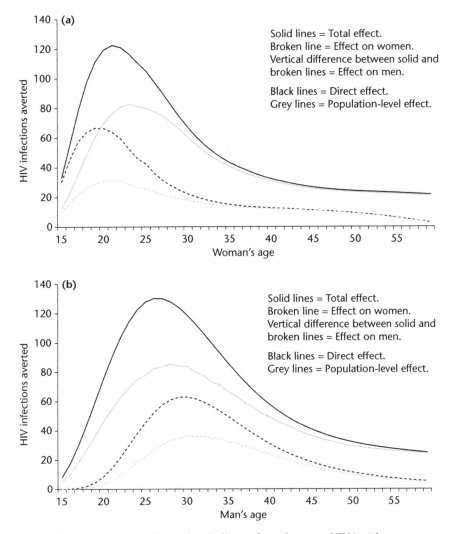

Figure 9.5. Direct and population-level effects of condoms on HIV incidence

Source: Author's calculations, based on ASSA (2011), a model of the South African HIV epidemic. Figure shows expected effect of 100,000 condoms utilized in 2010.

(a). Direct and population-level effects of condoms on HIV incidence, by woman's age (per 100,000 condoms)

(b). Direct and population-level effects of condoms on HIV incidence, by man's age (per 100,000 condoms)

divided in Figure 9.5.a in which results are indexed by the women's age (and male counterparts are drawn from a distribution specific to that age), and Figure 9.5.b where the results are indexed by the men's age. The effects are highest for sexual transactions involving women at about 22 or men at age 28, at over 120 HIV infections averted per 100,000 condoms used. While these peaks occur near the peak in sexual activity for both groups, there is no direct relationship between the efficiency of condoms and the frequency of sexual interactions (because one condom is good for one sexual interaction only). Instead, the pattern reflects the likelihood that a sexual activity involves sero-discordant partners—primarily a function of HIV prevalence in the respective age groups and among counterparts.

With regard to the effectiveness of condoms for HIV prevention across age groups, the estimates reflect common conceptions about the age pattern of sexual activity. Very young adults (both men and women) are almost always the ones who become infected in a sexual interaction. From their mid-20s to mid-30s, women tend to be the HIV-positive partner in a sero-discordant sexual interaction, and men tend to be the HIV-positive partner for (men's) ages 30–40. For older ages, the effectiveness of condoms declines more than HIV prevalence does, this reflects a sorting effect—while groups whose behaviour places them at a higher risk of contracting HIV play a large role in HIV transmission at younger ages, HIV prevalence in these groups increases steeply with age, so that there are fewer sero-discordant interactions at high ages.

The estimates summarized in Figure 9.5 also illustrate the need to differentiate between the direct effects and the population-level effects of HIV prevention interventions. Because of the high risk of subsequent HIV infections, these latter are considerably smaller than the former for young ages, for example peaking at 31 (instead of 67) HIV infections averted (per 100,000 condoms) for women, and at 56 (instead of 85) HIV infections for men.

The considerable role of the population-level effects, in addition to the direct effects of HIV prevention through condoms, complicates the assessment of the cost-effectiveness of condoms for HIV prevention. As shown in Figure 9.3, the secondary effects, following one HIV infection averted, are spread over more than 10 years. Additionally, the financial savings achieved by an HIV infection averted are spread over several decades, and—to take into account that the savings arise much later than the initial costs, some interest or discount rate is typically applied in the financial evaluation.

The findings on the effectiveness of condoms in HIV prevention, including estimates of the financial savings, are summarized in Table 9.1.[11] The estimated savings range from US$0.78 per condom (US$78,000 per 100,000 in Table 9.1) to US$5.03 per condom, which is much larger than estimates of the costs of providing condoms commonly used in HIV programme evaluation of up to US$0.20. Such a cost, for the least cost-effective example shown in

Table 9.1. HIV infections averted and cost savings from increased condom use

Age		Direct effect		Total effect		Gross savings (US$), discounted at		
Male	Female	Male	Female	Male	Female	3%	5%	7%
By female age								
28	20	53.0	66.5	48.4	39.6	451,313	329,648	252,077
32	25	62.9	42.4	61.0	31.6	454,351	328,063	248,614
36	30	44.8	22.1	43.5	20.4	304,394	218,256	164,546
41	35	28.1	15.0	26.9	14.7	195,304	139,680	105,135
45	40	19.5	12.7	18.5	12.6	145,351	103,807	78,059
By male age								
20	19	67.0	8.8	51.0	5.1	313,709	232,584	179,315
25	22	82.7	45.3	64.5	30.0	502,829	370,533	285,026
30	24	55.9	62.8	51.1	46.7	490,120	355,855	270,837
35	27	36.3	49.2	35.5	40.9	370,120	266,474	201,571
40	29	26.8	30.7	25.7	27.6	253,748	182,031	137,331

Note: Numbers refer to an increase in condom use by 100,000, distributed in proportion to sexual activity.
Cost savings assume annual treatment cost of US$400 and do not take into account further programme costs.
Source: Author's calculations, based on ASSA (2011), a model of the South African HIV epidemic.

Table 9.1 (sexual interactions involving women at age 40, applying a discount rate at 7 per cent), would be refinanced through reduced treatment costs within 8 years. In most cases, though, the amortization period would be much shorter, for example about two years for an interaction involving a 30-year old male, applying a 5 per cent discount rate.

In the above example, it is assumed that the coverage of condoms is even across ages and risk groups. It should be noted that this plausibly results in an *under*estimate of the average effectiveness of condoms, to the extent that condom coverage in groups subject to higher risk of HIV transmission and sero-discordant couples (some of whom would know their HIV status) is higher. Indeed, most discussions of HIV prevention policies (e.g. Bertozzi et al., 2006, or Jones et al., 2014) focus on provision of condoms to different risk groups. The analysis offered here additionally points to differences in the effectiveness of HIV prevention interventions by age *within* risk groups. On the other hand, the estimates could *over*estimate the effectiveness of *increasing* the coverage of condoms (i.e. the *marginal* effectiveness), if condom coverage is already high where the risk of HIV transmission is highest, and a scaling-up would extend the coverage across individuals at lower risk.

With regard to developing an analysis of the cost-effectiveness of specific HIV/AIDS interventions in support of optimal policy design, the analysis of the cost-effectiveness of condoms in HIV prevention could be utilized to refine the national HIV/AIDS strategy. In the three-step approach outlined in the introduction, the first step is the specification of a national HIV/AIDS strategy—in this example, this is embedded in the projections on the course of the epidemic, and the underlying assumptions on the coverage of treatment and other interventions. The second step is the analysis of the cost-effectiveness of a specific intervention within the parameters of the HIV/AIDS programme. The third step is to utilize the findings to improve the design of the HIV/AIDS programme. One plausible result could be that increasing access to condoms would be cost-saving, that is it would reduce the fiscal space absorbed by the HIV/AIDS programme. This could form the basis for agreeing on additional investments in expanding condom use, without necessarily reducing funding for other components of the HIV/AIDS programme. Another result could be that increasing access to condoms would be more cost-effective than aspects of the current HIV/AIDS strategy. In this case, re-allocating funds to interventions to expand condom use would improve outcomes or contribute to containing costs and attaining financial sustainability. Vice versa, condoms could turn out less effective than other components of the HIV/AIDS programme, and allocating funds to more effective interventions would enhance the overall effectiveness of the programme.

Prevention Measures Targeting Key Populations

HIV/AIDS is a disease that is primarily transmitted sexually. In order to understand the dynamics of the epidemic, it is therefore necessary to take into account the heterogeneity of sexual behaviour.[12] On the global level, the most important key populations[13] are people who inject drugs, sex workers, and men who have sex with men. UNAIDS (2014c) reports that:

- Globally, 13 per cent of people who inject drugs are living with HIV, and people who inject drugs account for 30 per cent of new HIV infections outside sub-Saharan Africa.

- HIV prevalence among female sex workers is estimated at around 12 per cent in low- and middle-income countries (13.5 times higher than for women of ages 15–49 in general), and as high as 37 per cent in sub-Saharan Africa (based on Kerrigan et al., 2013).

- Men who have sex with men are nineteen times more likely to be living with HIV than the general population. Median HIV prevalence of men who have sex with men is 19 per cent in Western and Central Africa, and 13 per cent in Eastern and Southern Africa.

The relevance of differences in sexual behaviour for the *cost-effectiveness* of HIV prevention interventions has been recognized early on. For example,

Kahn (1996) argues that the effectiveness of HIV prevention interventions across populations with different sexual behaviour in San Francisco differs by a factor of up to 400, and Over and Piot (1993) emphasize the role of heterogeneous sexual behaviour in the transmission of sexually transmitted diseases, and the role of 'core' (i.e. highly sexually active) groups vs. 'noncore' groups. Consequently, global strategies to contain and reverse the spread of HIV/AIDS have placed strong emphasis on prevention efforts towards 'vulnerable populations' (Schwartländer et al., 2001) or 'key populations' (Schwartländer et al., 2011). However, these broad prescriptions have not systematically been reflected in national HIV/AIDS spending allocations.[14]

Over the last few years, the role of interventions towards key populations in the global policy discourse has evolved in two areas. First, the UNAIDS investment framework (which in turn reflects deeper policy and strategic shifts) places increased emphasis on 'returns to investment', and enhancing 'equity and impact by focusing efforts on key locations and populations with the greatest needs' (UNAIDS, 2013a), and has encouraged a shift to planning over a longer time horizon. Second, building on improved national and subnational data on the state of the epidemic, HIV/AIDS strategies are being calibrated more finely to (sub)national drivers of the epidemic (under the heading of 'combination prevention', see Chapter 10).[15]

At the same time, there is a tension between recent policy documents, which place a strong emphasis on the *burden* of HIV/AIDS (as measured by HIV prevalence or incidence) in certain population groups, and the objective of 'maximizing the returns of investment in the HIV response' (UNAIDS, 2013a). This tension arises as some population groups at high risk of contracting HIV *are also more likely to pass on HIV*, so that their share in HIV incidence underplays the role of the respective population group in sustaining the epidemic (and, by extension, the potential returns to investment in HIV prevention in these population groups).

The remainder of this section first discusses the principle of directing HIV prevention efforts across population groups in accordance with the burden of HIV in the respective group, and the modes-of-transmission framework developed to operationalize this approach. Second, it reviews studies which take into account the transmission of HIV *across* population groups, and the impacts of HIV prevention interventions over time. Third, it connects to the earlier 'fiscal space' interpretation of HIV programmes, and discusses how approaches like the 'modes of transmission' framework can be improved to gain a better understanding of the cost-effectiveness of HIV prevention interventions across population groups, and their potential contributions to achieving financial sustainability.

The principles behind the 'modes of transmission' framework were described by Pisani et al. (2003). Effective HIV prevention programmes need to focus on the situations in which HIV infections occur, and these situations differ across countries or over time. Moreover, the distribution of HIV prevalence across the population can be very different from the distribution of HIV incidence, because of the natural dynamics of the epidemic or as a result of ongoing HIV prevention efforts. The first studies applying the modes-of-transmission framework were published in 2006, and a recent review identifies articles and reports covering twenty-nine countries.[16]

The core of the 'modes of transmission' framework is a spreadsheet that is used to divide the population by risk categories, set epidemiological parameters like HIV transmission probabilities, and specify—for each risk group— HIV prevalence and behavioural parameters like the annual number of sexual partners, the frequency of sexual acts with each partner, and the share of acts which are 'protected', that is, do not result in HIV infection because of the use of condoms. The most recent version (2012) of the spreadsheet also incorporates the effects of male circumcision and the reduction in HIV transmission owing to ART.[17] Based on these parameters, it returns estimates of the number of HIV infections for each risk group.

Typical results of a 'modes of transmission' analysis are presented in Table 9.2, which summarizes findings from studies on Zimbabwe (a 'generalized' epidemic, with HIV prevalence at 13.7 per cent) and Jamaica (a 'concentrated' epidemic, with HIV prevalence estimated at 1.8 per cent). HIV prevalence indeed is concentrated in Jamaica, estimated at 15 per cent for men who have sex with men, and 4.4 per cent for female sex workers (compared to 1.1 for the bulk of the population whose sexual behaviour is described as 'casual' or 'low-risk'). The situation is different in Zimbabwe, where HIV prevalence is estimated at 10 per cent or more for all risk groups. However, even here HIV prevalence is concentrated in some groups—for female sex workers, it is estimated to be four times, or 40 percentage points, higher than for the population overall.

With regard to HIV incidence, the picture is similar, but there are also important differences. The highest numbers of HIV infections in Jamaica, relative to the population size of the respective group, occur among men who have sex with men, clients of sex workers and their partners, and sex workers. The same applies for Zimbabwe (where injecting drug users play an absolutely small but—relative to population size—disproportionately large role).[18] In Zimbabwe, HIV incidence among individuals engaging in low-risk sexual behaviour is higher than for those engaging in casual heterosexual sex, this reflects the fact that the latter engage in higher-risk sexual behaviour per se, but also respond to this higher risk by a much higher rate of condom use (59 per cent vs. 6 per cent).

The 'modes of transmission' framework had been developed to align HIV prevention strategies with the pattern of risk, and adapt strategies as this

Table 9.2. Modes of transmission of HIV in Zimbabwe and Jamaica

	Zimbabwe				Jamaica			
	Population (% of total)	HIV prevalence (%)[a]	HIV incidence (%)[a]	Contribution to new infections (% of total)	Population (% of total)	HIV prevalence (%)[a]	HIV incidence (%)[a]	Contribution to new infections (% of total)
Injecting drug use (IDU)	0.1	12.4	13.1	1.4	n.a.	n.a.	n.a.	n.a.
Partners IDU	0.1	14.3	1.2	0.1	n.a.	n.a.	n.a.	n.a.
Sex workers	0.7	54.3	4.8	2.1	1.0	4.4	0.27	1.5
Clients	2.0	19.3	4.6	9.6	3.0	3.5	0.33	5.5
Partners of clients	1.0	20.9	1.9	2.0	1.8	1.1	0.38	3.9
MSM	1.5	16.8	3.8	6.2	2.0	15.0	3.17	31.2
Female partners of MSM	1.0	20.0	0.5	0.5	0.8	1.4	1.60	7.3
Casual heterosexual sex	10.5	17.0	0.9	9.7	44.0	1.9	0.09	22.6
Partners CHS	8.5	14.3	1.4	13.6	12.0	1.1	0.21	14.2
Low-risk heterosexual	40.9	14.3	1.2	54.8	25.4	1.1	0.09	13.8
Not currently at risk	33.7	10.0	0.0	0.0	10.0	1.1	0.00	0.0
Medical injections				0.1				0.0
Total	100.0	13.7	0.9	100.0	100.0	1.8	0.20	100.0

[a] HIV prevalence is shown as a percentage of the population belonging to the respective group. HIV incidence is shown as a percentage of the population not living with HIV in the respective group.

Sources: Fraser et al. (2010) and Barrow et al. (2012).

pattern of risk changes (Gouws et al., 2006). In this regard, it has been successful—it provides a snapshot of the epidemic that is accessible, and has contributed to re-allocations of expenditures towards key populations.[19] The principal shortcoming is the lack of *dynamics*. This shortcoming is fundamental in terms of designing effective HIV prevention policies, in two regards.

First, for any population at risk of contracting HIV it is unclear whether HIV prevention would more effectively target this population, or whether it is more effective to address a cause placing this population at risk. This shortcoming (and pragmatic solutions) is most obvious for the female partners of men who also have sex with men, and the partners of clients of sex workers. The issue is less clear for those deemed to be members of 'low-risk populations'—is it more effective to directly aim prevention interventions at 'low-risk' populations or to focus on the causes of transmission of HIV into the 'low-risk' population, or how can prevention interventions most effectively be combined?[20]

Second, what is the effectiveness of investments in HIV prevention among key populations, considering that a high risk of contracting HIV may also be associated with a high probability of passing on HIV? For example, in both Jamaica and Zimbabwe, an HIV-positive female sex worker is estimated to infect an average of 0.2 clients annually (who might in turn infect others). Thus, preventing HIV infections among female sex workers, against the objective of reducing HIV incidence overall, would carry a disproportionately large weight, beyond their share in the number of new HIV infections.

The latter point is developed more fully in a number of papers by Case et al. (2012) and Mishra et al. (2014a, 2014b, and 2014c). Case et al. (2012) observe that the 'modes of transmission' framework 'does not take into account the number of secondary infections that will result from new infections in a risk group'. Mishra et al. (2014a) compare a standard 'modes of transmission' model (as described in UNAIDS, 2012a) with a more complex model with richer interactions between risk groups (but still providing a snapshot of HIV incidence only), and a dynamic model, finding that the former models 'consistently underestimated the long-term contribution of epidemic drivers' (i.e. high-risk behaviour driving the epidemic), and that this bias increases the longer the time horizon considered.

Mishra et al. (2014c) discuss the policy implications of the bias contained in 'modes of transmission' studies—because it does not capture 'downstream' infections caused by HIV infections among people adopting high-risk behaviour, 'modes of transmission' studies tend to overemphasize HIV infections among population groups characterized by relatively low-risk sexual behaviour. Accordingly, and ironically, while the 'modes of transmission' framework had been designed to improve on what was considered haphazard and insufficient allocations of HIV prevention spending towards high-risk groups, it still places insufficient weight on HIV infections among high-risk groups.

These findings are consistent with those of studies addressing the effectiveness of HIV prevention interventions towards key populations adopting a longer time horizon. Many of the arguments from current studies are contained in the 1996 study by Kahn—the higher population-level impact of interventions targeting populations adopting high-risk sexual behaviour, the fact that the results on differences in effectiveness are stronger for longer time horizons, and the possibility that HIV prevention among key populations may be more effective in containing HIV among lower-risk groups than interventions targeting lower-risk groups directly. Anderson et al. (2014) identify behaviour change communications for men who have sex with men and for female sex workers as among the most cost-effective HIV prevention interventions in terms of minimizing HIV incidence across the population. Vassall et al. (2014), in an evaluation of the Avahan programme in India, estimate that an intervention targeting 150,000 high-risk individuals (largely female sex workers, but also men who have sex with men and injecting drug users) averted 61,000 HIV infections in 2004–2008, including 11,000 HIV infections averted in the general population. This would imply that one HIV infection averted among high-risk individuals *additionally* prevents about 0.1 HIV infections *annually* across the population over this period.[21]

The 'modes of transmission' framework can also be used to gain some insights on the consequences of HIV infections and HIV prevention interventions across population groups (Table 9.3). For example, as the 'modes of transmission' framework specifies the risk that a female sex worker *acquires* HIV from a client, it correspondingly specifies the statistical probability that an HIV-positive client *passes on* HIV to a female sex worker. This probability that an individual passes on HIV can be used to track the consequences of one HIV infection, for example between female sex workers and their clients, and on to clients' other partners.[22]

The advantage of using the 'modes of transmission' framework for estimating the consequences of one HIV infection across the population is the fact that it yields an explicit solution for the number of subsequent HIV infections caused by one initial HIV infection, which can be interpreted in a fairly straightforward manner in terms of underlying parameters and assumptions. There are, however, a number of drawbacks. First, the 'modes of transmission' framework does not contain an age structure. It is therefore necessary to specify how long an individual who contracts HIV remains active in the risk group and could pass on HIV (assumed here: 5 years). Also, an individual who becomes infected with HIV would otherwise remain in the risk group for some time (assumed: 10 years) and could contract HIV at a later time, reducing the effects of any specific HIV infections (or infections averted).[23] Second, the 'modes of transmission' model does not specify transitions of individuals between most risk groups. For example, it does not contain a theory of how

Table 9.3. Consequences of one HIV infection—subsequent infections, financial costs

	Excluding risk of later HIV infection				Including risk of later HIV infection			
	Total HIV infections	Own HIV infections	Other HIV infections	Financial costs (total)	Total HIV infections	Own HIV infections	Other HIV infections	Financial costs (total)
Zimbabwe								
Men who have sex with men	4.41	1.00	3.41	18,674	3.56	0.68	2.88	15,461
Female sex workers	2.04	1.00	1.04	10,858	1.27	0.61	0.66	6,270
Clients of female sex workers	1.53	1.00	0.53	7,070	0.86	0.62	0.24	5,240
Casual heterosexual sex—males	1.74	1.00	0.74	7,871	1.62	0.93	0.69	7,409
Casual heterosexual sex—females	1.49	1.00	0.49	6,841	1.33	0.89	0.44	6,563
Low-risk heterosexual sex—males	1.29	1.00	0.29	5,890	1.18	0.91	0.27	5,464
Low-risk heterosexual sex—females	1.20	1.00	0.20	5,553	1.04	0.86	0.17	4,866
Jamaica								
Men who have sex with men	4.72	1.00	3.72	19,686	3.98	0.72	3.26	16,933
Female sex workers	2.72	1.00	1.72	17,892	2.65	0.97	1.68	11,694
Clients of female sex workers	1.60	1.00	0.60	7,279	1.26	0.97	0.29	7,116
Casual heterosexual sex—males	1.54	1.00	0.54	6,996	1.53	0.99	0.54	6,944
Casual heterosexual sex—females	1.35	1.00	0.35	6,168	1.34	0.99	0.34	6,875
Low-risk heterosexual sex—males	1.37	1.00	0.37	6,223	1.36	0.99	0.37	6,176
Low-risk heterosexual sex—females	1.36	1.00	0.36	6,165	1.35	0.99	0.36	6,109

Source: Author's calculations, based on Barrow et al. (2012), and Fraser et al. (2010).

HIV enters the 'low-risk' population. Third, the 'modes of transmission' framework does not impose consistency in the number of sexual encounters. For example, the number of sexual encounters by males and by their female counterparts, respectively, might differ within a population group. This inconsistency in practice is less pervasive for the groups with the highest risk behaviour (female sex workers, men who have sex with men), but may affect results for other risk categories. Fourth, the 'modes of transmission' framework does not consistently control for sero-discordant couples (and does not need to, because it is a one-period model). In the dynamic analysis, this is taken into account by assuming that one-half of HIV infections among low-risk individuals do not cause any further HIV infections.

The results are presented in Table 9.3 in two forms—excluding the risk of a later HIV infection for the individual concerned, and including it, and the same two countries (Zimbabwe and Jamaica) as before. The first measure assumes that the beneficiary of an HIV prevention intervention (i.e. a person not contracting HIV because of it) does not contract HIV later on. The latter measure takes into account that the impact of an HIV prevention intervention is diminished if there is a high probability that beneficiaries subsequently become infected.

Excluding the individual risk of a later HIV infection, expected downstream infections augment the consequences of one HIV infection averted by around one-half for individuals with low-risk and casual sexual behaviour, but they are much higher for female sex workers and especially men who have sex with men. Taking into account the risk of a later HIV infection diminishes the impact of one specific HIV infection—for example, in case of Zimbabwe, there is a risk of almost 40 per cent of a subsequent HIV infection (resulting in values below one in the column 'own infection')—and consequently the number of downstream HIV infections is diminished as well. In most cases, taking into account the risk of a later HIV infection diminishes the consequences of one specific HIV infection, but leaves the ranking across risk groups unchanged. The important exception is the case of female sex workers in Zimbabwe—because of the very high underlying risk of contracting HIV, the consequences of any *specific* HIV infection are diminished so much that the overall effect ranks somewhere between the 'casual sex' and 'low-risk' groups.

In summary, with regard to the effectiveness of HIV prevention interventions, the 'modes of transmission' framework carries a number of important lessons:

- 'Downstream' HIV infections matter for the assessment of the cost-effectiveness of HIV prevention interventions across population groups. Notably, the population-level effects of HIV infections averted among female sex workers are more than double the direct effects if the direct effects are persistent; for men who have sex with men, the population-level effects in these examples are almost four times higher. In this regard, the findings from the analysis of the 'modes of transmission' framework mirror the conclusions of Kahn (1996), Case et al. (2012), and Mishra et al. (2014a, 2014b, and 2014c).

- However, it is not always correct that 'modes of transmission' studies place too much emphasis on low-risk populations because of the dispro-portionate dynamic effects of HIV infections among high-risk individ-uals, because the high-risk sexual behaviour means that the risk of subsequent HIV infections is higher.

- For the evaluation of HIV prevention interventions, this means that taking into account downstream infections and HIV transmission dynamics is critical. To what extent are the direct effects of an HIV prevention intervention augmented as people not infected with HIV also do not pass it on? To what extent are they diminished as people not infected as a result of the intervention may become infected later?

Whether it is necessary to include the risk of future infections in the risk group targeted by an HIV prevention intervention in the analysis depends on the type of intervention. For a one-off intervention (e.g. distributing condoms) it is necessary; for an intervention thought to eliminate aspects of risk behaviour permanently it may not be. In this latter case, though, the policy scenario might imply a continuation of HIV prevention policies, and it would be necessary to take into account the costs of this continuation.

With regard to optimal allocations of HIV prevention spending and the cost-effectiveness of HIV prevention interventions, there are a number of lessons. In almost all cases,[24] the total effect of an HIV prevention interven-tion (including downstream infections) is larger than the direct effects. Empir-ical analyses of cost-effectiveness based on specific populations over some fixed period therefore underestimate the cost-effectiveness of HIV prevention interventions.

Because the number of downstream infections tends to be higher for high-risk groups (in Table 9.3, consistently for men who have sex with men, but less so for female sex workers), the dynamic analysis lends additional support to findings like those by Amico et al. (2012), arguing that spending allocations towards 'most-at-risk' populations were insufficient in relation to their share in HIV incidence. Taking into account downstream infections, the incongru-ity between the role of different risk groups as drivers of HIV incidence and spending allocations comes out strongly.

Apart from their primary objective, HIV prevention interventions also contribute to reducing the long-term costs of the HIV response (see discussion in Chapter 7), and optimal HIV/AIDS programme allocations also need to take into account the long-term financial consequences of alternative HIV/ AIDS policies (illustrated in Chapter 8). This aspect of HIV prevention policies towards key populations is also accommodated in Table 9.3, which provides estimates of the costs caused by one new HIV infection across risk groups. Assuming a life-time cost of US$4,650 per person living with HIV (see end-note 11), the total costs caused by an HIV infection, including the costs from projected downstream infections, come out at between US$4,900 and US$15,500.[25] This means that in general an intervention that averts an HIV infection at a cost of at most US$4,900 is cost-saving and contributes to reducing the financial burden of the HIV/AIDS programme. The financial savings from preventing HIV infections among population groups with a high risk of HIV transmission, though, are much higher, estimated at more than US$15,000 for men who have sex with men in either country, and at US$11,700 for female sex workers in Jamaica.[26]

Medical Male Circumcision

Medical male circumcision has evolved into a cornerstone of HIV prevention strategies,[27] and is recognized in the 2011 UNAIDS investment framework and more recent policy documents such as the UNAIDS 'Gap Report' (2014c).[28] On the population level, a negative correlation between male circumcision rates and HIV prevalence in sub-Saharan Africa had been observed early on (see, e.g., Bongaarts et al., 1989), but a causal interpretation of this link was not generally accepted until several randomized trials concluded that the risk of acquiring HIV among circumcised males was reduced by about 60 per cent (Figure 9.6).[29]

From an economic perspective, male circumcision stands out because it is an intervention which occurs at a point in time, but provides partial

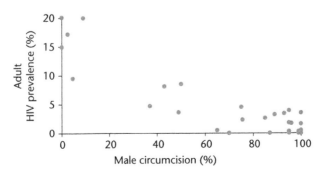

Figure 9.6. Correlation between male circumcision and HIV prevalence
Source: Bongaarts et al. (1989).

155

protection against contracting HIV for life. In contrast to interventions with a one-off impact (discussed in the section on condoms), the impacts on the individual circumcised are therefore spread out over several decades, and population-level effects (among sexual partners or children) are also spread over long time periods. The challenges in assessing the effectiveness and cost-effectiveness of HIV prevention interventions arising from the very slow disease transmission dynamics and long survival of people living with HIV are therefore particularly pervasive in the case of male circumcision.

(It should be noted that a vaccine—providing partial protection over a sustained period—has similar properties as male circumcision in terms of assessing the cost-effectiveness as an HIV prevention intervention. The most important differences are that a vaccine could be applied to women as well, and not only to men, and that the effectiveness of a vaccine could dissipate after some period and not last for life. Vaccines are not covered here because they do not play a role in HIV policies currently implemented, and because methodologically the discussion would strongly overlap with the discussion on male circumcision.)[30]

Inspired by the new empirical evidence, a number of studies explored the potential of male circumcision. Among these early studies, the one most relevant here is by White et al. (2008), employing a model calibrated for a Kenyan region with an HIV prevalence of 20 per cent. They show that the impact of male circumcision builds up over time—the number of HIV infections averted (per 1,000 circumcisions) increases from 53 after 5 years to 630 over a 40-year period, and the costs per HIV infection averted correspondingly decline from US$974 for the 5-year period to US$89 over the 40-year period. Among others, Hallett et al. (2008) highlighted that male circumcision also results in declines in HIV incidence among women and non-circumcised men (as circumcised men who do not become infected also do not pass on HIV).

An 'all-star' expert group,[31] reviewing evidence and policy studies for a range of African locations through 2009, found that it took between five and fifteen male circumcisions to avert one HIV infection, and that the cost of averting one HIV infection ranged from US$150 to US$900. Benefits, in terms of HIV infections averted, accrued not only to circumcised men, but also their female partners, and the costs of averting an HIV infection generally came out lower than the resulting savings in terms of the cost of treatment and other services, which means that male circumcision was a cost-saving intervention.

The emerging evidence and the endorsement by major organizations of male circumcision as an HIV prevention strategy (WHO and UNAIDS (2007), see also Reed et al. (2011) for a narrative of PEPFAR's evolving policies) have motivated a number of policy-oriented studies assessing the potential costs, impacts, and cost-effectiveness of scaling up male circumcision across countries. The most comprehensive of these are Njeuhmeli et al. (2011), focusing on thirteen priority countries for male circumcision, and Auvert et al. (2008), covering a very similar set of countries.[32] Because of the similarities in scope and purpose between these two studies, a comparison is fruitful in terms of highlighting some methodological differences and their consequences.

The study by Auvert et al. (2008) projects that reaching a coverage rate of male circumcision of 85 per cent, and sustaining it over another 15 years, would require about 44 million circumcisions, cost US$1.3 billion, and avert 8 million HIV infections, at an average cost of US$168 each. Because the costs of providing treatment and other medical services decline by US$3.6 billion over this period, the financial costs of the response to HIV/AIDS are reduced by US$2.3 billion over the 20-year period covered. According to Njeuhmeli and others (2011), reaching a coverage rate of male circumcision of 80 per cent and maintaining it through 2025 would require 28.7 million circumcisions, at a cost of US$2.0 billion, and avert 3.4 million HIV infections. The HIV infections averted would result in financial savings of US$18.5 billion, so that the scaling up of male circumcision would result in financial savings of US$16.5 billion.

The higher impact of male circumcision on HIV incidence projected by Auvert et al. (8 million HIV infections averted, vs. 3.4 million HIV infections averted) only partly reflects the higher number of circumcisions performed (44 million vs. 29 million). A principal reason is the longer time horizon in the study by Auvert et al. (20 years vs. 15 years in the study by Njeuhmeli et al.). This matters because male circumcision provides partial protection for life, a study adopting a longer time horizon therefore captures more of the benefits. This point is also underscored by Auvert et al., who observe that the costs per HIV infection averted decline by one-half, from US$338 to US$168, when a 20-year horizon rather than a 10-year horizon is considered.

The larger difference between the two studies regards the financial savings as a consequence of reduced HIV incidence. Auvert et al. (2008) project gross savings of US$3.6 billion, and net savings (after subtracting the costs of male circumcision) of US$2.3 billion, that is, an average net saving of US$50 per male circumcision, and US$300 per HIV infection averted. Njeuhmeli et al. (2011) estimate that the net financial savings amount to US$16.5 billion, that is, US$640 per male circumcision, and US$5,500 per HIV infection averted.

These very large differences (by a factor of thirteen for male circumcision, and eighteen for HIV infections averted) to some extent reflect that Auvert et al. (2008) assume a treatment coverage of only 30 per cent (not unreasonable for a paper written at the time), whereas Njeuhmeli and others base their estimate on the lifetime costs of treatment per patient (implying a treatment coverage of 100 per cent). The more important difference is methodological. Auvert et al. calculate savings in terms of current spending on treatment costs *during* the projection period—this captures only a fraction of the cost savings caused by reduced HIV incidence, because many individuals who would become infected over the projection period (in the absence of male circumcision) would not initiate treatment during the projection period, and most individuals would require treatment beyond the projection period. In contrast, Njeuhmeli et al. use an estimate of the lifetime costs of treatment of US$7,000 (much of which would occur *after* the end of the policy period), and attribute it to each HIV infection averted. The gross savings of US$18.5 billion are then obtained by multiplying HIV infections averted, applying a discount rate of 3 per cent, with the cost of US$7,000 per HIV infection.

The example of these two studies thus illustrates the relevance of a *forward-looking* analysis of the financial consequences of alternative HIV/AIDS policies (as previously discussed in Chapters 7 and 8). Because ART patients may receive treatment for several decades, an analysis looking only at the costs of an HIV prevention policy over some policy period and cost savings in terms of treatment costs over the same period systematically underestimates the financial savings achieved by reducng HIV incidence. In the case of male circumcision, this challenge is exacerbated by the fact that the impact of male circumcision on HIV incidence is not instantaneous, but spread over many years. The financial savings thus arrive subject to one lag (from male circumcision to HIV infections) stacked on another (from HIV infections to treatment costs).

Since about 2008, there has been considerable but also limited progress in expanding the uptake of male circumcision—in 2014, 3.2 million men were medically circumcised in 14 priority countries in East and Southern Africa,[33] bringing the total to 9.1 million since 2008 (WHO, 2015). These numbers, however, represent less than one-half of progress required towards an informal target of a circumcision rate of 80 per cent by 2016. The experience so far, and an increased emphasis on cost-effectiveness across the global HIV/AIDS response, have motivated a new round of work assessing more specifically the impacts of male circumcision *across* the population, and informing a more differentiated policy approach.

One such approach takes forward the approach used by Njeuhmeli et al. (2011), but extending the analysis to assess the impacts of male circumcision when specific age groups are targeted (Kripke et al., 2015a).[34] Typical findings are illustrated in Figure 9.7, which shows the impact of alternative hypothetical policies, calibrated for South Africa, in which only a specific age group is targeted (Kripke et al., 2015b). In this illustration, there are three factors determining the effectiveness of male circumcision. First, the intensity of sexual activity at different age groups—because of relatively high levels of sexual activity, the impacts of male circumcision at ages 20–34 is fastest (the relevant curves decline steepest initially). Second, circumcision at later ages means that the respective cohorts initiate sexual activity without benefiting

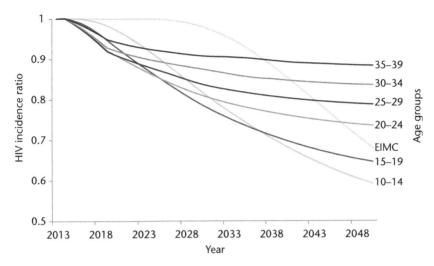

Figure 9.7. Effectiveness of male circumcision targeting specific age groups

Note: EIMC = Early infant male circumcision.

Source: Kripke et al. (2015b).

from male circumcision, so that the reduction in HIV incidence is diminished. Third, in the case of circumcisions of infants (age 0) and young adolescents (aged 10–14), the impact of male circumcision occurs with a lag, once members of the cohort initiate sexual activity. Additionally, the example illustrates that the impact of male circumcision evolves over very long periods—for circumcisions below the age of 24, more than half of the impact occurs after 15 years or later.

Haacker et al. (2016) complement the studies based on policy scenarios (for example, the one illustrated in Figure 9.7) in three directions. First, they incorporate estimates of the costs caused by each new HIV infection (and saved by an HIV infection averted), during the lifetime of a person who contracts HIV, derived from a costing of a national HIV/AIDS programme.[35] Second, they provide an *incremental* analysis, tracking the projected consequences of circumcising one male individual, at a specific age, in a specific year, over time. While policy scenarios are well suited to assess the costs and consequences of national policies, they return very imprecise estimates of the cost-effectiveness based on *average* outcomes and inputs over a policy period which—in studies of the effects of male circumcision—could be very long. Estimating the effect of circumcising one additional male individual gives a precise estimate of the *marginal* costs and effects, which are more precise indicators for testing the allocative efficiency of the national HIV/AIDS strategy than the *average* effects. Third, studies of policy scenarios are vulnerable to a cut-off problem—because the impact of male circumcision on HIV incidence

Table 9.4. Consequences of one medical male circumcision performed in South Africa in 2013: HIV infections averted, financial returns

Age at MC	Impact on HIV incidence			MCs per HIV infection averted	Cost of MC per HIV infection averted (US$)	Net savings from one MC (US$, @5% disc.)	Amortization period (years, @5% disc.)	Internal rate of return (%)
	Total	Direct	Indirect					
0	0.236	0.082	0.154	4.2	221	301	30.6	7.8
10	0.232	0.084	0.147	4.3	450	401	22.8	9.9
15	0.218	0.085	0.133	4.6	478	475	17.4	11.5
20	0.227	0.088	0.139	4.4	460	617	12.2	14.5
25	0.159	0.083	0.076	6.3	657	412	11.6	13.6
30	0.079	0.059	0.020	12.6	1,316	123	16.6	8.8
35	0.040	0.034	0.006	25.1	2,623	−2	n.a.	4.9
40	0.022	0.020	0.002	46.2	4,826	−52	n.a.	1.8
45	0.014	0.013	0.000	72.7	7,592	−74	n.a.	−0.9
50	0.009	0.009	0.000	113.3	11,819	−86	n.a.	−3.6
55	0.005	0.005	0.000	214.2	22,350	−95	n.a.	−6.8

Source: Haacker et al. (2016).

unfolds over a long period (for young adults, about two decades are required to capture most of the effects), the effects of male circumcision on HIV incidence are underestimated, especially for circumcisions occurring late in the policy period.[36] Focusing on the consequences of one additional male circumcision, the study runs the analysis as long as required to capture the impacts on HIV incidence completely.

Table 9.4 summarizes the findings by Haacker et al. (2016), calibrated for South Africa using a version of the ASSA2008 epidemiological model adapted to account for the effects of male circumcision. Up to age 20, the effects of one male circumcision on HIV incidence are similar—one male circumcision averts between 0.22 and 0.24 HIV infections. At higher ages, this effect diminishes steeply—by two-thirds for male circumcisions performed at age 30, and nine-tenths for male circumcisions at age 40. For the direct effects (i.e. the effects on the individual circumcised), the decline reflects three factors—declining remaining life expectancy, declining intensity of sexual activity (from about ages 25–30), and a sorting effect (individuals not infected with HIV at higher ages are statistically more likely to have adopted less risky sexual behaviour). Most of the decline, however, is accounted for by the *indirect* effects, that is the impacts on the sexual partners of circumcised men and so on through sexual transmission, and on infants through mother-to-child transmission—because there is a lag between an HIV infection and any subsequent HIV infections through the person infected first, the decline in sexual activity at higher age plays a larger role in indirect effects, and the remaining number of births (and potential for mother-to-child HIV transmission) declines as women get older.

Mirroring the declining effectiveness of male circumcision, the costs per HIV infection averted range from about US$450 for young adults to US$4,800 at age 40 (and more at higher ages). However, as each HIV infection averted also results in cost savings, male circumcisions at most ages result in a substantial net financial saving (the cost of circumcision, minus the resulting financial savings, discounted at a rate of 5 per cent in this illustration), which can be as high as US$600 per male circumcision (at age 20), exceed US$400 for young adults up to age 25, and remain positive—so that male circumcision is cost-saving—up to age 30.[37] While the financial returns to investments in male circumcision are spread over long periods, the costs are refinanced through reduced costs of treatment after only about 12 years for some age groups (ages 20 and 25). Even without taking into account the health benefits (HIV infections averted), providing male circumcision can be a good financial investment, carrying a financial rate of return exceeding 10 per cent for circumcisions between ages 15 and 25.

One aspect that stands out among the results presented in Table 9.4 is the cost-effectiveness of infant circumcision. The effectiveness—in terms of the number of HIV infections averted—is about the same as for young adults. Because of lower unit costs, the cost per HIV infection averted through infant circumcision therefore comes out far lower than for young adults. However, prevention effects and financial savings arrive with a long time lag. Because of discounting, the net savings from infant circumcision (US$300) are much lower than for young adults, and the financial costs are refinanced through financial savings after about 30 years.

In summary, the recent work on the effectiveness of male circumcision offers insights not only about refining approaches to male circumcision for maximum impact, but also underscores the role of male circumcision—a highly effective and frequently cost-saving intervention—in terms of reducing the financing burden of HIV/AIDS programmes and contributing to financial sustainability. While the available studies focus on countries with relatively high HIV prevalence, some of the findings—such as the large differences in the effectiveness of male circumcision by age—appear relevant for settings with lower HIV prevalence. Moreover, the results from South Africa—specifically the high financial net savings from male circumcisions for some age groups—suggest that male circumcision would be cost-saving at least for some age groups in settings with much lower HIV prevalence.

Treatment

From about 2003 to 2011, the drive to expand access to treatment and thus improve the health and life prospects of people living with HIV was one of the dominant themes of the global response to HIV/AIDS. One early milestone was the WHO's '3 by 5' initiative (WHO, 2003), aiming to extend treatment to 3 million people across developing countries by 2005. As of June 2015, the number of people receiving treatment has increased to 15.8 million globally, vastly extending the lifespan of people living with HIV, and at least partly reversing the steep declines in life expectancy observed overall in many countries affected by HIV/AIDS.[38] These impacts of treatment were discussed in Chapter 2 (illustrating the impact of HIV/AIDS on life expectancy, and the rebound in life expectancy associated with increased access to treatment), Chapter 6 (looking more specifically at the impact of the global response to HIV/AIDS across countries), and Chapter 7 (increasing life expectancy with earlier initiation of treatment).

Table 9.5 carries forward the narrative from Chapter 7 (specifically, Table 7.1, describing the costs and consequences of one HIV infection), and addresses the cost-effectiveness, in terms of life years gained, of treatment access under different eligibility criteria.[39] The calculations assume that 100 per cent of people eligible for treatment receive it, results for lower coverage rates, or a situation in which treatment initiation is spread across different coverage rates, can be obtained from Table 9.5 as a weighted average of the results for different rows.

The direct costs per life year gained are always higher than the annual costs of treatment, because individuals would survive for some time in the absence of treatment. For example, if an individual is placed on treatment at a CD4 count of 100, the expected remaining life span without ART is only about one year, and the costs per life year saved, at US$422, are close to the annual costs of treatment (assumed at US$400). For shifts in eligibility to a CD4 count of 200 or 350, the cost-effectiveness diminishes somewhat (for the *additional* life years gained when shifting from a CD4 count of 200 to 350, costs per life year gained rise to US$541). Overall, initiating treatment at a CD4 count of 350 rather than 100 extends the remaining life expectancy by 14 years (from 19 to 33), at a cost of US$7,100 (undiscounted) or US$2,500 (discounted at 5 per cent). Moving from eligibility at a CD4 count of 350 to 500, the cost-effectiveness of treatment with respect to life years gained is much diminished—life expectancy increases by about two years only, but individuals spend more than 5 additional years on treatment, so that the cost per life year gained comes out at US$1,110. As treatment is initiated earlier at higher CD4 counts, the differences in discounted costs are more pronounced—the cost of a life year gained by moving from treatment eligibility of 350 to 500 results in a cost of US$642 per life year gained, more than four times higher than for treatment initiation below a CD4 count of 200.

Table 9.5 also reflects one point made earlier—with wider treatment eligibility and increasing coverage of treatment, the health returns to preventing

Table 9.5. Cost-effectiveness of antiretroviral therapy—life years gained

	Life expectancy (years)	Probability of reaching treatment (%)	Average time on treatment (years)	Costs of treatment (US$, undiscounted)	Costs per life year gained (US$, undiscounted)		Costs of treatment (US$, 5% disc. rate)	Costs per life year gained (US$, 5% disc. rate)	
					Average	Marginal		Average	Marginal
No ART	12.1	0.0	0.0	0	0	0	0	0	0
ART from CD4 count of 100	19.0	37.5	7.2	2,898	422	422	874	127	127
ART from CD4 count of 200	25.5	63.0	14.5	5,818	435	449	1,796	134	142
ART from CD4 count of 350	33.2	87.1	24.9	9,974	474	541	3,354	159	203
ART from CD4 count of 500	35.1	94.9	30.3	12,108	527	1,110	4,588	200	642
ART at all CD4 counts	36.3	99.3	35.3	14,106	584	1,700	5,883	244	1,102

Note: Life expectancy is average remaining life expectancy from time of infection. Estimates assume that an individual initiates treatment with a probability of 100 per cent once he or she reach the eligibility threshold. More realistic scenarios can be obtained as a weighted average of the results presented in the rows of the table. Costs of treatment are assumed constant at US$ 400 annually.

Source: Author's calculations.

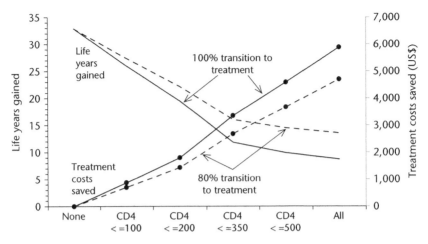

Figure 9.8. Treatment eligibility, coverage, and consequences of one HIV infection averted

Source: Author's calculations.

HIV infections diminishes, while the financial returns increase. Moving from a situation with no treatment access to one in which all people living with HIV receive treatment, the life years lost as a consequence of one HIV infection decline from 33 years to 9 years, while the treatment costs caused by each HIV infection increase from zero to US$5,900 (Figure 9.8).

Since about 2011, however, the emphasis of the global discourse on treatment access has shifted. In many countries, treatment coverage at least for the most pressing medical needs is now high. At the same time, the effects of treatment on HIV transmission, and consequently the potential of treatment as prevention (i.e. treatment beyond those who most urgently require it for medical reasons, to reduce the viral load of patients and the potential to pass on HIV) are now generally recognized, as documented in the Vancouver Consensus (Beyrer et al., 2015a, 2015b). Meanwhile, UNAIDS (2012b) has developed a new vision of 'ending AIDS', placing treatment as prevention at the centre of efforts to eliminate AIDS as a significant public health threat.[40] Under this vision, expanded treatment is considered the most potent instrument to reduce the number of new HIV infections—achieving the '90-90-90' target (90 per cent of people living with HIV know their status, 90 per cent of these receive treatment, and 90 per cent of the latter are virally suppressed) would enable a reduction in the number of new HIV infections to 500,000 globally by 2020.[41]

Treatment as prevention, however, is a fairly expensive instrument for HIV prevention, raising the possibility of a conflict between the objectives of emphasizing efficiency gains and returns to investment (as in the investment framework) and a strategy built around a rapid scaling-up of treatment as prevention. Because policy scenarios motivated by treatment as prevention involve substantial start-up costs, as a large number of people become newly eligible for and are placed on treatment, they also pose challenges for the financial sustainability of the HIV/AIDS strategy (unless donors and national governments are convinced that the projected health gains and eventual financial savings from reduced HIV incidence justify the initial increase in costs).

The principle of treatment as prevention has long been recognized in the prevention of *mother-to-child transmission*. In the absence of prevention, the rate of mother-to-child transmission is estimated at 15 to 30 per cent during pregnancy or at birth, and an additional 15 per cent subsequently if the mother is breastfeeding (de Cock et al., 2000). In the most developed countries, antiretroviral therapy had been used for prevention of mother-to-child transmission from the early 1990s, and was shown to reduce the rate of mother-to-child transmission to 4–6 per cent (and further down, as treatment options improved). In contrast, the short-course treatment regimens (administered just before and after birth) predominantly used in developing countries at the time (though not widely available) reduced HIV transmission at birth by about one-half (Mofenson and McIntyre, 2000; see also discussion of the impacts of global response to HIV/AIDS in Chapter 6).

With increased availability of antiretroviral treatment in general, the prevention of mother-to-child transmission has also become more comprehensive. For example, the WHO 2010 guidelines proposed two alternative drug regimens initiated in week 14 of the pregnancy, and continuing until after breastfeeding, and the 2013 guidelines recommend (under certain circumstances) that 'all pregnant and breastfeeding women with HIV should initiate ART as lifelong treatment'.[42] Recent empirical evidence suggests that these approaches can reduce HIV incidence at birth to around 1 per cent (NIAID, 2014), and that antiretroviral treatment is also effective in reducing HIV transmission during the breastfeeding period.[43]

With regard to *sexual transmission of HIV*, the effectiveness of treatment as prevention has been documented in several studies observing sero-discordant couples (of which one partner is HIV-positive, the other is not) over time. For example, Bunnell et al. (2006) report findings from a 'home-based ART program that included prevention counselling, voluntary counseling and testing (VCT) for cohabitating partners and condom provision'. Risky sexual behaviour in the sample declined by 70 per cent, but the bulk of the decline in HIV incidence from 45.7 to 0.9 per 1000 person years can be attributed to anti-retroviral treatment. In a study based on 3,400 sero-discordant couples from seven African countries (Donnell et al., 2010), ART was associated with a decline in the risk of HIV transmission of 92 per cent.

Observational studies such as the ones described suffer from at least two sources of bias. First, ART provision is generally correlated with some other services (if it is part of a bundle of care and prevention services, as described in the study by Bunnell et al. (2006), or if access to ART is correlated with some other services) or characteristics of the study subjects. Second, HIV transmission may not necessarily occur between discordant couples, but could involve third parties. Both these issues were addressed in the HPTN 052 trial (Cohen et al., 2011).[44] In this trial, 1,763 sero-discordant couples were enrolled and randomly assigned into groups where the HIV-positive individual received treatment either immediately ('early treatment') or following the onset of HIV-related symptoms ('delayed treatment'). To establish whether HIV infections were linked (i.e. derived from the HIV-positive partner of the couple) or involved a third party, HIV gene sequences for the relevant couples were compared. The trial recorded 35 HIV infections in the 'delayed treatment' group (annual incidence: 2.2 per cent), and 4 HIV infections in the 'early treatment' group (annual incidence: 0.3 per cent). Of these, 27 transmissions occurred in the 'delayed treatment' group (annual incidence: 1.7 per cent), and 1 HIV infection in the 'early treatment' group (annual incidence: 0.1 per cent) were linked—implying a reduction in HIV transmission by 96 per cent.

An alternative to treatment as prevention is the use of drugs for prophylaxis. This practice is long-established in the prevention of mother-to-child transmission (providing nevirapine to infants during the breastfeeding period) and as 'post-exposure prophylaxis', that is, providing a short course of drugs following an exposure to HIV (e.g. exposure to blood by health care professionals, unprotected sexual exposure, injecting drug use, and sexual assault).[45]

Pre-exposure prophylaxis—providing antiretroviral drugs to people not infected with HIV regularly and in the absence of a specific risk event—is attractive if it is effective in reducing HIV acquisition, and if the underlying risk of HIV infection is high (among most-at-risk populations or in countries with high HIV incidence overall). Pre-exposure prophylaxis has been shown to be effective in a sample of men who have sex with men with high intensity of sexual activity and among injecting drug users (reducing HIV incidence by 44 per cent and 49 per cent respectively).[46] The evidence on the effectiveness of pre-exposure prophylaxis in the general population is uneven. In three trial studies, pre-exposure prophylaxis reduced HIV incidence substantially, by between around 70 per cent for men and women in a study with samples from Kenya and Uganda (Baeten et al., 2012), and 60 per cent for a sample of men and women from Botswana (Thigpen et al., 2012), and by 39 per cent for women applying a antiretroviral vaginal gel in South Africa (Abdool Karim et al., 2010). However, two other studies did not show any effect (Van Damme et al., 2012, and Marazzo et al., 2015), a result attributed to low adherence.

The empirical evidence on the effectiveness of treatment as prevention has opened a road towards the elimination of AIDS, and lies at the heart of UNAIDS's drive towards 'ending AIDS'. This policy shift has motivated, and been reinforced, by a number of studies assessing the potential of expanding treatment access—beyond those who need it urgently for medical reasons—as a means to bringing down HIV incidence and controlling the epidemic. Also, some of these studies address the *cost*-effectiveness of treatment as prevention—because treatment is expensive, a scaling-up scenario is associated with large upfront costs, but these might eventually (and, depending on the discount rate, overall) be offset by financial savings or wider economic gains associated with reduced HIV incidence.

In interpreting such policy studies, it is important to keep in mind potential challenges which are not always captured in quantitative scaling-up scenarios. First, attaining high coverage rates of treatment overall (for all or most people living with HIV, even before the symptoms of AIDS become apparent) requires much expanded testing efforts, efficient referral into treatment, and high rates of retention.[47] In contrast, UNAIDS (2014c) estimated that less than half (45 per cent) the people living with HIV in sub-Saharan Africa know their HIV status (and about 75 per cent outside sub-Saharan Africa).[48] Avalos and Jefferis (2015) observe that HIV testing rates barely changed in Botswana (one of the leading countries in extending access to treatment) between 2008 and 2013—a period of steep expansion of access to treatment—and that 'HIV positive individuals continue to present late at health care facilities only after they have become ill' (median CD4 count at treatment initiation was 240 in 2014, well below the eligibility threshold of 350). For treatment to be effective as prevention (and otherwise), it also needs to be successful in terms of reducing viral load. In this regard, the available evidence is weak—in recent surveys, 76 per cent and 85 per cent of people receiving treatment were virally suppressed in Kenya and Swaziland, respectively.[49]

Building on the emerging empirical evidence on the effectiveness of treatment as prevention, Granich et al. (2009), in an exploratory analysis of potential population-level impacts, demonstrated that an expansive 'test-and-treat' strategy (testing *each* adult once a year, initiating treatment for *everyone* who tests HIV-positive), combined with some other HIV prevention measures, could reduce HIV incidence in a generalized epidemic (the model was calibrated based on South African data) from an initial 1.4 per cent to 0.1 per cent in about 10 years. A meta-modelling-analysis based on twelve models calibrated for South African data (Eaton et al., 2012) estimated that a scaling-up of treatment resembling the one under the actual HIV programme would result in a reduction in HIV incidence by between one-third and one-half over 8 years, and by between one-third and three-quarters by 2050.[50] For an expansive 'test-and-treat' scenario, with 95 per cent of adults receiving treatment, four of nine models predicted a decline in HIV incidence of approximately 90 per cent by 2050. On the policy side, the relevance of antiretroviral treatment in controlling HIV incidence is illustrated in the recent HIV investment case for Uganda, where the envisaged expansion of treatment alone would account for almost 60 per cent of the decline in HIV incidence projected under the preferred policy scenario in 2014–2025 (Uganda AIDS Commission, 2014).

Treatment is not only considered one of the most *effective* means of HIV prevention, it is also a fairly *expensive* HIV prevention intervention.[51] With regard to the design of HIV policies, this raises three questions (in addition to the questions on effectiveness discussed earlier). (1) What is the cost-effectiveness of treatment as prevention, especially at high CD4 counts where the impact on survival is much diminished so that HIV prevention is the primary motive for extending access to treatment? (2) What is the contribution of a scaling-up of treatment as prevention for the costs of an HIV/AIDS programme over the coming years, and what are the implications for financing? (3) To what extent are initial cost increases offset by later cost savings owing to reduced HIV incidence? Could 'treatment as prevention'—while raising the costs of the HIV/AIDS response in the short term—make a contribution towards financial sustainability?

The analysis of the cost-effectiveness of treatment as prevention poses some challenges which are similar to those encountered with regard to male circumcision. While male circumcision is a one-off intervention that has a lifetime effect, the decision to place a person on treatment is a *de facto* lifetime commitment—the effects of both interventions therefore unfold over long periods, and estimated effects could be sensitive to the time horizon applied in the analysis. However, treatment as prevention incurs a *recurrent* cost, which typically is higher annually than the one-off cost of performing a male circumcision. Methodologically, the two interventions differ as treatment as prevention is an intervention preventing recipients of treatment from passing on HIV, whereas male circumcision is an intervention that prevents (male only) individuals from acquiring HIV.

The effectiveness of treatment as prevention is illustrated in Figure 9.9, showing the number of secondary (adult) HIV infections caused by one primary infection, for different treatment eligibility criteria. To obtain such estimates, estimates of the probability that an individual passes on HIV, possibly differentiated by CD4 count, are required. For example, Donnell et al. (2010), one of the studies of HIV transmission among sero-discordant couples, estimate that the annual probability that an HIV-positive individual passes on HIV in South Africa is 8 per cent (CD4 count below 200), 3 per cent (CD4 count between 200 and 350), and 2 per cent (CD4 count above 350) for individuals not receiving treatment, and 0.4 per cent for individuals receiving treatment. The underlying sample, however, appears not to be representative

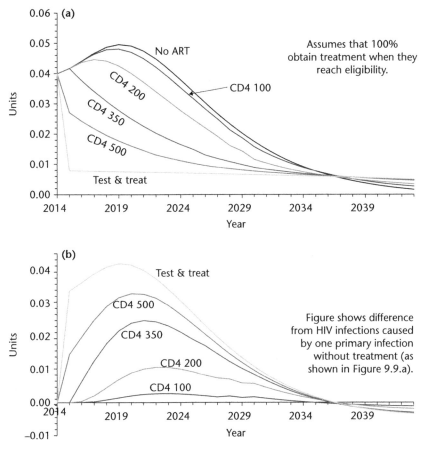

Figure 9.9. HIV transmission with different treatment eligibility criteria

Source: Author's calculations.

(a). HIV infections caused by one primary infection (units)

(b). HIV infections averted at higher treatment eligibility (units)

of the population—with these transmission rates, the average annual rate of transmission from people living with HIV in South Africa and not receiving treatment would be close to 3 per cent, whereas the 'Spectrum' file underlying the latest epidemiological estimates by UNAIDS for South Africa (UNAIDS, 2015a) suggests a rate of about 7 per cent.[52] For this reason, the estimates in Figure 9.9 apply double the transmission rates reported by Donnell et al. (2010). Under these assumptions, a person living with HIV would on average transmit HIV to 0.73 individuals without ART, but this rate declines to 0.47 with treatment eligibility at a CD4 count of 350, and 0.23 when all people living with HIV receive treatment irrespective of CD4 count.[53]

The analyses of the cost-effectiveness of antiretroviral therapy in terms of life years gained (Figure 9.8) and in terms of HIV infections averted (Figure 9.9) provides the ingredients for assessing the cost-effectiveness of antiretroviral therapy overall, including health gains and financial savings owing to HIV infections averted (Table 9.6).[54] The HIV infections averted result in additional life years gained and cost savings which could at least partly offset the costs of treatment. For example, if treatment eligibility is at a CD4 count of 500, HIV transmission is reduced by 0.4 per person living with HIV (compared to a setting with no treatment), and this decline in HIV incidence in turn adds 4.0 life years gained to the health outcomes,[55] and generates a financial saving of US$1,155 (Table 9.6).

One lesson from the results presented in Figure 9.9 and Table 9.6 is that treatment as prevention is expensive. The direct costs of preventing one HIV infection come out at over US$11,000 when treatment eligibility is extended above a CD4 count of 350. Taking into account the financial savings owing to reduced HIV incidence, and a delay in end-of-life care, does not change this picture fundamentally—the costs come out at around US$7,500. The cost-effectiveness in terms of life years saved of expanding treatment beyond a CD4 count of 350 is much diminished compared to the treatment effects at lower CD4 counts. The marginal costs per life year gained of moving to eligibility at a CD4 count of 500 (US$317) or providing treatment to all (US$478) are more than three times higher than the average costs per life year gained with eligibility at a CD4 count of 350. Savings in treatment costs from reduced HIV incidence offset a quarter of the costs of treatment when treatment is extended to all, but a lower share when treatment eligibility is more restricted. Savings from delays in end-of-life care play a role with treatment eligibility at low CD4 counts, but virtually no role (because of diminished gains in life expectancy and discounting) for treatment above a CD4 count of 500.

In contrast to the analysis above, applying a life-cycle approach, most attempts to assess the cost-effectiveness of treatment as prevention are based on national or global scaling up scenarios, comparing the costs and outcomes of a policy of expanding access to treatment, by CD4 count or towards specific population groups, with a baseline scenario characterized by unchanged eligibility or treatment coverage.[56] In general, these scenario-based studies provide less precise estimates of the cost-effectiveness of a specific HIV/AIDS intervention (because of the 'cut-off' problem, and as cost-effectiveness ratios are based on inputs and outcomes averaged over long periods, see the discussion in Chapter 8). Such policy studies, however, are critical to understanding the costs and consequences of alternative policies over time, and study the effects of and interactions between alternative interventions, including some targeting of different population groups, in a fully developed epidemiological and costing framework.

Substantial policy studies focusing on a scaling-up of treatment include a semi-official study of the consequences of implementing the 2013 WHO

Table 9.6. Treatment eligibility and the effectiveness and cost-effectiveness of treatment

	Life years gained (years)	Treatment costs (US$)	Costs per life year gained (US$)	HIV infections averted (units)	Costs per HIV infection averted (US$)	Owing to reduced HIV infections — Life years gained (years)	Owing to reduced HIV infections — Treatment costs (US$)	Costs of end-of-life care (US$)	Total costs (US$)	Total life years gained (years)	Total costs per life year gained (US$)	Total costs per HIV infection averted (US$)
Average cost-effectiveness												
ART from CD4 count of 100	6.9	874	127	0.063	13,933	1.63	-34	-219	621	8.5	73	9,904
ARTfrom CD4 count of 200	13.4	1,796	134	0.181	9,912	3.54	-217	-355	1,225	16.9	72	6,759
ART from CD4 count of 350	21.1	3,354	159	0.303	11,088	3.58	-667	-455	2,232	24.6	91	7,377
ART from CD4 count of 500	23.0	4,588	200	0.399	11,485	3.96	-1,155	-472	2,961	26.9	110	7,412
ART at all CD4 counts	24.2	5,883	244	0.501	11,749	4.37	-1,680	-482	3,721	28.5	130	7,431
Marginal cost-effectiveness												
ART from CD4 count of 100	6.9	874	127	0.063	13,933	1.63	-34	-219	621	8.5	73	9,904
ART from CD4 count of 200	6.5	922	142	0.118	7,783	1.90	-183	-136	603	8.4	72	5,093
ART from CD4 count of 350	7.7	1,558	203	0.121	12,844	0.04	-451	-100	1,007	7.7	130	8,301
ART from CD4 count of 500	1.9	1,234	642	0.097	12,725	0.38	-487	-17	729	2.3	317	7,522
ART at all CD4 counts	1.2	1,295	1,102	0.101	12,789	0.42	-525	-10	760	1.6	478	7,505

Note: Life expectancy is average remaining life expectancy from time of infection. Estimates assume that an individual initiates treatment with a probability of 100 per cent once he or she reach the eligibility threshold. More realistic scenarios can be obtained as a weighted average of the results presented in the rows of the table. Treatment costs are assumed constant at US$400 annually, and end-of-life care costs US$1,000. Total costs are treatment costs, minus savings in treatment costs from reduced HIV incidence, minus change in end-of-life care. All cost estimates apply a discount rate of 5 per cent.

Source: Author's calculations.

recommendations on eligibility for antiretroviral therapy on the global scale (Stover et al., 2014), a meta-study of the cost-effectiveness of treatment across several models and countries (Eaton et al., 2014), and a study by Granich et al. (2012) which is widely used in advocacy for treatment as prevention. These are complemented by a number of studies looking more specifically at the relative effectiveness of treatment as prevention, for example compared to pre-exposure prophylaxis (Cremin et al., 2013) or male circumcision (Bärnighausen et al., 2012a) or at the targeting of treatment as prevention (and of other interventions) across population groups (Delva et al., 2012) or regionally according to the scale and local drivers of HIV/AIDS (Anderson et al., 2014).

According to Stover et al. (2014), the WHO 2013 ART guidelines increased the number of people eligible for treatment in 2013 from 17.6 million to 28.6 million, and most of this increase is attributable to the increased eligibility threshold (CD4 count at 500 rather than 350, accounting for 6.4 million) and extending treatment to HIV-positive partners in sero-discordant couples irrespective of CD4 count (2.5 million). They estimate that scaling up treatment according to the new guidelines would result in a cost of US$29 billion between 2013 and 2025, but reduce the number of new HIV infections in this period by 3.1 million, or 17 per cent relative to a scenario where eligibility remains at a CD4 count of 350—at a cost of about US$9,600 per HIV infection averted.[57]

Eaton et al. (2014)—a follow-up to the 2012 paper discussed earlier in this section—summarize the findings on cost-effectiveness from several models across four countries (South Africa, Zambia, India, and Vietnam). No clear ranking in terms of cost-effectiveness between different strategies (earlier eligibility, expanded coverage) emerges. Usefully, they provide estimates for different time horizons, illustrating the crucial role of time frames in light of the complex dynamics of HIV/AIDS—moving from a time horizon of 5 years to 10 years, the costs per (disability adjusted) life year gained decline (i.e. improve) by about half, and they decline by half once again if the time horizon is extended from 10 years to 20 years. Importantly, the models surveyed by Eaton and others suggest that treatment as prevention is similarly effective in India and Vietnam, at much lower levels of HIV prevalence than in South Africa and Zambia—as treatment averts HIV infections by preventing individuals already living with HIV from passing on HIV, its effectiveness is only indirectly linked to the scale of HIV across the population.

The paper by Granich et al. (2012), calibrated on South African data, is interesting not only because it projects that expanding access to ART would result in large financial *savings* over time and that annual savings already exceed the additional costs of treatment after 2 years; it is also important because of its policy relevance, as it is frequently headlined by UNAIDS as showing that 'HIV treatment saves money' (UNAIDS, 2014c). The findings by Granich et al. (2012) are puzzling because the financial savings occur while the number of people receiving treatment increases. The reason for these findings appears to be that Granich and others assume a high cost of care of about US $700 for HIV-positive individuals *not* receiving treatment—exceeding the annual costs of first-line treatment. This assumption, however, appears to be based on a misreading of the empirical evidence. One of their sources (Harling and Wood, 2007) reports a healthcare cost per patient preceding treatment of US$400, but most of these individuals were in a very poor state of health and initiated treatment at an advanced stage of the disease.[58] Such costs cannot be generalized to all people living with HIV but not receiving treatment,[59] many of whom do not know their HIV status and do not experience any symptoms. The savings estimated by Granich and others (2012) therefore appear to be on the high side.

While treatment, in empirical studies and policy simulations, has been shown to be effective in preventing new HIV infections, it is also fairly expensive. This raises the question of how to utilize the potential of treatment, in combination with other interventions, in a cost-effective manner. These issues are discussed more generally in Chapter 10, but some studies specifically advance the understanding of treatment as prevention in relation to a small set of alternative or complementary strategies.

Cremin et al. (2013) study the effectiveness of treatment as prevention and of pre-exposure prophylaxis in a hyperepidemic setting (calibrated to the South African province KwaZulu-Natal, with an estimated HIV *incidence* rate of 2.5 per cent annually, one of the highest anywhere). The location is significant because unlike treatment as prevention, the effectiveness of which does not systematically depend on HIV prevalence, pre-exposure prophylaxis is particularly attractive in an environment with a high risk of *acquiring* HIV. However, according to the estimates by Cremin et al. (2013),[60] scaling-up treatment alone (at a cost of about US$6,000 per HIV infection averted) is much more cost-effective than providing pre-exposure prophylaxis across the population (or to the 15–24 year age group), at a cost of about US$20,000 per HIV infection averted. Moreover, the cost-effectiveness of pre-exposure declines as treatment is scaled up, and—when treatment coverage reaches 80 per cent of the population, the costs of averting an additional HIV infection by pre-exposure prophylaxis rise to around US$40,000. In consequence, pre-exposure prophylaxis for the general population is unlikely to be part of a cost-effective HIV prevention policy in KwaZulu-Natal (or anywhere else, considering that HIV incidence in KwaZulu-Natal is among the highest anywhere, and therefore the effectiveness of pre-exposure prophylaxis is unusually high).[61]

Bärnighausen et al. (2012a) address the cost-effectiveness of three policies in reducing HIV incidence and averting deaths in a model calibrated to South

African data for 2011–2020—expanding coverage of treatment for those with a CD4 count below 350 ('ART'), extending access to treatment to those with a CD4 count above 350 ('TasP'), and male circumcision ('MC'). With regard to HIV incidence, their results show that 'MC' is by far the most cost-effective intervention (between US$1,100 and US$1,900 per HIV infection averted, depending on the state of 'ART' and 'TasP'), followed by 'ART' (between US $6,300 and US$9,300) and 'TasP' (between US$11,900 and US$15,600). For deaths averted, 'ART' is the most effective intervention (between US$5,300 and US$7,200), followed by 'MC' (between US$4,700 and US$11,900), and 'TasP' (between US$11,600 and US$17,900).[62] A cost-effective HIV prevention policy based on these three tools would therefore focus on 'MC', followed by expanding coverage of ART, and only then allocate resources to 'TasP'.

Conclusions and Outlook

This chapter has developed elements of a forward-looking analysis of the effectiveness and cost-effectiveness of HIV/AIDS interventions—contributing to the goal of sharpening tools to identify the most effective and cost-effective HIV/AIDS strategies. It contrasts with the analysis in Chapter 8, addressing the effects and financial consequences of alternative HIV/AIDS strategies overall, by applying similar analytical tools to the analysis of the most important HIV prevention interventions. (There was no intention to provide an analysis of the cost-effectiveness of the complete range of HIV prevention interventions, the emphasis is on developing the methodology by applying it to certain well-researched examples.)

Two general findings emerge from the analysis presented or summarized in this chapter—(1) the importance of understanding the *dynamics* of the epidemic, across the population and over time, in understanding the effectiveness of HIV prevention interventions, and (2) the increasing relevance of HIV prevention interventions as long-term financial investments. Because the health consequences of new HIV infections are shrinking, but the financial consequences become more drawn-out (both a consequence of increased eligibility and coverage of treatment), indicators of cost-effectiveness commonly used in health economics become blunt, and the financial commitments implied by alternative interventions or strategies become more relevant.

The next chapter brings together the programme-level perspective from the previous chapter and the intervention-specific approach developed in the present chapter in a discussion of identifying optimal HIV/AIDS strategies.

10

Optimal HIV/AIDS Spending Allocations

HIV prevention policies have relied on a range of measures—for example targeting specific groups at high risk alongside measures addressing the entire population, combining biomedical interventions with behavioural interventions aimed at reducing the HIV transmission directly or by increasing the demand for HIV prevention services, and applying interventions addressing specific modes of transmission. Consequently, the planning and optimal design of an HIV/AIDS response involves selecting from and applying concurrently a wide set of HIV/AIDS interventions, taking into account their relative effectiveness and cost-effectiveness across the population and with regard to specific population groups, and their interdependencies. While the content of HIV prevention policies has evolved (e.g. as the potential of biomedical interventions like male circumcision and treatment as prevention became fully recognized), this principle of 'combination prevention' has remained relevant (discussed in the chapter's first section).

Most commonly, the design of an HIV/AIDS policy involves comparison between alternative scenarios, for example a 'baseline scenario' and an expanded national HIV/AIDS programme. While such scenarios carry information regarding the 'returns to investment' of the HIV/AIDS response overall, they are blunt tools with regard to identifying *optimal* strategies. However, such tools have also been used analytically, comparing the consequences of scaling up specific interventions and drawing lessons for the design of the HIV/AIDS programme. The second section discusses some recent applications, and shows how the forward-looking approach developed elsewhere in this book adds to the capabilities of such analyses.

In spite of the methodological challenges—the heterogeneity of sexual behaviour, the long time frames characterizing the epidemic, the complexity of HIV/AIDS programmes in terms of the number of interventions and their interdependencies, and the absence of a well-defined objective—a number of studies have applied some formal optimization routines in identifying 'optimal' HIV/AIDS strategies. The third section of the chapter reviews recent and current efforts applying explicit optimization techniques.

Combination HIV Prevention

Although elements of 'combination prevention' have been applied earlier, the first comprehensive statements date back to 2003 and 2004. The Global HIV Prevention Working Group (2003) argued that 'there is no single solution—no magic bullet—to prevent the spread of HIV. Instead, interventions must be used in combination to target the many diverse populations affected by HIV, and the various routes of HIV transmission', and emphasized the need to tailor 'combination prevention strategies to address national and local needs'.[1] This approach was endorsed in the *2004 Report on the Global HIV/AIDS Epidemic* (UNAIDS, 2004) which emphasized the 'ABCs of combination prevention', where 'A' stood for abstinence ('not engaging in sexual intercourse or delaying sexual initiation'), 'B' for 'being safer'—by being faithful to one's partner or reducing the number of sexual partners—and 'C' for 'correct and consistent condom use'. At the same time, UNAIDS (2004) recognized that these interventions would need to be refined in order to 'to fit the specific risk factors and vulnerabilities that characterized the epidemic in each country'.

The most significant change in the global response to HIV/AIDS over the following years was the steep increase in access to treatment across low- and middle-income countries (Chapter 5), and a realization that progress in bringing down HIV incidence had been modest (UNAIDS, 2007). The increasing coverage of treatment introduced a new element to the discourse on HIV prevention policies—expanding HIV prevention services as a contributor to the sustainability of the advances in antiretroviral therapy, by reducing the need for treatment and other services. (At that time, antiretroviral therapy was already used in the prevention of mother-to-child transmission of HIV, but its use in preventing the sexual transmission of HIV had not been generally recognized.) The effectiveness of male circumcision had become generally recognized (see Chapter 8), but male circumcision had not been integrated into HIV/AIDS services.

One important contribution in developing the 'combination prevention' approach was the 2007 'Practical Guidelines for Intensifying HIV Prevention' (UNAIDS, 2007), which spelled out the 'Know Your Epidemic/Know Your Response' approach—the principle to ground the HIV/AIDS response in a thorough understanding of the epidemic dynamics and social context, and distinguishing stylized epidemic scenarios (low-level, concentrated, generalized, and hyperepidemic scenarios) which would call for different approaches to HIV prevention. This approach was complemented by the development of modes-of-transmission analyses,[2] providing estimates of 'where the next 1000 infections will occur' (Hankins and de Zalduondo, 2010).[3]

Meanwhile, the content of 'combination prevention' changed, reflecting the need for a more comprehensive framework to capture the evolving practice of HIV services, and by 2009 it was taken to describe 'rights-based, evidence-informed, and community-owned programmes that use a mix of biomedical, behavioural, and structural interventions, prioritized to meet the current HIV prevention needs of particular individuals and communities, so as to have the greatest sustained impact on reducing new infections' (UNAIDS, 2010b).

The UNAIDS investment framework, introduced in 2011 (Schwartländer et al., 2011), reframed 'combination prevention' in three directions. First, it placed great emphasis on 'returns to investment'. Following a period in which global spending on HIV/AIDS increased and access to HIV/AIDS services improved steeply, there was a perception that often there was a mismatch between 'investments' (previously called 'spending') and relevant needs. One way in which the greater emphasis on returns to investment is realized is an expansion of the time horizon of the analysis, for example to 10 years in the paper introducing the investment framework. This reflects that the effects of HIV prevention interventions are dynamic and tend to increase over time (see Chapter 9), and that health outcomes like AIDS deaths follow HIV infections only with a considerable lag—to show 'returns to investment' in terms of such health outcomes, a fairly long time horizon is therefore required.[4] The 'investment framework' thus contrasts with the earlier 'know your epidemic' approach which focuses on the current distribution of HIV infections.

Second, the investment framework is centred around a range of 'basic programme activities'—behavioural and biomedical interventions with a proven impact in terms of stopping new HIV infections and keeping people alive—which include interventions targeting 'key populations at higher risk', prevention of mother-to-child transmission, behaviour change programmes, condom promotion and distribution, male circumcision, and treatment, care and support for people living with HIV. These are complemented by a range of 'critical enablers'—interventions and activities geared towards 'overcoming barriers to the adoption of evidence-based HIV policies and the factors that adversely affect HIV programmes by distorting their priorities, including social stigma, poor health literacy and a punitive legal environment' (UNAIDS, 2011).[5] It thus replaces the functional distinction of behavioural, biomedical, and structural interventions associated with combination prevention with a framework emphasizing effectiveness and contribution to programme objectives.

Third, the 'investment framework' widens the perspective on the 'returns to investment', placing more emphasis on the financial returns, that is, the 'savings incurred from avoidance of treatment costs, and pointing out that substantial economic gains will result as people stay healthy and productive' (Schwartländer et al. (2011), see also the discussion of economic returns in Chapter 8).

At the same time, the 'investment framework' is also a response to a perceived tightening in donor financing and demands for greater accountability, and has been embraced by major donors like the Global Fund, which demands that country applicants 'employ the HIV strategic investment approach in the development of Global Fund concept notes' (Global Fund, 2014a).

The emerging evidence on the effectiveness of certain biomedical interventions, notably male circumcision and treatment as prevention, has fuelled optimism that 'scientific research has identified the methods to develop combination programmes that could control the HIV pandemic' (Jones et al., 2014) and has raised the potential of 'Ending AIDS' (as a significant public health challenge).[6] This new agenda of 'Ending AIDS' carries forward the principles of 'combination prevention' and of building on a detailed knowledge of the local HIV epidemic.

Treatment as prevention (including a range of interventions geared at improving knowledge of HIV status, uptake of treatment, and retention on treatment) is seen as a necessary but not sufficient ingredient to achieving a steep reduction in HIV incidence (Cremin et al., 2013; Eaton et al., 2012), and it has featured prominently in national HIV/AIDS programmes developed over the last few years. In much the same way as described earlier, 'treatment as prevention' is then complemented by a combination of interventions in consideration of the scale of the epidemic, the drivers of the epidemic and the presence of certain risk factors, and the cultural context. However, with 'treatment as prevention' reducing the risk that an individual living with HIV passes it on, the optimal combination of other HIV prevention interventions may change, because of affinities with treatment as prevention (interventions enhancing uptake and adherence) or because a scaling-up of treatment as prevention reduces the effectiveness of other HIV prevention interventions (but not necessarily the cost-effectiveness, as with early initiation of treatment each HIV infection averted saves more money).

Assessing the Optimality of the HIV/AIDS Response 'Bottom-up'

The process of developing a national HIV/AIDS strategy generally involves comparisons between the costs and consequences of alternative strategies, most commonly casting an envisaged strategy against a baseline scenario, and describing cost-effectiveness in terms of the change in health outcomes (e.g. the number of HIV infections averted) and the increase in costs. Such programme-level comparisons, however, carry only very indirect information about the effectiveness of spending allocations within a programme, and the positive effect of some highly efficient interventions included in a scaling-up scenario could mask the lack of contributions from some ineffective interventions.

Comparing different scenarios, though, is a useful and simple tool to assess the potential contributions of specific HIV/AIDS interventions. For example, many of the studies on the effectiveness of male circumcision or treatment as prevention surveyed in Chapter 9 were using this technique. Less commonly, the technique has been used in the development of new HIV/AIDS programmes or of HIV investment cases—performing diagnostic scenarios across a range of interventions to establish the contributions to programme objectives and the cost-effectiveness of each, and feeding the results back into policy design. This is illustrated below with two examples. The recent investment case for Uganda (Uganda AIDS Commission, 2014) applies *diagnostic* scenarios in identifying cost-effective policies. A recent analysis on the HIV/AIDS programme of KwaZulu-Natal (Kripke et al., 2013), for which the work files have been made available by the authors,[7] is used to develop the technique more thoroughly and to connect to the discussion of the cost-effectiveness of alternative HIV/AIDS programmes in Chapter 8.

The Uganda investment case builds on a large number of diagnostic scenarios, analysing the consequences of scaling up one intervention at a time. This step is illustrated in Figure 10.1 for some key interventions. Together with expanded condom coverage, ART is the intervention with the highest potential for bringing down HIV incidence, followed by 'safe medical circumcision', HIV testing and counselling, prevention of mother-to-child transmission

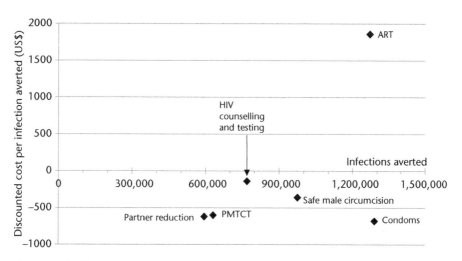

Figure 10.1. Uganda: Impact and costs of specific HIV interventions, 2014–2025
Source: Uganda AIDS Commission (2014).

Table 10.1. Uganda: Coverage of HIV/AIDS interventions under five scenarios, 2017

		Baseline	Medium	High	Test and treat	Feasible max.
Coverage in 2017 (%)	ART	43	70	90	90	80
	HIV counselling and testing	25	35	50	50	50
	Condoms	35	60	60	60	75
	Save male circumcision	30	60	60	60	80
	PMTCT	70	95	95	95	95
	Partner reduction	0	9	9	9	24
Treatment eligibility	ART at CD4	<500	<500	<500	All	<500
	Test and treat	PW HIV/TB SDC	PW HIV/TB SDC	PW HIV/TB SDC	All	PW HIV/TB SDC MARPs
	ART for Children	<15 years old	<15 years old	<15 years old	<15 years old	<15 years old

Notes: PW: Pregnant Women, HIV/TB: co-infected with HIV and TB, SDC: sero-discordant couples, MARPs: most-at-risk populations.
Source: Uganda AIDS Commission (2014).

(PMTCT), and reducing the number of sexual partners. With the exception of ART (which of course also directly contributes to reduced AIDS-related mortality), all other HIV prevention interventions come out as cost-saving, that is, the savings in terms of the costs of treatment and other HIV/AIDS services avoided as a consequence of reduced HIV incidence more than offset the costs of the HIV prevention intervention.

Based on such findings, the evaluation contained in the Uganda investment case focuses on five scenarios (Table 10.1)—a 'baseline', a 'medium' scenario that envisaged scaled-up HIV interventions across the board, a 'high' and a 'test and treat' scenario with successively increased treatment eligibility and coverage, and a 'feasible maximum' scenario with treatment coverage between the medium scenario and the high scenario,[8] but increased coverage of condoms and safe medical circumcision, and a steeper reduction in the number of sexual partners than envisaged in any of the other scenarios.

For these five scenarios, the impacts, costs, and cost-effectiveness are summarized in Table 10.2. The 'medium', 'high', and 'test and treat' scenarios successively reduce the number of HIV infections over the period 2014–2025 from 2.8 million in the baseline scenario to 836,000, and the number of AIDS-related deaths from 990,000 (baseline) to 271,000, while the overall costs increase from US$6.4 billion in the baseline scenario to US$10.4 billion. The 'feasible maximum' scenario achieves the steepest reduction in HIV incidence in any of the scenarios, although the number of deaths is higher than in the 'high' and 'test and treat' scenarios, and comes at a cost (US$8.7 billion) very close to the 'medium' scenario.

Table 10.2. Uganda: Cost-effectiveness of alternative HIV/AIDS policies

	HIV infections	Deaths	Costs (US$ mn)	Average costs[a]		Incremental costs[a]	
				Per HIV infection averted	Per AIDS death averted	Per HIV infection averted	Per AIDS death averted
Base	2,800,000	990,000	6,360				
Medium	1,250,000	512,000	8,460	1,355	4,393	1,355	4,393
High	865,000	300,000	10,160	1,964	5,507	4,416	8,019
Test and treat	836,000	271,000	10,400	2,057	5,619	8,276	8,276
Feasible maximum	642,000	417,000	8,700	1,084	4,084	395	2,526

Notes: The costs per HIV infection averted and deaths averted shown in the Uganda IC are somewhat higher than those shown here, probably because the former are based on discounted health outcomes (not shown), whereas they are calculated from the numbers in the table here.

[a] Average costs are calculated relative to the baseline scenario. Incremental costs are calculated relative to the preceding scenario, except for 'Feasible maximum' where they are calculated relative to 'Medium', because 'Max feasible' represents a scaling-up of a set of interventions relative to 'Medium', but a different profile of interventions compared to 'High' and 'Test and treat'. See Table 10.1 for details.

Sources: Uganda AIDS Commission (2014) and author's calculations.

Based on the analysis summarized here, the Uganda AIDS Commission recommended the 'feasible maximum' scenario. This recommendation is by no means a no-brainer, as it involves considerations regarding the overall costs of the programme and a weighing between outcomes like HIV infections averted vs. AIDS deaths averted. Some considerations may have contributed to this outcome:

- A perceived budget constraint. The ' feasible maximum' scenario could be an optimal outcome subject to an expectation that about US$8.7 billion would be available in 2014–2025; the 'high' and 'test and treat' scenarios could not be financed in this case.

- The high costs of deaths averted in the 'high' and 'test and treat' scenario, relative to the 'feasible maximum' scenario. Each additional AIDS death averted in these scenarios costs about US$12,000 (about 20 times GDP per capita), and this calculation does not yet take into account the superior outcomes of the 'feasible maximum' scenario in terms of HIV infections averted.

- The time horizon of 11 years is fairly short for an evaluation of an HIV/AIDS policy (see Chapter 8), and the 'feasible maximum' policy may yield improved benefits if a longer-term perspective is adopted. First, because lower HIV incidence would translate into a lower number of AIDS-related deaths. Second, projections of annual costs (not shown here) suggest that annual costs under the 'feasible maximum' scenario over time decline steeply relative to the other scenarios, as lower HIV incidence gradually translates into lower costs. If a longer time horizon is adopted, the programme costs under the 'feasible maximum' scenario would thus come out relatively lower.

Apart from the role of the time horizon, the discussion of the economic aspects of the decision problem faced by the Government of Uganda does not take into account two relevant aspects of the impacts and costs of alternative HIV/AIDS interventions. First, the cost-effectiveness of specific interventions depends on the HIV/AIDS policies pursued. Scaling up some HIV prevention interventions likely reduces the effectiveness of other HIV prevention interventions—because there are fewer HIV infections left to avert. The contributions of a specific HIV prevention evaluated as part of a scaled-up scenario could therefore come out much lower than under the baseline scenario. Second, HIV infections occurring or averted during the policy period have implications for HIV/AIDS spending which go far beyond this period—the analysis in Chapter 8 shows that only about one-third of spending caused by an HIV infection in 2014 occurs within 11 years (the length of the time horizon in the Uganda investment case).[9] Moreover, because most of the HIV infections averted in Uganda occur later in the policy period rather than in 2014, an even smaller proportion of cost savings is captured on average. The Uganda analysis therefore captures only a small proportion of the financial savings and consequently of the contributions to long-term financial sustainability.

These points are developed further with an example based on an analysis of the 'Provincial Strategic Plan for HIV and AIDS, STI and TB 2012–2016' (PSP) for KwaZulu-Natal (Kripke et al., 2013). Similar to the analysis in Uganda, the study assessed the costs and consequences of scaling up a range of HIV prevention interventions, one at a time, from a baseline scenario, and discussed their respective effectiveness and cost-effectiveness over the period 2012–2025. The present analysis, utilizing the work files graciously supplied by the authors, serves as a point of departure to develop several methodological aspects of analysing the cost-effectiveness of specific HIV/AIDS interventions, and drawing conclusions with regard to programme effectiveness.

- *Cost-effectiveness with regard to different health outcomes*. HIV infections are the most immediate outcome of HIV prevention interventions, but are relevant primarily because of their health consequences. However, the link between HIV infections and health outcomes is also a consequence of HIV policies pursued (treatment access).[10]

- *The role of the time horizon*. Because the impacts of a scaling-up of HIV prevention interventions tend to increase over time, the cost-effectiveness of an evaluation depends on the time horizon, and this point is illustrated by varying the time horizon between 2025 and 2035.

- *Declining returns*. To assess the interactions between the cost-effectiveness of specific interventions, and the relevance of declining returns to investments as the scale of the HIV/AIDS programme expands, the cost-effectiveness of specific interventions is evaluated around both the baseline scenario and the PSP.

- *Commitments*. The expenditures within the policy horizon capture only a small proportion of the cost savings in treatment, which extend over decades. This point is addressed by estimating the full cost savings over the lifetime of patients of HIV infections averted during the policy period.

To bring the earlier analysis (2013, based on 2011 data) in line with current challenges, two changes were made. First, the unit costs for treatment were changed from US$690 to US$320, in line with estimates produced for the HIV/AIDS investment case for South Africa.[11] Second, treatment at a CD4 count of 500 has been added as one of the HIV interventions. Because extending eligibility to and reaching full coverage at a CD4 count of 500 builds on reaching full coverage at a CD4 count of 350, the effect of extending eligibility to a CD4 count of 500 is shown relative to a scenario that already includes treatment at a CD4 count of 350.

Figures 10.2.a and 10.2.b illustrate the consequences of scaling up specific HIV prevention interventions from the baseline scenario.[12] Effectiveness is measured by HIV infections (or, in Figures 10.2.b, 10.2.d, and 10.2.f, deaths averted) over the period of interest. Cost-effectiveness is the change in programme costs associated with the relevant intervention, divided by the impact on the variable of interest. In most cases (Figures 10.2.a–10.2.f) they are calculated as programme-level costs associated with a particular intervention, that is, the costs of an intervention of interest (e.g. condom distribution), plus any resulting changes in costs across the programme, notably lower treatment costs. Typically, the latter offset some of the costs of the intervention; for highly effective HIV prevention interventions, the savings may exceed the direct costs and the intervention is 'cost-saving'. Both HIV infections and costs are discounted at a rate of 5 per cent.

Treatment (eligibility at a CD4 count of 350) stands out as the most effective HIV prevention intervention, but is one of the least cost-effective (181,000 HIV infections averted through 2025, at a unit cost of US$6,600). Expanding treatment eligibility further would prevent an additional 133,000 HIV infections, at a unit cost of US$9,200. Expanding male circumcision averts 100,000 HIV infections, but at a much lower cost of US$1,600 per HIV infection averted.[13] Scaling up other prevention interventions averts between 600 HIV infections (targeting female sex workers, reflecting only a small increase from an already high coverage) and 51,000 HIV infections (community mobilization), at a unit cost that ranges from US$153 for condom provision to US$8,200 (community mobilization).

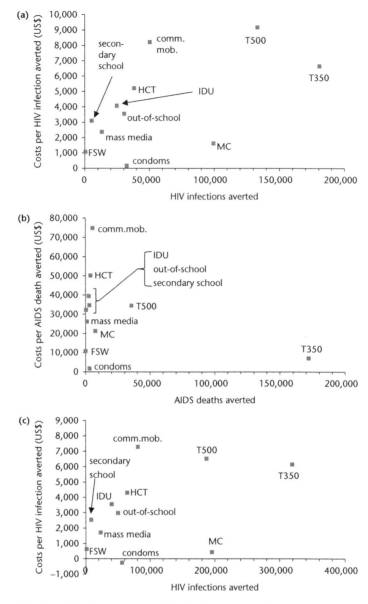

Figure 10.2. Cost-effectiveness of specific HIV prevention interventions

Source: Author's estimates, based on Kripke et al. (2013).

Notes: comm.mob. = Community mobilization, condoms = Condom promotion and distribution, FSW = Female sex worker interventions, HTC = HIV counselling and testing, IDU = Injecting drug user interventions, MC = Medical male circumcision, out-of-school = Prevention among out-of-school youth, secondary school = prevention through secondary schools, T350 = ART at CD4 <350, T500 = ART at CD4 <500.

(a). HIV infections averted through 2025, evaluated from baseline
(b). AIDS deaths averted through 2025, evaluated from baseline
(c). HIV infections averted through 2035, evaluated from baseline
(d). AIDS deaths averted through 2035, evaluated from baseline
(e). HIV infections averted through 2025, evaluated around PSP
(f). AIDS deaths averted through 2025, evaluated around PSP
(g). HIV infections averted through 2025, evaluated from baseline, fully accounting for financial savings from reduced HIV incidence
(h). HIV infections averted through 2025, evaluated around PSP, fully accounting for financial savings from reduced HIV incidence

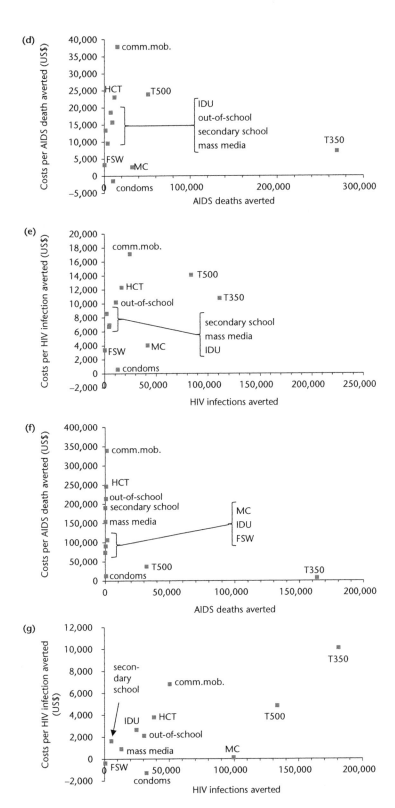

Figure 10.2. Continued

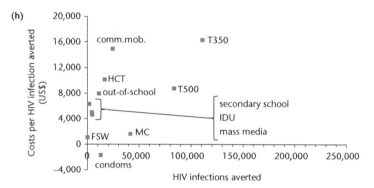

Figure 10.2. Continued

Treatment has a large impact on survival, potentially averting 208,000 deaths by 2025 (Figure 10.2.b).[14] The bulk of this (172,000) is a consequence of attaining full treatment coverage at a CD4 count of 350; extending eligibility to a CD4 count of 500 contributes another 36,000. The effectiveness of other HIV/AIDS interventions in terms of deaths averted is small, as they affect deaths only indirectly through HIV infections averted, and each HIV infection averted between 2010 and 2025 results in only 0.1 to 0.15 deaths averted in that period.

If the time horizon is extended to 2035, the results change in three ways. First, programme-level cost-effectiveness improves across the board as the longer time horizon captures more of the lower treatment costs as a consequence of the decline in HIV incidence. Second, the effects become bigger. Mainly this is a trivial consequence of counting over a longer period. However, it also reflects that the consequences of some interventions grow over time, so that cost-effectiveness improves. This applies especially to male circumcision where the costs per HIV infection averted decline from US$1,600 through 2025 to US$430 through 2035. Third, because the HIV infections averted increasingly feed through to reduced mortality, HIV prevention interventions (other than treatment) come out more effective in averting deaths—the costs per death averted decline by about one-half—but the effects of the HIV/AIDS programme on mortality are still dominated by policy choices on treatment access.

One potentially important factor in assessing the cost-effectiveness of specific interventions and using the information in designing an optimal HIV/AIDS response is the presence of interdependencies in the effectiveness of specific HIV interventions. This factor is relevant here—the effect of scaling up all interventions contained in the PSP (all shown, except measures targeting IDUs, out-of-school youths, and treatment from a CD4 count of 500) from the baseline individually add up to 420,000 by 2025, whereas the combined effect is a reduction in HIV infections of 350,000 only. Moreover, this discrepancy understates the relevance of declining returns to investments in the HIV/AIDS response because it reflects the *average* effect of expanding coverage across a number of interventions. The *marginal* contribution of one intervention to the PSP—scaling up one intervention once the other constituents of the PSP are already in place, leaving fewer HIV infections to be averted—is considerably lower than its effectiveness evaluated at the baseline.

Figures 10.2.e and 10.2.f illustrate this factor, evaluating the contribution of specific interventions around the PSP.[15] For non-treatment interventions, the effectiveness in preventing HIV infections is diminished by about 60 per cent relative to their effect against the baseline scenario (equivalently, the average costs per HIV infection averted increase by a factor of 2.5, from an average of about US$3,400 to US$8,300). For treatment, the impact on HIV incidence is diminished less, by 40 per cent, because treatment is the largest contributor to the effect of the PSP so its effect is diminished less by the scaling-up of other interventions. For programme-level costs, a factor that mitigates some of the decline in effectiveness is an increase in savings from one HIV infection averted. For the programme evaluation through 2025 this plays a modest role—on average, only US$270 (baseline) or US$560 (PSP) of the treatment cost savings owing to reduced HIV incidence occur within this period—but it becomes more relevant if the programme evaluation extends to 2035, with average savings in treatment costs per HIV infection averted of US$600 (baseline) and US$1,400 (PSP).

The determinants of the costs of treatment are more complex. For non-treatment HIV prevention interventions, there are the cost of the intervention and the savings from reduced treatment costs owing to reduced HIV incidence. For treatment, there are two additional factors. First, an increase in treatment eligibility usually means that a large number of people become newly eligible for treatment, a scaling-up scenario with this feature therefore typically involves a steep initial increase in costs. Second, while increased coverage of treatment results in reduced HIV incidence, each HIV infection becomes more expensive—with increased eligibility or coverage, people go on treatment earlier or are more likely to attain treatment. Financial savings from reduced HIV incidence occur only if the decline in HIV incidence is large enough to more than offset the higher costs from each HIV infection. In this example, the effects of reduced HIV incidence, and the higher costs per HIV infection largely cancel out, so the costs of attaining full coverage at a CD4 count of 350 or changing eligibility to a CD4 count of 500 are dominated by the treatment costs for people already living with HIV as of 2011.[16]

The discussion so far has illustrated how the cost-effectiveness of HIV prevention interventions can be described based on three factors—(1) the projected costs of the intervention, (2) the projected impact on the number of HIV infections, and (3) the change in treatment costs owing to reduced HIV incidence. For most HIV prevention interventions, this is straightforward; for treatment, it is also necessary to take into account the interaction between items (1) and (3). The analysis so far—whether over a policy period to 2025 or to 2035—however, does not capture that the implications of HIV/AIDS policies pursued now for treatment costs extend over decades, and are only partially contained within the policy period. For this reason, it is good practice to also consider the long-term treatment spending commitments which arise as a consequence of the HIV interventions considered. This point has been discussed with regard to HIV/AIDS programmes in Chapter 8. It is similarly relevant for the cost-effectiveness of alternative HIV prevention interventions because the cost savings from reduced HIV incidence within the policy period account for only a small proportion of the resulting changes in lifetime treatment costs. These lifetime treatment costs are estimated at US$2,500 in the baseline scenario, US$4,200 with full coverage at a CD4 count of 350, and US$5,100 with full coverage at a CD4 count of 500. However, evaluating around the PSP (with full coverage at a CD4 count of 350), only US$600 of savings from reduced HIV incidence (i.e. 14 per cent of the long-term savings from reduced HIV incidence) occur until 2025, and savings of US$1,600 (i.e. 39 per cent of the long-term savings) occur until 2035. Almost all (with a time horizon through 2025) or most of the financial savings from reduced HIV incidence therefore occur after the policy period.

Figures 10.2.g and 10.2.h illustrate the cost-effectiveness across HIV prevention interventions, fully taking into account the cost savings from reduced HIV incidence.[17] For non-treatment HIV prevention interventions, this results in a downward shift in the costs per HIV infection averted by about US$2,300 (evaluated around the PSP) or US$1,500 (evaluated from baseline). Differences in the size of the downward shift occur because of discounting (so the timing of expenditures and HIV infections averted matters) and because the timing of HIV infections averted affects how much of the savings occur within the policy period (and is already included in Figures 10.2.a and 10.2.e) or later.

For expanding coverage of treatment at a CD4 count of 350, the cost-effectiveness with regard to HIV infections averted deteriorates if long-term spending commitments are taken into account. This reflects that expanding treatment initiated at a CD4 count of 350 or below steeply improves survival— the projected costs of services to people already living with HIV in 2011 therefore increase steeply, and most of this occurs after 2025. Additionally, the costs caused by new HIV infections increase—the higher lifetime costs per HIV infection dominate the decline in HIV incidence. In contrast, the cost-effectiveness of providing treatment at a CD4 count of 500 rather than 350 improves when the long-term spending commitments are taken into account—the spending commitments per HIV infection averted increase only modestly (relative to eligibility at a CD4 count of 350) so the consequences with regard to people already living with HIV in 2011 are modest, and HIV incidence declines relatively steeply so that spending commitments from new HIV infections are lower than for eligibility at a CD4 count of 350.

One consequence of this downward shift in the costs per HIV infection averted across HIV prevention interventions, once the full costs caused by HIV infections are taken into account, is the fact that differences in returns to investment—measured as HIV infections averted per US$ spent—become more pronounced. For example, if one intervention over the policy period (e.g. until 2025) averts an HIV infection at a cost of US$8,000, and another at US$5,000, an investment of US$1 million would avert 125 or 200 HIV infections, a difference of 75, and the second intervention comes out 60 per cent more effective than the first. If the financial savings from reduced HIV incidence are fully taken into account, resulting in an offset of US$3,000 (additional savings occurring after the policy period, discounted in line with the government's practice), the net costs per HIV infection averted come out at US$5,000 and US$2,000, respectively, that is, the second intervention is 150 per cent more effective. In this example, investing US$1 million in HIV prevention interventions thus does not only prevent 125 or 200 HIV infections, respectively, but it also yields a financial saving of US$375,000 or US$600,000.

Thus, accounting fully for the savings owing to reduced HIV incidence accentuates the differences in cost-effectiveness across HIV prevention interventions, whereas measures based on current spending within some fixed policy period underplay the gains from allocating resources to HIV prevention interventions in the most effective manner. It should be noted that the analysis involves financial flows over long time periods, even decades. To draw the right conclusions with regard to the optimal design of an HIV prevention programme, it is necessary to understand the government's ability and willingness to accommodate these financial flows over time, and its preferences in terms of undergoing higher expenditures now, which, however, result in financial savings further on. A key variable summarizing the government's preferences and constraints regarding the spending consequences over time would be the discount rate. Because the financial consequences of HIV/AIDS investments are spread over unusually long periods, the discount rate plays a large role in the evaluation of alternative interventions and policies. For sensible policy analysis, it is essential to get the discount rate right, and to devote appropriate space in discussion with government officials to it.

Table 10.3 provides a scoreboard for assessing the impact and cost-effectiveness of various HIV prevention interventions. In line with the discussion above, HIV prevention interventions are evaluated around the PSP, rather than from the baseline, to take account of the decline in effectiveness of one

Table 10.3. Scoreboard for assessing programme and allocative efficiency

	Impact (HIV infections averted)	Costs	Savings (−)		Net costs	Returns to investment		
			Through 2025	Beyond 2025		Direct costs	Incl. savings through 2025	Incl. full savings
			(US$ millions)		(US$ millions)	(HIV infections averted per US$ 1 million)		
Prevention through secondary schools	1,974	18	−1.1	−4.6	12	109	116	146
Community mobilization	24,634	438	−17	−54	367	56	58	64
Condom promotion and distribution	12,725	15	−8	−29	−21	833	1,689	(cost-saving)
Female sex worker interventions (FSW)	225	0.9	−0.1	−0.5	0.2	252	295	600
HIV counselling and testing (HCT)	16,546	215	−11	−37	167	77	81	93
Injecting drug user interventions (IDU)	4,399	35	−4.9	−8	22	127	149	164
Mass media	4,716	35	−2.7	−11	22	133	144	193
Medical male circumcision (MC)	41,729	187	−19	−102	67	223	248	490
Prevention among out-of-school youth	10,990	119	−6.8	−25	87	92	98	117
Treatment 350	111,196	1,222	−25	613	1,810	91	93	61
Treatment 500	84,051	1,155	31	−454	732	73	71	120
Memorandum items								
Discount rate applied (per cent)	5.0							
Time horizon	2025							

Source: Author's estimates.

HIV prevention intervention as others are scaled up at the same time. The estimates illustrate the large role the financial savings owing to reduced HIV incidence play for the assessment of cost-effectiveness. For the least effective HIV prevention intervention covered, they account for one-sixth of the direct costs, for the most effective interventions, they offset most of the costs (and in one case exceed them). The table also illustrates the point that taking into account indirect cost savings accentuates differences in cost-effectiveness across HIV prevention interventions—for example, the estimated returns to prevention through secondary schools are 1.9 times higher (=105/56) than for community mobilization if only direct costs are considered, but 2.3 times (=176/68) higher when full savings are taken into account.

By translating impact, costs, and resulting financial savings into estimates of the return on investment, Table 10.3 represents a compact format for assessing the impact and cost-effectiveness of various HIV prevention interventions, and of the allocative efficiency of the HIV/AIDS programme. The information in this table (possibly expanded with a number of interventions which could possibly be included in the HIV/AIDS programme), can be used to improve spending allocations, or to consider the most appropriate level of investment over the policy period. As a snapshot of cost-effectiveness around a specific HIV/AIDS programme, though, it is a very incomplete tool for identifying optimal spending allocations (see the next section for further discussion of this point). Additionally, there are a number of points one should keep in mind when using a diagnostic tool such as the one in Table 10.3 (some more fundamental issues are discussed in the following section).

- *Changing unit costs.* The estimates presented in Figure 10.2 and Table 10.3 assume that unit costs are constant. This assumption would be unreasonable if unit costs increase as the coverage of certain services increases (and is extended to less accessible populations), or if economies of scale drive down unit costs as the number of individuals accessing services increases, or both. This shortcoming, however, could be addressed fairly easily within the framework presented here.

- *Interactions in the effectiveness of interventions.* The best known example is the interaction between HIV counselling and testing and expanding treatment access, or the 'critical enablers' which are 'necessary to support the effectiveness and efficiency' of the 'basic programme activities' in the UNAIDS investment framework (Schwartländer et al., 2011). Such links are not captured well in the epidemiological software underlying the estimates in Table 10.3, and their lack tends to be a weakness of models addressing the cost-effectiveness of HIV/AIDS interventions and assessing optimal spending allocations.

- *Changes in the effectiveness of interventions.* For epidemiological reasons, or if unit costs depend on the coverage, the cost-effectiveness of an HIV intervention may change as the intervention is (or other interventions are) scaled up. One pragmatic way of circumventing this problem is to use diagnostics such as cost-effectiveness or the returns to investment summarized in Table 10.3 to *gradually* change the spending allocations and then re-evaluate the policy.

Determining Optimal HIV/AIDS Strategies

Explicit optimization approaches have not been widely used in the design of HIV/AIDS programmes, for numerous reasons. The design of the HIV/AIDS programme involves a large number of players—including the government and other domestic political institutions, representatives of the national HIV/AIDS programmes, civil society, and external donors—whose possibly divergent interests need to be accommodated. Moreover, for many years, the emphasis in HIV/AIDS planning was on scaling up the HIV/AIDS programme and extending the coverage of essential services like prevention of mother-to-child transmission and treatment. Over this period, policy planning was dominated by 'national strategic plans' with a fairly short time horizon (about 4 years) outlining ambitious targets, which then served as a platform for fundraising.[18] This situation has changed gradually over the last years, as documented by the 'investment framework' and the underlying shift in emphasis by major stakeholders on improved accountability and 'returns to investment'.

However, there are also a number of more fundamental reasons for the dearth of optimization analysis in HIV policy design and evaluation. First, it is not clear with respect to what one would want to optimize. There is no 'vulgar metric' for health, a summary outcome that is generally accepted and captures policy makers' attention (Alleyne, 2009). Should HIV/AIDS policies be optimized with regard to HIV infections or AIDS deaths averted, life years saved, their contributions to national health outcomes like life expectancy? Are these health outcomes sufficient, or is it necessary to also take into account broader social and economic outcomes? To what extent should the analysis take into consideration the financial savings resulting from reduced HIV incidence? Depending on answers to these a priori questions, optimal HIV/AIDS policies could come out very differently.

Second, a complete optimization problem would require (i) determining optimal policies for each period under consideration, and (ii) valuing the endpoint, that is, the state of the epidemic and of the HIV/AIDS response at the end of the policy period. Both aspects are challenging because of the complex disease and transmission dynamics. As sexual activity and disease progression differs by age, the state of the epidemic cannot be described by just a few variables (male/female, HIV status and disease progression, treatment status, risk categories), but each of these variables would have an age distribution attached to it. Long-term survival of people living with HIV means that current challenges are shaped by past policies, and current policies affect the state of the epidemic for decades. For these reasons, optimal HIV/AIDS policies cannot be obtained recursively, one period at a time, but need to be determined simultaneously. This means that the number of variables which need to be optimized becomes very large—for example, if there are thirteen policy variables, and the analysis covers 15 years, the optimization problem cannot be divided into a sequence of fifteen optimization routines with thirteen variables each, but would require optimization over 195 (thirteen times fifteen) variables simultaneously. For the same reason, it is generally not possible to determine a simple policy rule which would be required to value the endpoint—the consequences of the policies pursued within the policy period depend on the policies pursued later.

For these reasons, efforts at determining an optimized or improved HIV/AIDS response take a number of pragmatic approaches to reduce the complexity of the optimization problem. These include:

- Disregarding the endpoint, for example by maximizing the number of HIV infections or AIDS deaths averted (or a combination) within the policy period, without valuing the state of the epidemic at the end of the policy period.

- The approach described in numerous places in this book, taking into account the spending *commitments* towards people living with HIV/AIDS, incorporates the financial liability implied by these spending commitments at the end of the policy period into the analysis, but also disregards the consequences for HIV transmission beyond the policy period.

- Restricting the policy variables, for example by stipulating that the interventions selected as part of a policy package must not change over the policy period, or that budget allocations (at least excluding treatment costs) remain fixed, and only considering specific coverage rates (e.g. assuming that an intervention is implemented either not at all or at full coverage).

- Unit costs and coverage rates of services are commonly assumed to be unrelated. This assumption is problematic if there are returns to scale (e.g. average unit costs of treatment decline during a scaling-up) or decreasing returns (e.g. if the unit costs increase as coverage is extended to the last 20, 10, or 1 per cent of the target population).

- Restricting disease dynamics, for example by assuming fixed transition rates between states. In sophisticated epidemiological models, such transition rates change over time (e.g. mortality among people living with HIV is low for the first years after infection, but then increases). Fixed transition rates considerably simplify the dynamics of disease progression—it is no longer necessary to track how much time individuals have spent in a specific state to calculate transition probabilities—but may result in difficulties in calibrating the model to available estimates and data on the state of the epidemic, and estimating the costs caused by new HIV infections.

- Setting aside age-related differences. This could be a sensible simplification if interventions applied across the population are considered. However, HIV incidence and the consequences of new HIV infections (see Chapter 9) differ very considerably by age. Estimates of the average effect of an intervention across ages could therefore mask large differences across ages, and capturing the effects of HIV prevention interventions across ages holds the potential for improving efficiency by targeting interventions to age groups where they are most effective, as illustrated in the discussion of male circumcision (Chapter 9).

The most common approach involves disregarding the endpoint, assessing the costs and consequences of alternative HIV/AIDS interventions within a policy period, without taking into account the consequences beyond it. The principal advantage of this approach is ease of implementation—it can be applied on top of any epidemiological and costing model, even if it had been designed for other purposes, varying some of the policy parameters and analysing the resulting changes in the variable of interest (e.g. HIV infections) and programme costs. The principal shortcomings are the sensitivity of the results with regard to the time horizon adopted, and the bias against the most cost-effective HIV prevention interventions that results from not accounting for the financial savings owing to HIV infections averted (as illustrated in the previous section, see Table 10.3).

Two applications of the 'Goals' model have been used above for illustration. In Uganda, the model was used to assess the costs and effects of alternative HIV/AIDS strategies, and their relative cost-effectiveness, and to inform the choice of a strategy that promised high returns subject to resource availability. The analysis for KwaZulu-Natal illustrated the use of modelling as a diagnostic tool (estimating the effectiveness and cost-effectiveness of the interventions forming part of the HIV/AIDS programme, and of other interventions which could be included), and using the ranking of the interventions—in terms of effectiveness and cost-effectiveness—for assessing whether the composition of the HIV/AIDS programme was broadly appropriate.

Picking a preferred strategy from a set of scenarios, or using a ranking of interventions around a baseline scenario to decide which should be included in a national HIV/AIDS strategy, are crude devices for identifying optimal HIV/AIDS strategies. The former approach can pick a preferred strategy from pre-selected strategies (but these may not include the optimal strategy). The latter can be misleading because of interactions in the efficiency and cost-effectiveness of specific HIV/AIDS-related interventions; the rankings of interventions in terms of cost-effectiveness therefore depend on the interventions being implemented.

There are two more comprehensive approaches to identifying optimal HIV/AIDS strategies. The first involves (1) running simulations across possible combinations of interventions; (2) identifying a health production function which describes the most cost-effective strategies to attain desired outputs; (3) picking a policy from the health production function according to some criterion (e.g. a budget constraint or marginal cost-effectiveness). This approach, however, requires the calculation of a large number of possible combinations; identifying optimal strategies through an iterative process of *improving* a strategy until no further improvements can be identified is more efficient.[19]

Hogan et al. (2005) address the cost-effectiveness of strategies to combat HIV/AIDS in sub-Saharan Africa and South East Asia (WHO regions 'AFR-E' and 'SEAR-D'), distinguishing seven interventions (and a range of coverage rates for most interventions).[20] In each region, cost-effectiveness rates across interventions (assessed one at a time) in terms of HIV infections averted or life years saved differ by a factor easily exceeding 100. Hogan et al. (2005) then identify an 'expansion path' containing thirteen combinations of interventions which for different spending levels are not dominated by some other combination.

This approach is also used by Anderson et al. (2014), seeking to determine optimal HIV prevention policies for Kenya. The analysis distinguishes four interventions (medical male circumcision, behaviour change, early antiretroviral therapy, and pre-exposure prophylaxis), which may be targeted at four population groups (sex workers, men, women, and men who have sex with men). Efficient HIV prevention strategies are summarized in a 'health production function' (corresponding to the 'expansion path' in the paper by Hogan et al., 2005) describing the optimal combination of interventions across spending levels (Figure 10.3). A policy not optimized with regard to reducing HIV infections would be located below the curve—the vertical distance would show the increase in HIV infections averted that could be achieved with the same funding, and the horizontal distance would illustrate the amount that could be saved while achieving the same outcome with regard to HIV infections averted.

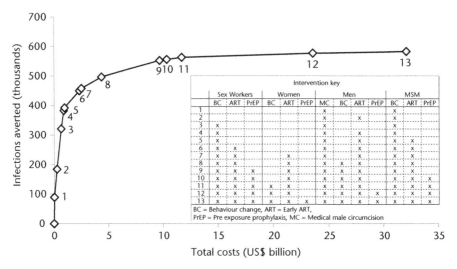

Figure 10.3. Kenya: Cost-effective national HIV prevention policies, 2015–2029
Source: Anderson et al. (2014).

The second—and more unique—contribution by Anderson et al. (2014) is the application of the model to estimate the state of the epidemic and 'health production functions' across Kenya's forty-seven counties. As the state of the epidemic differs vastly across counties—with estimated HIV prevalence (ages 15+) ranging from 0.2 per cent to 26.9 per cent, and five counties accounting for 40 per cent of HIV infections in the country—it is plausible that the efficiency of the HIV/AIDS response could be improved by adapting policies to regional or local circumstances and allocating resources to areas where they yield the highest benefits. Indeed, Anderson et al. (2014) find that an optimal HIV policy that takes into account these regional differences would reduce HIV infections between 2015 and 2030 by around one-quarter, relative to an optimal uniform national policy, at the same cost.

The efficiency gains from differentiating HIV prevention policies across counties are larger (in relative terms) when the budget becomes tighter. The differentiated HIV prevention policies show a rich pattern—nine different interventions are implemented in at least one county, whereas only four are used in the national scenario. Policies optimized across counties respond to the differences in the roles of female sex workers and men who have sex with men in HIV transmission, and in the state of male circumcision. Early ART for men is implemented in almost all counties in the differentiated policy, except some counties with low HIV incidence (where none of the HIV prevention interventions are implemented in the optimized differentiated policy—all funds are allocated to higher-burden counties), and in the two counties with the highest HIV prevalence (where the emphasis in on prevention of HIV transmission through female sex workers). Thus, the study by Anderson et al. (2014) provides a rich example for the gains that can be achieved by calibrating the HIV prevention policy in line with the regional state of HIV and with the drivers of HIV incidence.[21]

The analyses by Hogan et al. (2005) and Anderson et al. (2014) focus on a relatively small number of interventions. Even though, the number of possible combinations of interventions (which need to be calculated to establish non-dominated strategies) is large—about 10,000 in the study by Hogan et al., and 66,000 for the analysis by Anderson et al. For an analysis covering a wider range of interventions, or allowing more than just a few pre-selected coverage rates, this method becomes cumbersome, and an approach geared at identifying optimal policies through an algorithm that converges to an optimal solution iteratively becomes more efficient.[22] This latter approach is also not restricted by a pre-selected grid of coverage rates, and therefore returns more precise optimal strategies.

The most structured analysis determining an optimal HIV/AIDS strategy iteratively on top of a fully-developed epidemiological model has been undertaken in support of the South African HIV Investment Case, described by Meyer-Rath et al. (2015). The analysis builds on the THEMBISA model (a demographic and epidemiological model developed specifically for South Africa, see Johnson et al. (2014)), but the general approach is not specific to that model.[23]

The analysis is built around twenty-four interventions which could potentially be scaled up further or included in the national HIV/AIDS programme. At the outset, each intervention is evaluated individually, incremental to a baseline in which the coverage with all interventions remains at the 2013 levels. The most cost-effective intervention is then selected into the programme, and the process is repeated for the remaining HIV interventions, incremental to the new baseline with the first added intervention, and so on, and in each round the most cost-effective remaining intervention is added to the programme. This process was used to identify an optimal policy achievable within the current budget envelope, including—among other interventions—high coverage of male circumcision, a campaign geared at HIV testing and multiple partnerships, HIV testing for infants at 6 weeks, and coverage of antiretroviral therapy of 85 per cent below a CD4 count of 350 (in line with current guidelines in South Africa).[24] Meyer-Rath et al. (2015) estimate that this policy would help reduce HIV incidence to 0.3 per cent of the population at ages 15–49 by 2020, compared to 0.7 per cent in 2015 and 0.5 per cent projected under a baseline scenario for 2020. Methodologically, the approach yields an HIV/AIDS strategy that can no longer be obviously improved by shifting spending allocations between interventions.[25] Because ultimately the ranking of interventions occurs around the optimized response, the approach is more effective than one ranking the effectiveness of interventions around a baseline scenario. Among the shortcomings is the fact that the iterations are constrained to the pre-selected set of coverage rates (as in the papers discussed above by Anderson et al., Hogan et al., and Meyer-Rath et al.), and that the analysis is restricted to time-invariant strategies.

The Optima model and software, described by Kerr et al.[26] (2015), includes substantial in-built optimization capabilities (whereas the other analyses described so far were conducting some optimization analysis on top of a model not including these capabilities). It had originally been developed in the context of concentrated epidemics (and retains a high degree of flexibility in terms of specifying disease dynamics within and across population groups), but has more recently been applied in some countries facing a generalized epidemic.[27] The model allows unit costs to differ depending on coverage of the relevant service, and provides a tool to calibrate such curves to match available cost data. Because the model is very efficient in returning optimized results, it is useful to assess the robustness of an optimal HIV/AIDS strategy to different objectives (e.g. life years saved, deaths averted, or a combination), budget levels, or time horizons. In terms of HIV transmission, the model offers similar capabilities as a 'modes-of-transmission' template, but is more flexible and consistent. The model also incorporates aspects of a forward-looking analysis as described in Chapters 7 and 8 (partly based on contributions from the author of this book). Some of the drawbacks include a lack of accessibility,[28] a relatively simple dynamic structure,[29] and extensive input requirements (the latter partly a consequence of its flexibility). The model does not include an explicit demographic model and does not distinguish individuals by age (unless different age groups are set up as separate risk groups), so capturing age-related differences in HIV transmission and the effectiveness of HIV prevention interventions (which play a large role in Chapter 9) presents a challenge.

In conclusion, no dominant model on determining *optimal* HIV/AIDS strategies has emerged so far, as a consequence of the intricate and slow dynamics of the epidemic. Meaningful policy evaluations need to adopt an unusually long time horizon, as recognized in the HIV/AIDS policy discourse where time frames of about 15 years are common. Even these result in bias, as the consequences of current HIV/AIDS policies (e.g. in terms of the treatment need or transmission dynamics of the epidemic) are spread over decades, especially for interventions like male circumcision where the *direct* effect is also spread over a long period.

A number of pragmatic approaches have been applied, usually comparing the costs and effects of alternative policies over a specific policy period, or iteratively determining a policy that achieves certain policy targets at the lowest cost, or the best outcomes for a given budget, within this policy period. The analysis of the spending *commitments* implied by alternative HIV/AIDS policies outlined in Chapters 7–9 addresses one shortcoming of such evaluations—that current policies result in spending commitments towards people living with HIV/AIDS which extend beyond the policy period. Taking into account these spending commitments improves estimates of the cost-effectiveness of alternative policies, and identifies the *fiscal space* absorbed by these policies, linking the analysis of programme efficiency to the discourse on sustainable financing.

11

Sustainable Domestic Financing

The design of an HIV/AIDS programme, the financing burden, financial sustainability, and the modes of financing are interrelated. For example, the design of an HIV/AIDS programme affects the financing burden, and securing financial sustainability is one aspect of designing an efficient HIV/AIDS programme. The assessment of financial sustainability would take into account the financing burden and the available modes of financing. The design of an HIV/AIDS programme and financial sustainability are also connected through the outcomes of the programme and the costs of achieving them—the political will to provide funding depends on the returns to investments, in comparison to (and competition with) other funding priorities.

Some of these issues have appeared throughout the book—Part I deals with the impacts of HIV/AIDS from a health and development perspective, and provides a platform for linking HIV/AIDS programmes to national (or donors') development objectives. Part II of the book describes the impacts of the global response to HIV/AIDS and discusses current financing challenges. Chapters 7 to 10 describe techniques for assessing the cost-effectiveness of HIV/AIDS programmes and interventions, and specifically for taking into account the consequences of alternative HIV/AIDS policies in committing fiscal space. This chapter addresses financial sustainability and sustainable financing from the perspective of the domestic government, focusing on the following questions:

- *Can the HIV/AIDS programme be financed?* What is the magnitude of the costs of the HIV/AIDS programme compared to the available fiscal resources, and is it plausible that the government would be able to finance it?

- *Would the government/donors want to finance it?* What are the 'returns to investment' in the HIV/AIDS response, in relation to those of competing policy options?

- *How can this be financed?* If, or to the extent that, the government endorses the proposed HIV/AIDS programme, what are options for financing it?

The discussion of these questions is divided into four sections. The first section provides a simple fiscal perspective on HIV/AIDS spending and financing. The second section interprets the projected costs of the HIV/AIDS response as commitments of fiscal space and against the theory and practice of fiscal sustainability. The third section addresses contributions of HIV/AIDS policy design to sustainable financing, by identifying the most cost-effective HIV/AIDS strategies and scope for improving the technical efficiency of HIV/AIDS services. The final section gives an overview of domestic financing options and the policy discourse on the financing of HIV/AIDS programmes.

A Fiscal Perspective on Domestic HIV/AIDS Financing

The policy discourse on the domestic financing of the HIV/AIDS response is framed by the government's policy objectives with regard to expenditure policy and tax policy. This context is described, in a very stylized form, in Figure 11.1. The government's expenditure policy (for the moment excluding the HIV/AIDS response) is summarized by a curve X_0X_0', which orders potential spending in declining order of its contribution (per unit of spending) to the national policy objectives. HIV/AIDS introduces new spending needs, represented by a shift of the expenditure curve to the right (to X_1X_1'). To the

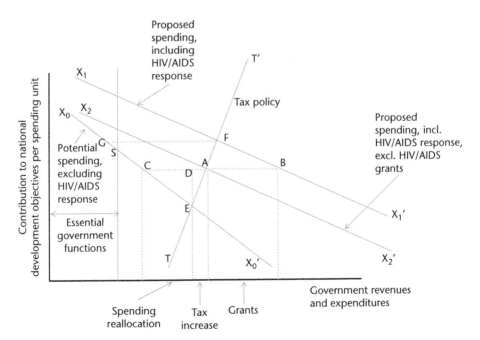

Figure 11.1. A fiscal perspective on HIV/AIDS financing

201

extent that the response to HIV/AIDS is financed by external grants, though, the implications for domestic funding are mitigated, and the curve that describes the government's effective spending opportunities and preferences shifts to X_2X_2'.[1] The availability of domestic fiscal resources is summarized by the 'tax policy' curve TT'. This is upward-sloping—generally there is some scope for raising additional revenues, but (because of the economic and political costs) the government would do so only if the gains (summarized by the expenditure curve) outweigh these costs.

Without HIV/AIDS-related spending needs and related external support, the government would settle on point E (at which expenditure policy X_0X_0' and tax policy TT' are consistent). The actual domestic policy outcome (including the HIV/AIDS response) is represented by point A, and total expenditure including grant-financed HIV/AIDS spending is located at point B. In this situation, an amount equivalent to the distance CB is spent on the HIV/AIDS response, of which CA is financed domestically, and AB through external grants. Compared to the counterfactual situation, the bulk of domestic HIV/AIDS spending in this example is financed by a re-allocation of expenditure from other sources (distance CD), and a smaller proportion from additional revenues (e.g. taxes, distance DA).

Although Figure 11.1 does not capture the intertemporal aspects of HIV/AIDS spending and of other expenditure and tax policies, it serves to illustrate some aspects of sustainability and the challenges of a transition to increased domestic financing. One of the questions regarding the sustainability of the response is whether the spending needs compromise essential government functions. In this example, this would mean that non-HIV/AIDS-related spending is located to the left of point S. The figure shows an example where this is the case in the absence of external support, which therefore contributes to domestic financial sustainability by mitigating the fiscal consequences of HIV/AIDS.[2]

The more complex question on financial sustainability is whether the HIV/AIDS programme is sustainable through a transition to increased domestic financing. In the situation described in Figure 11.1, this is questionable—a decline in external financing would shift X_2X_2' towards X_1X_1', and the policy outcome from point B towards point F (and non-HIV/AIDS spending described by point G, so low that essential government functions are compromised).

For a successful transition to increased domestic financing, a combination of two things would need to happen, and both are playing a large role in the current policy discourse—(1) progress towards ending AIDS and (2) improving cost-effectiveness and realizing efficiency gains in HIV/AIDS services. Progress towards ending AIDS would ultimately drive down the costs of the HIV/AIDS response, although this cost effect—as discussed elsewhere in this book—

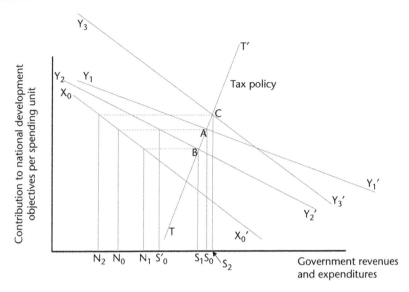

Figure 11.2. Efficiency gains and HIV/AIDS spending allocations

could trail progress in controlling the number of new HIV infections by a long period.

The consequences of efficiency gains for HIV/AIDS spending allocations are more complex (Figure 11.2), where the X curves represent non-HIV/AIDS spending, and the Y curves show total spending including the costs of the HIV/AIDS response. Improved efficiency (1) results in financial savings (for given outcomes), freeing budgetary resources part of which could benefit the HIV/AIDS response, and (2) the cost-effectiveness of HIV/AIDS interventions improves, so that HIV/AIDS interventions move up the list of expenditure priorities. The first effect only is illustrated by the shift from curve Y_1Y_1' to Y_2Y_2', freeing resources equal to $S_0'S_0$. Most of these resources gained result in additional spending—for non-HIV/AIDS purposes (N_0N_1) and towards the HIV/AIDS response ($S_0'S_1$). If this was the only effect, the new outcome would be represented by point B.

Because the improved efficiency means that money spent on the HIV/AIDS response also makes a higher contribution to national development objectives, the HIV/AIDS spending curve also shifts up, so that the new expenditure curve is Y_3Y_3', and the policy outcome is represented by point C. This improved efficiency causes a reallocation from non-HIV/AIDS spending (down by N_1N_2) and an increase in HIV/AIDS spending (by N_1N_2 plus S_1S_2).

Overall, spending on the HIV/AIDS response may increase or decline as a result of improved efficiency (and the final outcome C will lie to the right or left of the initial outcome A). However, as the immediate savings ($S_0'S_0$)

represent a gain *controlling for the outcomes* of the HIV/AIDS response, any outcome to the right of S_0' represents a scaling-up of the HIV/AIDS response. Similarly, in an environment with declining external funding (curve X_1X_1' shifts closer to curve X_2X_2' in Figure 11.1), improved efficiency would offset some of the decline in funding, and also help protect HIV/AIDS funding by better positioning aspects of the HIV/AIDS response in comparison to other spending possibilities.

Fiscal Sustainability and the Costs of the HIV/AIDS Programme

The purpose of assessing the consistency of an HIV/AIDS programme with fiscal sustainability is not to develop a criterion to dismiss a proposed HIV/AIDS strategy, but to complement the discussion of the shifts in global HIV/AIDS financing, and to inform policy discussions between the national government and donors on a 'fair share' of domestic vs. external financing (see Chapter 6, which takes a global perspective on these issues). There are two principal ways of assessing the financial sustainability of the HIV/AIDS response—(1) assessing the *current* costs of the HIV/AIDS response against some benchmark, and (2) looking at the costs of the HIV/AIDS response as long-term *financial commitments*.

The first approach is implied by comparisons between the outcomes and costs of the HIV/AIDS response on one hand, and of some other domain of public policy on the other hand. For example, one may ask if the costs of the HIV/AIDS response are justified, considering its contribution to the burden of disease, the state of health, and the level of health spending overall. For countries with high levels of HIV or very limited financial resources, it might also be necessary to ask whether the costs of the HIV/AIDS response would compress fiscal resources to a point that the effectiveness of the government is compromised.

The second approach adds three dimensions to the analysis. First, it accentuates that the response to HIV/AIDS represents a long-term spending commitment. Compared, for example, to a health shock like Ebola which resulted in high fiscal costs over a short period (a deterioration in the fiscal balance of several per cent of GDP in highly affected countries), the fiscal challenges posed by an HIV response—which absorbs a similar share of GDP over decades—are more significant. Second, because the costs of the HIV/AIDS response over time are interdependent, capturing long-term spending commitments gives a more accurate picture of the costs and effectiveness of alternative strategies (as explored in detail in Chapters 7–10). For example, the HIV/AIDS response may seem very expensive compared to the contribution of HIV/AIDS to the burden of disease, but this may be the case because it is effective in bringing down the HIV/AIDS-related burden of disease. And current investments in the HIV/AIDS response may reduce spending further on. Third, because the long-term spending commitments implied by the HIV/AIDS response have some characteristics of a financial liability, it is possible to draw on a body of literature on the sustainability of debt in assessing the sustainability of the HIV/AIDS response.

The remainder of this section focuses on this third aspect (which also formalizes and generalizes the first point). Before going down this road, though, it is useful to take a step back and clarify some of the key terms used here. Most importantly, is it appropriate to interpret the costs of an HIV/AIDS response as similar to a public debt? The argument for doing so rests on two aspects of HIV/AIDS. First, the treatment needs of people living with HIV/AIDS (and of the corresponding costs if the government commits to providing treatment) extend over several decades. Second, the commitment to provide treatment cannot easily be reversed. This applies most visibly to people already receiving life-saving treatment, but curtailing treatment eligibility would similarly result in a stream of additional AIDS deaths. Additionally, it is worth noting that most policy questions regarding the HIV/AIDS response are forward-looking and regard the design of appropriate strategies. In this context, it is sensible to assume that the government sticks to the policy studied, and treat the resulting spending commitments as firm for planning purposes even if the government would have the capability to change its policies—a later reversal would not constitute a sensible strategy ex ante.

For these reasons, the costs of the HIV/AIDS response can be interpreted as a *fiscal quasi-liability*—a long-term spending commitment like pension obligations and other social entitlements, which commits future government resources and (even though it does not constitute a formal debt) cannot easily be changed by the government (Haacker, 2011). This approach has been used in numerous places in this book: to assess the financial consequences of alternative HIV/AIDS policies, to analyse the net costs and cost-effectiveness of specific HIV prevention interventions, and to inform the design of an optimal HIV/AIDS strategy.

The interpretation of the costs of the HIV/AIDS response is related to the concept of *fiscal space* which is frequently used in the context of health financing. The most common definition of fiscal space is contained in Heller (2005), interpreting fiscal space 'as the availability of budgetary room that allows a government to provide resources for a desired purpose without any prejudice to the sustainability of a government's financial position'. The same source describes *fiscal sustainability* as the 'capacity of a government, at least in the future, to finance its desired expenditure programs, to service any debt obligations (including those that may arise if the created fiscal space arises from government borrowing), and to ensure its solvency'. The relevance here arises from the long-term perspective contained in both terms, expressing the need for consistency between the future flow of revenues and other financing instruments and the government's expenditure policies. The perspective in the present book, however, is different from the most common applications of fiscal space. The discussion in Heller (2005) focuses on *creating fiscal space* by identifying budgetary resources for desired additional expenditures. The discussion here focuses on the *absorption of fiscal space* by the HIV/AIDS programme, and the implied restriction on the government's capability to accommodate its various expenditure priorities.[3]

The costs of the HIV/AIDS programme have been interpreted as financial commitments elsewhere, especially by Over (2008, 2011), who considers the costs of treatment to be 'entitlements', particularly with regard to people already receiving treatment. While he recognizes that treatment programmes do not create legal entitlements, Over points to a 'moral imperative to treat' and to the role of the 'international community and the voting public in democratic countries' which 'will constrain donors from dropping patients from treatment rolls'. Less explicitly, Over also interprets the financial commitments more widely, including the projected costs of treatment to people not receiving it already, resulting in a 'ballooning entitlement burden' that would absorb a very significant part of US foreign assistance.

To the extent that the spending commitments under the HIV/AIDS response can be interpreted as fiscal quasi-liabilities, tools developed for assessing the sustainability of public debt can be applied to assess the magnitude and consequences of the costs of the HIV/AIDS response. The assessment of the government's fiscal position depends on a number of factors—fiscal revenues, expenditures, the level of and interest on public debt, and the general economic outlook.[4] The most common framework applied in such assessments is the 'debt sustainability analysis' (DSA) conducted by the IMF and the World Bank.[5] The DSA, for a country's external debt or its public debt, provides an assessment of the current level of debt and projections of how it is going to evolve, and contains a number of 'stress tests' to determine how the level of debt may evolve in an adverse scenario.

The DSA framework takes a pragmatic approach to what constitutes debt—while the focus is on formal debt, it also acknowledges liabilities implied by the social security system or unfunded public pension funds (IMF 2002, 2007) which are very similar to the quasi-liability posed by the HIV/AIDS response.[6] More broadly, the policy commitments to provide treatment and related services may constitute a 'constructive obligation' which creates a valid expectation that the government will fulfil these commitments (IPSASB, 2014).[7]

The fiscal quasi-liability posed by the spending commitments under the HIV/AIDS response may enter the debt-sustainability framework in two ways.

First, it is possible to interpret the liability as a liability similar to those implied by the social security system or unfunded public pension funds (IMF 2002, 2007), or interpreting the policy commitments to provide treatment and related services as a 'constructive obligation' which creates a valid expectation that the government will fulfil these commitments (IPSASB, 2014). As this liability, in the same way as debt service, binds fiscal resources and thus constrains the capacity to finance the government's policy objectives, its consequences are very similar to that of a formal debt.[8]

Under the DSA framework, the government's fiscal position is deemed sustainable 'if it satisfies the present value budget constraint' (i.e. projected revenues and expenditures on average add up over the foreseeable future) 'without a major correction in the balance of income and expenditure...' (IMF, 2002), taking into account not only feasibility, but also the social and political costs of such an adjustment. A high level of debt would compromise a country's capacity to finance its policy objectives, through the resources absorbed by debt service, and because an escalating level of debt would raise the risk of a large adjustment which could compromise the country's stability.[9] Translating this definition into the context of the costs of the HIV/AIDS response, fiscal sustainability of the HIV/AIDS response requires that the government would be able to finance the costs of the HIV/AIDS response (or the domestically financed portion) without a 'major fiscal adjustment'.

Regarding the magnitude of the costs of the HIV/AIDS response which fulfils this criterion, the practice of DSAs offers some benchmarks. IMF (2013a) provides estimates of the level of public debt above which 'the risk of public debt distress is heightened'. Depending on the country context,[10] these public debt benchmarks range from 38 per cent of GDP to 74 per cent of GDP for low-income countries (IMF, 2013a), and are estimated at 70 per cent of GDP for emerging markets (IMF, 2013b).[11] Furthermore, very few countries globally have a level of public debt around or exceeding 130 per cent of GDP, and most countries with debt at or close to that level would already experience acute debt distress.[12]

Table 11.1 summarizes estimates of spending commitments implied by the HIV/AIDS response, together with their main determinants and pointers to how the various estimates have been calculated. In many cases, the costs of the HIV/AIDS response represent a liability the financing of which would, or would have, required a major fiscal adjustment in the absence of external support (according to the yardsticks applied in DSAs). Whether current costs over a fixed period or spending commitments are considered makes a big difference for the estimation of the HIV/AIDS fiscal quasi-liability. For example, the costs of the HIV/AIDS response in Kenya until 2030 are estimated at 24–34 per cent of 2014 GDP, but if the lifetime spending commitments towards people living with HIV as of 2030 are added, the liability comes

Table 11.1. Spending commitments under the HIV/AIDS response, various countries

Country	HIV prevalence (ages 15–49, %)	GDP per capita (US$)	Costs of HIV/AIDS programme (% of GDP)	Cost coverage
Jamaica (2010)	1.9	4,800	5.2	Spending commitments towards 2010 PLWH
Kenya (2014)	6.0	1,500	23.6–34.0	Spending 2014–2030
			47.0–64.3	Same, plus spending commitments towards 2030 PLWH
			32.4–44.8	The latter, applying discount rate of 5%
Swaziland (2010)	27.1	3,700	151	Spending commitments towards 2010 PLWH
			293	Same, plus projected spending caused by future HIV infections
Uganda (2010)	7.0	510	83.5	Spending 2010–2025
			182	Spending commitments towards 2010 PLWH
			372	Same, including projected spending caused by future HIV infections
			109	Spending commitments towards 2010 PLWH, with 5% discount rate
			206	The latter, including projected spending caused by future HIV infections
Uganda (2014)	7.5	690	33.4	Spending 2014–2025

Sources: World Bank (2013) for Jamaica (2010); Haacker (2011), drawing on Lule and Haacker (2012) for Swaziland (2010) and Uganda (2010); National AIDS Control Council (2014a) for Kenya (2014); Uganda AIDS Commission (2014) for Uganda 2014. Unless stated otherwise, estimates apply discount rate of 3 per cent.

out at 47–64 per cent of 2014 GDP. Because of the long time horizons, the discount rate applied makes a large difference for the estimates of spending commitments under the HIV/AIDS response—an additional percentage point in the discount rate reduces estimated spending commitments by about one-quarter (see examples from Uganda (2010) or Kenya (2014) in Table 11.1).

One important question in assessing the magnitude of the liability posed by the HIV/AIDS response is whether the spending commitments caused by *projected* HIV infections (beyond some cut-off) should be included in the estimates. The practice throughout this book is to account for spending commitments caused by HIV infections which have already happened, or are projected to happen within some policy period (e.g. until 2030 in the example from Kenya). For the analysis of the cost-effectiveness of HIV interventions, focusing on the HIV infections caused or prevented in some policy period makes sense. For estimating the quasi-liability posed by the HIV/AIDS response, this approach underestimates the costs, because HIV infections will not drop to zero at the end of the policy period. The examples from Swaziland and Uganda show that also accounting for the costs caused by projected future infections results in much higher estimates of the costs of the HIV/AIDS response—about one-half of the costs are caused by past HIV infections, and one-half by HIV infections after the beginning of the policy period. A longer policy period reduces the bias, but does not eliminate it. There is no clear solution to this dilemma (which is related to the cut-off problem discussed in Chapter 10)—best practice includes the adoption of fairly long time horizons in policy analysis, assessing spending commitments as well as current spending, and developing an understanding of how sensitive the estimates are with regard to the length of the policy period or other parameters (e.g. the discount rate).

Efficiency and HIV/AIDS Programme Design

Improved efficiency of the HIV/AIDS response directly contributes to its financing because an increase in efficiency reduces the costs of attaining programme objectives, but also indirectly because higher efficiency moves HIV/AIDS interventions higher up in the pecking order of governments and other funders. There are several ways in which efficiency considerations have played a role in the design of HIV/AIDS policies—approaches addressing the optimal allocation of HIV/AIDS spending across different types of services ('allocative efficiency'), approaches which focus on systematic variations in the efficiency of services (e.g. by scale, mode of delivery, or location), and approaches which focus on variations which cannot be explained by some underlying factors and may point to inefficiencies or waste in service delivery. The latter two issues are the domain of 'technical efficiency'.[13]

The assessment of the cost-effectiveness of various HIV/AIDS services and the optimal allocation of HIV/AIDS spending—how to assess the financial returns as well as the health returns of investments in HIV treatment and prevention, assessing the spending commitments implied by alternative HIV/AIDS policies, and identifying strategies which are optimal according to some criterion—has been discussed extensively in Chapters 9 and 10 and need not be reviewed here. In the context of the financing of the HIV/AIDS programme, two aspects matter. First, improving allocative efficiency is a tool for attaining the objectives of the HIV/AIDS response at lower costs (or achieving more with available financing). Second, the tools described in Chapters 9 and 10 also interpret HIV/AIDS investments as financial instruments, which—in addition to their health outcomes—shape the costs of the HIV/AIDS response in later years. From this perspective, allocative efficiency also has an intertemporal dimension. With current investments affecting the long-term costs, improving allocative efficiency reduces the fiscal space absorbed by the HIV/AIDS response. Doing so may require higher investments in the short run; if this is the case, attaining allocative efficiency (in an intertemporal sense) and containing costs in terms of fiscal space add a motive for current HIV/AIDS investments.[14]

Assessing the cost-effectiveness or 'technical efficiency' of HIV/AIDS interventions requires data on costs and outputs, and an assessment on how these compare to some benchmark, or vary systematically in a way that could be exploited in HIV/AIDS programme design (e.g. according to delivery mode, or by scale of facility). Until recently, the understanding of the technical efficiency of HIV/AIDS services was very poor—a review of cost studies on HIV/AIDS-related health services identified 115 studies between 1999 and 2008, but most studies were performed in North America, and only nineteen in Africa (including thirteen from just one country, South Africa), and cost estimates in only forty of the 115 studies were based on a sample size over 100.[15] Moreover, these *cost* studies yielded little insight on *efficiency*.

This paucity of data from countries facing the most severe challenges reflects several factors, including weak cost monitoring systems in these countries in general, the rapid expansion of HIV/AIDS services over the last years, and the fact that the global HIV/AIDS agenda had been focusing on getting HIV/AIDS services on the ground, irrespective of their relative effects (Schwartländer et al., 2011). The situation has improved since then—a review by Siapka et al. (2014) identified eighty-four empirical studies on costs of basic HIV/AIDS services across low- and middle-income countries. However, only a subset allowed inference on efficiency (e.g. only nine studies were reported to have 'sufficiently large samples to apply econometric methods to explore any associations between scale and costs'). Those few studies tended to show the presence of economies of scale.

The most significant effort to assess the efficiency of HIV/AIDS services is the ORPHEA project, which is part of efforts supported by the Gates Foundation to fundamentally address HIV/AIDS programme efficiency and its determinants, and apply sophisticated commercial optimization techniques to the design of HIV/AIDS programmes.[16] Typical findings are summarized in Figure 11.3, comparing the unit costs of HIV testing and counselling across testing sites in four countries.

Figure 11.3 can be read in terms of the systematic variation in costs, and in terms of the variation across facilities with similar characteristics. The costs of testing per client tested differ by country (likely reflecting differences in salaries and related costs) and by facility according to the number of clients tested—a ten-fold increase in the number of clients tested reduces unit costs by about

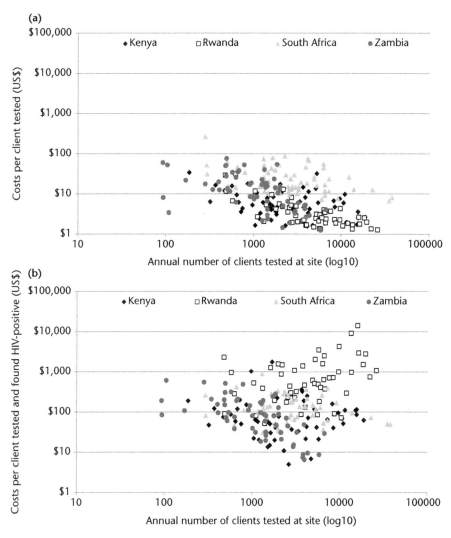

Figure 11.3. Unit costs of HIV testing and counselling across sites, four countries, by annual number of clients tested

Source: Bautista-Arredondo et al. (2014).
(a). Costs per client tested (US$)
(b). Cost per client tested and found HIV-positive (US$)

40 per cent.[17] However, there is little evidence for economies of scope, that is, differences in the unit costs of HIV testing and counselling depending on the size of the facility overall. With regard to the costs per client tested and found HIV-positive, the picture looks very different—cost-effectiveness now reflects HIV prevalence (e.g. the unit costs are highest in Rwanda, the country with

the lowest HIV prevalence among the four countries covered), and with the link between unit costs and the number of clients tested becoming much weaker—this likely reflects that smaller testing sites (where the costs per test tend to be higher) tend to be deployed in areas where HIV prevalence is high (and therefore the 'yield', in terms of people testing positive per test, is higher).[18]

The other way of reading Figure 11.3 is vertically—comparing the cost-effectiveness of sites with similar characteristics. On this count, the ORPHEA analysis reveals very large discrepancies, frequently around or exceeding a factor of ten for sites with similar numbers of patients. Such discrepancies could point to inefficiencies, and motivate a process of addressing their causes.

A very significant contributor to ongoing efforts to improve cost-effectiveness (and thereby contribute to financial sustainability) is PEPFAR, as part of its efforts to transform itself from an emergency response to one aiming at 'sustainable control of the epidemic' (PEPFAR, 2014c). From an economic perspective, there are two building blocks to this agenda—a drive to systemically *generate* economic and financial information, and their *use* 'with the same regularity that program managers use epidemiologic and pro-grammatic data' (Holmes et al., 2011, 2012). In terms of improving technical efficiency, PEPFAR combines a site-level analysis similar to the one shown in Figure 11.3 with a programme-level perspective, identifying the contributions to programme objectives across sites, and closing sites with low levels of activity.

Studies of the cost-effectiveness of HIV/AIDS interventions across facilities miss out on two sources of inefficiencies—those common across sites and inefficiencies in costs above the facility level, for example when an unusually large share of the costs of the HIV/AIDS programme is absorbed by overhead expenses. Studies based on cross-country data therefore may yield additional insights regarding the cost-effectiveness of HIV/AIDS programmes—identifying countries where, after taking into account a number of explana-tory variables, the cost-effectiveness of HIV/AIDS services is low.

Zeng et al. (2012, 2015) assess the cost-effectiveness of HIV/AIDS pro-grammes across low- and middle-income countries, based on outcomes in and costs of counselling and testing, treatment, and prevention of mother-to-child transmission. Cost-effectiveness is measured as outcomes for a given expenditure, relative to the observations with the highest level of effectiveness at that expenditure level. According to Zeng et al. (2012), average efficiency across sixty-one countries was about 50 per cent, countries with higher HIV prevalence tended to have higher efficiency, and efficiency was increasing with GNI per capita up to a level of about US$4,300 and then declining.

From the perspective of international funders, this means that the average health returns to each US$ invested have been higher in countries with lower income per capita, and in countries with higher HIV prevalence. With regard to potential efficiency gains or the scope for closing global funding gaps (discussed in Zeng et al., 2015), though, the analysis offers limited insights, because the relevant comparison for that purpose would be between *conditional* efficiency across countries, after taking into account factors like GDP per capita, HIV prevalence, and other factors which would have a bearing on the costs of HIV/AIDS interventions.

Sources of Domestic Funding

For an overview of domestic financing options for the HIV/AIDS response, it is useful to distinguish four different approaches—cutting government expenditures in other areas, increasing taxes, borrowing, and shifting some of the costs of the HIV/AIDS response to the private sector, for example through contributions to a national health insurance.[19] However, it is important to bear in mind that the dividing lines are not clear cut. Borrowing implies the need to raise taxes or curb expenditures at a later date; increasing taxes also reduces the scope for generating additional tax revenues for other policy objectives; and shifting some of the costs of HIV services to citizens is similar to increasing taxes.

Cutting Government Expenditures in Other Areas

Additional expenditures on HIV/AIDS can be financed within the budget envelope by reallocating resources from other policy objectives. For example, the Kenya AIDS Strategic Framework (NACC, 2014b) proposes that 2 per cent of government revenues be assigned to the HIV/AIDS response—this amount is then not available to other policy priorities. However, as Kenya is a rapidly growing country (GDP is increasing at a rate of about 6–7 per cent annually, and GDP per capita by 3–4 per cent (IMF, 2015)), an increase in HIV/AIDS expenditures could possibly be financed by assigning a disproportionate share of the anticipated *increase* in tax revenues to the HIV/AIDS response.[20]

There is no direct documentation on HIV/AIDS spending crowding out expenditures in other areas—in most countries, domestic HIV/AIDS spending accounts for a small proportion of shifts in public expenditures, so no formal empirical analysis is available. Some indirect evidence is available from the sphere of public health—countries facing severe HIV epidemics tend to experience a deterioration in some non-HIV health outcomes. The relevant literature, though, focuses on externally financed spending and only provides indirect evidence on the response of the domestic government. For example, Grépin (2012) documents deteriorating immunization outcomes in countries receiving large amounts of HIV/AIDS-related aid. These changes, though, have been more pronounced in countries with lower availability of physicians, suggesting that limited (non-financial) capacities in the health sector are an important part of the story.

Taxes

The policy discourse on domestic HIV/AIDS financing involves proposals for tax increases (or earmarking a proportion of existing taxes) to finance the HIV/AIDS response, as well as 'ring-fencing' these revenues through 'trust funds'.[21] The best-known example is from Zimbabwe, where the budget of the National AIDS Commission is largely financed through the 'AIDS levy', a 3 per cent mark-up on personal and corporate income taxes. Other examples for earmarking a portion of established taxes are from Kenya (a proposal for assigning 2 per cent of general tax revenues to the HIV/AIDS response) and Uganda, where the 2014 'HIV and AIDS Prevention and Control Act' assigned 2 per cent of excise taxes on beverages to the HIV/AIDS response.[22]

These taxes, and a number of more specific taxes (e.g. on air flights, financial transactions, luxury goods, mobile phones, 'sin' taxes targeting consumption of items like tobacco, alcohol, and junk food), have been proposed as vehicles for 'innovative financing' of the HIV/AIDS response (UNAIDS, 2013a; Wilson et al., 2014). This designation of taxes as innovative domestic financing is puzzling—much of public finance is about raising revenues through taxation in order to meet the government's policy objectives, and some of the taxes identified for the financing of HIV/AIDS programmes are among the most common domestic taxes.[23]

Two elements of the policy discourse on the domestic financing of HIV/AIDS spending, though, are unusual—*earmarking* specific tax revenues for the financing of the HIV/AIDS response, and administrating these revenues through '*trust funds*'.

Earmarking is appropriate if the budget process would otherwise be ineffective in allocating resources to specific purposes, to formalize a policy consensus about the distribution of certain revenues (e.g. assigning some revenues from resource extraction to local communities), or help build political support for raising taxes. With regard to HIV/AIDS, it can be argued that the stigma associated with HIV/AIDS and populations at high risk of contracting HIV, and the complex and long-term consequences of HIV prevention policies, result in inefficient budget allocations.

There are, however, several shortcomings of using earmarked taxes for HIV/AIDS financing. In general, earmarking is a very inflexible tool, and may result in inefficient budget allocations as needs are changing. This point is particularly relevant in the context of HIV/AIDS, where spending needs (because of a build-up in treatment costs, or because of changes in drug prices) may change considerably, and the earmarked taxes are not obviously linked to the demand for HIV/AIDS services. Moreover, in a situation where spending *needs* are projected to increase substantially over the coming years (as is the case in most HIV/AIDS programmes, owing to expanding access to treatment), there would be a mismatch between the profile of revenues and expenditures, and the government (or donors) would have to take additional measures to fund the HIV/AIDS programme. If, however, only a portion of domestic financing of the HIV/AIDS response is financed by earmarked taxes, and it needs to be topped up by discretionary funding, there is not much of a difference to a situation in which all HIV/AIDS spending is included in the yearly budget process.

The use of trust funds, or extrabudgetary funds, for special purposes is not unusual. In Kenya (one of the countries where an HIV trust fund financed by earmarked taxes is discussed), a survey at the Parliamentary Budget Office covered fifty-four such funds (Ojiambo et al., 2011), and Allen and Radev (2010) report that extrabudgetary funds (excluding social security) account for 9.4 per cent of government expenditures in transition and developing countries.[24] Trust funds do not contribute to sustainable financing of the HIV/AIDS response per se (unless they are backed by adequate financing, which could involve earmarked taxes).

Establishing a trust fund could help soliciting additional external revenues—if donors are reluctant to contribute to the HIV/AIDS response through the government budget, for example because of a perceived lack of transparency, setting up a fund with separate oversight and accounting procedures could alleviate such concerns and motivate donors to contribute. The intention to utilize the AIDS trust fund as a conduit for both domestic and external funding is apparent in the law on the AIDS trust fund in Tanzania, where one-half of the members of the Board of Trustees are drawn from major donors. The AIDS Trust Fund of Zimbabwe was also originally conceived to attract external grants and this dimension never took off because its establishment coincided with a breakdown in donor relations (Madzingira, 2008).

A trust fund could also be utilized to separate the broad funding decisions from questions of how the financial resources are going to be allocated. This could help circumvent the challenges associated with stigma noted above, and the governance of the trust fund could include a number of stakeholders in spending decisions. Finally, a trust fund could facilitate the financial manage-ment of the HIV/AIDS response. Some of the expenditures of the HIV pro-gramme (notably tenders for drug purchases) are bulky and occur infrequently. If budget allocations expire at the end of the financial year, this could complicate the financial management of the HIV/AIDS response.

In contrast, if unspent funds remain in the trust fund, considerations on the annual budget cycle need not constrain procurement.

Finally, an HIV trust fund could play a role in a transition to a national health insurance and universal health coverage. The consequences of HIV/AIDS for the costs of life or health insurance are well understood; and some of the earliest work on the demographic consequences of HIV/AIDS was undertaken on behalf of and at a life insurance company.[25] In expanding the coverage of a national health insurance towards universal health coverage, HIV/AIDS poses two challenges. First, it may present a substantial proportion of the costs of health services, and—to the extent that the insurance is covered by contributions rather than taxes—would complicate efforts to expand coverage to low-income groups.

Second, because of the dynamics of scaling up treatment and HIV transmission, the number of people receiving treatment and the number of new HIV infections evolve very differently—typically, the number of people receiving treatment in a policy scenario increases, while HIV incidence declines steeply (Figure 11.4). These dynamics separate the average costs of treatment (in the example in Figure 11.4, these are estimated at US$28 in 2014, rising to US$44 by 2020) and the actuarially fair premium for insuring against the health costs of contracting HIV (declining from US$80 in 2014 to US$31 by 2020). If insurance premiums are priced to cover the current costs of health services, this would mean that for HIV/AIDS services these premiums become considerably larger than the expected costs caused by contracting HIV (after 2018 in Figure 11.4.b). Under these circumstances, there are reasons to fund the costs of treating people already living with HIV/AIDS separately from insuring the risk of contracting HIV. In transition to a national health insurance with universal coverage, a trust fund could be set up to take the costs of treating people already living with HIV/AIDS off the books of the insurance scheme.

Borrowing

Loans have played an important role in global HIV/AIDS financing.[26] In the 1990s, World Bank loans were the most important source of external financing of HIV/AIDS programmes, and as of the end of February 2015, the World Bank had a portfolio of HIV/AIDS-related loans of US$1.7 billion on its books. The role of loans in external HIV/AIDS financing has receded as grant financing became widely available. Their share in global HIV/AIDS financing has declined from about 5 per cent in 2002 to 1 per cent in 2013, and loan disbursements have accounted for about US$120 million annually (1.6 per cent of external HIV/AIDS financing) in 2008–2013 (OECD, 2015).

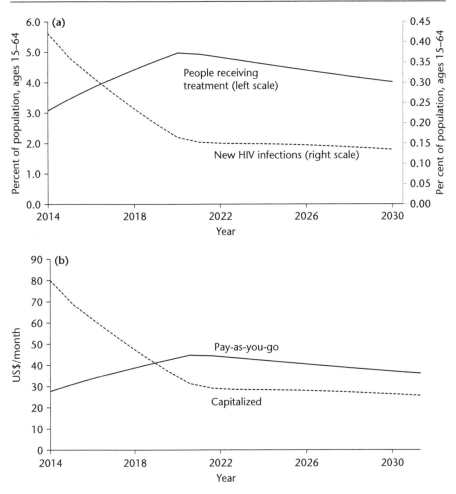

Figure 11.4. Kenya: Insurance premiums required to cover current treatment costs and costs caused by new HIV infections

Source: National AIDS Control Council, (2014a).
(a). Kenya: New HIV infections and people receiving treatment
(b). Kenya: HIV premiums required in pay-as-you-go and capitalized health insurance

Data on the role of borrowing in domestic HIV/AIDS financing is unavailable, as the government budget does not identify the sources of domestic funding, and as there are other options to meet the domestic financing needs of the HIV/AIDS response.[27]

Borrowing does not create additional fiscal space per se, but provides the government with additional resources early on, while constraining its resources later on through interest payments and as a loan is repaid. However, there are a number of circumstances under which borrowing can play a constructive role in HIV/AIDS financing:

- accommodating a sharp shock to government revenues, a spike in expenditures, or both;
- financing projects with a high rate of return;
- inter-generational equity aspects.

Some shocks—natural disasters, armed conflicts, or health emergencies—impose a steep fiscal cost and may at the same time disrupt the economy and therefore government revenues. The most significant recent example is the Ebola epidemic, which has resulted in a drop in GDP growth by several percentage points in the highly affected countries (Guinea, Liberia, and Sierra Leone) in 2014 and 2015, reduced tax revenues, and resulted in additional expenditure pressures, and the governments have accommodated this health (and fiscal) shock by increased borrowing—the fiscal deficit in each country increased by several per cent of GDP.[28] Notably, most of these impacts are not expected to last beyond 2015, that is the increased borrowing allowed the governments to accommodate the acute need by a temporary increase in borrowing, returning to a lower budget deficit once the health shock subsides.

HIV/AIDS, characterized by an extremely long disease trajectory and persistent spending commitments, is quite the opposite of Ebola regarding the persistence of the health and fiscal impacts—the HIV response does not give rise to sharp spikes in spending or sudden drops in expenditures. Distributing the financing burden over a longer period, as practised by the governments facing a severe Ebola outbreak, therefore does not provide a motive for borrowing in support of the HIV response.

Some spikes in expenditure can nevertheless arise for programmatic reasons. For example, a steep scaling up of male circumcision could result in higher costs over a couple of years (and much lower costs to maintain a targeted coverage rate once it is reached), or the HIV programme may envisage high spending upfront to bring down HIV incidence and the future costs of the HIV response. Under these circumstances, it could make sense to finance some of the HIV response by borrowing (through loans directly in support of the HIV programme or higher budget deficits) in the years when the highest costs occur, to avoid temporary adjustments in other expenditure items, and repay the borrowed funds when the costs of the HIV response—at least relative to GDP and fiscal revenues—come down.

Large investment projects are typically financed by loans, not only because they are bulky (so that it does make sense to spread the costs), but also because the benefits are spread over a long period. In this situation, borrowing is a means to elicit a contribution from the beneficiaries later on. Aspects of the response to HIV also have the character of investments for the benefit of a future generation—for example, if the goal of ending AIDS as a significant public health issue by 2030 is realized, then a person born today would face a much reduced lifetime risk of contracting HIV.

Finally, borrowing could enable HIV interventions which create additional fiscal space—where the financial returns to investment are more than enough to service and repay a loan. This is the case for HIV interventions which are deemed 'cost-saving', and the discussion in Chapters 9 and 10 has provided examples of interventions and circumstances where this could be the case. If some interventions are cost-saving, however, this is not a sufficient reason for *additional* funding—by borrowing or otherwise—because these interventions (e.g. condom provision) could be the bedrock of the HIV response and not marginal interventions affected by decisions about additional funding.

12

Concluding Notes

HIV/AIDS has caused a global health shock of extraordinarily large proportions, and the global response has been very effective in reversing the epidemic and mitigating its consequences. The worst country-level health shocks recorded since 1950 are dominated by HIV/AIDS. Of twenty-two episodes on record featuring a drop in life expectancy exceeding 4 years, twelve are primarily caused by HIV/AIDS; if the persistence of the health shock is also taken into account, eight of the ten worst reversals in life expectancy observed on the country level are associated with HIV/AIDS (Table 2.2).

These numbers of course already reflect the impact of the global response to HIV/AIDS, and especially the scaling up of treatment, which has reversed the health impacts of the epidemic. Without it, the bottom of the global distribution of health outcomes would feature a cluster of countries with life expectancy at about 50 years or below, dominated by countries facing a severe HIV/AIDS epidemic (Figure 6.4). In contrast, people living with HIV in South Africa can now expect a near-normal life span, provided that they initiate treatment relatively early, and in Botswana, where life expectancy overall was reduced by almost 20 years because of HIV/AIDS, the loss in life expectancy is now down to 5 years (Figure 2.8).

The global response has in part been motivated by concerns about the economic repercussions, based on the observations that HIV/AIDS primarily affected young (productive) adults and that the epidemic could reverse economic progress in countries where the level of economic development was already low. These concerns, however, have not materialized.

On the microeconomic level, the impacts of HIV/AIDS on affected individuals and families are well documented. 'People have undoubtedly suffered terrible personal loss and distress, but those who have survived have got by' (Seeley et al., 2010), high national HIV prevalence has not been associated with an increase in poverty rates (Figure 3.4), and the evidence for any impact of HIV/AIDS on GDP per capita is very weak. There is, however, a broad consensus that HIV/AIDS has slowed down GDP growth overall, as population growth has declined, and that—conversely—the HIV/AIDS response contributes to higher growth because a larger population can sustain higher output. Such economic gains, however, are of a different kind from the financial costs of the HIV/AIDS response—most of the GDP gains owing to reduced HIV/AIDS-related mortality are absorbed by the costs of living of people surviving longer because of the HIV/AIDS response, and only a small proportion of it is available to offset the economic costs of the HIV/AIDS response.

In summary, the epidemic has caused a devastating shock to the lives of people affected by HIV/AIDS and, in many countries, to aggregate national health outcomes, but the implications for national poverty rates or economic growth do not fundamentally add to the evaluation of the consequences of HIV/AIDS across countries.

The larger part of the book deals with the effectiveness and cost-effectiveness of HIV/AIDS interventions and policies. Cost-effectiveness was considered as somewhat disreputable in global HIV/AIDS policies, at least at the highest levels of policy formulation, where the impetus came from human rights and medical imperatives.[1] This changed around 2011 with the launch of the UNAIDS investment framework, which framed global HIV/AIDS strategies in terms of 'investment ... that will yield long-term dividends', efficiency gains, and cost-effectiveness (Schwartländer et al., 2011).

Cost-effectiveness analysis for HIV/AIDS programmes and interventions, though, presents unusual challenges, resulting from the very slow disease progression and transmission dynamics:

- The direct impacts of HIV prevention interventions are very different from the population-level impacts, and the latter evolve over time. The effects of an HIV prevention intervention can be much diminished by subsequent infection risk, but the effect of an HIV infection averted can also be magnified by subsequent 'downstream' infections averted (see, e.g., Table 9.3).

- Formal optimization approaches are frustrated by the excessive interdependencies over time—it is generally not possible to establish optimal spending allocations one period at a time, and there is no obvious measure to value the state of HIV/AIDS and the HIV/AIDS response at the end of the policy period.

- Over the last decade, the health consequences of HIV infections have diminished (because people living with HIV are likely to progress to treatment, and remain on it for decades), and the financial effects have become (at least relatively) more important and more pervasive (Figures 8.2 and 9.8).

The analyses reviewed and developed in this book respond to these challenges by consistently interpreting investments in the HIV/AIDS response as financial as well as health investments. Policy commitments under the HIV/ AIDS response are interpreted as financial commitments, and new HIV infections give rise to financial liabilities as the resulting costs of HIV/AIDS services absorb fiscal space. The costs of an HIV/AIDS policy over a specific period are interpreted as spending over that period, plus the financial liability posed by the needs of people living with HIV at the end of that period. This interpretation links programme effectiveness and the contributions of a policy towards the financial sustainability of the HIV/AIDS response, and yields more precise estimates of the cost-effectiveness of HIV/AIDS policies than the most common approaches to programme evaluation.

With regard to specific HIV interventions, the book develops two aspects of a forward-looking analysis of cost-effectiveness. First, it illustrates the use of modelling to translate estimates of the direct effects of HIV prevention interventions into estimates of total effects (including, through HIV transmissions averted, beyond the groups targeted by an intervention). Examples include the discussion of the consequences of HIV infections for different sexual risk behaviour (Tables 9.2 and 9.3), and the analysis of the population-level effects of male circumcision (Table 9.4).

Second, the book applies the analysis of the financial liabilities caused by new HIV infections to HIV prevention interventions. Fully accounting for these financial returns, and counting them against the financial costs of an intervention, accentuates differences in cost-effectiveness between HIV prevention interventions (Figure 10.2, Table 10.3), and some HIV interventions come out as good financial investments, even before taking into account any positive health outcomes (see Table 9.1 on condoms, Table 9.4 on male circumcision). This approach also provides a powerful tool for programme evaluation, by testing the marginal contributions of specific interventions to the programme, in terms of costs, health outcomes, and the fiscal space absorbed by the programme, providing pointers on how to improve the programme by reallocating resources or additionally invest in interventions with high cost-effectiveness or a potential to contain the fiscal space absorbed by the programme and contribute to financial sustainability.

Endnotes

Chapter 1

1. See Johnson et al. (2013), based on data from South Africa, and the discussion of the consequences of HIV infections in Chapter 7.
2. See United Nations General Assembly (2001) and WHO, UNAIDS, and UNICEF (2009) on 'universal access', and UNAIDS (2012b, 2014b) and UNAIDS-Lancet Commission on Defeating AIDS—Advancing Global Health (2015) on 'ending AIDS'.

Chapter 2

1. The examples are taken from Table 2.3, showing numerous countries where HIV/AIDS has caused a drop in life expectancy exceeding 10 years, and the estimates of accumulated HIV infection risk illustrated in Figure 2.5.
2. WHO and UNAIDS (2006) estimated that in 2003 only 2 per cent of people requiring treatment were receiving it in sub-Saharan Africa.
3. The early evidence on the scale of the epidemic in sub-Saharan Africa is discussed by Quinn et al. (1986).
4. Men who have sex with men, in the context of HIV/AIDS, are considered a high-risk population because HIV transmission risk during anal intercourse (about 1 per cent per sexual encounter) is much higher than for heterosexual vaginal intercourse (typically estimated at less than 0.1 per cent, in the absence of factors like other sexually transmitted diseases which may increase transmission risk).
5. See Hallett et al. (2006) for a more substantial discussion, and analyses of declines in HIV prevalence in urban Haiti, Kenya, Uganda, and Zimbabwe (in part attributed to behaviour change), and in Côte d'Ivoire, urban Ethiopia, Malawi, and Rwanda (where prevalence trends 'show no signs of changed sexual behaviour').
6. The decline in mortality among people living with HIV from 6.4 per cent in 2004 to 3.2 per cent in 2014 understates the impact of increased access to ART, as mortality (following past trends in HIV incidence) would likely have increased further.
7. The United Nations Population Division (UNPD) also produces annual estimates, but these are interpolated from the 5-year averages, and thus blur the health impacts even more than the 5-year averages.

8. The paper by Whiteside and Whalley (2007), especially its take on disasters, is frequently quoted in the literature on HIV/AIDS. One of the authors even wrote a case study (Whiteside and Henry, 2011) about the paper's success!

9. The discussion in the present section takes a short-term view on the location of the burden of disease. In the longer term, economic outcomes—the basis for the country classifications used here—could reflect the burden of disease. This point has been explored especially for malaria, where a number of studies (e.g. Gallup and Sachs, 2001; Acemoglu et al., 2001) proposed an adverse relationship between the disease burden on one hand, and economic growth or GDP per capita on the other hand. The strong association between malaria and low levels of income observed in Table 2.3 could therefore reflect the consequences of endemic malaria for economic development.

10. Sub-Saharan Africa also contains one high-income country (Equatorial Guinea), which carries a very low weight in light of its small population size of only about 820,000 in 2014, and about 840 AIDS-related deaths in 2014 (UNAIDS, 2015a).

11. The World Bank's definition of income groups relates to gross national income evaluated using smoothed exchange rates ('Atlas method'), whereas Figure 2.3 shows GDP per capita at current exchange rates. The classification of countries by income groups in Figure 2.3 is therefore not exact.

12. Whiteside and Smith (2009) arrive at similar conclusions, highlighting the impacts of HIV/AIDS in regions with high HIV prevalence, but also point to a number of low-income countries like Malawi, Mozambique, or Zambia where the response to HIV/AIDS is highly aid dependent.

13. Unless stated otherwise, epidemiological data on Kenya and Botswana are from UNAIDS (2015a), and on Jamaica from UNAIDS (2014d).

14. For generating estimates of the expected consequences of HIV/AIDS over an individual's life time, the UNAIDS Spectrum files were adapted to eliminate migration. A high rate of outward migration would otherwise reduce the estimated consequences of HIV/AIDS. This modification is especially important in Jamaica, with high rates of outward migration by young adults (i.e. the age group where HIV incidence is highest).

15. The UNAIDS Spectrum files extend to 2020 only. The long-term estimates for the three countries have been obtained by extending the time frame of the files into the future, assuming that HIV incidence remains constant after 2020. To the extent that HIV incidence continues to decline, the lifetime risk of contracting HIV is overestimated. For the cohorts born in 1970 or 1980, though, the resulting bias is small, as most HIV infections occur before 2020.

16. The relatively high risk for men in Jamaica reflects a serious epidemic among men who have sex with men.

17. UNAIDS (2014c) discusses the 'graying of AIDS' in low- and middle-income countries.

18. The concept of an AIDS transition has been introduced and discussed by Over (e.g. 2004, 2011), but is used in a different sense here.

19. An important point when comparing the state of health across less developed countries, where average mortality can be a misleading indicator of the state of

health, because high birth rates translate into a high share of the young population and (because mortality among the young is low) into low mortality overall.

20. The estimates were generated based on three variations of the UNAIDS country Spectrum files—the original files provided by UNAIDS ('actual'), a scenario in which HIV incidence was set to zero ('no AIDS'), and a scenario in which access to ART was set to zero ('AIDS, But No ART').

Chapter 3

1. A household affected by HIV/AIDS, throughout this chapter, is defined as a house-hold containing at least one person living with HIV or having experienced an AIDS-related death. An individual affected by HIV/AIDS is a member of such a household, but not necessarily a person living with HIV.

2. The health consequences of access to ART are addressed in more detail in Chapter 9.

3. The figure shows sub-Saharan Africa only, because country-level HIV prevalence in other regions is fairly low and therefore does not carry much information regarding economic correlates of HIV prevalence.

4. In addition to Mauritius (shown), Seychelles and Comoros would also be located in this group, but they do not appear because UNAIDS does not publish data on HIV prevalence.

5. While results are reported for a poverty line of \$1.25/day, the findings come out similarly for a poverty line of \$2/day. It is important to point out some limitations of the data on poverty and inequality. These are available from household surveys, at irregular intervals, and different years. The data on poverty and inequality on average date back to 2007; especially the data on Botswana—the oldest ones in the sample, dating back to 1994, should be taken with a grain of salt.

6. The correlation coefficients for HIV prevalence and the other variables are 0.33 for GDP per capita, 0.66 for the Gini index, and minus 0.10 for poverty. A cross-country regression for 40 countries for which all four variables are available comes out as

$$HIV\ Prev = \underset{(-4.6)}{-22.1} + \underset{(6.1)}{0.62 \cdot Gini} + \underset{(0.10)}{0.005 \cdot Pov} + \underset{(0.56)}{0.0002 \cdot GDPpc}$$

with t-ratios in parentheses, and an R^2 of 0.56. Only the Gini index comes out statistically significant. According to this regression, going from a Gini index of 33 to one of 64 (the minimum and maximum of the range observed here) is associated with an increase in HIV prevalence of 19 percentage points. A 10-percentage point increase in poverty is associated with a 0.05 percentage point increase in HIV prevalence, and an increase in GDP per capita of US\$1,000 is associated with a level of HIV prevalence that is 0.2 percentage points higher. If the insignificant variables are dropped from the equation, it becomes

$$HIV\ Prev = \underset{(-5.4)}{-22.3} + \underset{(6.8)}{0.64\ Gini}$$

with an R^2 of 0.55.

7. For some more general points regarding inference on health, income differences (both absolute and relative), and inequality, see Deaton (2003).

8. The quote is from Piot et al. (2007), who provide a broader discussion of 'AIDS, poverty, and human development', and summarize thinking reflected in the 2006 UNAIDS report.

9. Leclerc-Madlala (2008) provides an overview of HIV and age-disparate sex, describing the relevance and complex social determinants. However, a recent study (Harling et al., 2014), concludes that age-disparate sex is not the primary driver of HIV incidence among young women in KwaZulu-Natal.

10. At about this time, Wojcicki (2005) reviewed studies of socioeconomic determinants of HIV risk among women, not finding a clear pattern of association—of '36 studies, fifteen found no association between SES and HIV infection, twelve found an association between high SES and HIV infection, eight found an association between low SES and HIV infection and one was mixed' (with 'SES' standing for socioeconomic status).

11. Asiedu et al. (2012) is a good entry point to the literature. The paper provides a thorough discussion of socioeconomic correlates of HIV/AIDS, including sex, age, location (urban/rural), education, and wealth, focusing on four countries with high HIV prevalence (Lesotho, Malawi, Swaziland, and Zimbabwe).

12. A meta-analysis by Boily et al. (2009) does not find a clear difference between male and female risks of contracting HIV across low-income countries, but does not systematically control for co-factors.

13. Quoted from World Bank website, at http://go.worldbank.org/Z1HDOMB9J0, accessed on 9 August 2014.

14. One recent study (de Neve et al., 2015) finds a particularly large effect of an additional year of secondary education on HIV prevalence in Botswana—reducing HIV prevalence among young people by about one-third about 10 years after the intervention. This finding is particularly hard to reconcile with cross-sectional data on HIV prevalence—individuals with secondary education have much *higher* HIV prevalence (22.2 per cent) than individuals with primary education only (16.5 per cent) in the 2013 Botswana AIDS Impact Survey (Statistics Botswana, 2013).

15. According to preliminary results by Baird et al. (2015; an update to Baird et al., 2012) from a study in Malawi, the effects of cash transfers on HIV prevalence dissipated after 5 years.

16. This issue falls in the broader context of improving the efficiency of the HIV/AIDS response by better aligning HIV prevention interventions with evidence on the geographical distribution of HIV/AIDS, and the drivers of the epidemic (e.g. by risk groups) across locations. On the policy level, the emphasis on the 'importance of location and population' by UNAIDS (2014c) follows from the 'Know your epidemic, know your response' principle developed in UNAIDS (2007), and usefully discussed by Wilson and Halperin (2008).

17. Beegle and de Weerth (2008) provide a magisterial discussion on methods and analytical challenges in studying socioeconomic correlates of HIV/AIDS.

18. Most of the literature on the links between poverty and HIV/AIDS-related mortality is inspired by differences in AIDS-related mortality across countries, but does not systematically address the role of poverty. Among studies addressing the role of poverty more directly are Gitahi-Kamau et al. (2015), finding that HIV progressed

faster for individuals with income of less than US$1 per day in Kenya. Marazzi et al. (2008) document high mortality among individuals initiating treatment in the presence of malnutrition or anemia (after controlling for CD4 count at treatment initiation, and especially for individuals initiating treatment late).

19. Cutler et al. (2006) provide a good entry point to the literature on socioeconomic correlates of mortality; Ardington and Gasealahweb (2014) provide a study of mortality data from South Africa.

20. The papers by Bärnighausen et al. (2007) and Lopman and others (2007) are among the exceptions. Bärnighausen and others, studying HIV incidence in KwaZulu-Natal, conclude that 'in this overall poor community it is not the members of the asset-poorest households who are at highest risk of HIV acquisition but people who live in households belonging to the middle category of relative wealth', and that educational attainment significantly reduces the risk of HIV acquisition.

21. The literature on the household-level effects of HIV/AIDS is shaped by an extensive literature on the consequences of ill health for households. Alam and Mahal (2014) and McIntyre et al. (2006) provide thorough reviews of and introductions to this literature. Russell (2004) is still interesting because it combines a general discussion with a review of the consequences of specific diseases, including five early studies on the impacts of HIV/AIDS.

22. For a more substantial discussion of how access to treatment modifies the economic impacts of HIV/AIDS on individuals and households, see Thirumurthy et al. (2012).

23. This research is summarized in three papers—Goldstein et al. (2010), Graff Zivin et al. (2009), and Thirumurthy et al. (2008). Thirumurthy et al. (2011) provide a similar analysis using data from India.

24. This coping mechanism may be relevant more generally—if tasks are reassigned depending on physical capabilities, the social impacts of HIV/AIDS come out lower than impacts of HIV/AIDS on individual productivity.

25. While treatment eligibility at the site studied by Larson et al. (2013) begins at a CD4 count of 350, patients initiated treatment only at a mean CD4 count of 178 (women) and 153 (men). Comparison with the productivity losses documented by Fox et al. (2004)—with no treatment available—suggests that treatment in the study by Larson et al. (2013) is initiated around one year before death would occur.

26. Mahal and others state that the costs and income losses owing to HIV/AIDS accounted for 56 per cent of household income, and that out-of-pocket expenses for healthcare represented 54 per cent of the total economic burden of HIV. Out-of-pocket expenses for healthcare thus accounted for 30 per cent of household income.

27. Mather et al. (2004) provide a more thorough discussion, concluding that 'using incidence of prime-age adult mortality due to illness in rural household survey data is a reasonable and cost-effective way to identify households that are most likely affected by HIV/AIDS-related mortality'.

28. The studies by Bachmann and Booysen (2006) and Booysen (2004), based on repeated surveys of households affected by HIV/AIDS and a comparator group, are worth mentioning. Bachmann and Booysen find a large decline in expenditure among households affected by HIV relative to the reference cases; Booysen estimates transition matrices and documents an increased risk of becoming poor for

households affected by HIV. However, both studies are based on a relatively small sample and do not clearly distinguish the consequences of living with HIV and AIDS-related mortality.

29. The exception is the study on Malawi, with a time horizon of 13 years, but a much smaller sample size.

30. These points are discussed further by Yamano and Jayne (2004), one of the studies synthesized by Mather et al. (2004).

31. Unlike the paper by Yamano and Jayne (2004), the paper by Beegle et al. (2008) finds stronger effects for female adult deaths. Beegle et al. (2010) use the same data set to study the consequences of orphanhood.

32. Samuels and Drinkwater (2011) arrive at similar conclusions—'social units had adapted and . . . livelihoods had remained surprisingly resilient'.

33. The two papers referred are Bell et al. (2006), proposing that the disruptions to the accumulation of human capital caused by parental death would have a very severe impact on economic growth (see Chapter 4), and Schönteich (1999), suggesting that absence of supervision and increased impoverishment among orphans would 'increase their temptation to engage in criminal activity at an early age'.

34. UNICEF (2014) estimates that 15 per cent of the young population (ages 0–17) were orphans in the Democratic Republic of Congo (GDP per capita at US$370, AIDS orphans 1.1 per cent of young population) and in Guinea-Bissau (GDP per capita at US$520, AIDS orphans 2.1 per cent of young population) as of 2012.

35. See Mishra and Bignami-Van Assche (2008), who summarize data on orphans from eight DHS studies conducted between 2003 and 2006. Case et al. (2004) provide graphical illustrations of differences in orphan rates by age from earlier DHS studies from ten countries, conducted between 1992 and 2000.

36. The paper is the latest in a series of papers so far based on this data set, the others are Beegle, de Weerdt, and Dercon (2006 and 2009).

37. Data on poverty and inequality in the World Bank's World Development Indicators database are available at irregular intervals and are typically based on household income and expenditure surveys. Annual changes have been calculated as the difference in poverty rates or in the Gini index between two data points, divided by the number of years between the observations. Data are shown for sub-Saharan Africa only, because data from other regions would cluster at low HIV prevalence and literally blur the picture.

38. A regression based on 80 observations (pairs of successive observations on poverty rates) comes out as $Change\ in\ Poverty = -1.4\ -0.03\ HIV\ Prev + 0.00005\ GDPpc$ (t-ratios in $(-3.5)\ (-0.47)\ \ \ \ \ \ \ \ \ \ \ \ (0.2)$ parentheses), and an R^2 of 0.01, and $Change\ in\ Poverty = -1.4\ -0.03\ HIV\ Prev$, and an $(-3.5)\ (-0.64)$ R^2 of 0.005. For inequality (Gini index, 80 observations), the corresponding regressions yield $Change\ in\ Inequality = -0.5\ +0.09\ HIV\ Prev\ -0.0001\ GDPpc$ ($R_2 = 0.06$) and $(-1.75)\ (2.1)\ \ \ \ \ \ \ \ \ \ \ \ (-0.4)$ $Change\ in\ Inequality = -0.6\ +0.08\ HIV\ Prev$ ($R^2 = 0.06$). These results are influ- $(-1.8)\ (2.2)$ enced by one outlier with a year-on-year change in inequality of 8 percentage points, almost certainly the result of measurement error, without which the coefficient of HIV prevalence declines to 0.06 (t-ratio: 1.4), with an R^2 of 0.04.

39. Deaton (2003) discusses the evidence on the links between income, health, and inequality more fundamentally.

40. This economic reasoning is stated most clearly by Grimm and Harttgen (2008), who discussed the 'repugnant conclusion' in this context (adapted from Parfit 1984). The 'Lancet Commission on Investing in Health' also prominently applies an analysis based on lifetime welfare in general (Jamison et al., 2013).

Chapter 4

1. Even though, the HIV/AIDS-related spending might represent an improvement compared to a situation with no spending and an unfettered epidemic. The point here is only about accounting for the composition of GDP, whereas issues of cost-effectiveness and returns to HIV/AIDS 'investments' is the focus of Part III of this book.

2. The most explicit discussion in a macroeconomic analysis is contained in a study by Arndt and Lewis (2001), based on very preliminary evidence on the costs of HIV/AIDS.

3. See Aventin and Huard (2000) and Rosen et al. (2007) for estimates of the costs of HIV/AIDS to companies. Rosen et al. (2007) also discuss the cost-effectiveness of providing treatment to company employees as a means of reducing the costs of HIV/AIDS. Nattrass (2003) provides a review on the impact of HIV/AIDS on companies in South Africa, embedded in a discussion of macroeconomic studies.

4. See Rajan and Subramanian (2008) as an entry point to the literature.

5. Much of 'new growth theory' focuses on technological advances and research and development, and is geared at understanding the determinants of economic growth in advanced economies. The discussion in the present book focuses on aspects of new growth theory more relevant for developing economies.

6. Weil (2014) uses a similar model in his discussion of 'health and growth' in the *Handbook of Economic Growth*.

7. The transformation of Eq. (1) into Eq. (2) assumes that the production function is homogeneous of degree 1 with respect to K and L, i.e., $F(x \cdot K, x \cdot HL) = x \cdot F(K, HL)$.

8. In the longer run, it is also necessary to take in any changes in birth rates, for medical or economic reasons (desired fertility).

9. See Cuddington (1993a, 1993b), and Cuddington and Hancock (1994, 1995).

10. See Cuddington (1993b), Cuddington and Hancock (1995), and Over (1992).

11. Kambou et al. (1992) provide an accessible introduction to the methodology, and an application on the impacts of HIV/AIDS. Arndt and Lewis (2001) provide an accessible analysis of the sectoral impacts of HIV/AIDS in South Africa. Thurlow et al. (2009) discuss and contrast the impacts of HIV/AIDS in KwaZulu-Natal and in South Africa overall.

12. For illustration see Jefferis et al. (2008) on the macroeconomic consequences of HIV/AIDS in Botswana, comparing estimates from an aggregated growth model and a CGE model.

13. The others are the investment rate and educational attainment.

14. The point is not so much about the empirical validity of the findings by Bloom et al. (2004), but about a literal interpretation, and at least one of the authors would agree with it. On the interpretation of life expectancy in growth regressions, Temple (1999) observes that 'variables like life expectancy are often used in growth regressions, but their role is never justified by a well-articulated theory'. Weil (2007) points to challenges arising from the potential *inter*dependence of health and income, and indeed much of his empirical work addresses this problem. Deaton (2006) argues that the global evidence is more consistent with 'an explanation in which there are common third factors that are good both for growth and for health', than with a causal link between health and growth.

15. The authors report that all estimates were also undertaken using life expectancy instead of infant mortality as an indicator of the state of health, with similar results.

16. This specification may reflect concerns about the impact of HIV/AIDS on state capacities at the time. These concerns, however, have subsided, and the impact of HIV/AIDS on institutions has not played a role in later empirical work.

17. The analysis was updated by Mahal (2004), with data through 1998, who also tends to find negative but statistically insignificant coefficients.

18. This could be a better indicator for the economic impacts of HIV/AIDS than HIV prevalence—many reported AIDS cases are diagnosed at a fairly late stage of the disease, when productivity effects would be apparent, whereas HIV prevalence includes many undiagnosed and asymptomatic individuals, but also introduces a source of error as the share of AIDS cases reported may differ across countries.

19. Male circumcision is recognized to reduce the risk of acquiring HIV (Siegfried et al. (2009)), and the negative correlation between HIV prevalence and male circumcision across Africa has been recognized since the late 1980s (see Bongaarts et al., 1989, and Caldwell and Caldwell, 1993). Also see Chapter 9, on the cost-effectiveness of HIV/AIDS interventions.

20. When the sample is split with Eastern and Southern Africa (containing most countries with high HIV prevalence) on one hand, and the rest of Africa on the other, the coefficients change sign and become statistically insignificant.

21. A point also made by Lovász (2012).

22. This situation may be changing, though, with economically more advanced economies also more successful in extending access to treatment and reversing the adverse health consequences of HIV/AIDS. This point is discussed in more detail in Chapter 6.

23. Because of this, HIV/AIDS appears in a footnote only, making the point that 'the burst of HIV in Africa might well reverse this trend [towards convergence in life expectancies] in the future'.

24. The online appendix 3 of Jamison et al. (2013) provides a fairly accessible introduction to the value of statistical life, Viscusi (1993) provides a thorough review of the earlier literature, Viscusi and Aldy (2003) provide a survey and empirical analysis of estimates of the value of statistical life across countries.

25. As a stark example of the principle behind the 'value of statistical life', consider a piece that the *New York Times* ran on its front page on 14 April 2004 about US workers seeking employment in Iraq, during a surge of violence against foreign

contractors there. One job seeker, referring to a position as a truck driver (a particularly dangerous line of employment), says: 'I look at it from a business perspective.... When you're talking a possible $1,000 a day tax free, it's real attractive.' Other examples include an engineer receiving a 30 per cent bonus, or positions as mechanics and warehouse workers, 'some of which pay as much as $100,000 a year'.

26. This is consistent with standard theory of consumer behaviour and the declining marginal utility of consumption. An increase in mortality, in standard consumer theory, means that there is an increased risk that life's enjoyments will come to a premature end. In compensation, the individual would want to consume more in each period within the shortened expected time horizon. Because each additional unit of consumption buys less satisfaction, the amount required to restore the standard of living is disproportionately higher than the percentage decline in life expectancy.

27. Usher (1973, 1980) is credited with interpreting health gains and the evidence on the 'value of life' in a growth accounting context, the theoretical underpinnings were developed, among others, by Mishan (1971).

28. Sir George Alleyne may have tried to point this out to the author, after reading one of his earlier efforts (see Alleyne, 2009).

29. 'Swiftian' preferences were introduced by Jonathan Swift in *A Modest Proposal* (1729), a satirical and provocative essay suggesting that the wretched Irish should sell their children as meat, to generate some income to improve their lot, spare their children a dismal life, and contain the spread of Papism.

30. In contrast, Viscusi and Aldy (2003) estimate an elasticity of the value of statistical life with respect to income of about 0.5—this means that the value of statistical life in a country with a GDP per capita of US$1,500—relative to income—is 8 times higher than in a country with a level of GDP per capita of US$55,000. However, Becker and Elias (2007) point out that this result is driven by an outlier—one very large and implausible estimate from India, and that the elasticity is close to one (i.e. the value of statistical life is proportional to GDP per capita) if this observation is excluded. Ironically, the arguably more plausible estimate is arrived at by dropping the only observation from a low-income country.

31. Murphy and Topel (2006) assume that the relative valuation of health vs. income may change across the income distribution at a point in time, but that the value of statistical life increases over time in proportion to GDP per capita at any point of the income distribution.

32. The estimates on the loss of life expectancy were obtained from the latest available UNAIDS epidemiological country files (see Figure 2.8 for details and underlying estimates of life expectancy), comparing the UNAIDS estimates to a counterfactual scenario without HIV/AIDS created by the author.

Chapter 5

1. Quinn et al. (1986) give a good overview of the emerging evidence on HIV/AIDS in Africa at the time, documenting estimates of HIV prevalence and data on AIDS

cases, the sex and age distribution of people living with HIV, and the increases in the incidence of AIDS cases which had occurred over the preceding years.

2. The WHO's HIV/AIDS programme went through several permutations around its establishment 1986, and only from 1988 became the 'Global Programme on AIDS'. Lisk (2009) discusses its 'rise and fall'.

3. See Piot and Caraël (1988) for a review of the evidence at the time, discussing a number of risk factors and social correlates, but also pointing out that 'patterns of spread of HIV infection may widely vary from one area to another'.

4. See Fleming et al. (1988).

5. One unfortunate consequence from these experiences was that aspects like cost-effectiveness and efficiency played a subordinate role in HIV/AIDS programme design, at least until about 2009–2011 when perceptions about the availability of external funding started to change.

6. See Piot (2015) for lucid discussions on the transnational civil society movement and the right to treatment.

7. These tasks are summarized from ECOSOC (1994).

8. While the availability of data on the state of the epidemic across developing countries surpasses those for any other health condition, it should be noted that most of it is model-generated, calibrating an epidemiological model to fit available observations on HIV prevalence. Especially for variables for which no directly observed data are available (e.g. HIV incidence), the estimates are therefore subject to substantial error.

9. For consistency, current estimates of the state of HIV/AIDS in 2000 are quoted. Contemporary estimates of the number of people living with HIV were higher, with a global total of 34 million, of which 24 million were located in sub-Saharan Africa (UNAIDS, 2000).

10. Even the IMF issued a book on the economic repercussions of the epidemic (Haacker, 2004), the only book so far published by the IMF on a public health issue, discussing the social and economic impacts of HIV/AIDS and its fiscal consequences.

11. Goosby et al. (2012) provide a brief history of PEPFAR through 2011.

12. See Bongaarts et al. (1989) on male circumcision, and Montaner et al. (2006) on the potential effectiveness of 'treatment as prevention'. The effectiveness of either prevention intervention is discussed thoroughly in Chapter 9.

13. These issues are discussed at length in Chapter 9.

14. Altman and Buse (2012) similarly argued that 'the political reality is that AIDS cried wolf too often, and the more dire warnings have failed to materialise. In most parts of the world, AIDS is not a security or development crisis, and the perception that the response has received too much attention and funding is growing'.

15. The question addressed in the Copenhagen Consensus deliberations is how to spend an *additional* amount on pressing global challenges. As money already being spent on HIV/AIDS is reducing its impact, the returns to additional spending are diminishing.

16. These points are developed at length in Part III of this book.

17. These data are compiled from 'National AIDS Spending Assessments', 'progress reports' submitted by national governments to UNAIDS, and other documents. Summary data, including breakdowns by main spending category and funding source, are published through the 'aidsinfoonline' database maintained by UNAIDS (see www.aidsinfoonline.org).

18. For example, countries facing very high financing challenges might be unable or unwilling to implement a comprehensive HIV/AIDS response, and actual spending would understate the financing challenge.

19. The analysis in Chapter 6, though, linking outcomes of the HIV/AIDS response (treatment access) to these determinants, finds little evidence suggesting that such issues play a large role.

20. The equation was estimated in natural logs, with LN(spending) = 3.62 + 0.72*LN (HIV/GDPpc), based on latest available observations from ninety-eight countries. This equation explains the 80.7% variation of the dependent variable, and the explanatory variable is highly significant (*t*-ratio of 20.0). If LN(HIV) or LN(GDPpc) are included in the regression as additional explanatory variables, the coefficient is marginally significant (*t*-ratio of 1.7), and the R^2 increases marginally to 81.3.

21. See findings from ORPHEA study, discussed in Chapter 11, and summarized in Figure 11.3.

22. E.g., external financing for health overall would rarely exceed two-thirds of health spending, and it declines more steeply with GDP per capita.

23. In the terminology of HIV/AIDS policy, 'financial sustainability' is frequently equated with the question of whether an HIV/AIDS strategy (typically covering 3–5 years) can be financed. In the tradition of economic analysis applied here, though, sustainability is a long-term concept. From this perspective, an HIV/AIDS strategy is unsustainable if there is no plausible financing scenario beyond an arbitrary policy period.

24. Additionally, it is unclear how this index is used by UNAIDS (2010a), who observe that the 'median level of priority is 0.35' (which would mean that 50% fall below this level), and that the 'priority index of a large majority of countries (70%) ... falls below this average'.

25. See Global Fund (2014c) on its policy on allocating funding and the discussion of determinants of external financing later in this section.

26. The analysis by Haacker and Greener (2012) focuses on donor behaviour and uses the share of external financing as the dependent variable. As the share of external financing (in per cent) is simply equal to 100 minus the share of domestic financing, their analysis applies equally to the share of domestic financing.

27. See, e.g., Vassall et al. (2013) for a broad discussion. Stover et al. (2011) provide an illustration, projecting the costs of treatment for the cohort already receiving treatment in 2011 through programmes supported by the Global Fund (i.e. excluding the costs of patients initiating treatment from 2012). After 9 years (by 2020), two-thirds of these patients were projected to still be alive. Costs of treatment, however, decline by 10% only, because some patients switch to more expensive 'second-line' types of treatment.

28. Also see discussion in Chapter 11. Haacker (2015a) summarizes estimates of the macroeconomic and fiscal impact of Ebola, and discusses the financing of the costs and impact of Ebola and the HIV/AIDS response.
29. See Haacker (2011), Lule and Haacker (2012), and more recently Collier et al. (2015). A number of HIV/AIDS 'investment cases' have also been using this approach (e.g. NACC (2014a) for Kenya).
30. The paper by Haacker and Greener builds on an earlier analysis by Haacker (2009). Collier et al. (2015) follow a different empirical approach, linking the absolute amount of external funding to GDP per capita and HIV prevalence.
31. Haacker and Greener (2012) complemented the estimated rule with a criterion to minimize the sum of squares of domestic financing needs (in per cent of GDP), subject to a varying global budget constraint.

Chapter 6

1. Mahy et al. (2009) discuss the availability of measures of HIV incidence and AIDS-related mortality, for generalized and concentrated epidemics, and the resulting challenges for impact evaluation.
2. See Cohen et al. (2011, 2012a, 2012b) on treatment as prevention, and Auvert et al. (2005) on medical male circumcision.
3. The 'Goals' model is part of the 'Spectrum' software package (Avenir Health, 2014), but distinct from the 'AIDS Impact Model' (AIM) used to estimate the state of the epidemic by UNAIDS and national HIV/AIDS programmes. The AIM includes a full demographic model, and is used to calibrate estimates of the course and state of the epidemic based on available data on HIV prevalence (from national surveys, or antenatal clinics) over time. One of the outcomes is a trajectory of HIV incidence that, together with other factors like treatment access, best explains the available data. The Goals model takes the trends in HIV incidence supplied by the AIM as a starting point, provides estimates on how these trends would change as different HIV prevention interventions and treatment are varied from their baseline levels, and uses AIM to create a complete set of projections of the state of the HIV/AIDS epidemic.
4. To understand the consequences of the global HIV/AIDS response from a development perspective, it would also be important to understand how the benefits are distributed within countries. Consistent data on the distribution of access to HIV/AIDS services within countries, however, is unavailable.
5. The baseline number is based on data on the coverage of male circumcision summarized by Njeuhmeli et al. (2011).
6. This has been calculated assuming an effectiveness of male circumcision in reducing HIV transmission of 60 per cent, and assuming that the risk of contracting HIV is the same for individuals becoming circumcised and others—resulting most probably in an underestimate of the impact of male circumcision because a disproportionately large number of young men become circumcised, for whom the risk of contracting HIV tends to be higher.

7. In a multivariate regression across eighty-eight low- and middle-income countries with treatment coverage as dependent variable, the coefficients of both HIV prevalence and GDP per capita are significant. An increase in HIV prevalence of 1 per cent is associated with a treatment coverage rate that is 1.1 percentage points higher, and an increment in GDP per capita of US$1,000 is associated with a treatment coverage rate that is 0.8 percentage points higher. With these coefficients, and considering the variation of HIV prevalence and GDP per capita across these countries, HIV prevalence plays a larger role in explaining cross-country differences. Both variables, though, explain only 22 per cent of the variation in the data on treatment coverage.

8. See Johnson et al. (2013), concluding that people living with HIV in South Africa could enjoy a near-normal life expectancy, provided that they initiate treatment above a CD4 count of 200.

9. Averages are weighted by number of people living with HIV. The estimates of the state and consequences of HIV/AIDS in the absence of treatment have been obtained based on the epidemiological ('Spectrum') work files utilized and made available by UNAIDS (2014d), by setting treatment access equal to zero (but leaving HIV incidence unchanged). The resulting estimate is accurate in terms of capturing the survival effects of treatment, but may not capture some interactions arising from the HIV prevention aspects of treatment.

10. Lesotho is subsumed here, although it marginally exceeds the income threshold and is classified as a 'lower-middle-income country' by the World Bank. Income per capita, though, is much closer to the low-income countries than any of the middle-income countries discussed in this section.

11. In this section, excess mortality is defined as AIDS-related mortality among people living with HIV in a country, minus 1.2 per cent (the lowest mortality rate observed across developing countries where relevant data are available).

12. See May et al. (2010), Johnson et al. (2013), and Boulle et al. (2014). Estimates of the survival gains owing to antiretroviral therapy are also used in the analysis of the consequences of treatment in Chapter 9.

13. The data were available from the epidemiological 'Spectrum' country files from UNAIDS (2015a) for 86 countries. Data for 20 countries were obtained from epidemiological 'Spectrum' country files contained in UNAIDS (2014d).

14. The data used by UNAIDS and underlying Figure 6.4 uses demographic estimates from the World Population Prospects 2012, in which life expectancy in Sierra Leone (at 45 years) is a negative outlier. In the most recent version of the World Population Prospects, life expectancy in Sierra Leone has been revised to 50 years.

15. The analysis was based on 52 of 139 grants funded in Round 8 of the Global Fund, with a total allocation of just under US$1 billion.

16. See Section 6.3, and the discussion of the studies by Bendavid et al. (2012), Brugha et al. (2010), Grépin (2012), Kruk et al. (2012), and Lee and Platas-Izama (2015).

17. The three studies quoted are Car et al. (2012), Conseil et al. (2013), and Yu et al. (2008).

18. See the studies quoted in the previous footnote, and Biesma et al. (2009).

19. For a rare discussion of approaches to ex-post evaluation of the impacts of the global HIV/AIDS response, see McCoy et al. (2013).

20. UNAIDS (2015c) estimates that the number of people receiving treatment increased from 11.4 million at end-2012 to 13.0 million at end-2013, consistent with an average number of people receiving treatment of about 12 million in 2013.

Chapter 7

1. As signified by its prominent role in the Millennium Development Goals, or the characterization 'through its devastating scale and impact [as] a global emergency' by the UN General Assembly Special Session on HIV/AIDS in 2001.
2. Disbursements of global development assistance on HIV/AIDS increased from US $800 million in 2002 to US$7.2 billion in 2010, in which year it accounted for 40 per cent of all global development assistance in the areas of health and population policies (OECD CRS database).
3. Between 2003 and 2010, global access to antiretroviral therapy increased from 800,000 (of which only half were located in low- and middle-income countries) to 8 million, of which 90 per cent were located in low- and middle-income countries.
4. The link between the UNAIDS 'investment framework' and the new funding model of the Global Fund is bi-directional. Members of the Global Fund contributed to the 'investment framework', and elements of the 'investment framework' parallel the 2011 Global Fund strategy on 'investing for impact' (Global Fund, 2011a).
5. A good illustration of 'combination prevention' is the study by Anderson et al. (2014), which contrasts a uniform national prevention strategy with one that is differentiated according to the drivers of the epidemic across forty-seven counties. Tanser et al. (2009) identify wide variations in HIV prevalence across localities in KwaZulu-Natal.
6. I.e., to ensure that 90 per cent of people living with HIV know their status, 90 per cent of people knowing their status receive treatment, and 90 per cent of people receiving treatment are virally suppressed.
7. See Sidibé (2014) and UNAIDS (2014a, 2014b) for discussions of 'ending AIDS' and the '90-90-90' targets.
8. This is a point made similarly by Kremer (1998), who observes that 'it is difficult to assess the cost-effectiveness of anti-AIDS efforts, because it is difficult to estimate the number of additional infections due to each primary case and because it is very difficult to know how behaviour responds to such interventions as promotion of condoms'.
9. Even for those primary beneficiaries of an intervention who contract HIV later on, the intervention would be beneficial because an HIV infection delayed by some years extends life expectancy by a similar period. Moreover, a delay in HIV infections among primary beneficiaries may still result in onward HIV infections averted.
10. UNAIDS (2014a) provides brief pointers to such economic returns. Influential examples for the use of projected cost savings from scaling up HIV prevention services include Njeuhmeli et al. (2011) on medical male circumcision, Granich et al. (2012) on treatment as prevention, and Resch et al. (2011) on output gains from increased treatment coverage.

11. The references quoted are intended as more or less arbitrary snapshots, the issues are discussed further in Chapters 8 (Cost-effectiveness of HIV/AIDS programs), 9 (Cost-effectiveness of specific HIV/AIDS interventions), and 10 (Optimal HIV/AIDS spending allocations).

12. The discussion of the contribution of HIV/AIDS programmes to national development objectives (Chapter 8) develops this point further, and Chapter 6 provides a global perspective on health outcomes.

13. The financial analysis is developed further in the section on fiscal space in Chapter 8; Chapter 9 includes—among other aspects—further discussions on the financial consequences of various HIV/AIDS interventions.

14. The example is based on the UNAIDS (2015a) country 'Spectrum' file for South Africa. However, the file has been modified to carve out the effects caused by new HIV infections, and the assumptions underlying the scenarios are illustrative and not based on specific policies or cost estimates for South Africa.

15. This is considerably lower than the annual unit cost of treatment and other services, because of mortality before and after initiating treatment, and (for the earlier years) because some individuals progress to treatment eligibility and initiate treatment relatively late.

16. 'Lack of liquidity' means that investments in HIV prevention are long-term investments, and cannot be sold or reversed ('liquidated') if priorities change, because the returns to investments in HIV prevention are embodied in people not infected with HIV. In financial markets, such investments typically command higher interest rates than investments which can be easily turned back into money.

17. These estimates are based on the full life-cycle of a cohort who contract HIV in 2014.

Chapter 8

1. For more details on the HIV prevention interventions contained in the 'Goals' model, see Chapter 10 which contains a discussion of the effectiveness and cost-effectiveness of specific interventions across an HIV/AIDS programme.

2. See http://www.avenirhealth.org/software-spectrum and Avenir Health (2014) for documentation of the models. The 'AIDS Impact Model' is designed to generate estimates of the state of the epidemic consistent with available evidence like HIV prevalence from population surveys or antenatal clinics. Compared to the 'AIDS Impact Model', the 'Goals' software/model is simplified in some regards, but allows users to add assumptions on the current coverage and the scaling-up of a range of HIV prevention interventions.

3. The estimate of an average saving of US$3,900 per HIV infection averted is obtained by dividing the financial costs (US$46.5 billion, discounted at a rate of 3 per cent) by the *discounted* number of new HIV infections (10.3 million rather than the undiscounted figure of 12.1 million). The value of US$3,900 is coincidentally the one reported from Stover et al. (2001), but lower in real terms because of inflation.

4. The 2013 WHO guidelines (WHO, 2013) suggest earlier initiation of treatment at a CD4 count of 500, rather than 350 as in the 2010 guidelines, and also introduce additional eligibility criteria based on 'treatment as prevention' principles.

5. This point also plays a role in the analysis of specific interventions, especially for male circumcision, the impact of which is spread over the remaining life of the individual receiving it. See Chapter 9 for further discussion.

6. Schwartländer et al. (2011) simply compare the magnitude of the costs and the savings, but avoid subtracting the latter from the former to obtain net costs or savings, presumably because of the double-counting issue described here.

7. See Heller (2006), Hay and Williams (2006), Tandon and Cashin (2010), and Powell-Jackson et al. (2012).

8. Chapter 11 contains a discussion on the extent to which such spending commitments resemble a public debt and—in terms of their fiscal consequences—can be interpreted similarly.

9. This assumes that the government is able to shift resources between periods by borrowing or other financial operations.

10. As in the example in Figure 7.3, the illustration has been created using the UNAIDS country file for South Africa. However, the scenarios are generic (a 100 per cent chance to progress to treatment once an eligibility threshold is reached), and the cost assumption (US$400 annually) is not based on a costing of South Africa's HIV/AIDS programme.

11. The terms 'basic program activities' and 'critical enablers' were coined by Schwartländer et al. (2011), who discuss the scope of the respective costs more extensively.

12. See WHO (2013), Ministry of Health of Kenya (2014).

13. This estimate reflects a projected growth rate of about 6 per cent, in line with recent estimates and projections by the IMF (2015). As a consequence, the costs of the HIV/AIDS response, while increasing in absolute terms, decline relative to GDP from a peak of 1.8 per cent of GDP in 2020 to 1.4 per cent of GDP in 2030 under the investment framework. Under the baseline scenario, costs steadily decline from 1.5 per cent of GDP in 2014 to 1.1 per cent of GDP in 2030.

14. Lule and Haacker (2012) describe these spending commitments as fiscal 'quasi-liabilities', i.e., 'not a debt de jure, but a political and fiscal commitment that binds fiscal resources in the future and cannot easily be changed', and which are 'very similar to a pension obligation or certain social grants or services'.

15. The estimated costs for 2030 in Figure 8.3.f are lower than the costs of the HIV/AIDS response shown in Figure 8.3.a, because the former only include services to people living with HIV/AIDS, whereas the latter also comprise other categories of prevention spending.

16. This has been calculated by dividing the discounted savings from reduced HIV incidence (US$10.3 billion) by the discounted number of HIV infections averted (978,000) rather than the undiscounted number (1.3 million) quoted in the text, to obtain an estimate of the average cost savings from one HIV infection averted at the time the HIV infection would otherwise occur.

17. This point is discussed in more detail in the first section of Chapter 10, addressing methodological challenges in determining optimal HIV/AIDS spending allocations.

18. In Chapter 3, it is argued that while there is a substantial body of evidence on the impacts of HIV/AIDS or deaths more generally on affected households and individuals, there is no clear correlation between the impact of HIV/AIDS and national

poverty rates. This may reflect that some households may benefit from HIV/AIDS deaths elsewhere (e.g. if they gain control of a deceased's assets), and that dead people are not reflected in poverty rates—the epidemic may have a disproportionate impact on the poor and deepen the consequences of poverty, but improve measured poverty rates by killing poor people.

19. The gain in life expectancy of 1.2 years represents an increase in relative terms of about 2 per cent, at a cost of 0.3 per cent of GDP. In the economic valuations of health gains discussed in Chapter 4, an intervention that increases life expectancy by 1 per cent at less than 3–4 per cent of GDP would be considered welfare-enhancing. The criterion for cost-effectiveness applied by the WHO (one life year gained at a cost of less than 3 times GDP per capita) is broadly equivalent and—via the Commission on Macroeconomics and Health—builds on similar economic considerations (CMH, 2001; Hutubessy and others, 2003).

20. In some environments, the benefits of improved productivity would accrue to the employer, e.g. if treatment reduces the number of days an individual spends on paid sick leave. In this case, improved productivity would not have an effect similar to a social transfer to people living with HIV, and the gains would be more dissipated.

21. The duration of the negative impact of a death on per capita consumption of surviving household members is not necessarily congruent with the duration of the loss of support to surviving dependents. A decline in per capita income following a death may be the consequence of funeral costs and a resulting loss of assets, not of the loss of support. Another possibility is that previously unemployed household members take up employment opportunities following a breadwinner's death, including those vacated by the deceased person.

22. According to the latest data published by the World Bank (2015), government revenues excluding grants averaged 11 per cent in low-income countries in 2010, and 18 per cent in middle-income countries in 2011. Note that, in countries where government revenues are dominated by resource extraction, the impacts of increased survival on output and tax revenues could be less than proportional.

23. For an analysis adopting a more explicit macroeconomic framework, see Ventelou et al. (2012). A number of papers focusing on the financial returns to investments of HIV programes, without taking into account macroeconomic repercussions, are discussed in the second section of this chapter (with regard to HIV programme costs overall) and Chapter 9 (covering the scaling-up of specific interventions).

24. The gains from the paper by Resch et al. (2011) were attributed by a regression attributing the gains either to individuals who would have survived without treatment or to life years gained because of treatment in the respective year. This regression explains most of the variation in the results reported by Resch and others (R^2 = 0.996); the residual was then attributed to the two types of gains proportionately so that the totals match.

25. The role of the costs of orphan support is not entirely clear in this analysis. While grants to orphans are a fiscal cost, from the macroeconomic perspective applied in the paper by Resch et al. (2011) they are a transfer, i.e. a redistribution of resources within the population, and not an economic cost.

Chapter 9

1. The ASSA2008 model was developed by the Actuarial Society of South Africa (ASSA) and launched in 2011. It is available online (http://www.actuarialsociety.org.za/Socie-tyactivities/CommitteeActivities/DemographyEpidemiologyCommittee/Models.aspx). There are two versions—a 'lite' version, used here, which distinguishes individuals by risk categories, but not ethnic categories, whereas the full model also distinguishes four ethnic categories. Individuals are differentiated by sex, age (in 1-year brackets), and in six sexual risk categories—the 'Young' and the 'Old' are not sexually active, the 'Not' adults are not at risk of contracting HIV, there is one group 'RSK' adopting moderate sexual risk behaviour, and two high-risk groups—STD (associated with other sexually transmitted diseases), and PRO (behaviour associated with commercial sex workers).

2. This point will be discussed more thoroughly at the end of the section.

3. In the absence of complicating factors, such as the presence of other sexually transmitted diseases, the ASSA2008 model assumes a male-to-female transmission rate of 0.2 per cent per sexual act, and a female-to-male transmission rate of 0.1 per cent.

4. The effects shown in Figure 9.4 have been calculated in the same way as the *totals* reported in the discussion of Figure 9.3—i.e. adding up subsequent HIV infections associated with one initial HIV infection (or, equivalently, adding up HIV infections averted as a consequence of an intervention that directly averts one HIV infection).

5. These numbers are based on the ratio of new HIV infections (ages 15+) to the number of people living with HIV in that age group, based on UNAIDS estimates for 2014 (UNAIDS, 2014c). For countries with an HIV prevalence (ages 15–49) of 2.48 or higher in 2013, the unweighted average of the annual probability that an individual passes on HIV in 2013 was 5.4 per cent, with a standard deviation of 1.7. A regression of this probability on HIV prevalence returns an insignificant coefficient, and explains less than 1 per cent of the variation in the data.

6. Weller and Davis-Beaty (2002) also make the point about possible bias. Pinkerton and Abramson (1997) discuss the relevance of *consistent* condom use.

7. See Gregson et al. (2010) for Zimbabwe, Johnson et al. (2012) for South Africa, and Boily et al. (2013) for India.

8. See Foss et al. (2007), Chersich et al. (2013), and Ota et al. (2011) for reviews of the relevant literature, and Boily et al. (2013) for a recent case study.

9. See Foss et al. (2007); Foss et al. (2004).

10. Bertozzi et al. (2006) observe that 'given the central role that condom promotion, distribution, and social marketing has played in HIV prevention programs, the lack of data on the relative cost-effectiveness of such programs 20 years into their implementation is striking'.

11. The estimate of the financial savings from one HIV infection prevented is based on the projections of the costs caused by one HIV infection, under different eligibility criteria, discussed in Chapter 7. Specifically, it is assumed here that individuals have a 30 per cent chance of obtaining treatment once they reach a CD4 count of 500, and a 50 per cent chance to initiate treatment once they reach a CD4 count

of 350, i.e., an 80 per cent chance overall of reaching treatment once or before they reach a CD4 count of 350. With annual treatment cost set at US$400, and applying a discount rate of 3 per cent, this yields an estimated cost of US$4,650 per HIV infection.

12. This point is made similarly by Over and Piot (1993) with regard to sexually transmitted diseases in general.

13. In this chapter, the term 'key populations' is used to describe populations which play a large role in the transmission of HIV, and who therefore play a key role in HIV prevention policies. The usage of the term is thus narrower than the meaning adopted by UNAIDS (2014c), which also includes particularly vulnerable populations living with HIV (e.g. children). The meaning is differentiated from the term 'at-risk' or 'most-at-risk populations', as it also takes into account the risk of passing on HIV/AIDS.

14. Forsythe et al. (2009) provide an analysis of spending patterns across HIV prevention interventions across countries. Amico et al. (2012) find that 'only 7% of funding was spent on most-at-risk populations and less than 1% on male circumcision. Spending patterns did not consistently reflect current evidence and the HIV specific transmission context of each country.'

15. See the 'Kenya HIV Prevention Revolution Road Map' (NACC and NASCOP, 2014) and the related study by Anderson et al. (2014) for a well-developed example for 'combination prevention'.

16. The early study was by Gouws et al. (2006); the latest review covered here is by Mishra et al. (2014a).

17. The model is available at http://www.unaids.org/en/dataanalysis/datatools/incidencebymodesoftransmission and has been documented in UNAIDS (2012a).

18. The estimates on injecting drug users for Zimbabwe likely reflect misspecification, as it is hard to envisage an HIV incidence rate of 13.1 per cent in a community where HIV prevalence is only 12.4 per cent. Fraser et al. (2010) emphasize the lack of data on injecting drug users. Because injecting drug users account for only 1.4 per cent of all HIV infections in this study, misspecification in this area does not invalidate other findings.

19. See the review of the 'modes of transmission' approach by Gouws (one of the contributors to the development of the model) and Cuchi (2012).

20. The 'modes of transmission' framework is not well-suited to address these issues because of its short-term focus, and because it does not specify how HIV is entering the 'low-risk' population.

21. This has been calculated as follows. Vassall et al. (2014) report that 50,000 HIV infections were averted among high-risk populations over a 4-year period. Assuming that the HIV infections were averted on average around the mid-point of the 4-year period, this implies 100,000 person-years of high-risk individuals *not* living with HIV. These 100,000 person-years result in 11,000 HIV infections averted among the general population, i.e. 0.11 HIV infections averted annually for each HIV infection averted among high-risk individuals.

22. A preliminary version of the forward-looking analysis of the 'modes of transmission' framework with regard to Jamaica is contained in World Bank (2013).

23. The first assumption affects how long an individual can pass on HIV. The 5-year period during which an individual can pass on HIV has been set with several considerations in mind. Following an HIV infection, health will eventually deteriorate and sexual activity decline. This process will be halted or delayed if an individual proceeds to treatment, but treatment would also considerably reduce the HIV transmission probability. The second assumption regards the probability that an individual who becomes infected in some year would otherwise become infected later. An eventual transition to a lower-risk group is consistent with models in which sexual activity eventually declines with age. The dynamic model used by Mishra et al. (2012, 2014b) also contains such transitions out of high-risk groups. Note that the 10-year period is counted from the time an HIV infection may occur, so that the average total time of sexual activity within the risk group is higher.

24. The exception, shown in Table 9.3, is the case of clients of female sex workers in Zimbabwe.

25. The costs vary largely in proportion to the total number of HIV infections attributed to one initial HIV infection, but there are some differences because the costs are calculated based on a discount rate of 3 per cent. The costs caused by HIV infections occurring later thus carry a low weight.

26. In Zimbabwe, the financial savings from averting one HIV infection among female sex workers are much lower (at US$6,300) because the prevention impact is eroded by the high risk of subsequent HIV infections among female sex workers.

27. The term 'medical male circumcision' is used in the literature to differentiate from traditional circumcision, a traditional practice among some ethnic groups. However, not all types of traditional circumcision involve the complete removal of the foreskin and thus do not achieve the full potential benefits in terms of protection from HIV.

28. Schwartländer et al. (2011) include male circumcision, at least in generalized epidemics with a low underlying circumcision rate, among 'basic program activities'.

29. Caldwell and Caldwell (1993) provide a review of the early literature. A systematic review by Weiss et al. (2000) found that 21 (out of 27) studies showed a reduction in the risk of acquiring HIV by about one-half among circumcised men, and that the reduction in risk was stronger in studies controlling for potential confounding factors. However, Siegfried et al. (2003), while observing the 'strong epidemiological association' between male circumcision and HIV, concluded that there was 'insufficient evidence to support an interventional effect of male circumcision on HIV acquisition in heterosexual men'. Subsequently, findings from randomized controlled trials conducted in Kenya (Bailey et al., 2007), South Africa (Auvert et al., 2005), and Uganda (Gray et al., 2007) showed a reduction in HIV incidence among circumcised males of 50–60 per cent, resulting in general acceptance of the causal link between male circumcision and female-to-male HIV transmission.

30. Garnett (2014) provides an introduction on vaccines that protect against sexually transmitted diseases. Kaldor and Wilson (2010) discuss and compare the effectiveness of a vaccine and of male circumcision. Observing that male circumcision has an efficacy of 60 per cent, but can be targeted at only half the population, they assess the potential impact of a vaccine with an efficacy of 30 per cent among males

and females. (The rate of 30 per cent is motivated by preliminary outcomes of a medical trial.) They conclude that a vaccine, even at an efficacy of 30 per cent, could have a larger impact than scaling-up male circumcision. The principal reasons for this finding are that (i) the target population is twice as high, and direct benefits would accrue to women as well as to men, and (ii) the baseline coverage rate for an HIV vaccine is 0 per cent, whereas a share of the male population is already circumcised, so that the potential contribution to lowering HIV incidence from raising male circumcision rates is smaller than the potential contribution from expanding coverage of a vaccine from zero. Phillips et al. (2014) project that a vaccine with an efficacy of 30 per cent, in a model calibrated to a stylized Southern African country with an HIV prevalence of 25 per cent, could reduce HIV prevalence by two-thirds over 35 years.

31. See UNAIDS/WHO/SACEMA Expert Group on Modelling the Impact and Cost of Male Circumcision for HIV Prevention (2009).
32. Njeuhmeli et al. (2011) cover the thirteen priority countries identified by WHO and UNAIDS (2007), i.e. Botswana, Kenya (Nyanza Province), Lesotho, Malawi, Mozambique, Namibia, Rwanda, South Africa, Swaziland, Tanzania, Uganda, Zambia, and Zimbabwe. Auvert et al. (2008) additionally cover Burundi, Central African Republic, and Liberia.
33. The ones covered by Njeuhmeli et al. (2011), plus the Gambella Province of Ethiopia.
34. The effectiveness of male circumcision across different age groups has been discussed previously by White et al. (2008).
35. In this regard, the analysis resembles the one by Njeuhmeli et al. (2011), who attribute a cost saving of US$7,000 to each HIV infection averted, although the estimates here build more specifically on the costing of the national HIV/AIDS response, and the financial savings are age-dependent (because individuals initiating treatment at a higher age have a lower remaining life expectancy).
36. If a study measures savings in treatment cost within the policy period rather than making an allowance for the lifetime costs caused by one HIV infection, an even more pronounced cut-off problem arises with regard to cost savings resulting from HIV infections averted.
37. These savings, however, are spread over long periods, so that the projected financial returns are sensitive to assumptions on the interest rate used for discounting. This point is discussed more extensively by Haacker et al. (2016).
38. See Chapter 2 for a discussion of the health impacts of HIV/AIDS, and Chapters 5 and 6 on the global response to HIV/AIDS and the impacts of the global response. One study from South Africa (Johnson et al., 2013) concludes that 'HIV-positive adults can have a near-normal life expectancy, provided that they start ART before their CD4 count drops below 200 cells/μl. These findings demonstrate that the near-normal life expectancies of HIV-positive individuals receiving ART in high-income countries can apply to low- and middle-income countries as well.' In Botswana, life expectancy had declined from 63 years in 1990 to 45 years in 2002, but has recovered to 64 years as of 2014 (which still represents a loss of 7 years relative to a 'no-AIDS scenario' as life expectancy would arguably have risen in the absence of HIV/AIDS).

39. The *undiscounted* costs of treatment in Table 9.5 are higher than those shown in Table 7.1, because the analysis in Table 7.1 assumes a probability of 90 per cent that an individual will eventually progress to treatment. As Table 9.5 addresses the consequences of placing one individual on treatment, the implied probability is 100 per cent, and expected treatment costs are correspondingly higher. The discounted costs, especially for treatment initiated at low CD4 counts, are higher (1) for the same reason as undiscounted costs, and (2) because in Table 9.5 costs are discounted from the moment treatment is initiated, whereas they are discounted from the moment an HIV infection occurs, i.e. much earlier, in Table 7.1.

40. 'To end the AIDS epidemic by 2030 would mean that AIDS is no longer a public health threat. It means that the spread of HIV has been controlled or contained and that the impact of the virus on societies and on people's lives has been marginalized and lessened, ...' (UNAIDS, 2014b).

41. In addition to antiretroviral therapy, UNAIDS (2014b) lists condom use, combined with voluntary medical male circumcision, harm reduction measures, sexuality education, sexual and reproductive health services, and innovative social security programmes such as cash transfers as ingredients of a strategy towards ending AIDS.

42. The WHO 2010 guidelines (WHO, 2010; see also Mahy et al. (2010) for a discussion) recommend two alternative regimens, both from week 14 of the pregnancy. Option A includes treatment with zidovudine until birth, and nevirapine for the infant through the breastfeeding period; under Option B, the mother receives triple antiretroviral therapy from week 14 of the pregnancy until the end of the breastfeeding period. According to the WHO 2013 guidelines (WHO, 2013), all pregnant women should receive triple antiretroviral therapy until at least the end of the breastfeeding period; particularly in countries with high HIV prevalence, it additionally recommends that these women continue to receive ART.

43. Shapiro et al. (2010) find that three different types of antiretroviral therapy, initiated between weeks 18 and 34 of the pregnancy and continued through the breastfeeding period, reduced HIV incidence in a sample from Botswana to 0.8 per cent, and that an additional 0.3 per cent became infected in six months after birth. Hudgens et al. (2013), pooling results from several studies, demonstrate steep declines in HIV incidence among infants as the duration of antiretroviral prophylaxis (delivered to the infant) is extended—from 5.8 per cent after 28 weeks if nevirapine is discontinued 6 weeks after birth to 1.8 per cent if it continues for 28 weeks.

44. Because of the political relevance of the HPTN 052 trial in validating or reinvigorating the drive towards expanding access to treatment, a number of secondary papers are recommended. Cohen et al. (2012a) describe the research process underlying HPTN 052, and provide an accessible discussion of its results. Cohen et al. (2012b) interpret ongoing policy processes against the findings of HPTN. The study was selected by *Science* as Breakthrough of the Year 2011, hailed by Cohen (2011, author different from Cohen of Cohen et al., 2012a).

45. See WHO (2014) for a discussion of the state of the art on post-exposure prophylaxis and recommendations of best practice.

46. See Grant et al. (2010) for a study on men who have sex with men from Peru, Ecuador, South Africa, Brazil, Thailand, and the United States. Choopanya et al. (2013) focus

on injecting drug users in Bangkok. There are no studies available at present focusing specifically on female sex workers, but Bekker et al. (2015) provide a thorough discussion of the relevance of the evidence available for this population group.

47. See De Cock et al. (2009) for further discussion of challenges to a widespread use of treatment as prevention. Bärnighausen et al. (2012b) point at issues in economic evaluation, including the cost implications of intensified testing, and changing health consequences as treatment is initiated earlier.

48. UNAIDS (2014c) reports the global number of people knowing their HIV status (19 million out of 35 million people living with HIV, corresponding to 54 per cent), and the share of people knowing their status in sub-Saharan Africa (45 per cent). The rate of people knowing their status outside sub-Saharan Africa (75 per cent) is not reported by UNAIDS, but can be calculated from these numbers.

49. Viral suppression is defined here as a viral load below 1,000 copies/ml. See NASCOP et al. (2014) for the data on Kenya, and Justman et al. (2013) for Swaziland. An earlier systematic review (Barth et al., 2010) focusing on sub-Saharan Africa finds a similar rate of viral suppression (78 per cent) after 6 months of antiretroviral therapy, but a lower rate (67 per cent) after 24 months, and that the evidence is weak on viral suppression after longer periods on treatment.

50. The analysis assumes treatment coverage of 80 per cent for eligible individuals (CD4 count below 350) and retention on treatment of 85 per cent after 3 years. While calibrated to South African data, the analysis is highly stylized comparing a hypothetical no-ART scenario to another hypothetical scenario in which ART is introduced in 2012.

51. Kahn et al. (2011) provide a thorough discussion of the cost-effectiveness of treatment as prevention and a useful taxonomy of indicators commonly used in assessing the cost-effectiveness of health interventions.

52. This has been calculated in a version of the UNAIDS 2014 Spectrum file for South Africa (UNAIDS, 2014d) which has been adapted to set treatment coverage to zero. As treatment affects the composition of the population living with HIV and not receiving treatment, the actual average transmission rate from people living with HIV and not receiving treatment could be different.

53. One factor that is captured only crudely in the calculations underlying Figure 9.9 and Table 9.6 is the profile of sexual activity by age. Sophisticated demographic and epidemiological models would incorporate some assumptions in this direction. In the ASSA2008 (ASSA, 2011) model, for example, sexual activity peaks at age 23 for women, and 28 for men (see Chapter 7). The calculations underlying Table 9.6 assume that sexual transmission of HIV ceases at a certain time (30 years) following an HIV infection. The results, however, are robust to specific assumptions on the age profile of sexual activity, as the effects of treatment on HIV transmission are dominated by the impacts over about 10 years following an infection.

54. The analysis captures only the HIV infections caused directly by one primary HIV infection, and not HIV infections caused further on (by the sexual partners of the partners of the person who became infected in the first place, etc.). Incorporating them would require more elaborate modelling, but it would not change the results significantly, for two reasons. First, with each iteration, the effects would become

smaller—e.g. if treatment reduced HIV transmission by 0.33 (with eligibility at a CD4 count of 500), the 0.33 secondary HIV infections averted would result in 0.10 tertiary HIV infections averted (0.33 HIV infections averted, times 0.31 HIV downstream infections caused directly by each new HIV infection in this setting), and so on. Second, for the dynamic analysis, it is necessary to take into account that an individual *not* infected because of an intervention can therefore become infected later on—as discussed in Chapter 7, this 'own' effect offsets much of the potential downstream HIV infections.

55. The gain in life years from one HIV infection averted is calculated as the counterfactual remaining life expectancy at the time of HIV infection (assumed at 45 years) minus the life expectancy remaining from the time of HIV infection under the different treatment eligibility criteria.

56. Stover (2012) follows a similar life-cycle approach to the one applied here, focusing on the effects of treatment for different eligibility thresholds, but applies a more stylized model.

57. Stover et al. (2014) also give a number of 3.9 million HIV infections averted, apparently as a result of oversight following an update. The number of US$9,600 per HIV infection averted is the ratio of costs to HIV infections averted, each discounted at a rate of 3 per cent.

58. E.g. 58 per cent had a CD4 count below 100 and 44 per cent had already experienced an AIDS-defining illness.

59. E.g. Eaton et al. (2014) use an annual cost of non-ART health care for people living with HIV in South Africa of US$167 at a CD4 count below 200, but as low as US$13 for a CD4 count exceeding 350. Cleary et al. (2006), using data from Cape Town, estimate quarterly non-ART costs of care of almost US$239 for individuals with a CD4 count below 50, but much lower costs of US$145 for individuals with a CD4 count between 50 and 199.

60. Cost per HIV infection averted have been calculated based on Figure 2a in Cremin et al. (2013), the underlying data were generously provided by Cremin.

61. This conclusion is this author's interpretation of the findings by Cremin et al. (2013) and not necessarily shared by the authors of the underlying paper.

62. These numbers were obtained from Table 1 by Bärnighausen et al. (2012a). However, the numbers were transformed—whereas their Table 1 shows *average* cost-effectiveness ratios relative to a baseline scenario, these have been transformed into *marginal* cost-effectiveness ratios, i.e. cost-effectiveness relative to the next lower level in a sequence of coverage rates. Note that the discussion of male circumcision earlier in this chapter suggests that the analysis by Bärnighausen et al. understates the efficiency of male circumcision, as the 10-year horizon applied in their paper only partially captures the (lifetime) effects of male circumcision.

Chapter 10

1. For sub-Saharan Africa, the report emphasized 'youth-targeted behavioural interventions, scale-up of programs to prevent mother-to-child transmission, and supportive interventions to address poverty and gender inequities', whereas in Eastern Europe and Central Asia the focus was on harm reduction for injecting drug users.

2. The contribution of modes-of-transmission analyses to the development of effective HIV policies is mixed. While they arguably contributed to a better understanding of the state of the epidemic, they provide a snapshot of the state of the epidemic only and tend to give a disproportionately large weight to low-risk groups (contributing, for example, to the questionable focus on discordant couples in global HIV/AIDS strategies—see the discussion in Chapter 9).

3. While the following paragraphs follow the narrative of 'combination prevention' in global HIV/AIDS politics, the efforts to better ground the HIV/AIDS response in an understanding of the drivers of the epidemic continued. Significant recent contributions include the analysis by Tanser et al. (2014), documenting localized clustering of HIV infections, and a study by Anderson et al. (2014), which develops a regionally differentiated optimized HIV/AIDS response based on available data on the state of HIV/AIDS in Kenya across regions, and documenting the efficiency gains which could be realized by such a differentiated policy, compared to a uniform national strategy. Tanser et al. (2014) review the evidence on HIV among high-risk groups or specific locations within generalized epidemics, pointing to steep differences in HIV incidence within three countries (Kenya, South Africa, Uganda), and providing a rationale for targeted HIV prevention approaches (in addition to measures aimed at the general population) in hyperepidemic countries.

4. The role of the time horizon is discussed in Chapter 8 with regard to HIV/AIDS programmes overall, and appears throughout Chapter 9 with regard to transmission dynamics or the effects of specific HIV/AIDS prevention interventions.

5. Although the investment framework does not state this explicitly, this priority-setting and emphasis on the most effective interventions presents a contrast to the 'laundry list' appearance of 'national strategic plans' on HIV/AIDS of the day.

6. UNAIDS (2014b) defines that 'to end the AIDS epidemic by 2030 would mean that AIDS is no longer a public health threat. It means that the spread of HIV has been controlled or contained and that the impact of the virus on societies and on people's lives has been marginalized and lessened, owing to significant declines in ill health, stigma, deaths and the number of orphans. It means increased life expectancy, unconditional acceptance of people's diversity and rights, and increased productivity and reduced costs as the impact of AIDS diminishes.'

7. The analysis by Kripke et al. (2013) was conducted for the South African government, and the release of the work files for the present book was cleared by the Department of Health (Dr Yogan Pillay).

8. That is, with the exception of ART for most-at-risk populations, which is added as an additional eligibility criterion in the 'maximum feasible' scenario.

9. The estimate that only about one-third of the costs caused by new HIV infections occur within 11 years is based on the calculations underlying Figure 9.2. The rate, though, depends on the treatment eligibility criterion and varies, depending on treatment eligibility, e.g. from 30 per cent (eligibility from CD4 count of 350) to 38 per cent (CD4 count of 500).

10. This point is discussed intermittently in Chapter 8 (cost-effectiveness of HIV programmes) and Chapter 9 (especially in the section on treatment as prevention).

11. The South African HIV and TB Investment Case had not been published by the time this book went into typesetting. See Meyer-Rath et al. (2015) for a documentation of the economic analysis.

12. Figure 10.2.a corresponds to Figure 5 in Kripke et al. (2013). The figures appearing here, however, were generated from work files updated after Kripke et al. (2013) went into print, and reflect somewhat lower estimates of HIV incidence. For this reason, the effectiveness of HIV prevention interventions shown in Figure 10.2.a comes out lower than in Kripke et al. (2013). For example, the scaling up of treatment is estimated to avert 260,000 HIV infection in Kripke et al. (2013), but 210,000 based on the updated files.

13. The discussion in Chapter 9 suggests that this estimate of the cost per HIV infection averted through male circumcision is too high, considering that KwaZulu-Natal is the province with the highest HIV prevalence in South Africa. The discrepancy likely reflects that male circumcision is modelled only crudely in the 'Goals' module (coverage assumptions for the population of ages 15–49 overall only), whereas the estimates discussed in Chapter 9 show the returns on investments in male circumcision for specific age groups.

14. The default setup of the Spectrum software specifying treatment coverage in terms of the *stock* of people eligible for treatment, is not suitable for the analysis of cost-effectiveness in terms of deaths averted. Reduced HIV incidence, owing to the scaling up of an HIV prevention intervention, reduces the flow of people who become eligible for treatment. To maintain a targeted *stock* coverage rate, Spectrum then reduces the rate at which eligible individuals transition to treatment—i.e., lowering HIV incidence reduces the chance that an HIV-positive individual will access treatment. To neutralize this effect, treatment access is specified in terms of *flow* coverage, assuming that about 60 per cent of individuals will obtain treatment when they reach the eligibility threshold of 350, consistent with a stock coverage of about 80 per cent under the baseline scenario but neutralizing the negative feedback from HIV prevention to treatment access. The flow coverage is lower than the corresponding stock coverage because survival among people on treatment is higher.

15. The PSP includes all interventions shown except treatment between CD4 counts of 350 and 500, interventions targeting injecting drug users, and measures targeting out-of-school youths. For interventions included in the PSP, Figure 10.2 and Table 10.3 show the difference between the PSP and a scenario excluding the respective intervention; for others, it shows the effect of adding it to the PSP.

16. When the changes in treatment coverage and eligibility are evaluated around the PSP, the change in treatment costs owing to HIV infections averted during the policy period accounts for less than 5 per cent of the overall change in treatment costs. Evaluating treatment policies from the baseline scenario, the change in HIV incidence during the policy period accounts for about 1 per cent of the change in treatment costs until 2025, but this share rises to 10 per cent (expanding coverage at a CD4 count of 350) and 25 per cent (extending eligibility to a CD4 count of 500) if the policy period is extended to 2035.

17. For non-treatment HIV prevention interventions, this has been calculated by assigning the estimated lifetime costs of treatment per person to each HIV infection averted. See Chapter 8 for a discussion of the lifetime costs of treatment under different eligibility criteria. For changes in the coverage or eligibility of treatment, the change in treatment spending commitments were calculated as the change in costs of treating the population already living with HIV in 2011, plus the projected number of HIV infections times lifetime costs of treatment under the new coverage or eligibility criteria, minus the projected number of HIV infections times lifetime costs of treatment under the old coverage or eligibility criteria, discounted at the applicable rate.

18. Schwartländer et al. (2011) describe this policy context similarly: 'Until now, advocacy for resources has been done on the basis of a commodity approach that encouraged scaling up of numerous strategies in parallel, irrespective of their relative effects.... The commodity approach was not conducive for countries and donors to set priorities as shown by substantial differences in resource allocation for national HIV/AIDS responses between neighbouring countries with equivalent epidemics. Unsystematic prioritisation and investment were allowed to persist as interests and stakeholders competed for a proportion of available funding for HIV/AIDS, spreading resources thinly between many objectives.'

19. While the iterative approach is efficient in identifying locally optimal spending allocations, it may not identify a globally optimal strategy. This problem can be mitigated by selecting different strategies as a starting point and check if these different starting points result in different outcomes.

20. The interventions covered are: mass media, peer education for sex workers, school-based education, voluntary counselling and testing, prevention of mother-to-child transmission, treatment of sexually transmitted infections, and antiretroviral therapy.

21. The study by Anderson et al. (2014) is also an example of an academic analysis that is successful in informing national HIV/AIDS strategies. Reflecting the analysis, the Kenya 'Prevention Revolution Roadmap' provides guidelines for HIV prevention policies across counties, differentiating between three tiers of counties—nine high-incidence counties, with 23 per cent of the population, but accounting for 65 per cent of all HIV infections and annual HIV incidence above 0.4 per cent; twenty-eight medium-incidence counties (61 per cent of the population, accounting for 34 per cent of HIV infections; with HIV incidence between 0.1 per cent and 0.4 per cent) and ten low-incidence counties (16 per cent of population, 1 per cent of new HIV infections, HIV incidence below 0.1 per cent).

22. A third approach would be to calculate an optimal solution explicitly rather than through a numerical optimization. Because of the complexity of the underlying epidemiological models, and the presence of non-linearities, this approach is not feasible in the present context.

23. The Goals model was used as a secondary model for validation purposes in the South African Investment Case. To this end, the Goals software was adapted to include an optimization function similar to the one described here, but this version of the model is not in the public domain at present.

24. Additionally, Meyer-Rath et al. (2015) describe a scenario in which South Africa would meet the '90-90-90' target.

25. However, unlike a fully developed mathematical optimization routine, the analysis by Meyer-Rath et al. (2015) does not take into account the interactions in the cost-effectiveness of interventions (i.e. the cross-derivatives).

26. Including the author of this book.

27. A number of country studies are available online at http://optimamodel.com/publications.html.

28. A request by the author to obtain access to the model in February 2015 was referred to the World Bank (who funded its development). The World Bank responded only 3 months later, explaining that 'Optima access is provided to those who have completed one week Optima training course. We will inform you when the next training will be planned.' No further communications were received by the time of writing, in late 2015.

29. Whereas the transition rates between states of disease progression depend on the time an individual has spent in a state in other common applications, they are assumed constant in Optima.

Chapter 11

1. In this illustration, it is assumed that external funding is fixed. The analysis would look very similar if external funding depends on the commitment of domestic resources, as long as the activities underwritten by donors are broadly in line with the government's policy preferences, i.e. intra-marginal with respect to the spending priorities and preferences summarized in the expenditure curves.

2. In the absence of external support, the policy outcome is represented by point F. The spending allocation between non-HIV/AIDS and HIV/AIDS expenditures can be determined by drawing a horizontal line through point F. On this line, non-HIV/AIDS spending is represented by the distance from the vertical axis and the X_0X_0' curve, and HIV/AIDS spending by the distance between the X_0X_0' curve and point F.

3. The following sections address the creation of 'fiscal space', by pursuing the most cost-effective policies to achieve desired objectives or improving the cost-effectiveness of HIV/AIDS services, reallocating expenditures, and raising additional revenues.

4. The general economic outlook enters because higher economic growth results in a decline in the debt–GDP ratio, and makes it easier to repay public debt.

5. This is documented in some detail in IMF (2002) and Baldacci and Fletcher (2004). The practice of the DSA has been evolving, as documented most recently in IMF (2013a, 2013b). A brief overview of the DSA framework, with links to relevant documents, is available at https://www.imf.org/external/pubs/ft/dsa/.

6. DSAs rarely include pension obligations because of limited data availability. However, IMF (2002) explains that 'pensions are a particularly important direct or contingent liability for government' (in fifteen emerging market countries), and

that 'failure to anticipate (and offset) the fiscal gap caused by the introduction of funded pension schemes explains worse-than-anticipated debt ratios in a number of countries'.

7. In countries where the bulk of the HIV/AIDS response is financed externally, the projected costs may nevertheless constrain fiscal space if they constitute a contingent liability, i.e. the uncertainty on the future availability of external funding adds a risk to the fiscal outlook.

8. Similarly, in countries where the sustainability of public debt is under threat, additional financing needs under the HIV/AIDS response would accelerate the accumulation of debt or would have to be compensated by revenue measures or expenditure cuts elsewhere.

9. The description in this sentence follows IMF (2013c), though it is not quoted verbatim.

10. The IMF/World Bank public debt benchmarks differentiate according to the 'quality of policies and institutions', as measured by the CPIA index produced by the World Bank.

11. These benchmarks apply to the magnitude of public debt, including external and domestic public debt. The benchmarks applied in DSAs for the assessment of external debt are tighter (e.g. between 30 per cent of GDP and 50 per cent of GDP for low-income countries (IMF, 2013a)). The extent to which the spending commitments under the HIV/AIDS programme can be interpreted as an external debt (this would apply, e.g., to the purchase of drugs from external suppliers) would need to be evaluated carefully on a country-by-country basis. For this reason, the more robust benchmark for public debt overall is used here.

12. The exceptions are Greece, where public debt is currently estimated at 170 per cent of GDP as of 2014, and Japan where public debt stood at 140 per cent of GDP.

13. The lines between allocative efficiency and technical efficiency are blurred, however, as insights regarding the determinants of technical efficiency may result in reallocations of spending across sites, regions, or service delivery modes. In practice, therefore, allocative efficiency tends to regard the choices between different categories of services on the most aggregate level, whereas technical efficiency regards the costs of delivering specific services, including the choice of the most effective mode of delivery. See Bautista-Arredondo et al. (2008) for a fundamental discussion of the cost-effectiveness of HIV/AIDS services.

14. This point reappears in the discussion of domestic financing.

15. See Beck et al. (2010), and the discussion of the same data in Beck et al. (2012). The later survey by Galárraga et al. (2011) illustrates the rapid expansion in evidence, identifying twenty-nine studies on treatment costs in low- and middle-income countries, of which thirteen were published in 2008 or 2009.

16. See Bautista-Arredondo et al. (2008) for a fundamental discussion of cost-effectiveness in HIV/AIDS prevention programmes, Bautista-Arredondo et al. (2014) for an introduction to the ORPHEA project, and Bertozzi (2012) for a discussion of the 'Fed-Ex approach'—applying sophisticated optimization techniques to identifying the most cost-effective delivery options, and designing the system accordingly—as a model for HIV/AIDS programme design.

17. The elasticity of unit costs per client tested with respect to the number of clients tested comes out at –0.41 in a pooled model, and between –0.24 and –0.55 when the elasticities are allowed to differ across countries.

18. The elasticity of unit costs per client tested and found HIV positive with respect to the number of clients tested comes out at –0.13 in the pooled model, and between 0.45 and –0.78 when the elasticities are allowed to differ across countries.

19. Discussing domestic financing issues separately from external financing does not take into account that the two are related—donors are motivated by and may formally demand financial commitments from the government. These issues are discussed in Chapters 5 and 6 from a global perspective. Nevertheless, once there is clarity about the HIV/AIDS strategy and donor commitments, the government will need to accommodate the domestic financing needs.

20. In assessing how much of an increase in government revenues owing to economic growth can be assigned to new policy objectives, it is necessary to take into account that some of the increase will be absorbed by increasing salaries and—if high GDP growth in part reflects high population growth—an increased need for established government services. On the other hand, government revenues might increase faster than GDP through tax reform and improved revenue administration, or because the formal sector expands faster than GDP overall.

21. This section draws in part on a guidance note on 'trust funds' prepared under contract to UNAIDS (Haacker, 2015b). The material has been used with permission from UNAIDS. However, UNAIDS did not review the section, and may or may not agree with its findings.

22. See National AIDS Control Council (2014b) for Kenya, Manenji (undated) for Zimbabwe, and Government of Uganda (2014) on taxes earmarked for the Uganda AIDS Trust Fund.

23. The discourse on tax funding of HIV/AIDS spending appears to be drawing on the agenda on global health financing, notably the report of the Taskforce on Innovative International Financing of Health Systems (2009), where airline taxes and mobile phone taxes are proposed as means for soliciting funding for *global* health initiatives. The use of taxes for *domestic* government spending, as in the discourse on HIV/AIDS financing, of course, is all but innovative.

24. The estimate by Allen and Radev is based on data from twenty-three countries for which data were available in the IMF's Government Finance Statistics database, and might not be representative for countries facing severe HIV/AIDS financing challenges.

25. The 'Doyle model' of the impact of HIV/AIDS in South Africa was developed by Peter Doyle at Metropolitan life in 1989, and is a precursor to the ASSA2008 model used occasionally in this book.

26. This section draws on material developed under contract to UNAIDS for a guidance note on borrowing for HIV responses, which has been used with permission from UNAIDS. UNAIDS did not review the section, and may or may not agree with its findings.

27. See section on 'a fiscal perspective on domestic HIV/AIDS financing' in this chapter.

28. The macroeconomic and fiscal impacts of Ebola in these countries are discussed in several IMF staff reports, see IMF (2014a, 2014b, 2014c).

Chapter 12

1. See, e.g., Piot (2012) on cost-effectiveness and returns on investment, and early encounters with the World Bank; and Schwartländer et al. (2011) on the 'commodity approach'.

References

Abdool Karim, Quarraisha, et al., 2010, 'Effectiveness and Safety of Tenofovir Gel, an Antiretroviral Microbicide, for the Prevention of HIV Infection in Women', *Science*, Vol. 329, No. 5996, pp. 1168–74.

Acemoglu, Daron, Simon Johnson, and James A. Robinson, 2001, 'The Colonial Origins of Comparative Development: An Empirical Investigation', *American Economic Review*, Vol. 91, No. 5, pp. 1369–401.

Actuarial Society of South Africa (ASSA), 2011, 'ASSA 2008 AIDS and Demographic Models—User Guide (beta version)' (Cape Town: ASSA).

African Union, 2012, 'Roadmap on Shared Responsibility and Global Solidarity for AIDS, TB and Malaria Response in Africa' (Addis Abeba: African Union).

Ainsworth, Martha, and Deon Filmer, 2006, 'Inequalities in Children's Schooling: AIDS, Orphanhood, Poverty, and Gender', *World Development*, Vol. 34, No. 6, pp. 1099–128.

Ainsworth, Martha, and Mead Over (eds), 1998, *Confronting AIDS: Public Priorities in a Global Epidemic* (Luxembourg: Office for Official Publications of the European Communities).

Ainsworth, Martha, Kathleen Beegle, and Godlike Koda, 2005, 'The Impact of Adult Mortality and Parental Deaths on Primary Schooling in North-Western Tanzania', *Journal of Development Studies*, Vol. 41, No. 3, pp. 412–39.

Akbulut-Yuksel, Mevlude, and Belgi Turan, 2012, 'Left Behind: Intergenerational Transmission of Human Capital in the Midst of HIV/AIDS', *Journal of Population Economics*, Vol. 26, No. 4, pp. 1523–47.

Alam, Khurshid, and Ajay Mahal, 2014, 'Economic Impacts of Health Shocks on Households in Low- and Middle-income Countries: A Review of the Literature', *Globalization and Health*, Vol. 10, No. 1:21.

Alary, Michel, et al., 2014, 'Increased HIV Prevention Program Coverage and Decline in HIV Prevalence Among Female Sex Workers in South India', *Sexually Transmitted Diseases*, Vol. 41, No. 6, pp. 380–7.

Alkenbrack Batteh, Sarah E., Steven Forsythe, Gayle Martin, and Ty Chettra, 2008, 'Confirming the Impact of HIV/AIDS Epidemics on Household Vulnerability in Asia: The Case of Cambodia', *AIDS*, Vol. 22, Suppl. 1, pp. S103–11.

Allen, Richard, and Dimitar Radev, 2010, 'Extrabudgetary Funds', Technical Notes and Manuals No. 10/09 (Washington, DC: IMF, Fiscal Affairs Department).

Alleyne, George, 2009, 'Health and Economic Growth: Policy Reports and the Making of Policy', in: Michael Spence, and Maureen Lewis (eds), *Health and Growth* (Washington, DC: World Bank on behalf of Commission on Growth and Development).

Altman, Dennis, and Kent Buse, 2012, 'Thinking Politically about HIV: Political Analysis and Action in Response to AIDS', *Contemporary Politics*, Vol. 18, No. 2, pp. 127–40.

Amico, Peter, Benjamin Gobet, Carlos Avila-Figueroa, Christian Aran, and Paul De Lay, 2012, 'Pattern and Levels of Spending Allocated to HIV Prevention Programs in Low- and Middle-income Countries', *BMC Public Health*, Vol. 12:221.

Anderson, Gordon, 2005, 'Life Expectancy and Economic Welfare: The Example of Africa in the 1990s', *Review of Income and Wealth*, Vol. 51, No. 3, pp. 455–68.

Anderson, Sarah-Jane, et al., 2014, 'Maximising the Effect of Combination HIV Prevention through Prioritisation of the People and Places in Greatest Need: A Modelling Study', *The Lancet*, Vol. 384, Issue 9939, pp. 249–56.

Ardington, Cally, and Boingotlo Gasealahweb, 2014, 'Mortality in South Africa: Socio-economic Profile and Association with Self-reported Health', *Development Southern Africa*, Vol. 31, No. 1, pp. 127–45.

Ardington, Cally, Till Bärnighausen, Anne Case, and Alicia Menendez, 2014, 'The Economic Consequences of AIDS Mortality in South Africa', *Journal of Development Economics*, Vol. 111, pp. 48–60.

Arndt, Channing, and Jeffrey D. Lewis, 2001, 'The HIV/AIDS Pandemic in South Africa: Sectoral Impacts and Unemployment', *Journal of International Development*, Vol. 13, pp. 427–49.

Arora, Paul, et al., 2013, 'Female Sex Work Interventions and Changes in HIV and Syphilis Infection Risks from 2003 to 2008 in India: a Repeated Cross-sectional Study', *BMJ Open*, Vol. 3, No. 6: e002724.

Asiedu, Christobel, Elizabeth Asiedu, and Francis Owusu, 2012, 'The Socio-Economic Determinants of HIV/AIDS Infection Rates in Lesotho, Malawi, Swaziland and Zimbabwe', *Development Policy Review*, Vol. 30, No. 3, pp. 305–26.

Auvert, Bertran, et al., 2005, 'Randomized, Controlled Intervention Trial of Male Circumcision for Reduction of HIV Infection Risk: the ANRS 1265 Trial', *PLoS Medicine*, Vol. 2, No. 11: e298.

Auvert, Bertran, et al., 2008, 'Estimating the Resources Needed and Savings Anticipated from Roll-out of Adult Male Circumcision in sub-Saharan Africa', *PLoS Medicine*, Vol. 3, Issue 8: e2679.

Auvert, Bertran, et al., 2013, 'Association of the ANRS-12126 Male Circumcision Project with HIV Levels among Men in a South African Township: Evaluation of Effectiveness Using Cross-Sectional Surveys', *PLoS Medicine*, Vol. 10, No. 9: e1001509.

Avalos, Ava, and Keith Jefferis, 2015, 'Botswana at the Crossroads: Investment Towards Effective HIV Prevention, Health System Strengthening and the End of AIDS', draft, September 2015 (Gaborone: National AIDS Coordinating Agency).

Avenir Health, 2014, 'Spectrum Manual—Spectrum System of Policy Models', available online at http://www.avenirhealth.org/software-spectrum.php, accessed 17 June 2015 (Glastonbury, CT: Avenir Health).

Aventin, Laurent, and Pierre Huard, 2000, 'The Costs of AIDS to Three Manufacturing Firms in Cote d'Ivoire', *Journal of African Economies*, Vol. 9, No. 2, pp. 161–88.

Avila-Figueroa, Carlos, and Paul DeLay, 2009, 'Impact of the Global Economic Crisis on Antiretroviral Treatment Programs', *HIV Therapy*, Vol. 3, No. 6, pp. 545–8.

Bachmann, Max O., and Frikkie L. R. Booysen, 2006, 'Economic Causes and Effects of AIDS in South African Households', *AIDS*, Vol. 20, No. 14, pp. 1861–7.

Baeten, Jarad M., et al., 2012, 'Antiretroviral Prophylaxis for HIV-1 Prevention in Heterosexual Men and Women', *New England Journal of Medicine*, Vol. 367, pp. 399–410.

Bailey, Robert C., et al., 2007, 'Male Circumcision for HIV Prevention in Young Men in Kisumu, Kenya: A Randomised Controlled Trial', *The Lancet*, Vol. 369, pp. 643–56.

Baird, Sarah J., Ephraim Chirwa, Craig T. McIntosh, and Berk Özler, 2015, 'The Effects of Receiving Cash Transfers as Adolescents on Future Outcomes', World Bank AFR Seminar Series, 30 April 2015.

Baird, Sarah J., Richard S. Garfein, Craig T. McIntosh, and Berk Özler, 2012, 'Effect of a Cash Transfer Programme for Schooling on Prevalence of HIV and Herpes Simplex Type 2 in Malawi: A Cluster Randomised Trial', *The Lancet*, Vol. 379, pp. 1320–9.

Baldacci, Emanuele, and Kevin Fletcher, 2004, 'A Framework for Fiscal Debt Sustainability Analysis', in: Sanjeev Gupta, Benedict Clements, and Gabriela Inchauste, *Helping Countries Develop—The Role of Fiscal Policy* (Washington, DC: International Monetary Fund).

Bärnighausen, Till, Victoria Hosegood, Ian M. Timaeus, and Marie-Louise Newell, 2007, 'The Socioeconomic Determinants of HIV Incidence: Evidence from a Longitudinal, Population-based Study in Rural South Africa', *AIDS*, Vol. 21, Suppl. 7, pp. S29–38.

Bärnighausen, Till, David E. Bloom, and Salal Humair, 2012a, 'Economics of Antiretroviral Treatment vs. Circumcision for HIV Prevention', *Proceedings of the National Academy of Sciences of the United States of America*, Vol. 109, No. 52, pp. 21271–6.

Bärnighausen, Till, Joshua A. Salomon, and Nalinee Sangrujee, 2012b, 'HIV Treatment as Prevention: Issues in Economic Evaluation', *PLoS Med*, Vol. 9, No. 7: e1001263.

Barrow, Geoffrey, Sharlene Jarrett, Erva-Jean Stevens, et al., 2012, Modes of HIV Transmission in Jamaica (Kingston: UNAIDS and National HIV/STI Programme).

Barth, Roos E., et al., 2010, 'Virological Follow-up of Adult Patients in Antiretroviral Treatment Programmes in sub-Saharan Africa: A Systematic Review', *The Lancet Infectious Diseases*, Vol. 10, No. 3, pp. 155–66.

Bautista-Arredondo, Sergio, et al., 2014, 'Cost and Technical Efficiency of HIV Prevention Interventions in sub-Saharan Africa: the ORPHEA Study Design and Methods', *BMC Health Services Research*, Vol. 14: 599.

Bautista-Arredondo, Sergio, Paola Gadsden, Jeffrey E. Harris, and Stefano Bertozzi, 2008, 'Optimizing Resource Allocation for HIV/AIDS Prevention Programmes: An Analytical Framework', *AIDS*, Vol. 22, Suppl. 1, pp. S67–74.

Beaulière, Arnousse, et al., 2010, 'The Financial Burden of Morbidity in HIV-infected Adults on Antiretroviral Therapy in Cote d'Ivoire', *PloS One*, Vol. 5, Issue 6: e11213.

Beck, Eduard J., et al., 2010, 'The Cost of Treatment and Care for People Living with HIV Infection: Implications of Published Studies, 1999–2008', *Current Opinion in HIV and AIDS*, Vol. 5, No. 3, pp. 215–24.

Beck, Eduard J., Carlos Avila, Sofia Gerbase, Guy Harling, and Paul De Lay, 2012, 'Counting the Cost of Not Costing HIV Health Facilities Accurately. Pay Now, or Pay More Later', *PharmacoEconomics*, Vol. 30, No. 10, pp. 887–902.

Becker, Gary S., and Julio Jorge Elias, 2007, 'Introducing Incentives in the Market for Live and Cadaveric Organ Donations', *Journal of Economic Perspectives*, Vol. 21, No. 3, pp. 3–24.

Becker, Gary S., Thomas J. Philipson, and Rodrigo R. Soares, 2005, 'The Quality and Quantity of Life and the Evolution of World Inequality', *American Economic Review*, Vol. 95, No. 1, pp. 277–91.

Beegle, Kathleen, and Damien de Walque, 2009, Demographic and Socioeconomic Patterns of HIV/AIDS Prevalence in Africa, World Bank Policy Research Working Paper Series, No. 5076.

Beegle, Kathleen, and Joachim de Weerdt, 2008, 'Methodological Issues in the Study of the Socioeconomic Consequences of HIV/AIDS', *AIDS*, Vol. 22, Suppl. 1, pp. S89–94.

Beegle, Kathleen, Joachim de Weerdt, and Stefan Dercon, 2006, 'Orphanhood and the Long-run Impact on Children', *American Journal of Agricultural Economics*, Vol. 88, No. 5, pp. 1266–72.

Beegle, Kathleen, Joachim de Weerdt, and Stefan Dercon, 2008, 'Adult Mortality and Consumption Growth in the Age of HIV/AIDS', *Economic Development and Cultural Change*, Vol. 56, No. 2, pp. 299–326.

Beegle, Kathleen, Joachim de Weerdt, and Stefan Dercon, 2009, 'The Intergenerational Impact of the African Orphans Crisis: A Cohort Study from an HIV/AIDS Affected Area', *International Journal of Epidemiology*, Vol. 38, No. 2, pp. 561–8.

Beegle, Kathleen, Joachim de Weerdt, and Stefan Dercon, 2010, 'Orphanhood and Human Capital Destruction: Is there Persistence into Adulthood?' *Demography*, Vol. 47, No. 1, pp. 163–80.

Behrman, Julia Andrea, 2015, 'The Effect of Increased Primary Schooling on Adult Women's HIV Status in Malawi and Uganda: Universal Primary Education as a Natural Experiment', *Social Science & Medicine*, Vol. 127, pp. 108–15.

Bekker, Linda-Gail, et al., 2015, 'Combination HIV Prevention for Female Sex Workers: What Is the Evidence?' *The Lancet*, Vol. 385, Issue 9962, pp. 72–87.

Bell, Clive, Shantayanan Devarajan, and Hans Gersbach, 2006, 'The Long-run Economic Costs of AIDS: A Model with an Application to South Africa', *World Bank Economic Review*, Vol. 20, No. 1, pp. 55–89.

Bellavance, François, Georges Dionne, and Martin Lebeau, 2009, 'The Value of a Statistical Life: A Meta-analysis with a Mixed Effects Regression Model', *Journal of Health Economics*, Vol. 28, No. 2, pp. 444–64.

Bendavid, Eran, Charles B. Holmes, Jay Bhattacharya, and Grant Miller, 2012, 'HIV Development Assistance and Adult Mortality in Africa', *Journal of the American Medical Association*, Vol. 307, pp. 2060–7.

Bertozzi, Stefano, 2012, Keynote address at International AIDS Economics Network, Washington, DC, July 2012, obtained online at http://www.iaen.org/iaen2012.cfm accessed 30 March 2015.

Bertozzi, Stefano, et al., 2006, 'HIV/AIDS Prevention and Treatment', in: Dean T. Jamison, et al. (eds), *Disease Control Priorities in Developing Countries* (2nd edn) (Washington, DC: World Bank).

Beyrer, Chris, et al., 2015a, 'The Vancouver Consensus', http://vancouverconsensus.org/, accessed 14 December 2015.

Beyrer, Chris, et al., 2015b, 'The Vancouver Consensus: Antiretroviral Medicines, Medical Evidence, and Political Will', *The Lancet*, Vol. 386, Issue 9993, pp. 505–7.

Bicego, George, Shea Rutstein, and Kiersten Johnson, 2003, 'Dimensions of the Emerging Orphan Crisis in sub-Saharan Africa', *Social Science & Medicine*, Vol. 56, No. 6, pp. 1235–47.

Biesma, Regien G., et al., 2009, 'The Effects of Global Health Initiatives on Country Health Systems: A Review of the Evidence from HIV/AIDS Control', *Health Policy and Planning*, Vol. 24, pp. 239–52.

Bloom, David E., and Ajay S. Mahal, 1997, 'Does the AIDS Epidemic Threaten Economic Growth?' *Journal of Econometrics*, Vol. 77, No. 1, pp. 105–24.

Bloom, David E., David Canning, and Dean T. Jamison, 2004a, 'Health, Wealth, and Welfare', *Finance and Development*, Vol. 41, No. 1, pp. 10–15.

Bloom, David E., David Canning, and Jaypee Sevilla, 2004b, 'The Effect of Health on Economic Growth: A Production Function Approach', *World Development*, Vol. 32, No. 1, pp. 1–13.

Boily, Marie-Claude, et al., 2009, 'Heterosexual Risk of HIV-1 Infection Per Sexual Act: Systematic Review and Meta-analysis of Observational Studies', *The Lancet Infectious Diseases*, Vol. 9, No. 2, pp. 118–29.

Boily, Marie-Claude, et al., 2013, 'Positive Impact of a Large-scale HIV Prevention Programme Among Female Sex Workers and Clients in South India', *AIDS*, Vol. 27, No. 9, pp. 1449–60.

Bongaarts, John, and Mead Over, 2010, 'Global HIV/AIDS Policy in Transition', *Science*, Vol. 328, Issue 5984, pp. 1359–60.

Bongaarts, John, Priscilla Reining, Peter Way, and Francis Conant, 1989, 'The Relationship between Male Circumcision and HIV Infection in African Populations', *AIDS*, Vol. 3, No. 6, pp. 373–8.

Bonnel, R., 2000, 'HIV/AIDS and Economic Growth: A Global Perspective', *South African Journal of Economics*, Vol. 68, No. 5, pp. 820–55.

Booysen, Frederik Le R., 2004, 'Income and Poverty Dynamics in HIV/AIDS Affected Households in the Free State Province of South Africa', *South African Journal of Economics*, Vol. 72, No. 3, pp. 522–45.

Bor, Jacob, Frank Tanser, Marie-Louise Newell, and Till Bärnighausen, 2012, 'In a Study of a Population Cohort in South Africa, HIV Patients on Antiretroviral Therapy Had nearly Full Recovery of Employment', *Health Affairs*, Vol. 31, No. 7, pp. 1459–69.

Boulle, Andrew, et al., 2014, 'Mortality in Patients with HIV-1 Infection Starting Antiretroviral Therapy in South Africa, Europe, or North America: A Collaborative Analysis of Prospective Studies', *PLoS Medicine*, Vol. 11, Issue 9: e1001718.

Bourguignon, Francois, and Christian Morrison, 2002, 'Inequality among World Citizens: 1820–1992', *American Economic Review*, Vol. 92, No. 4, pp. 727–44.

Brugha, Ruairí, Joseph Simbaya, Aisling Walsh, Patrick Dicker, and Phillimon Ndubani, 2010, 'How HIV/AIDS Scale-up Has Impacted on Non-HIV Priority Services in Zambia', *BMC Public Health*, Vol. 10, No. 1:540.

Bunnell, Rebecca, et al., 2006, 'Changes in Sexual Behavior and Risk of HIV Transmission after Antiretroviral Therapy and Prevention Interventions in Rural Uganda', *AIDS*, Vol. 20, No. 1, pp. 85–92.

Bureau for Economic Research (BER), 2001, 'The Macroeconomic Impact of HIV/AIDS in South Africa', BER Research Note No. 10 (Stellenbosch: BER).

Buse, Kent, and Greg Martin, 2012, 'AIDS: Ushering in a New Era of Shared Responsibility for Global Health', *Globalization and Health*, Vol. 8, No. 1:28.

Caldwell, John C., and Pat Caldwell, 1993, 'The Nature and Limits of the sub-Saharan African AIDS Epidemic: Evidence from Geographic and Other Patterns', *Population and Development Review*, Vol. 19, No. 4, pp. 817–48.

Car, Josip, et al., 2012, 'Negative Health System Effects of Global Fund's Investments in AIDS, Tuberculosis and Malaria from 2002 to 2009: Systematic Review', *JRSM Short Reports*, 3(10).

Case, Anne, and Christina Paxson, 2009, 'Early Life Health and Cognitive Function in Old Age', *American Economic Review: Papers & Proceedings*, Vol. 99, No. 2, pp. 104–9.

Case, Anne, and Christina Paxson, 2011, 'The Impact of the AIDS Pandemic on Health Services in Africa: Evidence from Demographic and Health Surveys', *Demography*, Vol. 48, No. 2, pp. 675–97.

Case, Anne, Christina Paxson, and Joseph Ableidinger, 2004, 'Orphans in Africa: Parental Death, Poverty and School Enrolment', *Demography*, Vol. 41, No. 3, pp. 483–508.

Case, Anne, Anu Garrib, Alicia Menendez and Analia Olgiati, 2013, 'Paying the Piper: The High Cost of Funerals in South Africa', *Economic Development and Cultural Change*, Vol. 62, No. 1, pp. 1–20.

Case, Kelsey K., et al., 2012, 'Understanding the Modes of Transmission Model of New HIV Infection and Its Use in Prevention Planning', *Bulletin of the World Health Organization*, Vol. 90, No. 11, pp. 831–8.

Chang, Larry W., et al., 2013, 'Combination Implementation for HIV Prevention: Moving from Clinical Trial Evidence to Population-level Effects', *The Lancet Infectious Diseases*, Vol. 13, No. 1, pp. 65–76.

Chapoto, Antony, and T. S. Jayne, 2008, 'Impact of AIDS-related Deaths on Farm Households' Welfare in Zambia', *Economic Development and Cultural Change*, Vol. 56, No. 2, pp. 327–74.

Chersich, Matthew F., et al., 2013, 'Priority Interventions to Reduce HIV Transmission in Sex Work Settings in sub-Saharan Africa and Delivery of These Services', *Journal of the International AIDS Society*, Vol. 16:17980.

Chicoine, Luke, 2012, 'AIDS Mortality and Its Effect on the Labor Market: Evidence from South Africa', *Journal of Development Economics*, Vol. 98, No. 2, pp. 256–69.

Choopanya, Kachit, et al., 2013, 'Antiretroviral Prophylaxis for HIV Infection in Injecting Drug Users in Bangkok, Thailand (the Bangkok Tenofovir Study): a Randomised, Doubleblind, Placebo-controlled Phase 3 Trial', *The Lancet*, Vol. 381, Issue 9883, pp. 2083–90.

Cleary, Susan M., Di McIntyre, and Andrew M. Boulle, 2006, 'The Cost-effectiveness of Antiretroviral Treatment in Khayelitsha, South Africa—A Primary Data Analysis', *Cost Effectiveness and Resource Allocation*, Vol. 4:20.

Cleary, Susan, et al., 2013, 'Investigating the Affordability of Key Health Services in South Africa', *Social Science and Medicine*, Vol. 80, pp. 37–46.

Cogneau, Denis, and Michael Grimm, 2008, 'The Impact of AIDS Mortality on the Distribution of Income in Côte d'Ivoire', *Journal of African Economies*, Vol. 17, No. 5, pp. 688–728.

Cohen, Jon, 2011, 'Breakthrough of the Year—Treatment as Prevention', *Science*, Vol. 334, Issue 6063, pp. 1628.

Cohen, Myron S., et al., 2011, 'Prevention of HIV-1 Infection with Early Antiretroviral Therapy', *New England Journal of Medicine*, Vol. 365, No. 6, pp. 493–505.

Cohen, Myron S., Marybeth McCauley, and Theresa R. Gamble, 2012a, 'HIV Treatment as Prevention and HPTN 052', *Current Opinion in HIV and AIDS*, Vol. 7, No. 2, pp. 99–105.

Cohen, Myron S., et al., 2012b, 'HIV Treatment as Prevention: How Scientific Discovery Occurred and Translated Rapidly into Policy for the Global Response', *Health Affairs*, Vol. 31, No. 7, pp. 1439–49.

Collier, Paul, Olivier Sterck, and Richard Manning, 2015, 'The Moral and Fiscal Implications of Anti-retroviral Therapies for HIV in Africa', CSAE Working Paper No. 2015-05, Centre for the Study of African Economies, University of Oxford.

Commission on Macroeconomics and Health (CMH), 2001, 'Macroeconomics and Health: Investing in Health for Economic Development' (Geneva: WHO).

Conseil, A., S. Mounier-Jack, J. W. Rudge, and R. Coker, 2013, 'Assessing the Effects of HIV/AIDS and TB Disease Control Programmes on Health Systems in Low- and Middle-income Countries of Southeast Asia: A Semi-systematic Review of the Literature', *Public Health*, Vol. 127, No. 12, pp. 1063–73.

Corrigan, Paul, Gerhard Glomm, and Fabio Mendez, 2005, 'AIDS Crisis and Growth', *Journal of Development Economics*, Vol. 77, No. 1, pp. 107–24.

Couderc, Nicolas, and Bruno Ventelou, 2005, 'AIDS, Economic Growth and the Epidemic Trap in Africa', *Oxford Development Studies*, Vol. 33, No. 3–4, pp. 417–26.

Crafts, Nicholas, 2007, 'Living Standards', in: Nicholas Crafts, Ian Gazeley, and Andrew Newell (eds.), *Work and Pay in 20th Century Britain* (Oxford and New York: Oxford University Press).

Crafts, Nicholas, and Markus Haacker, 2004, 'Welfare Implications of HIV/AIDS', in: Markus Haacker (ed.), *The Macroeconomics of HIV/AIDS* (Washington, DC: International Monetary Fund).

Cremin, Íde, et al., 2013, 'The New Role of Antiretrovirals in Combination HIV Prevention: A Mathematical Modelling Analysis', *AIDS*, Vol. 27, No. 3, pp. 447–58.

Cuddington, John T., 1993a, 'Modeling the Macroeconomic Effects of AIDS, with an Application to Tanzania', *World Bank Economic Review*, Vol. 7, No. 2, pp. 173–89.

Cuddington, John T., 1993b, 'Further Results on the Macroeconomic Effects of AIDS: The Dualistic, Labor-surplus Economy', *World Bank Economic Review*, Vol. 7, No. 3, pp. 403–17.

Cuddington, John T., and John D. Hancock, 1994, 'Assessing the Impact of AIDS on the Growth Path of the Malawian Economy', *Journal of Development Economics*, Vol. 43, pp. 363–8.

Cuddington, John T., and John D. Hancock, 1995, 'The Macroeconomic Impact of AIDS in Malawi: A Dualistic, Labor Surplus Economy', *Journal of African Economics*, Vol. 4, No. 1, pp. 1–28.

Cutler, David, Angus Deaton, and Adriana Lleras-Muney, 2006, 'The Determinants of Mortality', *Journal of Economic Perspectives*, Vol. 20, No. 3, pp. 97–120.

De Cock, Kevin M., et al., 2000, 'Prevention of Mother-to-child HIV Transmission in Resource-poor Countries: Translating Research into Policy and Practice', *Journal of the American Medical Association*, Vol. 283, No. 9, pp. 1175–82.

De Cock, Kevin M., Charles F. Gilks, Ying-Ru Lo, and Teguest Guerma, 2009, 'Can Antiretroviral Therapy Eliminate HIV Transmission?' *The Lancet*, Vol. 373, Issue 9657, pp. 7–9.

De Neve, Jan-Walter, Günther Fink, S. V. Subramanian, Sikhulile Moyo, Jacob Bor, 2015, 'Length of Secondary Schooling and Risk of HIV Infection in Botswana: Evidence from a Natural Experiment', *Lancet Global Health*, Vol. 3, e470–7.

de Paoli, Marina Manuela, Elizabeth Anne Mills, and Arne Backer Grønningsæter, 2012, 'The ARV Roll-out and the Disability Grant: A South African Dilemma?' *Journal of the International AIDS Society*, Vol.15 (February), Art. 6.

de Walque, Damien, 2007, 'How Does the Impact of an HIV/AIDS Information Campaign Vary with Educational Attainment? Evidence from Rural Uganda', *Journal of Development Economics*, Vol. 84, No. 2, pp. 686–714.

Deaton, Angus, 2003, 'Health, Inequality, and Economic Development', *Journal of Economic Literature*, Vol. 41, No. 1, pp. 113–58.

Deaton, Angus, 2006, 'Global Patterns of Income and Health: Facts, Interpretations, and Policies', NBER Working Paper No. 12735 (Cambridge, MA: NBER).

Delva, Wim, 2012, et al., 'HIV Treatment as Prevention: Optimising the Impact of Expanded HIV Treatment Programmes', *PLoS Medicine*, Vol. 9, No. 7:e1001258.

Dixon, Simon, Scott McDonald, and Jennifer Roberts, 2001, 'AIDS and Economic Growth in Africa: A Panel Data Analysis', *Journal of International Development*, Vol. 13, No. 4, pp. 411–26.

Donnell, Deborah, et al., 2010, 'Heterosexual HIV-1 Transmission After Initiation of Antiretroviral Therapy: A Prospective Cohort Analysis', *The Lancet*, Vol. 375, Issue 9731, pp. 2092–6.

Durevall, Dick, and Annika Lindskog, 2012, 'Economic Inequality and HIV in Malawi', *World Development*, Vol. 40, No. 7, pp. 1435–51.

Eaton, Jeffrey W., et al., 2012, 'HIV Treatment as Prevention: Systematic Comparison of Mathematical Models of the Potential Impact of Antiretroviral Therapy on HIV Incidence in South Africa', *PLoS Medicine*, Vol. 9, Issue 7: e1001245.

Eaton, Jeffrey W., et al., 2014, 'Health Benefits, Costs, and Cost-effectiveness of Earlier Eligibility for Adult Antiretroviral Therapy and Expanded Treatment Coverage: A Combined Analysis of 12 Mathematical Models', *The Lancet Global Health*, Vol. 2, No. 1: e23–34.

ECOSOC, see United Nations Economic and Social Council.

Ellis, Linette L., 2006, 'The Economic Impact of HIV/AIDS on Small, Medium and Large Enterprises', *South African Journal of Economics*, Vol. 74, No. 4, pp. 682–701.

Ellis, Linette, and Jenny Terwin, 2005, 'The Impact of HIV/AIDS on Selected Business Sectors in South Africa' (Stellenbosch: Bureau for Economic Research, Stellenbosch University).

England, Roger, 2007, 'Are We Spending Too Much on HIV?' *British Medical Journal*, Vol. 334, p. 344.

Farmer, Paul, et al., 2001, 'Community-based Approaches to HIV Treatment in Resource-poor Settings', *The Lancet*, Vol. 359, No. 9306, pp. 404–9.

Feldacker, Caryl, Michael Emch, and Susan Ennett, 2010, 'The *Who* and *Where* of HIV in Rural Malawi: Exploring the Effects of Person and Place on Individual HIV Status', *Health & Place*, Vol. 16, No. 5, pp. 996–1006.

Ferreira, Pedro Cavalcanti, Samuel Pessôa, and Marcelo Santos, 2011, 'The Impact of AIDS on Income and Human Capital', *Economic Inquiry*, Vol. 49, No. 4, pp. 1104–16.

Fleming, Alan F., Manuel Carballo, David W. FitzSimons, Michael R. Bailey, and Jonathan Mann (eds), 1988, *The Global Impact of AIDS* (New York: Alan R. Liss).

Floyd, Sian, et al., 2012, 'The Effect of Antiretroviral Therapy Provision on All-Cause, AIDS and non-AIDS Mortality at the Population Level—A Comparative Analysis of Data from Four Settings in Southern and East Africa', *Tropical Medicine & International Health*, Vol. 17, No. 8, e84–93.

Forman, Lisa, 2011, 'Global AIDS Funding and the Re-emergence of AIDS "Exceptionalism"', *Social Medicine*, Vol. 6, No. 1, pp. 45–51.

Forsythe, Steven, John Stover, and Lori Bollinger, 2009, 'The Past, Present and Future of HIV, AIDS and Resource Allocation', *BMC Public Health*, Vol. 9, Suppl. 1:4.

Fortson, Jane G., 2008, 'The Gradient in sub-Saharan Africa: Socioeconomic Status and HIV/AIDS', *Demography*, Vol. 45, No. 2, pp. 303–22.

Fortson, Jane G., 2011, 'Mortality Risk and Human Capital Investment: The Impact of HIV/AIDS in sub-Saharan Africa', *The Review of Economics and Statistics*, Vol. 93, No. 1, pp. 1–15.

Foss, Anna M., Charlotte H. Watts, Peter Vickerman, and Lori Heise, 2004, 'Condoms and Prevention of HIV', *British Medical Journal*, Vol. 329, Issue 7456, pp. 185–6.

Foss, Anna M., Mazeda Hossain, Peter T. Vickerman, and Charlotte H. Watts, 2007, 'A Systematic Review of Published Evidence on Intervention Impact on Condom Use', *Sexually Transmitted Infections*, Vol. 83, No. 7, pp. 510–16.

Fox, Matthew. P., et al., 2004, 'The Impact of HIV/AIDS on Labour Productivity in Kenya', *Tropical Medicine & International Health*, Vol. 9, No. 3, pp. 318–24.

Fraser, Nicole, et al., 2010, 'Zimbabwe—Analysis of HIV Epidemic, Response and Modes of Transmission' (Harare: Zimbabwe National AIDS Council).

Galárraga, Omar, et al., 2011, 'Unit Costs for Delivery of Antiretroviral Treatment and Prevention of Mother-to-Child Transmission of HIV', *Pharmacoeconomics*, Vol. 29, No. 7, pp. 579–99.

Galárraga, Omar, Veronika J. Wirtz, Yared Santa-Ana-Tellez, and Eline L. Korenromp, 2013, 'Financing HIV Programming: How Much Should Low- and Middle-income Countries and their Donors Pay?' *PLoS One*, Vol. 8, Issue 7: e67565.

Gallup, John Luke, and Jeffrey D. Sachs, 2001, 'The Economic Burden of Malaria', *American Journal of Tropical Medicine and Hygiene*, Vol. 64, No. 1 (Suppl.), pp. 85–96.

Garnett, Geoff P., 2014, 'The Theoretical Impact and Cost-effectiveness of Vaccines that Protect against Sexually Transmitted Infections and Disease', *Vaccine*, Vol. 32, No. 14, pp. 1536–42.

Gitahi-Kamau, Nyawira T., et al., 2015, 'Socio-economic Determinants of Disease Progression among HIV Infected Adults in Kenya', *BMC Public Health*, Vol. 15:733.

Global Fund to Fight AIDS, Tuberculosis and Malaria (Global Fund), 2011a, *The Global Fund Strategy 2012–2016: Investing for Impact* (Geneva: Global Fund).

Global Fund, 2011b, 'Turning the Page from Emergency to Sustainability. The Final Report of the High-Level Independent Review Panel on Fiduciary Controls and Oversight Mechanisms of the Global Fund to Fight AIDS, Tuberculosis and Malaria' (Geneva: Global Fund).

Global Fund to Fight AIDS, Tuberculosis and Malaria (Global Fund), 2011c, 'Policy on Eligibility Criteria, Counterpart Financing Requirements, and Prioritization of Proposals for Funding from the Global Fund', Global Fund Twenty-Third Board Meeting, 11–12 May 2011, Document No. GF/B23/14, Attachment 1 (Geneva: Global Fund).

Global Fund to Fight AIDS, Tuberculosis and Malaria (Global Fund), 2012, *Strategic Investments for Impact—Global Fund Results Report 2012* (Geneva: Global Fund).

Global Fund to Fight AIDS, Tuberculosis and Malaria (Global Fund), 2013a, The Global Fund to Fight AIDS, Tuberculosis and Malaria Fourth Replenishment (2014–2016)—Needs Assessment (Geneva: Global Fund).

Global Fund to Fight AIDS, Tuberculosis and Malaria (Global Fund), 2013b, 'New Funding Model: Eligibility, Counterpart Financing and Prioritization Policy Revision', Global Fund Thirtieth Board Meeting, 7–8 November 2013, Document No. GF/B30/6—Revision 1 (Geneva: Global Fund).

Global Fund to Fight AIDS, Tuberculosis and Malaria (Global Fund), 2014a, *Global Fund Information Note: Strategic Investments for HIV Programs* (Geneva: Global Fund).

Global Fund to Fight AIDS, Tuberculosis and Malaria (Global Fund), 2014b, 'Eligibility List 2014' (Geneva: Global Fund).

Global Fund to Fight AIDS, Tuberculosis and Malaria (Global Fund), 2014c, 'Overview of the Allocation Methodology (2014–2016): The Global Fund's New Funding Model' (Geneva: Global Fund).

Global HIV Prevention Working Group, 2003, 'Access to HIV Prevention – Closing the Gap'.

Goldstein, Markus, Joshua Graff Zivin, and Harsha Thirumurthy, 2010, 'The Household Impacts of Treating HIV/AIDS in Developing Countries', in: Justin Yifu Lin and Boris Pleskovic (eds), *Annual World Bank Conference on Development Economics Global, People, Politics, and Globalization* (Washington, DC: World Bank), pp. 385–405.

Goosby, Eric, et al., 2012, 'The United States President's Emergency Plan for AIDS Relief: A Story of Partnerships and Smart Investments to Turn the Tide of the Global AIDS Pandemic', *Journal of Acquired Immune Deficiency Syndromes*, Vol. 60, Suppl. 3, pp. 51–6.

Gouws, Eleanor, and Paloma Cuchi, 2012, 'Focusing the HIV Response Through Estimating the Major Modes of HIV Transmission: A Multi-country Analysis', *Sexually Transmitted Infections*, Vol. 88, Suppl. 2, pp. i76–85.

Gouws, Eleanor, Peter J. White, John Stover, and Tim Brown, 2006, 'Short Term Estimates of Adult HIV Incidence by Mode of Transmission: Kenya and Thailand as Examples', *Sexually Transmitted Infections*, Vol. 82, Suppl. 3, pp. iii51–5.

Government of Uganda, 2014, 'The HIV and AIDS Prevention and Control Act, 2014' (Kampala: Government of Uganda).

Graff Zivin, Joshua, Harsha Thirumurthy, and Markus Goldstein, 2009, 'AIDS Treatment and Intrahousehold Resource Allocation: Children's Nutrition and Schooling in Kenya', *Journal of Public Economics*, Vol. 93, No. 7, pp. 1008–15.

Granich, Reuben M., Charles F. Gilks, Christoher Dye, Kevin M. De Cock, and Brian G. Williams, 2009, 'Universal Voluntary HIV Testing with Immediate Antiretroviral Therapy as a Strategy for Elimination of HIV Transmission: A Mathematical Model', *The Lancet*, Vol. 373, Issue 9657, pp. 48–57.

Granich, Reuben, et al., 2010, 'Highly Active Antiretroviral Treatment as Prevention of HIV Transmission: Review of Scientific Evidence and Update', *Current Opinion in HIV and AIDS*, Vol. 5, No. 4, pp. 298–304.

Granich, Reuben, et al., 2012, 'Expanding ART for Treatment and Prevention of HIV in South Africa: Estimated Cost and Cost-effectiveness 2011-2050', *PLoS One*, Vol. 7, Issue 2: e30216.

Grant, Robert M., et al., 2010, 'Preexposure Chemoprophylaxis for HIV Prevention in Men Who Have Sex with Men', *New England Journal of Medicine*, Vol. 363, No. 27, pp. 2587–99.

Gray, Ron, et al., 2012, 'The Effectiveness of Male Circumcision for HIV Prevention and Effects on Risk Behaviors in a Posttrial Follow-up Study', *AIDS*, Vol. 26, pp. 609–15.

Gray, Ronald H., et al., 2007, 'Male Circumcision for HIV Prevention in Men in Rakai, Uganda: A Randomised Trial', *The Lancet*, Vol. 369, pp. 657–66.

Greener, Robert, Keith Jefferis, and Happy Siphambe, 2000, 'The Impact of HIV/AIDS on Poverty and Inequality in Botswana', *South African Journal of Economics*, Vol. 68, No. 5, pp. 393–404.

Gregson, Simon, et al., 2010, 'HIV Decline in Zimbabwe Due to Reductions in Risky Sex? Evidence from a Comprehensive Epidemiological Review', *International Journal of Epidemiology*, Vol. 39, pp. 1311–23.

Grépin, Karen A., 2012, 'HIV Donor Funding has Both Boosted and Curbed the Delivery of Different non-HIV Health Services in sub-Saharan Africa', *Health Affairs*, Vol. 31, No. 7, pp. 1406–14.

Grimm, Michael, and Kenneth Harttgen, 2008, 'Longer Life, Higher Welfare?' *Oxford Economic Papers*, Vol. 60, No. 2, pp. 193–211.

Haacker, Markus (ed.), 2004, *The Macroeconomics of HIV/AIDS* (Washington, DC: IMF).

Haacker, Markus, 2009, 'Financing HIV/AIDS Programs In Sub-Saharan Africa', *Health Affairs*, Vol. 28, No. 6, pp. 1606–16.

Haacker, Markus, 2011, 'HIV/AIDS as a Fiscal Liability', Proceedings of the German Development Economics Conference, Berlin 2011, No. 35.

Haacker, Markus, 2015a, 'Guidance Note: Borrowing for Financing HIV Responses' (Geneva: UNAIDS).

Haacker, Markus, 2015b, 'Guidance Note: Trust Funds for Financing HIV Responses' (Geneva: UNAIDS).

Haacker, Markus, and Robert Greener, 2012, 'Financing HIV Programmes: The Role of External Support', paper prepared for UNAIDS 'Economics Reference Group', 29 November 2011.

Haacker, Markus, Marelize Gorgens, and Nicole Fraser-Hurt, 2016, 'Effectiveness of and Financial Returns to Voluntary Medical Male Circumcision for HIV Prevention in South Africa: An Incremental Cost-effectiveness Analysis', forthcoming, *PLoS Medicine*.

Hajizadeh, Mohammad, Drissa Sia, S. Jody Heymann, and Arijit Nandi, 2014, 'Socio-economic Inequalities in HIV/AIDS Prevalence in sub-Saharan African Countries: Evidence from the Demographic Health Surveys', *International Journal for Equity in Health*, Vol. 13, No. 1:18.

Hallett, Timothy B., et al., 2006, 'Declines in HIV Prevalence Can Be Associated with Changing Sexual Behaviour in Uganda, Urban Kenya, Zimbabwe, and Urban Haiti', *Sexually Transmitted Infections*, Vol. 82, Suppl 1, pp. i1–8.

Hallett, Timothy B., et al., 2008, 'Understanding the Impact of Male Circumcision Interventions on the Spread of HIV in Southern Africa', *PLoS Medicine*, Vol. 3, Issue 5: e2212.

Hallett, Timothy B., et al., 2009, 'Assessing Evidence for Behaviour Change Affecting the Course of HIV Epidemics: A New Mathematical Modelling Approach and Application to Data from Zimbabwe', *Epidemics*, Vol. 1, No. 2. pp. 108–17.

Halperin, Daniel T., 2001, 'Is Poverty the Root Cause of African AIDS? *AIDS Bulletin*, Vol. 10, No. 2, pp. 10–15.

Halperin, Daniel T., et al., 2011, 'A Surprising Prevention Success: Why Did the HIV Epidemic Decline in Zimbabwe?' *PLoS Medicine*, Vol. 8, Issue 2: e1000414.

Hankins, Catherine A., and Barbara O. de Zalduondo, 2010, 'Combination Prevention: A Deeper Understanding of Effective HIV Prevention', *AIDS*, Vol. 24, Suppl. 4, pp. S70–80.

Hargreaves, James R., et al., 2008, 'Systematic Review Exploring Time Trends in the Association Between Educational Attainment and Risk of HIV Infection in sub-Saharan Africa', *AIDS*, Vol. 22, No. 3, pp. 403–14.

Hargreaves, James R., Calum Davey, and Richard G. White, 2013, 'Does the "Inverse Equity Hypothesis" Explain How both Poverty and Wealth Can Be Associated with HIV Prevalence in sub-Saharan Africa?' *Journal of Epidemiology and Community Health*, Vol. 67, No. 6, pp. 526–9.

Harling, Guy, and Robin Wood, 2007, 'The Evolving Cost of HIV in South Africa: Changes in Health Care Cost with Duration on Antiretroviral Therapy for Public Sector Patients', *Journal of Acquired Immune Deficiency Syndromes*, Vol. 45, No. 3, pp. 348–54.

Harling, Guy, et al., 2014, 'Do Age-disparate Relationships Drive HIV Incidence in YoungWomen? Evidence from a Population Cohort in Rural KwaZulu-Natal, South Africa', *Journal of Acquired Immune Deficiency Syndromes*, Vol. 66, No. 4, pp. 443–51.

Harris, Katherine, Victoria Hosegood, and Andrew A. Channon, 2014, 'Gender Disparity in HIV Prevalence: A National-level Analysis of the Association between Gender Inequality and the Feminisation of HIV/AIDS in sub-Saharan Africa', *African Population Studies*, Vol. 28, No. 2 (supplement), pp. 1132–45.

Hay, Roger, and Gareth Williams, 2006, 'Fiscal Space and Sustainability from the Perspective of the Health Sector', in: Kathy Cahill, et al., *High Level Forum on the Health Millennium Development Goals: Selected Papers*, 2003–2005 (Geneva: World Health Organization).

Hecht, Robert, et al., 2010, 'Financing of HIV/AIDS Programme Scale-up in Low-income and Middle-income Countries, 2009–31', *The Lancet*, Vol. 376, Issue 9748, pp. 1254–60.

Heller, Peter S., 2005, 'Understanding Fiscal Space', IMF Policy Discussion Paper No. 05/4 (Washington, DC: IMF).

Heller, Peter S., 2006, 'The Prospects of Creating "Fiscal Space" for the Health Sector', *Health Policy and Planning*, Vol. 21, No. 2, pp. 75–9.

Heymann, Jody, and Rachel Kidman, 2009, 'HIV/AIDS, Declining Family Resources and the Community Safety Net', *AIDS Care*, Vol. 21, Suppl. 1 (Special Issue: JLICA AIDS Care), pp. 34–42.

Hogan, Daniel R., et al., 2005, 'Cost Effectiveness Analysis of Strategies to Combat HIV/AIDS in Developing Countries', *British Medical Journal*, Vol. 331, pp. 1431–7.

Holmes, Charles B., Rifat Atun, Carlos Avila, and John M. Blandford, 2011, 'Expanding the Generation and Use of Economic and Financial Data to Improve HIV Program Planning and Efficiency: A Global Perspective', *Journal of Acquired Immune Deficiency Syndromes*, Vol. 57, Suppl. 2, pp. S104–8.

Holmes, Charles B., et al., 2012, 'PEPFAR's Past and Future Efforts to Cut Costs, Improve Efficiency, and Increase the Impact of Global HIV Programs', *Health Affairs*, Vol. 31, No. 7, pp. 1553–60.

Hosegood, Victoria, et al., 2007, 'The Effects of High HIV Prevalence on Orphanhood and Living Arrangements of Children in Malawi, Tanzania, and South Africa', *Population Studies*, Vol. 61, No. 3, pp. 327–36.

Hudgens, Michael G., et al., 2013, 'Pooled Individual Data Analysis of 5 Randomized Trials of Infant Nevirapine Prophylaxis to Prevent Breast-milk HIV-1 Transmission', *Clinical Infectious Diseases*, Vol. 56, No. 1, pp. 131–9.

Hutubessy, Raymond, et al., 2003, 'Generalized Cost-effectiveness Analysis for National-level Priority-setting in the Health Sector', *Cost Effectiveness and Resource Allocation*, Vol. 1, No. 1, Art. 8.

Individual Members of the Faculty of Harvard University, 2001, 'Consensus Statement on Antiretroviral Treatment for AIDS in Poor Countries.'

Institute for Health Metrics and Evaluation (IHME), 2014, 'Global Burden of Disease Study 2013 (GBD 2013) Age-sex Specific All-cause and Cause-specific Mortality 1990–2013' (Seattle: IHME).

International Monetary Fund (IMF), 2002, 'Assessing Sustainability' (Washington, DC: IMF).

International Monetary Fund (IMF), 2007, 'Manual on Fiscal Transparency' (Washington, DC: IMF).

International Monetary Fund (IMF), 2013a, 'Staff Guidance Note on the Application of the Joint Bank-Fund Debt Sustainability Framework for Low-income Countries' (Washington, DC: IMF).

International Monetary Fund (IMF), 2013b, Staff Guidance Note for Public Debt Sustainability Analysis in Market-access Countries (Washington, DC: IMF).

International Monetary Fund (IMF), 2014a, 'Guinea: Requests for Disbursement under the Rapid Credit Facility and for Modification of Performance Criteria under the Extended Credit Facility Arrangement—Staff Report' (Washington, DC: IMF).

International Monetary Fund (IMF), 2014b, 'Sierra Leone: Ad Hoc Review under the Extended Credit Facility Arrangement and Request for Augmentation of Access, Modification of Performance Criteria and Financing Assurances Review—Staff Report' (Washington, DC: IMF).

International Monetary Fund (IMF), 2014c, 'Liberia: Ad Hoc Review under the Extended Credit Facility Arrangement and Request for Augmentation of Access and Modification of Performance Criteria—Staff Report' (Washington, DC: IMF).

International Monetary Fund (IMF), 2015, World Economic Outlook database, April 2015 edition (Washington, DC: IMF).

International Public Sector Accounting Standards Board (IPSASB), 2014, *Handbook of International Public Sector Accounting Pronouncements* (New York: International Federation of Accountants).

Jamaica National HIV/STI Programme (JNHP), 2012, 'HIV Modes of Transmission Model Distribution of New HIV Infections in Jamaica for 2012: Recommendations for Efficient Resource Allocation and Prevention Strategies' (Kingston: JNHP).

Jamison, Dean T., et al., 2013, 'Global Health 2035: A World Converging Within a Generation', *The Lancet*, Vol. 382, pp. 1898–955.

Jefferis, Keith, Anthony Kinghorn, Happy Siphambe, and James Thurlow, 2008, 'Macroeconomic and Household-level Impacts of HIV/AIDS in Botswana', *AIDS*, Vol. 22, Suppl. 1, pp. S113–19.

Johnson, Leigh F., Timothy B. Hallett, Thomas M. Rehle, and Rob E. Dorrington, 2012, 'The Effect of Changes in Condom Usage and Antiretroviral Treatment Coverage on Human Immunodeficiency Virus Incidence in South Africa: A Model-based Analysis', *Journal of Royal Society Interface*, Vol. 9, pp. 1544–54.

Johnson, Leigh F., et al., 2013, 'Life Expectancies of South African Adults Starting Antiretroviral Treatment: Collaborative Analysis of Cohort Studies', *PLoS Medicine*, Vol. 10, Issue 4:e1001418.

Johnson, Leigh F., et al., 2014, 'THEMBISA Version 1.0: A Model for Evaluating the Impact of HIV/AIDS in South Africa', Centre for Infectious Disease Epidemiology and Research Working Paper, University of Cape Town.

Joint United Nations Programme on HIV/AIDS (UNAIDS), 1998, *Report on the Global HIV/AIDS Epidemic* (Geneva: UNAIDS).

Joint United Nations Programme on HIV/AIDS (UNAIDS), 2000, *Report on the Global HIV/AIDS Epidemic—June 2000* (Geneva: UNAIDS).

Joint United Nations Programme on HIV/AIDS (UNAIDS), 2004, *2004 Report on the Global HIV/AIDS Epidemic* (Geneva: UNAIDS).

Joint United Nations Programme on HIV/AIDS (UNAIDS), 2006, *2006 Report on the Global AIDS Epidemic* (Geneva: UNAIDS).

Joint United Nations Programme on HIV/AIDS (UNAIDS), 2007, 'Practical Guidelines for Intensifying HIV Prevention—Towards Universal Access' (Geneva: UNAIDS).

Joint United Nations Programme on HIV/AIDS (UNAIDS), 2010a, 'Global Report: UNAIDS Report on the Global AIDS Epidemic 2010' (Geneva: UNAIDS).

Joint United Nations Programme on HIV/AIDS (UNAIDS), 2010b, 'Combination HIV Prevention: Tailoring and Coordinating Biomedical, Behavioural and Structural Strategies to Reduce New HIV Infections', UNAIDS Discussion Paper (Geneva: UNAIDS).

Joint United Nations Programme on HIV/AIDS (UNAIDS), 2010c, 'AIDS Scorecards: Overview: UNAIDS Report on the Global AIDS Epidemic 2010' (Geneva: UNAIDS).

Joint United Nations Programme on HIV/AIDS (UNAIDS), 2011, 'A New Investment Framework for the Global HIV Response' (Geneva: UNAIDS).

Joint United Nations Programme on HIV/AIDS (UNAIDS), 2012a, 'Modeling the Expected Short-term Distribution of New HIV Infections by Modes of Transmission' (Geneva: UNAIDS).

Joint United Nations Programme on HIV/AIDS (UNAIDS), 2012b, 'Together We Will End AIDS' (Geneva: UNAIDS).

Joint United Nations Programme on HIV/AIDS (UNAIDS), 2013a, 'Smart Investments' (Geneva: UNAIDS).

Joint United Nations Programme on HIV/AIDS (UNAIDS), 2013b, 'Investment Case Toolkit' (Geneva: UNAIDS).

Joint United Nations Programme on HIV/AIDS (UNAIDS), 2014, *Ambitious Treatment Targets: Writing the Final Chapter of the AIDS Epidemic* (Geneva: UNAIDS).

Joint United Nations Programme on HIV/AIDS (UNAIDS), 2014b, 'Fast Track—Ending the AIDS Epidemic By 2030' (Geneva: UNAIDS).

Joint United Nations Programme on HIV/AIDS (UNAIDS), 2014c, *The Gap Report* (Geneva: UNAIDS).

Joint United Nations Programme on HIV/AIDS (UNAIDS), 2014d, 2014 Country Spectrum files (Geneva: UNAIDS).

Joint United Nations Programme on HIV/AIDS (UNAIDS), 2015a, 2015 Country Spectrum files (Geneva: UNAIDS).

Joint United Nations Programme on HIV/AIDS (UNAIDS), 2015b, How AIDS Changed Everything. MDG 6: 15 Years, 15 Lessons of Hope from the AIDS Response (Geneva: UNAIDS).

Joint United Nations Programme on HIV/AIDS (UNAIDS), 2015c, Estimates of the State of the Global HIV Epidemic, obtained online at aidsinfoonline.org (Geneva: UNAIDS).

Joint United Nations Programme on HIV/AIDS (UNAIDS), 2015d, Country-level HIV/AIDS Spending Estimates, obtained online at aidsinfoonline.org (Geneva: UNAIDS).

Jones, Alexandra, et al., 2014, 'Transformation of HIV from Pandemic to Low-endemic Levels: A Public Health Approach to Combination Prevention', *The Lancet*, Vol. 384, Issue 9939, pp. 272–9.

Justman, Jessica, et al., 2013, 'Population HIV Viral Load in Swaziland: Assessing ART Program Effectiveness and Transmission Potential', conference presentation, 20th Conference on Retroviruses and Opportunistic Infections, 3–6 March 2013, Atlanta GA.

Kahn, James G., 1996, 'The Cost-effectiveness of HIV Prevention Targeting: How Much More Bang for the Buck?' *American Journal of Public Health*, Vol. 86, No. 12, pp. 1709–12.

Kahn, James G., Elliot A. Marseille, Rod Bennett, Brian G. Williams, and Reuben Granich, 2011, 'Cost-effectiveness of Antiretroviral Therapy for Prevention', *Current HIV Research*, Vol. 9, No. 6, pp. 405–15.

Kaldor, John M., and David P. Wilson, 2010, 'How Low Can You Go: The Impact of a Modestly Effective HIV Vaccine Compared with Male Circumcision', *AIDS*, Vol. 24, No. 16, pp. 2573–8.

Kambou, Gerard, Shantayanan Devarajan, and Mead Over, 1992, 'The Economic Impact of AIDS in an African Country: Simulations with a Computable General Equilibrium Model of Cameroon', *Journal of African Economies*, Vol. 1, No. 1, pp. 109–30.

Kerr, Cliff C., et al., 2015, 'Optima: A Model for HIV Epidemic Analysis, Program Prioritization, and Resource Optimization', *Journal of Acquired Immune Deficiency Syndromes*, Vol. 69, No. 3, pp. 365–76.

Kerrigan, Deanna, et al., 2013, The Global HIV Epidemics Among Sex Workers (Washington, DC: World Bank).

Kremer, Michael, 1998, 'AIDS: The Economic Rationale for Public Intervention', in: Martha Ainsworth, Lieve Fransen, and Mead Over (eds.), 1998, *Confronting AIDS: Evidence from the Developing World* (Luxembourg: Office for Official Publications of the European Communities).

Kripke, Katharine, et al., 2013, 'Impact and Cost of HIV/AIDS Prevention and Treatment in Kwazulu-Natal, South Africa 2011–2025' (Washington, DC: Futures Group, Health Policy Initiative, Costing Task Order).

Kripke, Katharine, et al., 2015a, 'Age Targeting of Voluntary Medical Male Circumcision Programs Using the Decision Makers' Program Planning Toolkit (DMPPT) 2.0', unpublished.

Kripke, Katharine, et al., 2015b, 'Cost and Impact of Voluntary Medical Male Circumcision in South Africa: Focusing the Program on Specific Age Groups and Provinces', unpublished.

Kruk, Margaret E., et al., 2012, 'PEPFAR Programs Linked to More Deliveries in Health Facilities by African Women Who Are Not Infected with HIV', *Health Affairs*, Vol. 31, No. 7, pp. 1478–88.

Larson, Bruce A., et al., 2013, 'Antiretroviral Therapy, Labor Productivity, and Gender: A Longitudinal Cohort Study of Tea Pluckers in Kenya', *AIDS*, Vol. 27, No. 1, pp. 115–23.

Laxminarayan, Ramanan, et al., 2006, 'Advancement of Global Health: Key Messages from the Disease Control Priorities Project', *The Lancet*, Vol. 367, Issue 9517, pp. 1193–208.

Leclerc-Madlala, Suzanne, 2008, 'Age-disparate and Intergenerational Sex in Southern Africa: The Dynamics of Hypervulnerability, *AIDS*, Vol. 22, Suppl. 4, pp. S17–25.

Lee, Melissa M., and Melina Platas-Izama, 2015, 'Aid Externalities: Evidence from the Case of PEPFAR', *World Development*, Vol. 67, pp. 281–94.

Lisk, Franklyn, 2009, *Global Institutions and the HIV/AIDS Epidemic* (Abingdon and New York: Routledge).

Lopman, Ben, et al., 2007, 'HIV Incidence and Poverty in Manicaland, Zimbabwe: Is HIV Becoming a Disease of the Poor?' *AIDS*, Vol. 21, Suppl. 7, pp. S57–66.

Lovász, Enrico, 2012, 'The Impact of HIV on Economic Growth in sub-Saharan Africa: Evidence of Spatial Externalities', unpublished paper, available at SSRN: ssrn.com/abstract=2257696 or http://dx.doi.org/10.2139/ssrn.2257696.

Lovász, Enrico, and Bernhard Schipp, 2009, 'The Impact of HIV/AIDS on Economic Growth in sub-Saharan Africa', *South African Journal of Economics*, Vol. 77, No. 2, pp. 245–56.

Lule, Elizabeth, and Markus Haacker, 2012, *The Fiscal Dimension of HIV/AIDS in Botswana, South Africa, Swaziland, and Uganda* (Washington, DC: World Bank).

McCoy, David, et al., 2013, 'Methodological and Policy Limitations of Quantifying the Saving of Lives: A Case Study of the Global Fund's Approach', *PLoS Medicine*, Vol. 10, No. 10:e1001522.

McDonald, Scott, and Jennifer Roberts, 2006, 'AIDS and Economic Growth: A Human Capital Approach', *Journal of Development Economics*, Vol. 80, No. 1, pp. 228–50.

McIntyre, Diane, Michael Thiede, Göran Dahlgren, Margaret Whitehead, 2006, 'What Are the Economic Consequences for Households of Illness and of Paying for Health Care in Low- and Middle-income Country Contexts?' *Social Science & Medicine*, Vol. 62, No. 4, pp. 858–65.

Madise, Nyovani J., et al., 2012, 'Are Slum Dwellers at Heightened Risk of HIV Infection than Other Urban Residents? Evidence from Population-based HIV Prevalence Surveys in Kenya', *Health & Place*, Vol. 18, No. 5, pp. 1144–52.

Madzingira, Nyasha, 2008, 'The Zimbabwe National AIDS Levy Trust (The AIDS Levy)', Southern Africa Development Community (SADC) AIDS and HIV Best Practice Series.

Magadi, Monica A., 2011, Understanding the Gender Disparity in HIV Infection across Countries in sub-Saharan Africa: Evidence from the Demographic and Health Surveys, *Sociology of Health & Illness*, Vol. 33, No. 4, pp. 522–39.

Magadi, Monica A., 2013, 'The Disproportionate High Risk of HIV Infection among the Urban Poor in sub-Saharan Africa', *AIDS and Behavior*, Vol. 17, No. 5, pp. 1645–54.

Magadi, Monica, and Muluye Desta, 2011, 'A Multilevel Analysis of the Determinants and Cross-national Variations of HIV Seropositivity in sub-Saharan Africa: Evidence from the DHS', *Health & Place*, Vol. 17, No. 5, pp. 1067–83.

Mahal, Ajay, 2004, 'Economic Implications of Inertia on HIV/AIDS and Benefits of Action', *Economic and Political Weekly*, Vol. 39, No. 10, pp. 1049–63.

Mahal, Ajay, David Canning, Kunle Odumosu, and Prosper Okonkwo, 2008, 'Assessing the Economic Impact of HIV/AIDS on Nigerian Households: A Propensity Score Matching Approach', *AIDS*, Vol. 22, Suppl. 1, pp. S95–101.

Mahy, Mary, Matthew Warner-Smith, Karen A. Stanecki, and Peter D. Ghys, 2009, 'Measuring the Impact of the Global Response to the AIDS Epidemic: Challenges and Future Directions', *Journal of Acquired Immune Deficiency Syndromes*, Vol. 52, Suppl. 2, pp. S152–9.

Mahy, Mary, et al., 2010, 'What Will It Take to Achieve Virtual Elimination of Mother-to-Child Transmission of HIV? An Assessment of Current Progress and Future Needs, *Sexually Transmitted Infections*, Vol. 86, Suppl. 2, pp. ii48–55.

Manenji, Albert, undated, 'Sustainable Financing for HIV: The Experience of Zimbabwe', presentation.

Marazzi, Maria Cristina, et al., 2008, 'Excessive Early Mortality in the First Year of Treatment in HIV Type 1-Infected Patients Initiating Antiretroviral Therapy in Resource-Limited Settings', *AIDS Research and Human Retroviruses*, Vol. 24, No. 4, pp. 555–60.

Marazzo, Jeanne M., et al., 2015, 'Tenofovir-Based Preexposure Prophylaxis for HIV Infection among African Women', *New England Journal of Medicine*, Vol. 372, No. 6, pp. 509–18.

Mather, David, et al., 2004, 'A Cross-country Analysis of Household Responses to Adult Mortality in Rural sub-Saharan Africa: Implications for HIV/AIDS Mitigation and Rural Development Policies', MSU International Development Working Paper No. 82, Michigan State University.

May, Margaret, et al., 2010, 'Prognosis of Patients with HIV-1 Infection Starting Anti-retroviral Therapy in sub-Saharan Africa: A Collaborative Analysis of Scale-up Programmes', *The Lancet*, Vol. 376, Issue 9739, pp. 449–57.

Meintjes, Helen, Katharine Hall, Double-Hugh Marera, and Andrew Boulle, 2010, 'Orphans of the AIDS Epidemic? The Extent, Nature and Circumstances of Child-Headed Households in South Africa', *AIDS Care*, Vol. 22, No. 1, pp. 40–9.

Meyer-Rath, Gesine, et al., 2015, 'South Africa's Investment Case—What Are the Country's "Best Buys" for HIV and TB?' Presentation at 7th South African AIDS Conference, Durban, 10 June 2015.

Miller, Ted R., 2000, 'Variations between Countries in Values of Statistical Life', *Journal of Transport Economics and Policies*, Vol. 34 (May), pp. 169–88.

Ministry of Health (Kenya), 2014, Guidelines on Use of Antiretroviral Drugs for Treating and Preventing HIV Infection (Nairobi: Ministry of Health).

Mishan, E. J., 1971, 'Evaluation of Life and Limb: A Theoretical Approach', *Journal of Political Economy*, Vol. 79, No. 4, pp. 687–705.

Mishra, Vinod, and Simona Bignami-Van Assche, 2008, 'Orphans and Vulnerable Children in High HIV-prevalence Countries in sub-Saharan Africa', DHS Analytical Studies No. 15 (Calverton, MD: Macro International Inc.).

Mishra, Vinod, et al., 2007, 'HIV Infection Does not Disproportionately Affect the Poorer in sub-Saharan Africa', *AIDS*, Vol. 21, Suppl. 7, pp. S17–28.

Mishra, Sharmistha, et al., 2012, 'Impact of High-risk Sex and Focused Interventions in Heterosexual HIV Epidemics: A Systematic Review of Mathematical Models', *PLoS One*, Vol. 7, No. 11:e50691.

Mishra, Sharmistha, et al., 2014a, 'Validation of the Modes of Transmission Model as a Tool to Prioritize HIV Prevention Targets: A Comparative Modelling Analysis', *PLoS One*, Vol. 9, No. 7:e101690.

Mishra, Sharmistha, et al., 2014b, 'Distinguishing Sources of HIV Transmission from the Distribution of Newly Acquired HIV Infections: Why Is It Important for HIV Prevention Planning?' *Sexually Transmitted Infections*, Vol. 90, No. 1, pp. 19–25.

Mishra, Sharmistha, et al., 2014c, 'HIV Epidemic Appraisals for Assisting in the Design of Effective Prevention Programmes: Shifting the Paradigm Back to Basics', *PLoS One*, Vol. 7, No. 3:e32324.

Mofenson, Lynne M., and James A. McIntyre, 2000, 'Advances and Research Directions in the Prevention of Mother-to-Child HIV-1 Transmission', *The Lancet*, Vol. 355, Issue 9222, pp. 2237–44.

Montaner, Julio S. G., et al., 2006, The Case for Expanding Access to Highly Active Antiretroviral Therapy to Curb the Growth of the HIV Epidemic, *The Lancet*, Vol. 368 (5 August), pp. 531–6.

Murphy, Kevin M., and Robert Topel, 2006, 'The Value of Health and Longevity', *Journal of Political Economy*, Vol. 114, No. 5, pp. 871–904.

National AIDS Control Council (NACC), 2014a, 'The Costs and Returns to Investment of Kenya's Response to HIV/AIDS: An HIV Investment Case Technical Paper' (Nairobi: NACC).

National AIDS Control Council (NACC), 2014b, Kenya AIDS Strategic Framework 2014/2015–2018/2019 (Nairobi: NACC).

National AIDS Control Council (NACC) and National STI and AIDS Control Programme (NASCOP), 2014, 'Kenya HIV Prevention Revolution Road Map—Count Down to 2030' (Nairobi: Ministry of Health).

National Center for HIV/AIDS, Viral Hepatitis, STD, and TB Prevention, undated, 'HIV Mortality Slides 1987–2010', online at http://www.cdc.gov/HIV/library/slidesets/index.html, accessed June 2015 (Atlanta: Centers for Disease Control and Prevention).

National Institute of Allergy and Infectious Diseases (NIAID), 2014, 'NIH-Sponsored Study Identifies Superior Drug Regimen for Preventing Mother-to-Child HIV Transmission', press release, 17 November 2014 (Bethesda, MD: NIAID).

National STI and AIDS Control Programme (NASCOP), et al., 2014, 'Kenya AIDS Indicator Survey 2012: Final Report' (Nairobi: Ministry of Health).

Nattrass, Nicoli, 2003, 'AIDS, Growth and Distribution in South Africa', *South African Journal of Economics*, Vol. 71, No. 3, pp. 428–54.

Nattrass, Nicoli, 2006, 'Trading off Income and Health? AIDS and the Disability Grant in South Africa', *Journal of Social Policy*, Vol. 35, No. 1, pp. 3–19.

Ng, Marie, et al., 2011, 'Assessment of Population-Level Effect of Avahan, an HIV-Prevention Initiative in India', *The Lancet*, Vol. 378, No. 9803, pp. 1643–52.

Njeuhmeli, Emmanuel, et al., 2011, 'Voluntary Medical Male Circumcision: Modeling the Impact and Cost of Expanding Male Circumcision for HIV Prevention in Eastern and Southern Africa', *PLoS Medicine*, Vol. 8, No. 11:e1001132.

Nunnenkamp, Peter, and Hannes Öhler, 2011, 'Throwing Foreign Aid at HIV/AIDS in Developing Countries: Missing the Target?' *World Development*, Vol. 39, No. 10, pp. 1704–23.

Ojiambo, Millicent, Rosemary Irungu, and Peter Kitheka, 2011, 'Fund Accounts in Kenya: Managing Complexities of Public Financial Management' (Parliamentary Budget Office. Nairobi, Kenya).

Organisation for Economic Cooperation and Development (OECD), 2015, Creditor Reporting System database, online at http://stats.oecd.org/ accessed 31 March 2015.

Organization of African Unity, 2001, 'Abuja Declaration on HIV/AIDS, Tuberculosis and Other Related Infectious Diseases', African Summit on HIV/AIDS, Tuberculosis and Other Related Infectious Diseases, Abuja, Nigeria, 24–27 April 2001.

Ota, Erika, et al., 2011, 'Behavioral Interventions to Reduce the Transmission of HIV Infection among Sex Workers and their Clients in High-income Countries', *Cochrane Database of Systematic Reviews*, Issue 12. Art. No. CD006045.

Over, Mead, 1992, 'The Macroeconomic Impact of HIV/AIDS in sub-Saharan Africa' (Washington, DC: World Bank).

Over, Mead, 2004, 'Impact of the HIV/AIDS Epidemic on the Health Sectors of Developing Countries', in: Markus Haacker (ed.), *The Macroeconomic of HIV/AIDS* (Washington, DC: International Monetary Fund).

Over, A. Mead, 2008, 'Prevention Failure: The Ballooning Entitlement Burden of US Global AIDS Treatment Spending and What to Do About It', Center for Global Development, Working Paper No. 144 (Washington, DC: Center for Global Development).

Over, Mead, 2011, *Achieving an AIDS Transition* (Washington, DC: Center for Global Development).

Over, Mead, and Geoffrey P. Garnett, 2012, 'Treatment—Assessment Paper', in: Bjørn Lomborg (ed.), 2012, *Rethink HIV—Smarter Ways to Invest in Ending HIV in sub-Saharan Africa* (Cambridge: Cambridge University Press).

Over, Mead, and Peter Piot, 1993, 'HIV Infection and Sexually Transmitted Diseases', in: Dean T. Jamison, W. Henry Mosley, Anthony R. Measham, and Jose Luis Bobadilla (eds), 1993, *Disease Control Priorities in Developing Countries* (Oxford and New York: Oxford University Press).

Padian, Nancy S., et al., 2011a, 'HIV Prevention Transformed: The New Prevention Research Agenda', *The Lancet*, Vol. 378, Issue 9787, pp. 269–78.

Padian, Nancy S., et al., 2011b, 'Evaluation of Large-scale Combination HIV Prevention Programs: Essential Issues', *JAIDS Journal of Acquired Immune Deficiency Syndromes*, Vol. 58, No. 2, pp. e23–8.

Papageorgiou, Chris, and Petia Stoytcheva, 2008, 'What is the Impact of AIDS on Cross-country Income so far? Evidence from Newly Reported AIDS Cases', unpublished paper (Washington, DC: IMF).

Parfit, Derek, 1984, *Reasons and Persons* (Oxford: Oxford University Press).

Parkhurst, Justin O., 2010, 'Understanding the Correlations Between Wealth, Poverty and Human Immunodeficiency Virus Infection in African Countries', *Bulletin of the World Health Organization*, Vol. 88, No. 7, pp. 519–26.

PEPFAR, see President's Emergency Plan for AIDS Relief.

Philipson, Thomas J., and Rodrigo R. Soares, 2005, 'The Economic Cost of AIDS in sub-Saharan Africa: A Reassessment', in: Guillem López-Casasnovas, Berta Rivera, and Luis Currais, *Health and Economic Growth—Findings and Policy Implications* (Cambridge, MA and London: MIT Press).

Phillips, Andrew N., et al., 2014, 'Potential Future Impact of a Partially Effective HIV Vaccine in a Southern African Setting', *PLoS One*, Vol. 9, No. 9:e107214.

Pinkerton, Steven D., and Paul R. Abramson, 1997, 'Effectiveness of Condoms in Preventing HIV Transmission', *Social Science and Medicine*, Vol. 44, No. 9, pp. 1303–12.

Pinto, Andrew D., et al., 2013, 'Patient Costs Associated with Accessing HIV/AIDS Care in Malawi', *Journal of the International AIDS Society*, Vol. 16: 18055.

Piot, Peter, 2005, 'Why AIDS is Exceptional', Speech given at the London School of Economics, London, 8 February 2005.

Piot, Peter, 2012, *No Time to Lose—A Life in Pursuit of Deadly Viruses* (New York and London: W.W. Norton).

Piot, Peter, 2015, *AIDS Between Science and Politics* (New York: Columbia University Press).

Piot, Peter, and Michel Caraël, 1988, 'Epidemiological and Sociological Aspects of HIV-infection in Developing Countries', *British Medical Bulletin*, Vol. 44, No. 1, pp. 68–88.

Piot, Peter, Robert Greener, Sarah Russell, 2007, 'Squaring the Circle: AIDS, Poverty, and Human Development', *PLoS Medicine*, Vol. 4, No. 10:e314.

Pisani, Elizabeth, et al., 2003, 'Back to Basics in HIV Prevention: Focus on Exposure', *British Medical Journal*, Vol. 326, No. 7403, pp. 1384–7.

Powell-Jackson, Timothy, Kara Hanson, and Di McIntyre, 2012, 'Fiscal Space for Health—A Review of the Literature', Resyst Working Paper No. 1, London School of Hygiene and Tropical Medicine.

President's Emergency Plan for AIDS Relief (PEPFAR), 2012, 'PEPFAR Blueprint: Creating an AIDS-free Generation' (Washington, DC: PEPFAR).

President's Emergency Plan for AIDS Relief (PEPFAR), 2014a, 'PEPFAR Annual Report—10th Annual Report to Congress' (Washington, DC: PEPFAR).

President's Emergency Plan for AIDS Relief (PEPFAR), 2014b, '2014 Report on Costs of Treatment in the President's Emergency Plan for AIDS Relief (PEPFAR)' (Washington, DC: U.S. Department of State).

President's Emergency Plan for AIDS Relief (PEPFAR), 2014c, 'PEPFAR 3.0—Controlling the Epidemic: Delivering on the Promise of an AIDS-free Generation' (Washington, DC: U.S. Department of State).

Quinn, Thomas C., Jonathan M. Mann, James W. Curran, and Peter Piot, 1986, 'AIDS in Africa: an Epidemiologic Paradigm, *Science*, Vol. 234, No. 4779, pp. 955–63.

Rajan, Raghuram G., and Arvind Subramanian, 2008, 'Aid and Growth: What Does the Cross-country Evidence Really Show?' *Review of Economics and Statistics*, Vol. 90, No. 4, pp. 643–65.

Reed, Jason R., et al., 2011, 'Voluntary Medical Male Circumcision: An HIV Prevention Priority for PEPFAR', *Journal of Acquired Immune Deficiency Syndromes*, Vol. 60, Suppl. 3, pp. S88–95.

Reniers, Georges, et al., 2014, 'Mortality Trends in the Era of Antiretroviral Therapy: Evidence from the Network for Analysing Longitudinal Population based HIV/AIDS Data on Africa (ALPHA)', *AIDS*, Vol. 28, Suppl. 4, pp. S533–42.

Resch, Stephen, et al., 2011, 'Economic Returns to Investment in AIDS Treatment in Low- and Middle-income Countries', *PLoS One*, Vol. 6, No. 10:e25310.

Resch, Stephen, Theresa Ryckman, and Robert Hecht, 2015, 'Funding AIDS Programmes in the Era of Shared Responsibility: An Analysis of Domestic Spending in 12 Low-income and Middle-income Countries', *The Lancet Global Health*, Vol. 3, No. 1, pp. e52–e61.

Roe, Terry L., and Rodney B. W. Smith, 2008, 'Disease Dynamics and Economic Growth', *Journal of Policy Modeling*, Vol. 30, No. 1, pp. 145–68.

Rosen, Sydney, et al., 2007, 'The Private Sector and HIV/AIDS in Africa: Taking Stock of 6 Years of Applied Research', *AIDS*, Vol. 21, Suppl. 3, pp. S41–51.

Russell, Steven, 2004, 'The Economic Burden of Illness for Households in Developing Countries: A Review of Studies Focusing on Malaria, Tuberculosis, and Human

Immunodeficiency Virus/Acquired Immunodeficiency Syndrome', *The American Journal of Tropical Medicine and Hygiene*, Vol. 71, No. 2, Suppl., pp. 147–55.

Sala-i-Martin, Xavier X., 1997, 'I Just Ran Two Million Regressions', *American Economic Review*, Vol. 87, No. 2, pp. 178–83.

Salinas, Gonzalo, and Markus Haacker, 2006, 'HIV/AIDS: The Impact on Poverty and Inequality', IMF Working Paper No. 06/126 (Washington, DC: International Monetary Fund).

Samji, Hasina, et al., 2013, 'Closing the Gap: Increases in Life Expectancy among Treated HIV-Positive Individuals in the United States and Canada', *PLoS One*, Vol. 8, No. 12: e81355.

Samuels, Fiona, and Michael Drinkwater, 2011, ' "Twelve Years on": The Impacts of HIV and AIDS on Livelihoods in Zambia', *Annals of Anthropological Practice*, Vol. 35, No. 1, pp. 148–66.

Schönteich, Martin, 1999, 'Age and AIDS: South Africa's Crime Time Bomb?' *African Security Review*, Vol. 8, No. 4, pp. 34–44.

Schwartländer, Bernhard, et al., 2001, 'Resource Needs for HIV/AIDS', *Science*, Vol. 292, No. 5526, pp. 2434–6.

Schwartländer, Bernhard, Ian Grubb, and Jos Perriëns, 2006, 'The 10-Year Struggle to Provide Antiretroviral Treatment to People with HIV in the Developing World', *The Lancet*, Vol. 368, pp. 541–6.

Schwartländer, Bernhard, et al., 2011, 'Towards an Improved Investment Approach for an Effective Response to HIV/AIDS', *The Lancet*, Vol. 377, Issue 9782, pp. 2031–41.

Seeley, Janet, et al., 2008, 'Using In-depth Qualitative Data to Enhance our Understanding of Quantitative Results Regarding the Impact of HIV and AIDS on Households in Rural Uganda', *Social Science & Medicine*, Vol. 67, No. 9, pp. 1434–46.

Seeley, Janet, Stefan Dercon, and Tony Barnett, 2010, 'The Effects of HIV/AIDS on Rural Communities in East Africa: A 20-year Perspective', *Tropical Medicine & International Health*, Vol. 15, No. 3, pp. 329–35.

Sen, Amartya, 1999, 'Health in Development', Keynote Address to the Fifty-second World Health Assembly (Geneva: World Health Organisation).

Shapiro, Roger L., et al., 2010, 'Antiretroviral Regimens in Pregnancy and Breast-feeding in Botswana', *New England Journal of Medicine*, Vol. 362, No. 24, pp. 2282–94.

Shelton, James D., Michael M. Cassell, and Jacob Adetunji, 2005, 'Is Poverty or Wealth at the Root of HIV?' *The Lancet*, Vol. 366, pp. 1057–8.

Shiffman, Jeremy, David Berlan, and Tamara Hafner, 2009, 'Has Aid for AIDS Raised All Health Funding Boats?' *Journal of Acquired Immune Deficiency Syndromes*, Vol. 52, Suppl. 1, pp. S45–8.

Shisana, Olive, et al., 2014, *South African National HIV Prevalence, Incidence and Behaviour Survey, 2012* (Cape Town: HSRC Press).

Siapka, Mariana, et al., 2014, 'Is There Scope for Cost Savings and Efficiency Gains in HIV Services? A Systematic Review of the Evidence from Low-and Middle-income Countries', *Bulletin of the World Health Organization*, Vol. 92, No. 7, pp. 499–511 and 511A–511AD.

Sidibé, Michel, 2014, 'The Last Climb: Leaving No One Behind', Speech given at 20th International AIDS Conference Opening Session (Geneva: UNAIDS).

Sidibé, Michel, José M. Zuniga, and Julio Montaner, 2014, 'Leveraging HIV Treatment to End AIDS, Stop New HIV Infections, and Avoid the Cost of Inaction', *Clinical Infectious Diseases*, Vol. 59, Suppl. 1, pp. S3–6.

Siegfried, Nandi, et al., 2003, 'Male Circumcision for Prevention of Heterosexual Acquisition of HIV in Men', Cochrane Database of Systematic Reviews 2003, Issue 3.

Siegfried, Nandi, Martie Muller, Jonathan J. Deeks, and Jimmy Volmink, 2009, 'Male Circumcision for Prevention of Heterosexual Acquisition of HIV in Men', Cochrane Database of Systematic Reviews 2009, Issue 2.

Smit, Ben, Linette Ellis, and Pieter Laubscher, 2006, 'The Macroeconomic Impact of HIV/AIDS under Alternative Intervention Scenarios (With Specific Reference to ART on the South African Economy)' (University of Stellenbosch: Bureau of Economic Research).

Statistics Botswana, 2013, 'Preliminary Results—Botswana AIDS Impact Survey IV (BAIDS IV), 2013', Stats Brief No. 2013/28 (Gaborone: Statistics Botswana).

Stover, John, 2012, 'Treatment—Perspective Paper', in: Bjørn Lomborg (ed.), *Rethink HIV—Smarter Ways to Invest in Ending HIV in sub-Saharan Africa* (Cambridge: Cambridge University Press).

Stover, John, et al., 2001, 'The Global Impact of Scaling up HIV/AIDS Prevention Programs in Low- and Middle-income Countries', *Science*, Vol. 311, No. 5766, pp. 1474–6.

Stover, John, et al., 2011, 'Long-term Costs and Health Impact of Continued Global Fund Support for Antiretroviral Therapy', *PLoS One*, Vol. 6, No. 6:e21048.

Stover, John, et al., 2014, 'The Impact and Cost of the 2013 WHO Recommendations on Eligibility for Antiretroviral Therapy', *AIDS*, Vol. 28, Suppl. 2, pp. S225–30.

Swift, Jonathan, 1729, A Modest Proposal for Preventing the Children of Poor People in Ireland, From Being a Burden on Their Parents or Country, and for Making Them Beneficial to the Publick.

Tagar, Elya, et al., 2014, 'Multi-country Analysis of Treatment Costs for HIV/AIDS (MATCH): Facility-Level ART Unit Cost Analysis in Ethiopia, Malawi, Rwanda, South Africa and Zambia', *PLoS One*, Vol. 9, Issue 11:e108304.

Tandon, Ajay, and Cheryl Cashin, 2010, 'Assessing Public Expenditure on Health From a Fiscal Space Perspective', Health, Nutrition and Population (HNP) Discussion Paper (Washington, DC: World Bank).

Tanser, Frank, Till Bärnighausen, Graham S. Cooke, and Marie-Louise Newell, 2009, 'Localized Spatial Clustering of HIV Infections in a Widely Disseminated Rural South African Epidemic', *International Journal of Epidemiology*, Vol. 38, No. 4, pp. 1008–16.

Tanser, Frank, Tulio de Oliveira, Mathieu Maheu-Giroux, and Till Bärnighausen, 2014, 'Concentrated HIV Subepidemics in Generalized Epidemic Settings', *Current Opinion in HIV and AIDS*, Vol. 9, No. 2, pp. 115–25.

Taskforce on Innovative International Financing of Health Systems, 2009, 'More Money for Health, and More Health for the Money'.

Temple, Jonathan, 1999, 'The New Growth Evidence', *Journal of Economic Literature*, Vol. 37, No. 1, pp. 112–56.

Thigpen, Michael C., et al., 2012, 'Antiretroviral Preexposure Prophylaxis for Heterosexual HIV Transmission in Botswana', *New England Journal of Medicine*, Vol. 367, No. 5, pp. 423–34.

Thirumurthy, Harsha, Joshua Graff Zivin, and Markus Goldstein, 2008, 'The Economic Impact of AIDS Treatment: Labor Supply in Western Kenya', *Journal of Human Resources*, Vol. 43, No. 3, pp. 511–52.

Thirumurthy, Harsha, et al., 2011, 'Two-year Impacts on Employment and Income among Adults Receiving Antiretroviral Therapy in Tamil Nadu, India: A Cohort Study', *AIDS*, Vol. 25, No. 2, pp. 239–46.

Thirumurthy, Harsha, Omar Galárraga, Bruce Larson, and Sydney Rosen, 2012, 'HIV Treatment Produces Economic Returns through Increased Work and Education, and Warrants Continued US Support', *Health Affairs*, Vol. 31, No. 7, pp. 1470–7.

Thurlow, James, Jeff Gow, and Gavin George, 2009, 'HIV/AIDS, Growth and Poverty in KwaZulu-Natal and South Africa: An Integrated Survey, Demographic and Economy-wide Analysis', *Journal of the International AIDS Society*, Vol. 12:18.

Uganda AIDS Commission (UAC), 2014, 'A Case for More Strategic and Increased Investment in HIV/AIDS Programmes for Uganda 2015–2025' (Kampala: UAC).

UNAIDS, see Joint United Nations Programme on HIV/AIDS.

UNAIDS–Lancet Commission on Defeating AIDS—Advancing Global Health, 2015, 'Defeating AIDS—Advancing Global Health', *The Lancet*, Vol. 386, Issue 9989, pp. 171–218.

UNAIDS/WHO/SACEMA Expert Group on Modelling the Impact and Cost of Male Circumcision for HIV Prevention, 2009, 'Male Circumcision for HIV Prevention in High HIV Prevalence Settings: What Can Mathematical Modelling Contribute to Informed Decision Making?' *PLoS Medicine*, Vol. 6, Issue 9:e1000109.

United Nations Economic and Social Council (ECOSOC), 1994, 'Joint and Co-Sponsored United Nations Programme on Human Immunodeficiency Virus/Acquired Immunodeficiency Syndrome (HIV/AIDS)', Resolution No. 1994/24 (New York: ECOSOC).

United Nations Fund for Children (UNICEF), 2013, Towards an AIDS-Free Generation—Children and AIDS, Sixth Stocktaking Report (New York: UNICEF).

United Nations Fund for Children (UNICEF), 2014, *The State of the World's Children 2015: Reimagine the Future* (New York: UNICEF).

United Nations General Assembly, 2001, 'Declaration of Commitment on HIV/AIDS', Twenty-Sixth Special Session, Resolution No. S26-2 (New York: United Nations General Assembly).

United Nations General Assembly, 2011, 'Political Declaration on HIV and AIDS: Intensifying Our Efforts to Eliminate HIV and AIDS' (New York: United Nations).

United Nations General Assembly, 2015, 'Transforming our World: the 2030 Agenda for Sustainable Development' (New York: United Nations).

United Nations Population Division (UNPD), 2015, 'World Population Prospects: The 2015 Revision' (New York: United Nations).

Usher, Dan, 1973, 'An Imputation to the Measure of Economic Growth for Changes in Life Expectancy', in: Milton Moss (ed.), *The Measurement of Economic and Social Performance*, National Bureau for Economic Research Studies in Income and Wealth, Vol. 38 (New York: Columbia University Press).

Usher, Dan, 1980, *The Measurement of Economic Growth* (New York: Columbia University Press).

Van Damme, Lut, et al., 2012, 'Preexposure Prophylaxis for HIV Infection among African Women', *New England Journal of Medicine*, Vol. 367, No. 5, pp. 411–22.

Vassall, Anna, et al., 2013, 'Financing Essential HIV Services: A New Economic Agenda', *PLoS Medicine*, Vol. 10, No. 12:e1001567.

Vassall, Anna, et al., 2014, 'Cost-effectiveness of HIV Prevention for High-risk Groups at Scale: An Economic Evaluation of the Avahan Programme in South India', *The Lancet Global Health*, Vol. 2, No. 9, pp. e531–40.

Ventelou, Bruno, et al., 2012, 'The Macroeconomic Consequences of Renouncing to Universal Access to Antiretroviral Treatment for HIV in Africa: A Micro-simulation Model', *PLoS One*, Vol. 7, No. 4:e34101.

Vermund, Sten H., and Richard J. Hayes, 2013, 'Combination Prevention: New Hope for Stopping the Epidemic', *Current HIV/AIDS Reports*, Vol. 10, No. 2, pp. 169–86.

Viscusi, W. Kip., 1993, 'The Value of Risks to Life and Health', *Journal of Economic Literature*, Vol. 31, No. 4, pp. 1912–46.

Viscusi, W. Kip, and Joseph E. Aldy, 2003, 'The Value of a Statistical Life: A Critical Review of Market Estimates Throughout the World', *Journal of Risk and Uncertainty*, Vol. 27, No. 1, pp. 5–76.

Warren, Ashley E., Kaspar Wyss, George Shakarishvili, Rifat Atun, and Don de Savigny, 2013, 'Global Health Initiative Investments and Health Systems Strengthening: A Content Analysis of Global Fund Investments', *Globalization and Health*, Vol. 9, No. 1:30.

Weil, David N., 2007, 'Accounting for the Effect of Health on Economic Growth', *Quarterly Journal of Economics*, Vol. 122, No. 3, pp. 1265–306.

Weil, David N., 2014, 'Health and Economic Growth', in: Philippe Aghion and Steven N. Durlauf, *Handbook of Economic Growth*, Volume 2 (Oxford: Elsevier).

Weiss, Helen A., Maria A. Quigley, and Richard J. Hayes, 2000, 'Male Circumcision and Risk of HIV Infection in sub-Saharan Africa: A Systematic Review and Meta-analysis', *AIDS*, Vol. 14, No. 15, pp. 2361–70.

Weller, Susan C., and Karen Davis-Beaty, 2002, 'Condom Effectiveness in Reducing Heterosexual HIV Transmission', *Cochrane Database of Systematic Reviews*, Issue 1, Art. No.CD003255.

Werker, Eric, Amrita Ahuja, and Brian Wendell, 2009, 'Male Circumcision and AIDS: The Macroeconomic Impact of a Health Crisis', Harvard Business School Working Paper: 07-025.

White, Richard G., et al., 2008, 'Male Circumcision for HIV Prevention in sub-Saharan Africa: Who, What and When?' *AIDS*, Vol. 22, No. 14, pp. 1841–50.

Whiteside, Alan, 2002, 'Poverty and HIV/AIDS in Africa', *Third World Quarterly*, Vol. 23, No. 2, pp. 313–32.

Whiteside, Alan, and Fiona E. Henry, 2011, 'The Impact of HIV and AIDS Research: A Case Study from Swaziland', *Health Research Policy and Systems*, Vol. 9, Suppl. 1:59.

Whiteside, Alan, and Julia Smith, 2009, 'Exceptional Epidemics: AIDS Still Deserves a Global Response', *Globalization and Health*, Vol. 5, No. 1:15.

Whiteside, Alan, and Amy Whalley, 2007, 'Reviewing "Emergencies" for Swaziland Shifting the Paradigm in a New Era' (Mbabane, Swaziland: National Emergency

Response Council on HIV/AIDS; and Durban: Health Economics and HIV/AIDS Research Division, University of KwaZulu-Natal).

Wilson, David, and Daniel T. Halperin, 2008, 'Know Your Epidemic, Know Your Response: A Useful Approach, If We Get It Right', *The Lancet*, Vol. 372 (9 August 2008), pp. 423–5.

Wilson, David, Jessica Taaffe, Nicole Fraser-Hurt, and Marelize Gorgens, 2014a, 'The Economics, Financing and Implementation of HIV Treatment as Prevention: What Will it Take to Get There?' *African Journal of AIDS Research*, Vol. 13, No. 2, pp. 109–19.

Wilson, David P., et al., 2014b, 'Allocating Resources Efficiently to Address Strategic Objectives: Optimization of HIV/AIDS Responses', unpublished draft.

Wojcicki, Janet Maia, 2005, 'Socioeconomic Status as a Risk Factor for HIV Infection in Women in East, Central and Southern Africa: A Systematic Review', *Journal of Biosocial Science*, Vol. 37, No. 1, pp. 1–36.

World Bank, 2013, 'Assessing the Financial Sustainability of Jamaica's HIV/AIDS Program' (Washington, DC: World Bank).

World Bank, 2014, World Development Indicators, edition of 1 July 2014 (Washington, DC: World Bank).

World Bank, 2015, World Development Indicators, updated 28 July 2015 (Washington, DC: World Bank).

World Health Organization (WHO), 2003, *Treating 3 Million By 2005: Making it Happen: The WHO Strategy* (Geneva: WHO).

World Health Organization (WHO), 2010, 'Antiretroviral Drugs for Treating Pregnant Women and Preventing HIV Infection in Infants: Recommendations for a Public Health Approach—2010 Version' (Geneva: WHO).

World Health Organization (WHO), 2013, 'Consolidated Guidelines on the Use of Antiretroviral Drugs for Treating and Preventing HIV Infection, June 2013' (Geneva: WHO).

World Health Organization (WHO), 2014, 'Post-Exposure Prophylaxis for HIV— Supplementary Section to the 2013 WHO Consolidated Guidelines on the Use of Antiretroviral Drugs for Treating and Preventing HIV Infection' (Geneva: WHO).

World Health Organization (WHO), 2015, 'WHO Progress Brief: Voluntary Medical Male Circumcision for HIV Prevention in 14 Priority Countries in East and Southern Africa— July 2015', online at http://www.who.int/hiv/pub/malecircumcision/brief2015/en (Geneva: WHO).

World Health Organization (WHO) and Joint United Nations Programme on HIV/AIDS (UNAIDS), 2006, 'Progress on Global Access to HIV Antiretroviral Therapy: A Report on "3 by 5" and beyond' (Geneva: WHO).

World Health Organization (WHO) and Joint United Nations Programme on HIV/AIDS (UNAIDS), 2007, 'New Data on Male Circumcision and HIV Prevention: Policy and Programme Implications', WHO/UNAIDS Technical Consultation, Male Circumcision and HIV Prevention: Research Implications for Policy and Programming, Montreux, 6–8 March 2007, Conclusions and Recommendations (Geneva: WHO).

World Health Organization (WHO) and Joint United Nations Programme on HIV/AIDS (UNAIDS), 2011, 'Joint Strategic Action Framework to Accelerate the Scale-up of

Voluntary Medical Male Circumcision for HIV Prevention in Eastern and Southern Africa 2012–2016' (Geneva: UNAIDS).

World Health Organization (WHO), Joint United Nations Programme on HIV/AIDS (UNAIDS), and United Nations Fund for Children (UNICEF), 2009, 'Towards Universal Access: Scaling up Priority HIV/AIDS Interventions in the Health Sector: Progress Report 2008' (Geneva: WHO).

World Health Organization (WHO), Joint United Nations Programme on HIV/AIDS (UNAIDS), and United Nations Fund for Children (UNICEF), 2013, 'Global Update on HIV Treatment 2013: Results, Impact and Opportunities' (Geneva: WHO).

Yamano, Takashi, and T. S. Jayne, 2004, 'Measuring the Impacts of Working-age Adult Mortality on Small-scale Farm Households in Kenya', *World Development*, Vol. 32, No. 1, pp. 91–119.

Young, Alwyn, 2005, 'The Gift of the Dying: The Tragedy of AIDS and the Welfare of Future African Generations', *Quarterly Journal of Economics*, Vol. CXX, No. 2, pp. 423–66.

Yu, Dongbao, Yves Souteyrand, Mazuwa A. Banda, Joan Kaufman, and Joseph H. Perriëns, 2008, 'Investment in HIV/AIDS Programs: Does it Help Strengthen Health Systems in Developing Countries?' *Globalization and Health*, Vol. 4, No. 8.

Zeng, Wu, Donald S. Shepard, Jon Chilingerian, and Carlos Avila-Figueroa, 2012, 'How Much Can We Gain from Improved Efficiency? An Examination of Performance of National HIV/AIDS Programs and Its Determinants in Low- and Middle-income Countries', *BMC Health Services Research*, Vol. 12, No. 1:74.

Zeng, Wu, Donald S. Shepard, Carlos Avila-Figueroa, and Haksoon Ahn, 2015, 'Resource Needs and Gap Analysis in Achieving Universal Access to HIV/AIDS Services: A Data Envelopment Analysis of 45 Countries', *Health Policy and Planning*, first published online 9 November 2015.

Index